THE MAGNIFICENT LOSERS
HISTORY'S GREATEST UNSUCCESSFUL REFORMERS, REVOLUTIONARIES AND FIGHTERS FOR FREEDOM AND JUSTICE

Gregg Coodley, M.D.

Copyright@2017
Gregg Coodley
All rights reserved

Published by Bendrogo Publishing
Portland, Oregon

ISBN: 978-0-9990770-0-9

Library of Congress Control Number: 2017908717

MORE REVIEWS OF THE MAGNIFICENT LOSERS

"Magnificent Losers is a brilliant corrective to the Great Man theory of history, perhaps more necessary today than ever. In a series of finely crafted biographical vignettes, Coodley chronicles the lives of some 20 leaders, thinkers and activists across more than 2000 years of history whose ideas represented concepts of justice and reform that were far ahead of their time…in Coodley's insightful retelling, these aren't the losers of history, but its advance guard. The ideas they championed were worth fighting for, as they helped lay the foundation for a more equal and just society that we're still struggling to attain."

W.C. McRae, Author, *Pacific Northwest: Lonely Planet Travel Survival Kit*

"Gregg Coodley chronicles the deeds of a host of largely forgotten heroes, who, in their time, lost and often died in their struggles for freedom, justice and equality. The ideas they fought for… thrive today in no small part because of their sacrifices…These are inspiring stories of courage, persistence and virtue that speak to the pressing needs of our own time."

Rick Seifert, Journalist, Community Leader and University Teacher

"This book is a collection of many tidbits of history…The heroes of the stories are indeed Magnificent Losers, some of whom changed history."

Charles Kuttner, M.D.

"This book could not arrive at a more opportune time when many of us need to be reminded that our work for social justice is not in vain…It makes a persuasive case through the force of many examples that our efforts may well bear fruit long after we are gone, and in doing so it holds out hope."

Stephen Karakashian, Co-Author, *Redeeming the Past: My Journey from Freedom Fighter to Healer*

"Perhaps, as Churchill said, history is written by the victors. But social progress may well be inspired by the vanquished. Gregg Coodley has put together a fascinating and entertaining collection…They serve as a reminder that "losers"- particularly those who pay the highest price for their ideals- may do more than "winners" to move the arc of human history towards compassion."
Michael Z. Cahana, Senior Rabbi, Congregation Beth Israel

"Gregg Coodley has undertaken an ambitiously wide ranging, surprising and often provocative historical tour of men and women who struggled and often succeeded at changing their world for the better. He has delivered their stories to us both compellingly and concisely."
Fergus M. Bordewich, Author, *The First Congress: How James Madison, George Washington and a Group of Extraordinary Men Invented the Government*

"History's hidden heroes come to life in the book, a series of vignettes of 20 men and women from ancient Rome to 20th century Europe and America who devoted their lives to social equality, national independence or the advancement of women and workers. Some faced defeat or compromise. Others met early deaths. All created legacies that inspired later generations. The book's achievement is to build biographies from multiple sources that show how activists across time committed their lives to begin work that outlived their lifetimes. Read to learn and be inspired."
Bob Liebman, Professor of Sociology, Portland State University

In memory of my parents, Eugene and Gloria Coodley

Acknowledgments

I am indebted to many people for their generous comments and assistance in the creation of this book. I owe the idea to Ted Blazsek. I appreciate the advice of Nora Coon, Nils McCune, David Sarasohn, David Heidler and Gary Binder for their invaluable suggestions that have made this a much better book. I want to thank the staff at Author Accelerator for their feedback, including Jennifer Nash, Lana Storey, Lizette Clarke and most of all Michael Raymond. I appreciate the replies of James Nelson to my questions as I embarked on the writing. I never could have put this together without the technical assistance of Dennis Bjelland and Danny Henderson, who helped me time and again.

I want to thank Judy Jewell for her superb editing and formatting of the manuscript. I also want to thank Nancy Gerth for her excellence in creating the index for the book.

The materials for the book came in a large part from the Multnomah County Library as well as their service to obtain materials from other libraries. I am deeply grateful to the staff of the Multnomah County Library, particularly at the Hillsdale and Central Library branches, including the Hillsdale reference staff of Liz Von Gehren, Betsy Fontenot, Dale Smith and Tom French.

I appreciate my sister Cheryl Coon and brother-in-law, James Coon, who read the book and offered encouragement and suggestions. I am very grateful to my sister Lauren Coodley, an excellent historian in her own right, who offered advice and guidance month after month as I wrote and edited the book. I am indebted to my children David and Mimi for their help with the maps for the book. I want to thank my children Sam, Scout and Sarah, for their support. Finally, I want to thank my wife, Karen, who in addition to offering feedback, put up with two years of me being distracted by the process of writing and editing, while always encouraging me to keep going with the book.

Table of Contents

Chapter 1: Tiberius and Gaius Gracchus
    Reforming Rome: 137–122 BCE, Rome 5
Chapter 2: Boudica
    Warrior Queen, 61 CE, Britain 19
Chapter 3: Rabbi Akiba and the Judean Revolts
    Challenging the Roman Empire, 131 CE, Judea 29
Chapter 4: Mazdak
    The First Communist, 524 CE, Persia 35
Chapter 5: John Ball and Wat Tyler
    The Peasants' Revolt, 1381 CE, England 41
Chapter 6: Stenka Razin
    Russia in Revolt, 1670 CE, Russia 56
Chapter 7: Joseph Warren
    The Forgotten Founding Father, 1775 CE, Massachusetts 67
Chapter 8: Tupac Amaru
    The Great Uprising, 1781 CE, Peru 87
Chapter 9: Wolfe Tone
    The Battle for Irish Independence, 1798 CE, Ireland 97
Chapter 10: Toussaint L'Ouverture
    The Greatest Slave Revolt, 1801 CE, Haiti 109
Chapter 11: Tecumseh
    Holding Back the Tide, 1813 CE, United States 125
Chapter 12: Henry Clay
    Thrice or Six-time Defeated Presidential Candidate,
    1824 CE, United States 139
Chapter 13: Louis Kossuth
    Liberal Nationalism, 1848 CE, Hungary 155
Chapter 14: Elizabeth Cady Stanton
    Fighter for Women's Rights, 1848 CE, United States 172
Chapter 15: Oliver Otis Howard
    The Freedman's Bureau, 1866 CE, United States 185
Chapter 16: Giuseppe Garibaldi
    Soldier for Humanity, 1882 CE, Italy 203
Chapter 17: Eugene Debs
    The Rights of Labor, 1894 CE, United States 219
Chapter 18: William Jennings Bryan
    The Great Commoner, 1896 CE, United States 243

Chapter 19: Emilio Aguinaldo
   The First Philippine Republic, 1898 CE, Philippines 261
Chapter 20: Jean Jaurès
   Justice, Not War, 1914 CE, France 275

List of Maps
1. The Roman Republic, 132 BCE
2. Britain 61, CE
3. Judea
4. Sassanian Empire
5. London during Peasant's Revolt, 1381 CE
6. Russia, 1670 CE
7. Boston Area, 1775 CE
8. South America, 1781 CE
9. Ireland
10. St. Dominigue (Haiti)/The Caribbean, 1801 CE
11. Northwestern United States, 1812 CE
12. The United States, 1824 CE
13. Hapsburg Austrian Empire, 1848 CE
14. New York State
15. Eastern United States, 1866 CE
16. Italy, 1848 CE
17. Midwestern United States
18. The United States, 1896 CE
19. Northern Luzon, 1898 CE
20. Europe, 1914 CE

INTRODUCTION

HISTORY focuses on the winners. We read about presidents who were elected and kings who ruled. Victorious generals are celebrated while the defeated are forgotten. We remember leaders who successfully initiated profound changes, such as Abraham Lincoln ending slavery in the United States or Franklin Delano Roosevelt's New Deal.

Yet there were many leaders who "fought the good fight" and lost. This book focuses on some of the heroes and heroines down through the years who fought for freedom, justice or reform. In conventional terms, they ultimately were unsuccessful. They did not win the last battle or achieve the success for which they hoped. Yet for many, their ideas were vindicated later and their causes proved ultimately successful. Often this happened after their lifetimes, sometimes after centuries.

Success, however, shouldn't be the main yardstick of whether the effort was worth the fight. These reformers who gave everything of themselves, yet were not successful, are just as worthy of being celebrated and remembered as those who won battles.

The magnificent losers of this book had lives that spanned twenty centuries and the length of the Earth. For it is important to recognize that it is not simply one era or one nation where people sought to fight injustice, speak for those unable to speak for themselves and repair the world. By looking at people from many continents and time periods, we can see that the desire for independence and justice is indeed a universal battle.

What qualities link these heroes and heroines? First, all fought for more than just personal power. Each was motivated by something more, by some idea greater than themselves. Second, each believed that their world was seriously flawed. They also believed that the problems of their society or nation could be improved and that it was within their power to try to do so. Third, all were interested in fixing the world of today rather than accepting injustice today as the price for promised rewards in any heaven to come. Fourth, each rallied other people to follow them and join them in their struggle. These were not lone prophets, scorned by everyone in their society. Finally, all were unsuccessful when the forces opposed to change proved the stronger. Yet, perhaps they didn't lose after all.

For the ideas they fought for did not die with them. Tiberius Gracchus's proposal to give land to the poor has been often copied over the next two millennia. His brothers Gaius introduced the idea that a nation was responsible for the feeding of its citizens, a concept that has been part of modern ethos in such programs as food stamps and famine relief. The 6th-century Persian reformer Mazdak is almost unknown outside his native land, but his doctrine that property should be held in common inspired millions in the 19th and 20th centuries. The hedge priest John Ball's vision of the essential equality of man was an outrageous heresy in 14th century England, but it is gospel in the 21st century. Touissaint L'Ouverture, Tupac Amaru and Elizabeth Cady Stanton died with their respective dreams of the equality of blacks, Native Americans and women unfulfilled, but such dreams, at least in theory, have become mainstream thought today.

The magnificent losers presented here might best be summed up in the words of a reformer both successful and unsuccessful, President Theodore Roosevelt. Roosevelt wrote, "It is not the critic who counts; not the man who points out how the strong man stumbles, or where the doer of deeds could have done them better. The credit belongs to the man who is actually in the arena, whose face is marred by dust and sweat and blood; who strives valiantly; who errs, who comes short again and again, because there is no effort without error and shortcoming; but who does actually strive to do the deeds; who knows great enthusiasms, the great devotions; who spends himself in a worthy cause; who at best knows in the end the triumph of high achievement, and who at the worst, if he fails, at least fails while daring greatly, so that his place shall never be with those cold and timid souls who neither know victory or defeat."

The heroes of this book failed while daring greatly. Their courage in fighting for a better world matters more than their degree of success, for indeed they spent themselves in a worthy cause.

Roman Republic
133 BCE

Chapter 1: Tiberius and Gaius Gracchus
Reforming Rome, Rome, 137–122 BCE

TIBERIUS GRACCHUS stood in the Forum in Rome, looking out upon the crowd. Tiberius, not yet 30 years old, had been elected a tribune, the representative of the common people, the year before, in 134 BCE. Now he prepared to challenge the powerful aristocrats who had long run Rome through their control of the Senate. Straightening his toga, Tiberius climbed onto the lower steps of the huge Temple of Jupiter so that people could see him. A few steps below gathered the common people of Rome, the plasterers and cart-drivers, the men who furnished the labor to build the aqueducts and the bakers who made the delectable pastries that the Romans were so fond of. These people had come a distance, down from their multistory tenements on the Aventine Hill and from their hovels in Transtibernia, across the Tiber River, where the poor of Rome resided. It was worth it to hear what Tiberius might say. For Tiberius, as a tribune, could propose legislation in the Assembly, the other part of the Roman legislature besides the Senate. Rome was no longer the small town it started as three hundred years before, but instead was the greatest power in the Mediterranean. With growth in power and wealth had come growing inequality between rich and poor. Rumor had it that Tiberius had a plan to help the common people.

The crowd thought of Tiberius as one of themselves, for the Gracchus family was undoubtedly of plebian or common ancestry. Despite this origin, the Gracchi had risen high in Rome based on their merit. Tiberius' father, twice consul, the executive officer of Rome, was celebrated for his military victories.[1] Tiberius' mother Cornelia was the daughter of the fabled Scipio Africanus, the man who conquered Carthage, Rome's deadliest foe. Tiberius himself, as a young army officer, had been the first man to scale the walls of Carthage itself.

The crowd hushed as he began to speak. Tiberius highlighted the desperate plight of the ordinary citizens who made up the mass of the Roman army.

"The savage beasts have their particular dens…," he began in a calm, but impassioned voice, "The men who bear arms and expose their lives for the safety of their country…having no houses or settlements of their own, are constrained to wander from place to place with their wives and children...They fight indeed and are slain, but it to maintain the luxury and wealth of other men...They are styled masters of the world, but have not one foot of ground which they can call their own."[2]

Tiberius then proposed giving land to the poor of Rome to establish their own farms. Neither Tiberius or his listeners could know that his words and deeds, and those of his brother Gaius, would inspire reformers for the next two thousand years.[1-7]

Tiberius Gracchus was born around 161 or 162 BCE, followed a few years later by his brother Gaius. Their father died in 150 BCE, leaving their mother Cornelia to raise the children alone. It is unclear whether it was the influence of Cornelia or the boys' Greek tutors, who emphasized democracy and rational thought, or if there was some other factor that led both Tiberius and Gains to dedicate their lives to helping the weaker and poorer members of Roman society.

After putting in his mandatory ten years of army service, Tiberius was elected to his first political position around age 26, an age not atypical for the day. He served as quaestor or second in command in a campaign in Spain. The Roman historian Plutarch described him, writing, "Tiberius was gentle and composed in his cast of features, expression and demeanor...Tiberius was...conciliatory...and his language chosen with extreme care."[2]

After his return to Rome, Tiberius successfully ran for the position of tribune, a step up the political ladder for an ambitious politician. Yet, Tiberius was motivated by more than ambition, instead being determined to fix the evils he saw plaguing Rome.

The multiple, almost continuous wars of Rome changed Roman society. The Roman army during this time was a citizen army rather than the professional army it was to become in the years of the Roman Empire. Whenever Rome was engaged in a war the citizens were required to serve in the army for the length of the conflict. The years away from the farm resulted in financial failure for many small farmers, who often had to leave their fields fallow while serving in the army. Increasingly, many had to sell their land and move to Rome to look for jobs as laborers. Others remained in the countryside working for large landowners.[1] Since only those with property, i.e., land, could serve in the army, the number of available recruits fell with the decrease in the number of small farms.[3]

The Roman victories also resulted in the capture and enslavement of tens of thousands of people from the defeated nations. With the price of foreign slaves so low, it became economical for the wealthy to set up large profitable plantations called *latifundia*, farmed by slaves. The *latifundia* specialized in profitable cash crops such as olive oil or grapes. Tiberius' younger brother Gaius later wrote that his brother was shocked to see, while en route to the Roman province of Hispania (modern Spain) in 137 BCE, the replacement of so many small farms by huge estates being worked by foreign slaves.[4] The replacement of grain-producing small farms by these estates meant that an increasing proportion of the food need to feed the growing population of Rome needed to be imported from farther away, the majority from the Roman island of Sicily.[1]

The Roman historian Appian summarized the situation well, writing, "The powerful were becoming extremely rich, and the number of slaves in the country was reaching large proportions while the…people were suffering from depopulation and a shortage of men, worn down as they were by poverty and taxes and military service. And if they had any relief from these tribulations, they had no employment, because the land was owned by the rich who used slave farm workers instead of free men."[5]

In the city of Rome, the foreign tribute garnered from the successful wars financed large-scale building programs employing many of the urban poor. When a period of peace led to this tribute being exhausted in 146 BC, public building came to a stop in Rome, throwing many out of work. Then in 135 BCE a slave revolt broke out in Sicily. The revolt interrupted the grain supply from Sicily, leading to an acute shortage of food in Rome. The poor of the greatest power of the Western world faced starvation.[1]

Tiberius had a plan to help them. He believed that increasing the number of small farmers would increase the pool of recruits for the army. It would also ensure a more reliable, closer and thus less expensive food supply. From the conquest of neighboring states in Italy, Rome had a large quantity of public land, which had originally been intended for the poor. A law passed in 366 BCE prevented any individual from owning more than three hundred acres. Yet the wealthy had bought up more land than they were allowed, first under the name of fictional tenants and then openly.[2] The Senate, controlled by wealthy landowners, ignored this violation of the law.

Now, in 133 BCE, Tiberius proposed in the Assembly, the legislature of the common people, a law making the public land available for distribution in small lots for farms to the poor of Rome. Tiberius told the Assembly that it was "just...to divide the common land among the common people."[1] The rich Romans who were using this land would have to surrender a portion of it for division among the poor, yet they were given the concession that they could keep another part of the public land for themselves.[1]

The wealthy who held large acreages of public land bitterly opposed Tiberius' proposal, being unwilling to compromise. Many of them used it as part of their plantations, planting vineyards and olive orchards on it and using it for storage of crops and housing for their slaves. Appian wrote, "The rich gained possession of most of the undistributed land and after a while were confident that no one would take it back from them."[5]

Tiberius persuaded the Assembly to pass his land reform. There was one catch. In addition to proposing laws each of the ten tribunes could veto such laws. Tiberius was shocked when his close friend and tribune Marcus Octavius vetoed his land bill. Tiberius tried to reason with him, but Octavius, without explaining his reasons, would not change his mind. Perhaps due to pressure from many powerful and wealthy men, Octavius had stopped Tiberius' reforms in its tracks.[1]

Tiberius was committed to helping the poor. After a brief interval, Tiberius again persuaded the Assembly to pass his proposal, but once more Marcus Octavius, without explanation, vetoed it.

Rome had an alternate mechanism to enact legislation. Passage by the Senate would also make a proposal law. Tiberius now had his proposal introduced in the Senate. Tiberius hoped that his family ties to the Claudians, one of the most influential families in the Senate and in Rome, would be enough to move the law forward in the Senate. Since the proposed law would take away land from many senators, the Senate contemptuously ignored the proposal.[1,2]

Yet while the patrician elite balked at reform, hunger gnawed increasingly at the poor. Tiberius saw around him in Rome the desperation and hunger of the lower classes.

For a third time, Tiberius went back before the Tribal Assembly. Tiberius addressed Octavius in affectionate terms, clasping his hands and pleading with him to give way.[2] Octavius again refused. Tiberius now suggested an unprecedented step. He asked the Assembly to remove Octavius via a special recall election. Tiberius argued that since either he or

Octavius did not truly represent the Roman people, the people, in the form of the Assembly, should decide which of the two should resign. The Assembly met to decide this question. As the votes were cast, Tiberius several times stopped the proceedings to beg Octavius to change his mind and, "not to throw into chaos a project that was morally right."[5] The assembly cast their votes. After the thirty-four votes had gone unanimously against him, Octavius had to be dragged from the rostrum. A new tribune, a supporter of Tiberius, was elected to replace Octavius. The Assembly then passed into law Tiberius' proposal.[1]

Yet it took more than land to turn a poor man into a successful small farmer. Such a farmer would also need some sort of shelter or home, tools such as plows and hoes, oxen to pull the plow and seed for planting. It would take money to help the poor get these minimum resources necessary to succeed as a farmer. However, all money was controlled by the Senate. The aristocrats who controlled the Senate had no intention of helping fund a program that many despised.

At this moment, the king of Pergamum, a state in western Asia Minor, who had been allied with Rome, died. The king left his kingdom and the resources of it to Rome. Tiberius announced that the money from this windfall would be distributed to those who had received land. Tiberius further announced that the affairs of the new Roman province of Pergamum would be decided by the Assembly rather than the Senate. These actions challenged both the Senate's control over the treasury as well as its traditional control over the provinces. Many aristocrats argued that these actions made Tiberius, as the dominant tribune and the leader of the Assembly, the real power in Rome.[1] For many of the old families the idea of such power being held by a commoner, let alone one with ideals, was outrageous. Nor did the senators accept that they must play second fiddle to the Assembly.

Tribunes, like counsels, served for only one-year terms. It was somewhat unusual, but not unprecedented for an individual to serve two terms in a row. Tiberius may have felt that a single year in office was not sufficient to complete his reforms. He certainly knew that new tribunes holding different opinions could overturn everything he had achieved. Tiberius now announced that he would run again.

Given his popularity with the people, Tiberius' bid for reelection raised the specter among the wealthy that he might remain in office for years.

Tiberius might be popular enough to persuade the Assembly to pass further measures antithetical to the wealthy aristocrats of the Senate. Consequently, the rich patricians attacked Tiberius in increasingly personal and vehement terms. He was accused of violating the Roman constitution by amassing improper powers as a tribune and violating the sanctity of the tribunate by engineering the recall of Octavius.[1]

Tiberius argued that he had not been unjust in his treatment of Octavius, stating, "If it is just for a man to be elected tribune by a majority of tribes, is it not even more just to be deprived by an unanimous decision."[1] He continued, "If a tribune should depart from his duty, oppress the people, cripple its powers and take away its right to vote, he has by his own actions deprived himself of his honorable office by not fulfilling the conditions on which he accepted it."[2]

By the day of the election, the hostility between Tiberius' supporters and opponents was palpable throughout Rome. Up until this point civic disputes in Rome had not resulted in violence for centuries. As the populace lined up with their tribes to vote, the opponents of Tiberius disrupted the proceedings, pushing and shoving people as they tried to vote.[1] The result was a near riot.

Fulvius Flaccus, a senator and ally of Tiberius, now spoke to him. Flaccus warned him that Tiberius' opponents in the Senate were plotting to kill him. Tiberius told the news to his nearby supporters, but many in the crowd were unable to hear him amidst the tumult. Trying to explain what was happening to those farther away, Tiberius raised his hand to his head, indicating that his life was in danger.[2] Tiberius' enemies spun the gesture differently, sending a messenger to the Senate with the report claiming that Tiberius was asking for a crown, i.e., to become king. Since Rome had abolished its monarchy many centuries before, the Senate feared nothing as much as anyone who aspired to become king. Yet it likely that Tiberius' opponents merely used this as a useful pretext rather than believing he really sought to become king.

Angry senators now called upon the presiding officer of the Senate, the consul Scaevola, to take armed action against Tiberius and his supporters. Scaevola, not believing that Tiberius had broken the law or desired a crown, refused.[1]

Then Cipio Nasica, a senator and the Pontifex Maximus, the high priest of Rome, spoke in the Senate, urging the opponents of Tiberius to act.

Nasica, a cousin of Tiberius, was one of the largest owners of public lands and felt bitterly resentful at having to give them up.[2,4] Enraged at Scaevola's inaction, Nasica shouted, "Now that the Consul has betrayed the State, let every man who wishes to uphold the laws follow me."[2]

Many senators followed Nasica out of the Senate, determined to act. Outside the Senate, they armed their servants and followers with clubs and staves, and then charged into the crowd who were still trying to vote. The people in Nasica's path, out of respect for religion, parted in the face of the enraged high priest. Nasica and his supporters, swinging clubs, cornered Tiberius near the door of the Temple of Jupiter. Ignoring the supposed sanctity of the person of the tribune, they bludgeoned Tiberius to death.

Many of Tiberius' supporters in the crowd were also killed.[4] That night the corpses of Tiberius and some three hundred of his followers were dumped in the Tiber River, which bordered Rome.[1,2,5] Plutarch wrote, "This is said to be the first outbreak of civil strife in Rome which ended in the bloodshed and death of citizens since the expulsion of the kings."[2] The willingness of the wealthy elite to use violence and murder to achieve their objectives set a fateful precedent that would eventually help destroy the Republic.

A senatorial court, led by the other consul, P. Popillus Laenas, condemned to death many of Tiberius' supporters, including Tiberius' teacher Diophanes, who had remained his advisor.[1] This court devised unusual deaths for the condemned. One man was killed by being locked in a huge clay pot with poisonous snakes.[2] The Senate took back control over the treasury and the provinces.

The common people were angered by the murder of their champion Tiberius. There was a backlash against Nasica. Whenever he appeared in public, people shouted abuse and curses at him. Nasica fled Rome, despite his duties as Pontifex Maximus which demanded his presence in the city, and died soon afterwards.[2]

Gaius Gracchus, perhaps age 21 at the time of his brother's murder, was doing his military service. When this service was completed he waited for two more years before deciding to enter the political arena at around age 28. The later Roman consul and orator Cicero wrote that Gaius had planned to shun any office when his brother appeared to him in a dream, saying, "Why do you hesitate, Gaius? There is no escape. Fate has decreed the same destiny for us both, to live and die in the service of the people."[2] Gaius felt conflicted between an unwillingness to suffer his brother's fate and his desire to continue Tiberius' reforms.

At last, aiming to complete what his brother had started, Gaius decided to enter politics. Elected quaestor in 127 BCE, Gaius served on the island of Sardinia. Opponents of the Gracchi tried to keep Gaius away from Rome by prolonging his service in Sardinia. At last, in 124 BCE Gaius resigned to return to Rome to run for election as a tribune. Initially, he was attacked by many Senators for resigning while his commander, the consul, remained in Sardinia. Gaius, "pointed out that he had served in the army for no less than twelve years, although other men were obligated to serve only ten. He had spent more than two years as quaestor, although the law allowed him to return after one. He also claimed that he was the only man in the army who had taken a full purse out with him and taken it back empty [i.e., that he had not enriched himself while in office]."[2] Gaius cleared himself completely.

In Gaius' campaign for election as a tribune, he faced the near unanimous hostility of the nobility due to their memory of his brother. Nevertheless, Gaius was elected tribune in 124 BCE, for the ordinary people of Rome, the masons, the carpenters and day laborers, remembered how his brother Tiberius had been the first leader to acted to help the weak and poor. Plutarch wrote, "Once he (Gaius) had taken up office, he quickly asserted his predominance over the other tribunes, for he was incomparably the finest orator in Rome."[2] Plutarch noted how Gaius differed from his brother, noting that in contrast to Tiberius' mild calmness, "Gaius was…impassioned… Gaius' oratory tended to electrify his audience."[2]

The poor struggled to pay for food, for the price of grain bought from far away was very dear. To address this problem Gaius persuaded the Assembly to pass a law providing for the sale of grain in Rome at a set subsidized price. This measure benefited the urban poor by limiting the price of grain. The difference between the set price and the market price was subsidized by the State.[1,6] Gaius also addressed the practical aspects of this, creating the infrastructure needed for the sale of subsidized grain including the purchasing, storage and distribution of the grain.[4] Rome became and remained the only place in the ancient Mediterranean world where the state took regular responsibility for assuring a food supply for its citizens.[4]

Conservative aristocrats then and later criticized the cost of this program. A story of the day tells of Lucius Calpurnius Piso Frugi, a wealthy ex-consul, who opposed Gaius' law. After the law's passage, Gaius spotted

Frugi in line for his allotment of grain. Gaius asked why he was there since he opposed the grain subsidy. Frugi answered, "I'm not keen, Gracchus, on you getting the idea of sharing out my property man by man, but it that's what you are going to do, I'll take my cut."[4]

The second major law that Gaius had passed affirmed that courts that were empowered to inflict the death penalty could only be established by a vote of the people i.e. the Assembly. The Assembly was reacting to the Senate's court of inquisition, which executed many former supporters of Tiberius after his death.

During his army service, Gaius had seen the poorer soldiers suffering from the cold in inadequate clothing.[1,2] Gaius now pushed through a measure furnishing uniforms, at public expense, to the soldiers.

Gaius also tried to reduce judicial corruption, which resulted in preferential treatment for the rich and powerful. Senators were almost never convicted of any crime, no matter how overwhelming the evidence, due to the reluctance of juries made up of their fellow senators to convict them. Gaius pushed through a measure changing such courts to include an equal mixture of senators and equestrians, the middle class of wealthy plebeians.[1] He later passed a measure eliminating senators completely from such juries.

Gaius Gracchus was reelected easily as tribune in the summer of 123 BCE, leading him to push further reforms and improvements to help the poor.[4] Gaius remained concerned about the hardships of the growing number of poorer citizens of the city. In addition to building storehouses to hold grain, Gaius improved the roads leading to Rome to allow an easier flow of produce into the city. The construction also provided work for unemployed laborers. To relieve the overflowing population of Rome, Gaius enacted a plan to start new Roman colonies abroad.

Gaius was sympathetic not just to the poor, but also to Rome's Italian allies, who supplied much of the manpower for Rome's wars, but were denied any political voice.[3,5] To illustrate that Rome was often unfair to its allies, Gaius told the story of how a Roman consul and his wife were traveling through Italy when they came to town of Teano. The wife wanted to use the baths usually used by the men of the town. The mayor of Teano had the regular bathers ejected and the baths prepared for the consul's wife. However, she complained that the bath was not ready in time or clean enough. Consequently, the consul had the mayor stripped, tied to a stake and beaten with sticks.[4]

Gaius and his fellow tribune Fulvius Flaccus, the old ally of his brother, proposed letting Rome's allies become full voting citizens of Rome.[1,3,5] The citizenship proposal was vetoed by another tribune, M. Livius Drusus, who refused to discuss the law or explain his action. The powerful of Rome suspected the motives of anyone who attempted to extend citizenship and the right to vote, believing that the new citizens would support those who had given them the vote. Moreover, many of the common people of Rome opposed expanding rights for the non-Roman allies, fearing that they would compete for jobs and even food.[3]

Gaius now went to supervise the founding of a Roman colony near the site of the now-destroyed city of Carthage. While Gaius had championed this project, it took him away from Rome for several months. During this time, his opponents in the Senate and among the tribunes worked aggressively to undermine support for Gaius.

Drusus, the tribune who had vetoed expanded citizenship, used Gaius' absence to undermine him. With the support of the Senate, he proposed weaker measures that took the place of Gaius' proposals. The Senate was willing to swallow Drusus' tepid reforms if this would undercut Gaius' preeminence.

Gaius returned from North Africa to find an emboldened opposition. Trying to win back popular support, Gaius moved from his house on Palatine Hill to a slum area near the Forum. Some of the other tribunes, hosting games in Forum, had constructed choice seats for the wealthy that obstructed the view of the common citizens. Gaius had these seats torn down, outraging many of his fellow tribunes. It was to prove a fatal mistake.

Gaius decided to run for a third term as tribune. His opponents accused Gaius of corruption in the management of his projects, as well as favoring outsiders over ordinary Romans. These spurious charges were too much for Gaius to overcome. Gaius was defeated in his bid for reelection.

Plutarch attributed this defeat to Gaius alienating the other tribunes, writing, "This action (the tearing down of the seats erected by other tribunes) cost him his election to the tribunate for the third time, because although he won a majority of votes, his colleagues falsified the returns and the declaration of the results."[2] Even worse, a bitter enemy of Gaius named Lucius Optimus, an extreme conservative, was elected as one of the two consuls, the executive officers of the state.[1]

The conservatives moved quickly once Gaius had left office to try to annul his laws in the Assembly. They hoped to provoke Gaius into committing some act of violence, which would give them the excuse to destroy him.[2]

Large crowds gathered at the Assembly for what both sides saw as crucial votes to repeal Gaius' reforms. Quintus Antyllius, an attendant of Optimus, now insulted Gaius and his supporters, shouting, "Stand back you rogues and make way for honest citizens."[2] Antyllius followed this with an obscene gesture. An unknown assailant stabbed Antyllius with a writing stylus, killing him.[1] It was alleged that this murder was due to a "sharp look that Gaius gave Antyllius," thus encouraging one of his followers to kill Antyllius.[5] If indeed this was the case, it would soon be clear that the pen was not mightier than the sword.

Using this killing as a pretext, Optimus asked the Senate for extraordinary authority, in the words of Cicero, "to defend the State."[1] At Optimus' behest, the Senate passed the first ever *senatus consultum ultimum*, which told the consuls, "to make sure that the state should come to no harm."[4] This decree was to become an excuse for violence and lynch mobs. Gaius and Flaccus now faced summary execution. They were asked to surrender and beg for mercy from the Senate.[1]

The next day Gaius Gracchus and Flaccus said goodbye to their wives and families and took refuge at the Temple of Diana on the Aventine Hill. Distraught, Gaius' wife Licinia told him as he left, "When you leave me today, Gaius, I know you are not going to the rostra to speak as a tribune… No, you are going to expose yourself to the men who murdered Tiberius…our country will be none the better for taking your life, for injustice has triumphed in Rome and it is violence and the sword which settle all disputes."[2]

Flaccus sent his son to the Senate to try to negotiate to try to negotiate a compromise to save the lives of Gaius and Flaccus. Confident of his power, Optimus refused. Optimus had gathered armed forces, comprised of patricians and their servants, and mercenary archers from the island of Crete. These forces assaulted the Temple of Diana, slaughtering Flaccus and many of his and Gaius' adherents. Gaius escaped the Temple and crossed the Tiber, but there he was caught and killed. Optimus' forces then sought out and butchered other supporters of Gaius. Some three thousand were killed.[2]

The heads of Gaius and Flaccus were brought to Optimus for a promised reward, to be based on the weight of the heads. It was reported that Septimuleius, who brought in the head of Gaius, bored a hole in it and filled it with lead before presenting it to the consul.[1] The bodies of the slaughtered were tossed into the Tiber. The following days brought further executions along with confiscation of the property of Gaius' supporters. Their wives were forbidden to mourn.[2] Much later, Optimus was convicted of accepting bribes from a foreign ruler and ended his life in disgrace.[2,8]

Over the next few years, several of the most important laws of the Gracchi, including the agrarian and grain laws, were annulled.[1] A law was passed allowing holders of the public land to sell it. Immediately the rich began to buy from the poor or find pretexts to evict them.[5]

Over the next century, the aristocrats of the Senate became ever more entrenched in their power. The failure to grant citizenship to Rome's allies resulted in a bloody civil war some thirty years later, finally resulting in expanded citizenship. The patricians increasingly fought among themselves for power and the riches that went with it. The citizen army was replaced by professional soldiers with more loyalty to their commander than to the institutions of Rome. Ultimately the Roman Republic collapsed, to be replaced by an empire where power was even more concentrated.

Roman conservatives held up the Gracchi as disruptors of the social order. Yet, their reforms might have saved the Republic. Fairer distribution of the society's wealth might have kept the poor attached to the Republic, rather than feeling than they had nothing to lose when they followed later demagogues. Expansion of the ranks of the farmers might have allowed the citizen army to continue. The wealthy senators who were unwilling to share any power with the poor would find themselves powerless under the Emperors. The descendants of the aristocrats who trampled over the laws and bodies of the Gracchi would find far less rational opponents in emperors like Caligula and Nero.

The Gracchi would be remembered for years by the common people. Statues were erected of them at prominent locations and the sites where they had been killed were declared to be holy ground. Their mother Cornelia became known as one of the great epitomes of Roman motherhood.[2]

For the last 2000 years, Tiberius and Gaius have been remembered both for their attempts at reform and the cost of their efforts. Versions of Tiberius' land reform have been proposed, fought over and sometimes implemented in societies from Russia to the Philippines. Almost any reform or revolutionary agenda in agrarian societies over the succeeding centuries included giving land to the poor in hopes that they could be successful farmers. Gaius implemented the first systematic program in which a nation took responsibility for feeding all its citizens. Gaius' grain subsidy was a forerunner of the modern welfare state.

Even in losing, the Gracchi created the idea that societies could be reformed to improve the lot of the poorer citizens. Their ideas have long outlived them. Their killers and opponents have been forgotten.

Chapter 2: Boudica
Warrior Queen, 61 CE, Britain

THE MEN of the Iceni and Trinovante tribes shivered as they waited at dawn in that cold, damp morning in 61 CE to meet Queen Boudica. The two tribes of Britons eyed each other with suspicion as they stood in a muddy field in southeast Britain. Yet both tribes hated their Roman conquerors more.[9–14] The next step would depend on Boudica, Queen of the Iceni, whom many of the men had never seen. Was she the leader who would free them from the Roman yoke?

At last Boudica appeared. Her hair hung loosely to her waist. Around her neck, she wore a golden torc, crafted by one of the skilled metalworkers of the Iceni. In her hand, she grasped a huge spear. Boudica looked out over the crowd for a time, brushed some strands of tawny hair away from her face and then at last began to speak, "But to speak the plain truth, it is we who made ourselves responsible for all these evils, in that we allowed them [the Romans] to set foot on the island in the first place, instead of expelling them at once as we did to their famous Julius Caesar."[14]

Some hundred years before, a young Roman politician, Gaius Julius Caesar, decided to try military conquest as a route to power. In 58–57 BCE Caesar conducted a masterful campaign capturing most of previously unconquered Gaul, the area now making up northern France and Belgium. Gaul, like much of Europe, was dominated by a people known as the Celts, who had a common tongue, but were divided into fiercely competing tribes. Caesar noted that the Gauls had been aided by mercenaries from the closely related Celtic tribes in Britain.[9,10]

Caesar followed up his conquest of Gaul by launching an invasion of Britain in 55 BCE. Although the Romans fought their way ashore, a massive storm badly damaged the Roman fleet. Dismayed at the prospect of being cut off, the Romans retreated to Gaul.[9] The next year Caesar attempted a second invasion, with a much larger army of some 30,000 Romans. Once again Caesar's initial success was spoiled by a storm. Caesar wrote, "Nearly all the ships had been damaged and cast up upon the shore."[10] Caesar sailed away, leaving Britain free of the Romans for a generation

In 43 CE, Rome, by now an empire following the collapse of the Roman Republic, invaded Britain again. The Roman commander, Aulus Plautius, decisively defeated the British tribes of southeast England at the

Medway River. Emperor Claudius himself arrived with reinforcements to finish the conquest a few months later. The divisions among the tribes was a key factor in the Roman victory as the Roman historian Tacitus noted, that the British tribes "fight separately and separately are defeated."[15] The Romans established their capital of this new province of Britain at Camulodunum (modern Colchester).

The tribe of the Iceni, under the rule of King Prastagus and Queen Boudica, dominated the region now known as East Anglia on Britain's eastern shore. The Iceni accepted Roman rule. Tribes such as the Iceni that submitted to Rome lived peaceably if they acknowledged Roman authority and paid their taxes. The ruler and nobility of such tribes continued in power, their wealth enhanced by the trade brought by Roman rule. The Romans introduced silken robes and marble floors, new luxuries that many Britons eagerly embraced. The Romans felt that southern and eastern Britain were safely under their control.

In contrast, tribes that rebelled were mercilessly put down, sometimes slaughtered to the last man while their women and children were sold into slavery. Resistance to the Romans was encouraged by the Druids, who served as priests, magicians and judges among the Britons.[16] The Druids had powerful influence among the Britons, who believed in a world filled with supernatural beings and gods.

In 59-60 CE, the Romans decided to destroy the seat of power of the Druids on the island of Anglesey, just off the west coast of Britain. Under the Roman governor, Suetonius Paulinus, the bulk of the Roman army was moved to the west coast. Defying a line of cursing Druids standing on the shore, the Romans swarmed out of their boats, conquering Anglesey and slaughtering the Druids and all their followers.[9,13] The slaughter of the Druids further embittered many Britons against Rome.

Amidst their success, the Romans brought trouble upon themselves. King Prastagus of the Iceni, fabled for his great wealth, died in 60 CE.[17] Prastagus left half his kingdom to Rome and half to his two daughters, under the supervision of their mother, Queen Boudica.[9,13] This arrangement was not atypical among the client kingdoms of the Romans.

The Romans, however, felt that his whole kingdom was theirs to dispose of. For reasons that remain unclear, their reaction was particularly harsh and brutal. The Romans looted the king's house, seized his estates and those of the Iceni nobility, while enslaving many of the latter. Then the

Romans flogged Queen Boudica before raping her daughters.[13] The Roman action was particularly foolish when the bulk of their army was hundreds of miles away on the west coast of Britain.

Led by Boudica, the Iceni rebelled. The tribe to their south, the Trinovantes, joined them. The Romans had seized the Trinovante capital of Camulodunum to become their capital, forcing the Trinovantes to pay special taxes for the construction of Roman buildings.[9] The Romans had taken their best lands while scorning them as little better than slaves.[13] The Roman abuse led the Trinovantes to join the incensed Iceni.

Queen Boudica inspired her listeners among the Iceni and Trinovantes enough for the two tribes to take the unprecedented step of choosing her, a woman, as their leader.[16] Boudica proposed uniting the tribes of Britons to drive Rome completely out of Britain. Boudica now spoke to her united army, saying, "Those over whom I rule are Britons, men that know not how to till the soil or ply a trade, but who are thoroughly versed in the art of war…As the Queen, then, of such men and such women, I supplicate and pray for victory, preservation of life and liberty against men [the Romans] insolent, unjust, insatiable, impious—if indeed we ought to term these people men who bathe in warm water, eat artificial dainties, drink unmixed wine, anoint themselves with myrrh, sleep on soft couches with boys for bedfellows…and are slaves to a lyre player [the Emperor Nero] and poor one too."[14] Boudica now led the two tribes toward the Roman capital of Camulodunum.

Camulodunum, dominated by the columned Temple of Claudius, had 10,000 inhabitants. It was filled with houses, shops, a marketplace, baths and a theater, but lacked walls or other defenses.[9]

Having just slaughtered the Druids, Paulinus and most of the Roman army were over three hundred miles away on the western shore of Britain. His second in command, the Roman procurator Caius Decianus, from Londinium, dispatched a mere two hundred poorly armed soldiers to the almost defenseless Camulodunum. Then Decianus fled by ship to Gaul.

Boudica led the Britons to smash through the handful of Roman soldiers defending Camulodunum. The Britons massacred the population of Romans and pro-Roman Britons, then looted and burned down the city. The last surviving Romans held out for two days behind the stone walls of the Temple of Claudius before they too were killed.[9,15] The Romans, who treated their defeated foes mercilessly, nevertheless complained about the tortures the Britons inflicted on the Romans in the city. Roman historian Cassius Dio wrote of women having their breasts sliced off, then stuffed in their mouths, while dead Roman babies were carried about spits.[14]

Petilius Cerealis, commander of the Ninth Legion, some 5000 men in all, hurried from his base in the Midlands with a large detachment of the Legion to relieve Camulodunum. Boudica ambushed Cerealis en route, wiping out the Roman infantry. Fifteen hundred Romans were killed. Cerealis fled back northwest with a few surviving cavalrymen.[9,13]

The army of Britons now tramped quickly to the Roman trading port of Londinium, nestled on the banks of the River Thames. Londinium was purely a trading town with no military presence or defensive walls. However, it was a symbol of Rome, full of wealth from trade and only forty miles south of Camulodunum. The population of Londinium numbered some 30,000, including many Britons who had accepted Roman rule and adopted Roman customs. Boudica was determined to slay all the Romans and uproot all traces of Roman influence from the land.

Paulinus, the Roman governor, had returned from Anglesey to Londinium with a handful of cavalry, but the bulk of the Roman army was still far to the west. Paulinus realized that with his handful of men he could not defeat the approaching army of Britons so he ordered the population to flee the city. Those who were too weak or infirm or unwilling to leave remained.

Boudica sent her forces into Londinium. Those Romans or pro-Roman Britons who remained in the city were tortured before being killed. Boudica's soldiers looted the city, then burned it to the ground.

Boudica and her army now headed northwest to assault a third Roman city, Verulamium (the modern St. Albans). This town was the capital of the Catuvellauni tribe. This tribe had rapidly adopted Roman customs and ideas. They also were the traditional enemies of the Trinovantes. As Boudica and her army approached Verulamium, the outnumbered Catuvellauni fled. Thus, it was a largely empty town that the Britons set afire, but what had been the third largest town in Roman Britain.[9]

Roman rule in Britain appeared at an end. Roman historian Cassius Dio later wrote, "A terrible disaster occurred in Britain. Two cities were sacked, 80,000 of Romans and of their allies perished, and the island was lost to Rome. Moreover, all of this was brought upon the Romans by a woman, a fact which in itself covered them with the greatest shame."[14]

Now Boudica and her army moved northwest to face the main Roman army in Britain, finally approaching from the west. Both sides had an incentive to fight an immediate decisive battle. Boudica's army required so much food that it had to move constantly to new areas to obtain food or else disperse. For their part, the Romans wanted to quash the rebellion before more tribes joined it.

The Britons far outnumbered the Romans, but the Roman forces consisted of trained and well-armed soldiers, unlike the Britons. Paulinus managed to pull together some 10,000 men from the Fourteenth and Twentieth Legions and various auxiliary forces. While the British tribes had a cadre of elite warriors, the majority were farmers and herdsmen with little experience in battle. Boudica reportedly had an army of 230,000, although this almost certainly inflated total included women and children.[9]

Paulinus chose the battlefield, the exact location of which remains uncertain. He chose a position approached by a narrow defile, or steep-sided gorge, which would have limited the number of Britons that could attack the Romans at any one time. The geography would obviate the Britons' greater numbers while also limiting the Britons' ability to use their chariots, which were a major part of their weaponry. While the Romans all had armor, shields, short swords and throwing javelins, only the aristocracy among the Britons was trained for war, with armor and full weaponry. The mass of Britons were armed only with homemade swords and spears.

Paulinus placed his cavalry at the flanks with the legionaries at the center. The Britons, who probably outnumbered him at least ten to one, were grouped in their tribal bands with their chiefs. The whole tribe accompanied its warriors to battle. Behind the Briton warriors lay their families, animals and possessions in loaded wagons.

Boudica, wearing a multicolored tunic and a cloak secured by a brooch at her throat, then mounted her chariot. Accompanied by her daughters, she drove to the front line and addressed her warriors. Boudica cried out, "But now it not as a woman descended from illustrious ancestry, but as one of the people that I am avenging my lost freedom, my lashed body, the outraged honor of my daughters. Roman greed has developed to such an extent that not even our persons, nor even our age or our virginity are left unpolluted. But heaven is on the side of just vengeance: one legion which dared to fight has been destroyed; the rest are cowering in their camps or anxiously seeking a means of escape. They will not stand even the din and shout of so many thousands, let alone our attack and our weapons."[9,13] The British warriors, dyed blue with woad for the battle, cheered the queen. Boudica, accompanied by her daughters, then rode in her chariot up and down the ranks of her troops, urging revenge against the Romans.[16]

Coming to a section of her waiting troops, Boudica lifted a spear and told them, "It is better to have poverty with freedom than wealth with servitude, for what can be worse than the treatment we have suffered since these men came over to Britain… We have such an excess of bravery that we consider our tents to be safer than their walls and our shields better at protecting us than their whole suits of armor… So—let us prove to them that they are hares and foxes trying to rule over dogs and wolves."[9] Boudica then performed a divination in which she released a hare from under her cloak. It ran towards the Britons, a sign that victory would be theirs.[16]

Addressing the Roman ranks, Suetonius Paulinus told his men, "Before you, you can see more women than warriors. Cowardly, unarmed, they will give up the moment they see the weapons and bravery of their conquerors who have given them such a drubbing so many times before… Keep your ranks tight, and once you've discharged your javelins, then continue the slaughter with shields and swords, never stopping to think about plunder; when you've won yourselves a victory you can have it all."[9,13]

At last Boudica released the attack. Fueled by copious quantities of ale, the Britons then charged toward the waiting Romans. The Romans unleashed a storm of hurled javelins. The javelins pierced the poorly armored Britons by the score, felling large numbers. The Romans followed with a second volley. As Britons fell, this further narrowed the space for the remainder to go forward. When the Britons at last reached the Romans, the Romans pushed forward in thick wedge formation, their shields overlapping to form a solid wall. Behind the thin layer of well-armed professional warriors of the Iceni and Trinovantes followed thousands of simple farmers and herdsmen. The Britons found it difficult to swing their long swords effectively in the close-packed combat. The short swords of the Romans did murderous damage to the Britons. Little by little the Britons were pushed back. As the Britons' best warriors fell to the Roman shield wall, those behind at last lost heart. Finally, the Britons could take no more and turned to flee. However, their retreat was impeded by their own wagons and families that waited behind at the edge of the battlefield. The Romans came on, slaughtering all in their path. It is estimated that a thousand Romans and

40,000 Britons fell in the battle.[9, 13] This would make it the largest one-day death toll of any battle fought in Britain.

Boudica managed to escape the carnage, but died soon thereafter. Tacitus reported that she ended her life with poison. Dio said that she became ill and died. A romantic writer might say that she died of a broken heart. The fate of her daughters is unknown.

The battle effectively ended the rebellion, although the Romans spent the rest of the winter putting down the last embers of defiance. The Romans killed 80,000 more Britons in stamping out the revolt.[16,17] Roman apologists excused this killing, saying, "Suetonius [Paulinus] had prevented Britain from falling back into its aboriginal barbarism."[17]

A few years later Paulinus was replaced by a new governor, Petronius Turpilianus, who emphasized reconciliation. His efforts and those of his successors ensured that no further rebellions occurred.[15,16] Londinium was rebuilt and became the major city of the province, eventually being renamed London. Britain would remain a largely peaceful and increasingly Romanized part of the Roman Empire for over another 300 years, almost up to the Empire's final collapse in the 5th century CE. Boudica would have scorned this as a poor substitute for freedom from Rome.

Ironically, Boudica would have been forgotten had she not been immortalized by the Roman historians, principally Tacitus and Cassius Dio. The Britons banned writing, which they believed stole the power from spoken words. While the British bards were famed for their storytelling, perhaps none of these bards survived to pass on the story.

Boudica became a symbol of British resistance to foreign oppression. She is the first monarch remembered as ruler of the Britons, as opposed to of a single tribe in Britain. She should be given credit for helping form this national identity as Britons.

As a warrior queen her story was resurrected under the realm of Elizabeth I. Elizabeth was depicted as another Boudica, this time guarding Britain against a Spanish invasion.[9] Boudica was memorialized by British writers from Spenser to Milton. Tennyson wrote his poem "Boudica" in 1860. In 1902 the sculpture, *Boudica and Her Daughters*, by Thomas Thorneycroft, showing the queen and her daughters in her chariot, was erected in London, where it remains. Boudica has been the central character in several British films and plays, as well in museum exhibits in Britain.[9] All the details of the historical Boudica will never be established for sure. Yet few losing commanders have ever been more remembered.

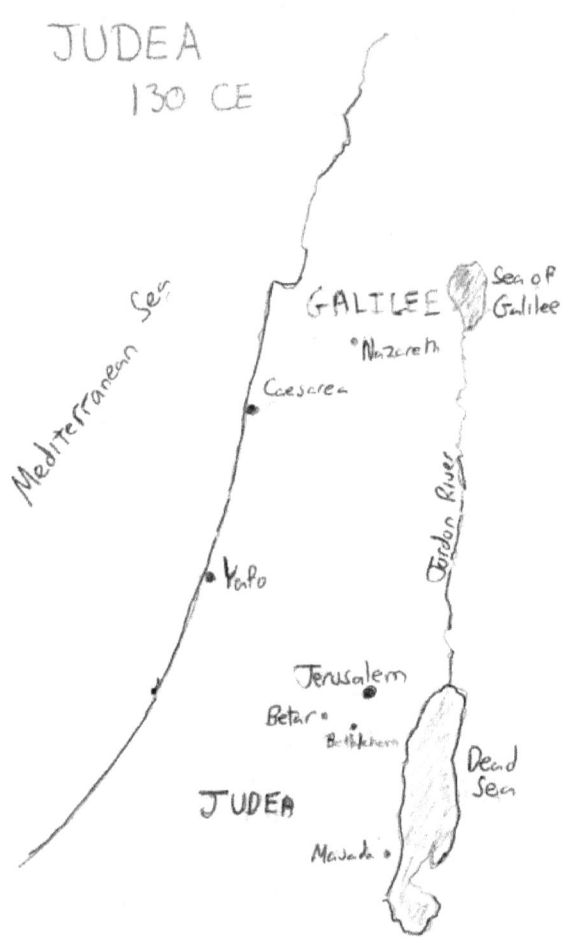

Chapter 3: Rabbi Akiba and the Judean Revolts
Challenging the Roman Empire, Judea, 131 CE

RABBI AKIBA'S STUDENT was dumbfounded. In 130 CE the Roman Empire was near the peak of its power, stretching from Britain to Syria. Yet here was Rabbi Akiba, the wisest man in Judea, proposing to challenge Rome's control. This is insanity, thought the student. Yet, indeed Akiba and his friend Simeon Bar Kochba were to lead the last of three great Judean revolts that challenged the authority and control of Rome.[18-29]

Akiba may have thought about the events of the preceding century and a half. Judea had enjoyed a brief period of independence after the five Maccabee brothers led a successful, twenty-five-year-long struggle against the rule of Syria. However, after the death of the last brother, Simon, a popular, effective leader, his descendants fought among themselves for power, with few exceptions caring little for the people they ruled. A battle for succession between two brothers, Hyrcanus II and Aristobulus, led both to appeal to the Romans, who by then had conquered Syria, for support. The Roman general Pompey, the dominant leader in the east of the Roman Republic, chose to support Hyrcanus II, helping him conquer the Judean capital of Jerusalem. Judea became a client state of Rome.[29]

Akiba knew that it was the greed and rapacity of the Romans that led to the first great revolt, for increasingly the men Rome appointed as procurators, the administrators of Judea, saw the job as an opportunity for private spoils. The Roman procurator Gesius Florus precipitated the first Jewish revolt against Rome in 66 CE when he removed a large amount of gold from the Temple treasury claiming financial distress. In response, the population mocked Florus "going around with baskets [and] begged coppers for the poor starveling."[21] Enraged, Florus ordered his troops to sack the marketplace in Jerusalem and kill all they met, resulting in an estimated 3600 deaths.[21]

The ensuing war lasted four years. The Romans first advanced in the Galilee, where they captured town after town, many after heavy fighting with large loss of life on both sides. The Romans burned the villages, then broke the agricultural terraces so the soil washed away, leaving a barren land.[22] The war ended when the Romans, after a long siege, took Jerusalem and destroyed the Jewish Temple there. An estimated one million Jews died in Jerusalem alone.[21]

The Jews expected that at some point the Temple in Jerusalem could be rebuilt. However, the Romans refused. What remained of Jerusalem became a city under military occupation with a strong permanent Roman garrison. A special tax was imposed on Jews throughout the empire as punishment for the revolt in Judea.[29] These measures ensured that intense Jewish resentment of the Romans would persist.

Akiba was sixteen, a poor, illiterate shepherd at the time of the first revolt, and did not participate in this revolt. He lived near the coast, an area that was spared the degree of destruction and deaths in the Galilee and Jerusalem.[25]

The destruction of the Temple meant that the Jews had to adapt their religion in its absence. Many Jews migrated to other parts of the Roman Empire. The hereditary priesthood was replaced by teachers called rabbis, who rose based on their ability. The rabbis established a school at Yavneh where they studied, taught and wrote down the Torah (the Bible) and the commentary on it. This consequence of the revolt was to change Akiba's life.

At some point after this first revolt, Akiba's life changed significantly. The poor shepherd fell in love with Rachel, the daughter of a wealthy man. Rachel agreed to marry him only if he would commit to learning to read and write. Her father, angered by her marriage to an illiterate shepherd, disinherited Rachel. Akiba was unable to fulfill his promise for many years. One day Akiba saw a fissure in a rock caused by a trickle of water. Akiba later said that he thought, "Water is soft, yet it has made an impression on this hard rock. Surely the Torah will make an impression even on my dull mind if I keep trying."[24] Quickly Akiba learned to read and soon surpassed the teacher in their village. Rachel urged him to travel to the village of Yavneh to study under the greatest rabbis of the time. The legend is that she cut off and sold her long hair to help pay for this.[24] Akiba traveled to Yavneh to study. When he returned to Rachel twelve years later it was as a great rabbi, surrounded by hundreds of students.[24,26] Akiba told his students that he owed it all to his wife Rachel. When asked who is truly a rich man, Akiba replied, "He who has a good wife."[24]

Akiba founded his own rabbinic school at B'nai Brak. He also traveled throughout the Roman Empire, serving as a teacher while fundraising for money to give to the poor. He also was part of a rabbinic delegation that traveled to Rome itself. Legend is that the other rabbis were saddened by the noise coming from Rome while Jerusalem lay desolate. Akiba, however, began to laugh. He explained, "If this is what God has given to those who anger Him, how much more will He give to those who fulfill his will."[25] Akiba was optimistic that one day Judea would become independent again, although he could not say how.

The second great Jewish revolt against Rome occurred in 112 CE, among the huge Jewish population living outside Judea, who made up an estimated 10% of the population of the Roman Empire at the end of the first century CE.[23] The immediate precipitant is unclear. By 115 CE this revolt was smashed with thousands of deaths.[18,23,24,29] Akiba, who was not involved in this revolt, was convinced that it was foolish to challenge Roman rule. Yet Akiba remained optimistic about the future and about the rebuilding of the Temple, saying, "Even as the day is now overcast and now bright again, so shall darkness be made bright."[25]

Akiba became the leading rabbi in Judea, renowned for his wisdom. Gathering together all the competing interpretations, Akiba arranged the vast amount of the oral commentary on the Torah into a logical order, organized by subject matter, allowing its transmission to students. He systemized and preserved the unwritten laws and traditions of Judaism.[20,25] A saying of the time was that the power of Moses was weak until his teachings were interpreted by Akiba.[20] Akiba became the spiritual and intellectual leader of the Jewish community throughout Judea.

Akiba believed that Jewish law should try to remedy inequality in society.[18] As a judge in the rabbinic courts, Akiba was known for interpreting the laws to favor the poor.[25] Akiba argued that religious rituals should be open to the poor equally with the rich. He tried to limit slavery and fought for an improved social position for women. Akiba was known for his modesty, concern for others and optimism, emphasizing the goodness of God and expectation of better things to come.[25]

Rabbi Akiba was troubled by the Roman rule over his country. The people were oppressed by heavy taxes and harsh Roman laws. Moreover, the Temple, which had been the religious center of Judaism, remained in ruins. To the younger firebrands who talked of overthrowing Roman rule, Akiba counselled patience. Perhaps the Romans would eventually let the Temple be rebuilt. Years passed. Akiba was now almost 80 years old, very rare at that time. His wife Rachel and oldest son had already died.[24]

Trajan, who ruled for nearly twenty years and oversaw immense military expansion, was succeeded as emperor by Hadrian. Hadrian saw the roots of the Jews' rebelliousness against Rome in their religion. Why else would they risk their lives in these revolts to regain their freedom?[18] Hadrian decided to suppress this religion. Akiba and the people of Judea initially were overjoyed when word came that Hadrian would permit the rebuilding of Jerusalem and the Temple. Then came the news that Jerusalem was to be rebuilt as Aelia Captolina, a city for the Romans, from which the Jews were excluded.[29] The Temple would be rebuilt as the Temple of Jupiter, chief of the many Roman gods. Hadrian also outlawed the Jewish custom of circumcision, further inflaming the population.[20,25,29]

Almost immediately the people of Judea rose in rebellion against the Romans. Hadrian's actions persuaded Akiba, no matter any misgivings, that the Jews must rise against Roman rule. Akiba was desperate to find a commander to lead the fight against the Romans. He heard about Simeon, a man from the town of Kosiba, who had gathered a small army in a valley in the mountains.

Akiba went to see Simeon and his army, made up largely of farmers and laborers, with his own eyes. Akiba found in Simeon a magnetic personality who inspired great devotion from his men.[23,24] Akiba now remembered a verse out of the Torah, "A star [Kochba] shall arise out of Israel."[24] Akiba laid his hand on Simeon's head and blessed him, saying, "Not Simeon Bar [of] Kosiba shall you be called, but Bar Kochba, Son of a Star."[24]

Akiba differed from many of the other rabbis of the time in his belief that there was active and regular divine intervention in the world. He felt that what was needed was a true commitment to the Divine Kingdom, a commitment he found in Bar Kochba. Akiba felt that the Divine Kingdom, or the so-called end of days, would be ushered in by human beings.[27] Other rabbis challenged Akiba's view of Bar Kochba as the possible messiah. Rabbi Yohanan Ben Torta said, "Akiba! Grass will grow in your cheeks and the son of David will still not have come."[27] Whether or not Akiba believed Simeon to be the messiah, he felt that Simeon was the commander to take on the Romans.

Akiba and Simeon were quite different men. Where Akiba was gentle and calm, Simeon was full of confidence, daring and fearless. When some Jews attacked Simeon for putting more reliance on his sword than on God,

Akiba supported Simeon. In turn Simeon and his troops strictly observed the Sabbath. It was the combination of the two leaders that persuaded the population to back the rebellion.

With Akiba's support, hundreds of new recruits came to join Bar Kochba. In 132 CE Bar Kochba attacked the Roman army in Judea. Shocking the Empire, Bar Kochba's army of farmers and craftsmen defeated the professional soldiers of the Roman legions. The Roman 22nd Legion was wiped out. It disappeared from the future lists of the legions.[27] Unfortunately for posterity, the details of the war are few. Akiba encouraged all who would listen to join the revolt for this would surely be the Jews' last chance to overthrow Roman rule in Judea.

The Romans recalled their ablest general, Julius Severus, from Britain to try to recapture Judea. Legion records suggest that as many as twelve legions from across the empire, totaling some 50,000 men, were sent to suppress the revolt.[26] While the Romans had full armor and weapons, Bar Kochba's forces had only handmade weapons or what they had captured from the Romans. Bar Kochba divided the country into districts under local leaders, waging a guerilla campaign against the Romans. In response, Severus slowly and systematically recaptured or laid waste district after district, town after town. Roman historian Cassius Dio wrote, "By depriving them [the Jews] of food and shutting them up, he was able, rather slowly to be sure…to crush, exhaust and exterminate them."[14] The ongoing battles led to massive casualties on both sides. The Romans systematically razed the Jewish villages they captured. Tens of thousands of noncombatants among the Jews died from famine and disease. Dio concluded, "Nearly the whole of Judea was made desolate… Many Romans, moreover, perished in this war."[14]

The war lasted three years. Eventually the superior numbers, training and equipment of the Romans won out. Finally, in 135 CE, Bar Kochba and the remains of his army were wiped to the last man at the fortress of Betar.[19,24] An estimated half a million Jews died in this war, with many of the survivors sold into slavery.[20]

The Romans prohibited the remaining Jews from studying or keeping any of the laws of the Torah. Anyone violating this edict would be put to death. Rabbi Akiba defied this law, meeting each day with a few students, determined to pass on his knowledge. At last Akiba was arrested.

During his imprisonment, he reportedly was frequently questioned by the Roman governor, Tineius Rufus, about Judaism. In one exchange, Rufus asked Akiba, "If your god so loves the poor, why does he not take care of them himself."[25] Akiba answered, "This gives us an opportunity to carry out his work."[25]

After a long imprisonment, Akiba was condemned to death by torture. Akiba believed that one must accept what God metes out, be it "of good or of punishment."[25] Thus, when his flesh was pulled out with red hot pincers, Akiba was defiant, refusing to cry out in pain. Rather he died continuing to chant prayers to his last breath.[24]

After this third revolt, the Romans prohibited any Jews from living in Judea. The province was renamed Syria Palestina.[20] Hadrian prohibited the religion of Judaism itself, although this ban was relaxed by later emperors. Neither Hadrian nor any succeeding emperor permitted the rebuilding of the Temple in Jerusalem.

Bar Kochba and Akiba, by one perspective, had suffered a catastrophic defeat. Many rabbinical chroniclers would besmirch Bar Kochba's memory for having led the Jews into such an apocalypse, while minimizing Akiba's role in the uprising. Yet, Akiba also gave Judaism its first great martyr, a model for tenacity in the face of torture and death for thousands who would face a similar path in the next two millennia. Moreover, the two men's fight for independence against overwhelming opposition was not forgotten.

Against all odds, perhaps uniquely among nations, the Jews and Judaism survived 1900 years without a homeland or nation. The oral commentary that Akiba systematized became an important part of the Talmud, which helped preserve Jewish identity during the centuries when they were scattered far from their homeland. In 1948 with the establishment of Israel, the Jews came home. The Roman Empire had fallen some 1500 years earlier.

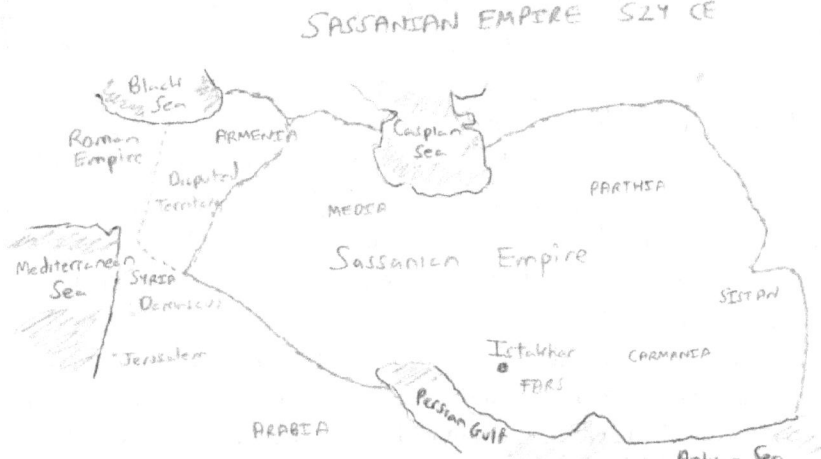

Chapter 4: Mazdak
The First Communist, 524 CE, Persia

THE POOR MAN mourned his dead sons. Both sons had followed the Zoroastrian priest and reformer Mazdak, who argued that men should be treated equally. Mazdak also asserted that property should be held in common. Mazdak's doctrines angered the wealthy and powerful men of Persia. The elite had struck back, killing Mazdak and a hundred thousand of his followers, the poor man's sons among them. Why had Ahura Mazda, the supreme deity, the god of goodness, allowed this to happen in his sons and to Persia?[30-35]

The year was somewhere around 530 CE. The Sassanian Dynasty had reestablished the Persian Empire in 224 CE. Soon after, Zoroastrianism became the official state religion in the empire.

It is unclear where or when Zoroaster, the founder of this religion, lived.[30,33] Zoroaster's ethics emphasized human choices. In a universe that is a battleground between good and evil, it up to the individual to choose between them. History is progressing to an ultimate battle in which good will ultimately prevail. Zoroaster postulated an evil deity, Anra Mainyu, as well as minor gods, the daevas and yazotas, who are on the side of evil and good respectively.[30] Zoroaster was one of the first religious leaders to emphasize personal moral choices.

Zoroaster was also reportedly the first to suggest that what happened to individuals after death would depend on their actions in life. The good would ascend to the heavenly realm of Ahura Mazda while evil people would go to a hell under the rule of Anra Mainyu.[30]

No man was to shake up the Persian Empire as much as a Zoroastrian priest named Mazdak. Mazdak is a mysterious figure, with almost no details existing about his life.[30-3] There is evidence of a Book of Mazdak, but no copy of this or any other books from the entire period of the Sasanian Dynasty has survived.[30]

Mazdak presented his teachings as a reinterpretation of the Avesta, the Zoroastrian texts. Mazdak taught that light (goodness) and darkness (evil) are mingled by chance in the human and natural world. Hence even the lowliest person might be lucky enough to be dominated by good and hence receive salvation.[30] Since the poor were not necessarily worse than the rich in terms of goodness, Mazdak argued that the poor should share resources equally with the wealthy.

Mazdak antagonized the Zoroastrian priesthood by rejecting any formal religious duty or ritual. Mazdak said that the mark of a righteous person "was that he embodied [goodness] in which case he attains the state of [a] divine lord in [this] inferior world and can do so without any religious obligation."[30] When in power Mazdak was reported to have ordered the abolition of all temples except the three major ones. He aimed at a simplification of the Zoroastrian priestly hierarchy with an attending restriction on church property.[32]

Mazdak preached a pacifist lifestyle including vegetarianism. Mazdak taught abstemiousness, devotion and the sacredness of animal life.[35] This did not imply a life of total self-denial. Mazdak is said to have "allowed, at least for the bulk of believers, enjoyment of life in moderation and without competition and without causing suffering to others.[32] Mazdak taught his followers to perform deeds of kindness, and to refrain from killing or causing people sorrow. Mazdak also emphasized hospitality to one's guests, granting them whatever they desired.[30]

The most detailed source about Mazdak is the *Shahnameh*, written by Abolqasem Ferdowski around 980 CE, which tells the history of Persia from prehistory through the Arab conquest in 651 CE. Ferdowski wrote, "A man named Mazdak, who was eloquent and knowledgeable and possessed great abilities, came to the court. King Qobad listened to his wise words and made him the King's chief minister and treasurer."[31]

When a drought occurred, making food scarce throughout Persia, the people gathered outside the palace of King Qobad. Mazdak listened to their concerns and asked them to return the next day. Mazdak then went to King Qobad and asked him a question. Mazdak asked, "Suppose there's someone who's been bitten by a poisonous snake and he's about to die: What to say, my lord, should happen to a man who has the antidote but who insists on hoarding it, and will not give the bitten man the means to help him live?"[31] The king replied, "The man who had the antidote is a murderer. He should be hanged at the gates as punishment for the dead man's blood."[31] When the crowd of hungry people returned the next day, Mazdak again went to the king and asked another question, saying, "Picture a man in chains: for want of bread he wastes away and soon he will be dead. Now he's denied bread by a passerby who lets the miserable captive die. Should this man suffer punishment? Or would you say that he did was just and good?"[31] The king replied, "Destroy the wretch; by not acting he has another man's blood on his hands." Mazdak left King Qobad and went to the gates of the palace.

There he addressed the crowd, saying, "Take the grain that has been hoarded and hidden away; put it at men's disposal in the streets and throughout the town; let each man take his share!"[31] The people proceeded to strip the royal granaries bare. The overseers went to the king, complaining that Mazdak was responsible. King Qobad summoned Mazdak and asked him to account for the looting of the granaries. Mazdak replied, "I told the suffering citizens what I'd heard from the king. I talked to the king of the world about the poisonous snake and about the man who had the antidote. The king told me that the man who had the antidote had committed a sin, and that if someone shed his blood there would be nothing wrong in this. For a hungry man bread is the antidote to his sufferings, one that he won't need when he's well fed again. If you are a just ruler, your majesty, you won't hoard grain in your granaries. How many hungry men have died with empty bellies because of those granaries."[31] This argument persuaded King Qobad to support Mazdak and his ideas of social justice.[31]

The reason the king supported Mazdak's ideas has been debated. Some historians have argued that he genuinely wanted to help the common people, while others have speculated that he was seeking to counter the power of the aristocracy. The Persian kings depended on the aristocrats to supply most of the troops for the Persian state's recurrent wars with Rome.[33]

Mazdak's ideas have led later historians to call Mazdak the first communist.[35] Ferdowski wrote, "[Mazdak] said that those who had nothing were equal with the powerful and that one man should not own more than another."[31] Mazdak also proclaimed that "women, houses and possessions were to be distributed, so that the poor would have as much as the rich."[31] Mazdak declared "that God placed the means of subsistence on earth so that people divide them among themselves equally…but people wronged one another and sought domination over one another… It is absolutely necessary that one take from the rich for giving to the poor, so that all will become equal in wealth. Whoever possesses an excess of property, women or goods he has no more right to it than another."[32] Mazdak believed that redistribution of property to the poor was an act of piety that would please God.[32]

Mazdak's arguments won him many adherents, but also much hatred from the aristocracy. Ferdowski wrote, "The poor and anyone who lived by the sweat of his brow were with him…[while] the nobility faced ruin."[31]

Mazdak said, "There are five things that lead us away from justice…these five are envy, the longing for vengeance, anger, desire, and the fifth, which becomes a man's master, greed. If you can conquer these five demons, the way to God lies open to you…if women and wealth are not to harm the true faith, they must be held in common… It is these two that generate envy, greed and desire…anger and a longing for vengeance."[31]

Quobad's son, Prince Kesra, did not support Mazdak or his ideas. The *Shahnameh* tells of a decisive meeting between Quobad, Kesra, Mazdak and an assembly of the people. At the meeting, an unnamed Zoroastrian priest rebukes Mazdak, saying, "You are a seeker after knowledge, but the new religion you have made is a pernicious one. If women and wealth are to be held in common, how will a son know his father, or a father his son. If men are to be equal in the world, social distinctions will be unclear; who will want to be a commoner, and how will nobility be recognized? If a laboring slave and the king are the same, when a man dies, who is to inherit his goods? This talk of yours will ruin the world, and such an evil doctrine should not flourish in Iran. If everyone is a master, who is he to command…None of those who established religions have talked in this way.

You have secretly put together a demonic faith; you are leading everyone to hell."[31]

The *Shahnameh* has the king, after hearing these words, turning away from Mazdak's teachings in disgust. Ferdowski wrote, "He [the king] handed Mazdak and his followers, who included a hundred thousand men of good standing over to Kesra and said, 'Do with these men as you will.'"[31]

Kesra then killed Mazdak's followers by burying their heads while they were stood upside down in the ground. Mazdak was strung up on a tall gallows, hanging upside down. He was killed with a shower of arrows.[31]

An alternate history is that Kesra, backed by the anti-Mazdak nobility, succeeded in winning the battle for succession over his two older brothers, who supported Mazdak's ideas. He then killed Mazdak and his supporters.[32,35] In either case, Kesra then rolled back Mazdak's reforms, returning property to the nobility.[32]

There is also controversy as to whether Mazdak really intended that women and property be held in common. Some writers believe that Mazdak did indeed intend to abolish private property and marriage.[34] Other historians believe Mazdak did not push collective ownership, but rather engaged in redistribution, taking from the rich to give to the poor. In this view Mazdak argued that no one should have more than another and that the surplus should be taken away to achieve this equality.[34] Historian Ehsan Yarshater, editor of the *Cambridge History of Iran*, wrote, "What seems more plausible is that Mazdak preached a series of measures to strip the higher classes of their privileges and to help the poor. Among such measures were most probably the breaking up of large estates, prohibition of hoarding, adjustment of landlord's shares from crops, lowering of class distinctions and instituting public foundations for the benefit of the needy."[32] Mazdak also aimed for having rural communities pool their resources to meet everyone's needs.[32]

The *Cambridge History of Iran* also argues that Mazdak's views on women have been misrepresented, stating, "As for Mazdak's teachings with regards to women, most probably he approved of them marrying outside their own class. He may have prohibited having more than one wife and called for the abolition of harems…he may have relaxed the marriage laws…to the orthodox Zoroastrians such modifications would mean disturbing the lines of descent and destroying family and class distinctions."[32]

Whether due to Mazdak's influence or not, under Kings Qobad and Kesra measures were pushed through that weakened the power of the nobility. The army would in the future be paid for and directly under the control of the king. The reign of Kesra marked the pinnacle of Sassanid rule.[33]

The centuries that followed Mazdak's death would be marked by intermittent rebellions by people claiming to share Mazdak's beliefs. Some of Mazdak's doctrines were absorbed by various Islamic sects. Yarsahater wrote, "The presence of Mazdakites in practically all parts of Iran during the early centuries of Islam is well attested."[32]

In Central Asia, a prophet named al-Moqanna maintained control over the region of Sogdiana from 766–780. It was said that his religion was simply "all the laws and institutes which Mazdak had established."[30] In 1844 an English missionary, Joseph Wolff, met a group of Persian Sufis in Central Asia. They told him, "The time will come when there shall be no difference between rich and poor, between high and low, when property shall be in common, even wives and children."[30] Thus, some of Mazdak's teachings had survived at least 1300 years.

Mazdak's fight for justice and equality was unsuccessful. Even as Mazdak himself has been forgotten by most of the world, some of his ideas, particularly that all men should be equal, survived and has been put forth by other people in other countries. The ideal of communism, of property held in common, has exerted a powerful influence into current times.

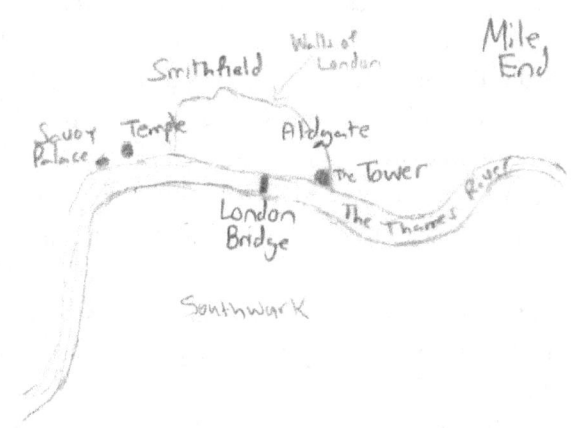

Chapter 5: John Ball and Wat Tyler
The Peasants' Revolt, 1381 CE, England

IN THE YEAR 1381 the news traveled from village to village in southern England. Men whispered, "John Ball hath rungen thy bell," code words that the time was right to rebel. Quickly the villagers of England grabbed their longbows if they had them, their scythes and stout clubs if they did not. From hamlet and town, the men marched toward the capital of London. These were the yeoman of England. Their numbers had been slashed by the Black Plague that earlier in the century had killed a fourth to a half of the population. Still, it was their longbows that had won the great victories over the French, at Crecy and Poiters, in the Hundred Years War. The nobility of England viewed them as little better than animals. The common folk now set out to change that.[36–43]

England was not a happy country. The long wars of the English kings with France had drained the treasury. The French fleet ravaged the southern coast of England while the English fleet had fallen into disarray.[43] These disasters only added to the existing woes of the long-suffering peasantry who made up most of the population.

For the land the peasants farmed belonged to the great noble families of England, the king and the Catholic Church, then the only religion in England. Songs were sung about "the covetous bishops and proud prelates of the Church…who longed only for possessions and temporal goods."[37] Many of the peasants were held almost as slaves, called villeins. They could cultivate some acres of their lord's land in exchange for also cultivating another portion of lord's land from which the lord retained all the crops. This was called the corvee. The noble owner, in addition, had what was called the "boons," the right to ask the peasant to do extra work, without compensation, on his land whenever he saw fit. Thus, the peasant might be forced to harvest the lord's crops even at the cost of watching his own not yet harvested crops be destroyed by weather or other circumstances.[36] In some case the service due had been converted into cash payments to the lord along with service at harvest.[43]

The villein was bound to the land. He could not leave without the lord's consent. His children were similarly bound. The villein needed the lord's permission to marry.[36] In addition, the lord of every manor "had the right to erect a gallows and try peasants, rebels, thieves and bandits."[37] The villein had no right to plead in court against his lord and was subject to his will.[41,43] Tenants frequently had to pay fines for alleged infringements of manorial rules.[43]

The Black Death had killed large numbers of the peasants. Since so many had died, their labor became more valuable. The landowners were forced to offer increased money to attract labor. The nobility complained that the peasants wanted more for their efforts than in the past. The contemporary chronicler Henry Knighton wrote, "There was such a dearth of servants and laborers that men were quite bewildered as to what they should do about it."[43]

Parliament, which then consisted only of nobility and high-ranking churchmen, passed the Statute of Labourers in 1349, which forbid employers from paying more for labor than they had before the pestilence.[40] All agricultural workers had to appear twice a year in front of local officials to swear to abide by this law.[43] The poet John Gower spoke for many of the elite when he said, in commenting on the peasantry, "They are sluggish, they are scarce and they are grasping. For the very little they do they demand the highest pay."[37] Complaining about the demanding peasants, William Langland, author of *Piers Plowman*, wrote around this time, "Laborers deigned not to dine a day on wort a night old. Penny ale will not do…but [only] fresh flesh or fish fried or baked…unless he be highly paid he will chide [complain]."[41]

These new laws stipulated that a man could not seek new employers or ask for higher pay. He must remain on the manor where he had been born and work for his lord on the terms that had been present before the coming of the plague. Many peasants ignored this provision to move into other districts or into the towns where they could earn higher pay.[40,41] One member of Parliament stated, "If their master reprove them for bad service or offer pay them for the said service according to the form of said statutes, they fly and run suddenly…to strange places unknown to their said masters."[41] The law held that if the sheriff failed to catch the runaway worker, he should declare him an outlaw, whom any man might slay on sight.[41]

Decreased food production, resulting from the labor shortage, resulted in a higher cost of living. The profits from the higher grain prices went to the nobility while the peasant would toil for the same wage, yet face higher prices.[36] Statutes also required all able-bodied persons to work and imposed penalties on those who were idle.[37,40] Landowners, sitting as justices of the peace, kept a portion of the money from fines levied on workers breaking the law, thus creating an even stronger incentive for enforcing the law. The labor laws were greatly resented by the population. One of the main goals of the rebels would be the abolition of the Statute of Labourers.[43]

The nobility in Parliament was aware of peasant unhappiness, but was unwilling to alleviate it. Parliament complained about the villeins' behavior in 1377, writing as a preamble of a statute that "the villeins…affirm themselves to be quite and utterly discharged of all service…will not suffer any distress or other justice to be made upon them."[41] Parliament concluded, "If due remedy be not…provided upon the same rebels, greater mischief…may thereof spring through the Realm."[41]

The treasury remained empty due to the cost of the war with France. To raise revenue, the so-called "Good Parliament" passed a poll tax in 1377.

The tax, although initially different for different incomes, eventually became equal for everyone whether the noble owner of thousands of acres and multiple estates or the poorest villein. This tax was levied multiple times between 1377 and 1381, with last tax being the highest.[40] The tax was more galling because the enormous sums spent in the prior four years had not prevented repeated military defeats.[43] The new tax, by being the same for every person, shifted the burden from the wealthy to the poorer classes.

In 1381, the accumulated discontent of the peasantry broke into the open in the Peasants' Revolt, the biggest single uprising of the common people in English history. Some historians claim that a better name would be the "People's Revolt," noting that it included artisans, poor priests, free farm laborers, idle soldiers, wage earners, craftsmen and the village elite, including stewards, bailiffs and constables.[39,43] One of the great leaders of the revolt was John Ball.

John Ball, originally from Yorkshire, was a hedge priest, which meant a priest without a church or any formal position. He roamed England, sleeping where he could (hence the jibe hedge priest) and preaching in villages or sometimes in the woods nearby. Ball and other preachers often talked about the wickedness of some of the wealthy, with one commenting, "the tournaments of the rich are the torments of the poor."[44] Ball is first mentioned in February 1364, when the king withdrew a special protection that Ball had, because "[he] wanders the countryside preaching articles contrary to the faith of the church to the peril of his soul and souls of others, especially laymen."[43]

Ball preached the essential equality of men. The poet William Morris wrote a book, *The Dream of John Ball*, in which Ball tells a group of peasants, "What else shall ye lack when ye lack masters? Ye shall not lack for the fields you have tilled nor the houses ye have built, nor the cloth ye have woven…and man shall help man, and the saints in heaven shall be glad, because men no more fear each other."[36]

To the Church, Ball was dangerous. If all men were equal, what would the need for the hierarchy of the Church? Ball was three times imprisoned by Simon Sudbury, Archbishop of Canterbury. Sudbury accused Ball of slandering him and had him excommunicated in 1364.[43] At the time of the Revolt, Ball was imprisoned in the archbishop's prison in Maidstone in Kent.

Ball urged those who listened to be patient. It was said that when the time was right, John Ball would sound the bell. Sympathizers used certain phrases to communicate with each other. One peasant would say, "John the Miller grinds small, small, small." Another, if he believed in the message of John Ball, would answer, "The king's son of heaven shall pay for all."[36]

There were scattered conflicts in several towns in 1380, the year prior to the great revolt. Riots occurred in Winchester, Shrewsbury and York.[43] The year was also marked by a poor harvest.[43]

The yield collected from the poll tax in January 1381 was disappointing to the government. The number of eligible taxpayers was significantly reduced from four years before, suggesting widespread evasion. Rather than scaling back on its military plans, the government decided to send out new tax collectors with the power to investigate local communities and people for nonpayment.[43] The inequity of the tax was aggravated by corruption among the tax collectors, who would sometimes claim a tax had not been paid while the money vanished into their pockets.[39]

The Peasants' Revolt started in Essex. The men of the three villages of Fobbing, Corringham and Stanford-le-Hope reported that they had already paid the poll tax and refused to pay again. The tax collector, John Brampton, ordered his men-at-arms to arrest the men. Brampton was notorious for imprisoning men accused of breaking the labor laws and only releasing them when paid a bribe.[43] The people of the area chased Brampton and his minions away. A higher official, Robert Belknap, returned with henchmen to try to enforce order, but was driven away. Several legal officials were killed.[39] Having crossed the line in defiance of royal authority, the men of Essex rose in rebellion, their leader a priest known as Jack Straw.[36]

Throughout the revolt, the peasants evidenced hostility to any lawyers. Called Black Robes for their characteristic black gowns, lawyers were viewed as creatures of the powerful, using the laws to afflict the common people.[34,44] Many lawyers were killed during the revolt, including the Chief Justice of England, Sir John Cavendish.[36,40,41] It was reported that every lawyer's house along the line of march of the peasants was destroyed.[44]

In Kent, the revolt began in June 1381. Essex and Kent were two of the places hardest hit by the plague and where the labor laws had been most strictly enforced, so the outbreak of the revolt there was no coincidence.[40] Legend is that a man named Wat, by occupation a tiler in the town of Dartford, became incensed when a poll tax collector insisted that Wat's daughter was old enough to pay the tax. The tax collector stripped the girl of her clothes to prove this. Wat the tiler, or Wat Tyler, smashed in the tax collector's head with a hammer. Historians argue whether this man, or another Wat Tyler from Maidstone, was the Wat Tyler that led the revolt.[36] John Legge, the king's sergeant-at-arms, had been appointed a tax collector for the area that included Dartford.[43] Legge was notorious for demanding to see if girls had reached the age of puberty, so the Wat Tyler story may have an underlying factual basis.[43]

Another story is that the Kentish revolt began at Gravesend on June 3 when the king's tutor, Sir Simon Burley, captured an escaped villein, refused the people's offer to buy his freedom except for an exorbitant sum, and threw the escapee into Rochester Castle.[39,41,43]

Whichever incident was the true precipitant, it caused a great uproar in Kent. Hundreds of men gathered, many from neighboring villages. Some carried bows or pikes, but many had only crude handmade weapons.[36] Despite their outrage, the peasants decided that all men who lived within twelve miles of the coast should stay to guard that coast against a French invasion.[39] The next morning, June 7, the rest marched south some twenty miles to Maidstone, where John Ball was being held. The Archbishop's prison was broken into and Ball freed. The tax rolls of the county were burned.[40] Now John Ball and Wat Tyler sent out messengers to try to arouse the peasants. Across England men went on foot to the villages of the land, saying, "John Ball hath rungen thy bell."[36] The motives of the people were clear to contemporary writers, even those hostile to the revolt. Thomas Walsingham, who served as chronicler for Abbey of St. Albans, wrote that they had risen "for freedom, to be made equal to their Lords, and never again to be held in servitude to any man."[39,43]

In Suffolk, the people's grievances were with the Abbey of Bury St. Edmunds. The abbey, owner of much of the surrounding countryside, employed the peasants on its estates under the same harsh terms as any of the lay nobility. The abbey also lent money, and its head, Prior John, was said to have "thumbs callused from the tightness with which he applied the screws to debtors."[36] Led by a priest named John Wrawe, the peasants stormed of Prior John's manor house, condemned him in a mock trial and cut off his head. His naked body was tossed on a dunghill. The peasants then ransacked the abbey to find the records of the people's debts. These papers were burned.[36]

In Cambridge, the townspeople burned the charters of the university, blaming it for its tight hold on the town. In St. Albans, the uprising was directed against the local abbey, which held a monopoly on the milling of corn, forbidding anyone from grinding their own or taking it elsewhere. The peasants broke in and smashed the millstones of the abbey.[36] Abbeys and monasteries were among the last to commute the requirement of servile labor by the peasants on their lands.[44]

In Norfolk, the revolt was led by Geoffrey the Litster, who called himself the "King of the Commons" and insisted that nobles that were captured had to serve him at meals.[36] Uprisings also broke out in Somersetshire, Yorkshire, Suffolk, Ipswich, Ely, Bridgewater, North Leicestershire, York and Beverly.[41,43]

The Kentish men in revolt stormed the formidable castle at Rochester, at the mouth of the Medway River on June 6.[43] These high stone walls proved little barrier to the determined common folk, who overwhelmed the garrison with sheer numbers and forced its surrender.[39] Another force made its way south to Canterbury. Here, on June 10, they were welcomed by the mayor and townspeople. They searched the archbishop's palace in vain for Archbishop Sudbury, who as Chancellor of England was hated by the people for his role in government. In the absence of the archbishop, who was in London, the peasants burned all records they could find of the people's debts to the church.[36,43]

On June 11, the peasants of Kent turned to march to London. There was no wholesale killing of the upper classes, although some unpopular lords were murdered.[41] Particularly targeted were officials involved in tax collection.[43] Tenants also seized the opportunity to burn manorial records in belief that this might free them from the services requested by their lords.[43]

The King of England, Richard II, was a fourteen-year-old boy. Much as the American colonists believed prior to the start of the American Revolution, the peasants believed that the king would be sympathetic to their cause. They blamed the king's ministers and especially the king's uncle, John of Gaunt, for misgovernment and the failure of the war against the French.[41,44] A story tells how a group of peasants encountered the mother of the king, her wagon stuck in the mud. The peasants helped lift the wagon out of the mud and allowed the Queen Mother to proceed unharmed. The people took as their rallying cry, "With King Richard and the true commons."[36]

Historians dispute the number of peasants in revolt, with numbers ranging from 30,000 to 100,000 men, out of a nation of three million. By comparison the largest city at the time, London, had a population of 40,000 to 50,000.[43] Court records showed that many of those involved in the revolt were indeed the leaders in their villages, acting as bailiffs, constables and jurors.[40]

In any event, it was a large force of peasants that came to Blackheath, south across the river from London, on June 12. Even the smallest estimates of perhaps 10,000 would match the size of the English army in the battles of Crecy, Poitiers and the later Agincourt. The peasant army now surrounded the capital in all directions.

The chroniclers of the time complained that the nobility was passive at the onset of the revolt. Walsingham wrote, "The lords remained quietly at home as though they were asleep while the men of Kent and Essex swelled the ranks of their army."[41] The contemporary French historian Froissart noted that an army of knights under the Duke of Cambridge was at Plymouth when the revolt began. Froissart wrote that this army hastened to put to sea, lest it be prevented in doing so by a rising of the people, as the ransom hunting in France (from the capture of wealthy French nobles) was more important than the safety of the kingdom.[39]

At Blackheath, the peasants halted while their leaders tried to contact the king and his officials in London. The morning after their arrival John Ball addressed the assembled host. Ball is reported to have said, "Good people, things will never be well in England as long as goods are not held in common. And as long as there are villeins and gentlemen [the nobility]. Why do they hold us in serfage? They go clothed in velvet and warm in their furs and their ermines while we are covered with rags. They have wine and spices and fine bread, and we have oat cake and straw and water to drink. They have leisure and fine houses; and we have pain and labor, the rain and the wind in the fields. And yet, it is of us and our toil that these men hold their state."[36]

John Ball continued, pointing out the injustices under which the people suffered. Finally, John Ball concluded with a couplet for which he would be famous for centuries to come: "When Adam delved and Eve span, who was then the gentleman?"[36] Froissart wrote that Ball also said, "Let us go to the King, he is young, and show him what servitude we be in, and show him how we will have it otherwise…if we go together…when the King sees us, we shall have some remedy, either by fairness or otherwise.[39]

While waiting for an answer from the king, the peasant army proceeded to attack the town of Southwark, clustered on the southern bank of the Thames. Here several prisons—the Marshalsea, the King's Bench, the Compter and the Clink—were broken into and the prisoners freed. The army also burned down the Stews, the center of prostitution at the time in London. One of the major owners of the brothels there was the Lord Mayor of London, William Walworth. He would play a key role in the events to come.[36]

At this point, King Richard and his advisors met to consider what to do. While the group hesitated as to what to do, Mayor Walworth raised the drawbridge between two of the piers of the London Bridge. The Thames River was a formidable barrier blocking the Kentish peasants' entry into London. Walworth then urged the king to launch the Trained Bands, the militia of London, against the peasants. However, the others doubted Londoners' loyalty. The ordinary workers tended to oppose all authority. Even the men of property were unhappy and of doubtful allegiance.[36]

The king decided to send out three aldermen to Blackheath to treat with the rebels. Two of them spoke to the mass of peasants, urging them to return home. The third alderman, John Horne, met with Wat Tyler and the other leaders. Horne reportedly said, "Pay no heed to these who came with me. They speak with crooked tongues. You have your cause won, for the whole of London is ready to rise. Cause a tumult around the gates and at the Bridge and you'll find the city ready for you."[36,41]

Three of Tyler's men accompanied Horne back into London, where they were present at a secret meeting of disaffected residents. Meanwhile Horne went to Mayor Walworth to report that the rebels wanted a peaceful settlement. Horne was reported to have said, "I'll wager my head that they won't do any damage if they're allowed inside the walls."[36]

The peasants now sent Sir John Newton, the captured commander of Rochester Castle, with a message to the king. Newton said, "They profess loyalty to the King. They want a chance to lay before him the grievances they hold against his councilors and ministers of state."[36] Newton returned to the peasants with a message that the king would go the next day to Greenwich to listen to what the peasants had to say.

The next day, June 13, the king and his councilors set out down river in the royal barge, followed by four other barges. At Greenwich, the river bank was filled with masses of peasants. The barges were stopped some distance from shore. King Richard addressed the people, saying, "Sirs, I have come to listen. What want ye?"[36] The people demanded that the king come ashore to talk to them. His councilors and the king decided that would be too dangerous, declaring that an audience was impossible under the circumstances. Some accounts have the Earl of Salisbury saying that the peasants were not suitably dressed to face the king.[36] One chronicle reported that the rebels "made such a great clamor that it really seemed as if the devil himself had joined their company."[40] The barges turned around and began to slowly row upriver back to London. There were enough peasants carrying longbows to have wiped out the royal party. Yet not a single arrow was launched. The peasants were sincere in their loyalty to the king.[36]

The peasant army marched upriver to the London Bridge. The commander at the bridge, an alderman named Walter Sibley, looked at the horde on the other side and ordered his small company to retreat, after dropping the drawbridge in place. It is unclear if Sibley had been in on the plan of the prior night to allow the peasants entry to London. Thousands of peasants, gathered into companies based on their home town or county, marched unhindered across the bridge into London. They met no opposition. The peasants were welcomed by the population and given food.[36] Another alderman, William Tonge, opened the Aldgate to let the men of Essex into the city from the north.[39]

Wat Tyler and the other leaders of the army issued strict orders against thievery and killing. One of the first targets of the peasants was the Savoy, the sumptuous palace of the king's uncle John of Gaunt. Gaunt's household and mistress were permitted to leave the palace before the peasants destroyed it with gunpowder and fire. Enforcing the edict against theft, the peasants tossed a man who had taken a silver goblet from the palace to drown in the river.[36] The manor house of Treasurer Robert Hales at Highbury was burned down.[39] Hales was also master of the Order of St. John of Jerusalem. Apparently to spite the treasurer, the buildings and priories of that society were destroyed.[41]

The peasants then proceeded to the legal center of the nation, the New Temple, where all the state and legal papers were kept. All that could be found were burned. The Black Robes, the lawyers, had fled in advance. The prisons of the Fleet and Newgate were then broken into and the prisoners released. The release of the city's criminals contributed to lawlessness. Many of them took advantage of the anarchy to pay off old grudges. Groups of drunken rioters roamed the city. Many Flemish immigrants living in London were slain, as were many lawyers.[36,41] Nevertheless, there was no wholesale attack on the wealthier residents of London or destruction of their property.[39]

The bulk of the peasants marched to the Tower of London, surrounding this Norman-built fortress, in which were the king and his councilors. During the night, Richard and his advisors debated what to do. Walworth urged an armed sortie to defeat the peasants, but he was overruled. The Earl of Salisbury said, "Sire, if you could appease them by fair words and grant them what they wish, it will be so much the better; for should we begin what we cannot go through, we shall never be able to recover it. It will be all over with us and our heirs and England will be a desert."[41] The earl's plan for conciliation was adopted by the king.[41,42]

Two knights were sent to the peasant leaders offering that the king would consider all grievances submitted to him in writing. The knights' announcement was met with derision. "Get ye back," the knights were told, "and bring us a fair offer. The King must talk to his loyal commons face to face."[36]

The king then agreed to meet with the peasant leaders the next morning, June 14, at Mile End, an open stretch of ground outside the walls of London. It was said that the Royal Council consented to the meeting in hopes that all the peasants would march outside the walls. The plan called for Richard to agree to all the peasant demands so they would disperse. These promises could then be annulled later.[36,39] In at least one feature the plan failed. The rebel army kept guards on all the gates of London and around the Tower.

At Mile End, King Richard remained on horseback as Wat Tyler listed the people's demands. The whereabouts of John Ball during this time are unclear. Richard agreed to five important points:

    1. Villeinage was to be abolished.

    2. The corvee was abolished (the obligation to work for the lord of the manor on demand).

    3. The peasants would have the status of tenants and pay four pence an acre per year to the owner.

4. Restrictions on buying and selling would be removed.
5. A general amnesty would be extended to all participants in the uprising.

Point four abolished the monopolies of the guilds, the great religious houses and the secular elites of the towns. Ironically, given their role in inciting the rebellion, the agreement did not address the issue of taxes nor the unpopular labor laws. Nor would King Richard agree to demand to punish unpopular ministers.[43]

For many hours, some thirty clerks from Westminster wrote out the charters containing this agreement. A copy was provided to the representatives of each of the shires represented.[39] After receiving these charters many peasants headed homeward, feeling that their cause had triumphed.[36,39]

After Richard and his party rode out of the Tower of London to this meeting, the garrison neglected to raise the drawbridge or lower the portcullis, the iron gate barring entry into the fortress. The peasants swarmed inside the Tower. Here they seized those viewed as the chief oppressors of the people. Archbishop and Chancellor Simon Sudbury and Treasurer Robert Hales were executed as was John Legge, collector-in-chief of the poll tax. Richard Imworth, warden of Marshalsea prison, known for his use of torture, was dragged by a mob out of Westminster Abbey and killed.[41] The Queen Mother was again allowed to leave unharmed from the Tower.[36,41] Henry Bolingbroke, son of John of Gaunt, and the future Henry IV, somehow escaped being killed in the Tower.

Wat Tyler was described as handling the negotiations with skill and moderation. The chroniclers of the revolt, almost all nobles or high churchmen hostile to the uprising, claimed that Tyler now let the power go to his head. Walsingham wrote that Tyler boasted that "in four days' time all the laws of England would be issuing from his mouth."[44] Another chronicle had Wat declaring, "There are twenty thousand of my stout fellows to go with me and help enforce my will."[36] The veracity of these quotes is doubtful.

The next day saw a diminishing of violence, although most of the shops and homes remained shuttered. The Royal Council sent Wat a message, suggesting a further conference with the king later that day in Smithfield, again outside the walls of London. Smithfield was the site of many prior executions. The royal party this time numbered some two hundred, mainly knights, wearing armor concealed under their cloaks and clothing. They took up position on the east side of this wide plain while the peasants, still some thousands in numbers, were on the other side.[36,39]

Wat Tyler, accompanied only by a banner bearer, rode out from the peasant ranks. He arrived within speaking distance of the king and then dismounted. One report had him shaking the king's hand, saying, "Sir King, within a fortnight you shall enjoy the thanks and loyalty of all true Commons."[36] The exact content of the ensuing conversation is unclear. It seemed to center on the peasant requests for further reforms. Wat was reported to have asked that the lands held by the church be confiscated and returned to lay ownership. There was to be only one bishop in England. The tenants of the church-owned properties were among those feeling most aggrieved. There was also a request to abolish the manorial courts. The forest laws, which restricted hunting and use of the forests to the nobility on the penalty of death, were to be abolished. King Richard was said to have replied that he would grant all that he had the right to concede, "saving the regalities of my crown."[36,43,44]

A long silence was said to have ensued. Wat then remounted to return to the ranks of the peasants. Someone in the royal party called out, "I recognize this fellow. He's a notorious highwayman and robber." Wat denied this charge, only to have the speaker repeat the charge. It was said that Wat then rode into the ranks of the king's men, brandishing a dagger. There Mayor Walworth blocked him and sliced his sword into Wat's neck inflicting a grievous wound. Wat Tyler rode only a few feet more, back toward the peasants, before falling out of the saddle.[36]

It is hard to imagine that Tyler would turn from negotiating to suddenly charge two hundred armored knights armed only with a dagger. It is more likely that the events that unfolded were a carefully staged trap.[42] The accounts of what happened all came from the royal party so the truth is unknown.

The peasants, while too far away to hear, saw Wat ride a few feet back toward them, then tumble, severely wounded, off his horse. The peasants charged toward the royal ranks, many fitting arrows to their bowstrings. Then King Richard rode out to meet them. "What need ye, my masters," he cried. "Ye seek a leader. I am your captain and your king. Follow me." The peasants stopped and then followed the king back to their prior positions and then a bit farther north to Islington.[36,40] No other episode in the revolt so shows the peasants' trust in the king.

A heavily armed force under the command of Sir Robert Knowles, a veteran commander from the wars with France, now pushed their way through the city and into the plain where the king waited with the peasants. Seeing this force of armed men, the remaining peasants fled.[36,44] The king and his ministers had regained control in London.

Tyler was taken to St. Bartholomew's Hospital and executed later that night. The emboldened nobility now suppressed the rebellion in the countryside with sword and blood.

On June 22, King Richard appointed Sir Robert Tresilian as chief justice. Tresilian proceeded to exact full retribution on the peasant leaders. At St. Albans, two juries refused to find against these leaders. Tresilian selected a third jury, threatening the jurors with death if they failed to follow his will. Tresilian made it clear that every man that came before him would be found guilty.[36,41] William Grindecobbe, a peasant who had returned from London with a charter of rights, was promised his life if he could persuade others to return their charters. Grindecobbe refused, saying, "If I die, I shall die for the cause of freedom we have won, counting myself happy to end my life by such a martyrdom."[36]

In July, King Richard annulled the charters he had issued. When Parliament met again in November, the king reported that if he had issued the charters under duress, but, "If you desire to enfranchise and set at liberty the said serfs by your common assent, as the king has been informed some of you desire, he will consent to your prayer." Parliament instead decided to revoke all the rights the king had granted.[36] Historian Juliet Barker argued that Richard sympathized with the rebels and would have stood by the concessions if not forced to retract from pressure from the nobility.[43] Parliament was "unanimous in their condemnation for the rebels, their demand for severe punishment and their approbation of the withdrawal of the King's enforced promises of immunity."[38] To crack down further on the peasants, Parliament passed laws that no child born on the land could be apprenticed or sent to school.

Contemporary chroniclers reported the king as sharing the nobles' views. Walsingham reported that King Richard answered a group of peasants in Essex who asked him to respect the agreements, stating, "You wretches are detestable on both land and on sea. You seek equality with the lords, but you are unworthy to live. Give this message to your fellows: villeins you are and villeins you will always be. You will remain in bondage, not as before, but incomparably harsher. For as long as we live we will strive to suppress you and your misery shall be an example to posterity."[36,40]

John Gower summed up the feeling of the nobility when he wrote that the peasant aspirations were the work of the devil, "according to their foolish notions that in the future there would be no lords, but only king and peasants."[37]

The king sat beside Tresilian during the trial of John Ball. Even his fiercest opponents concede that Ball conducted himself with dignity. Allowed to speak, he expressed his belief that the equality of man was what God had planned and that all feudal laws eventually must be abolished. Two days later John Ball was hanged, and drawn and quartered, being tortured before he was executed. Accounts differ drastically on the number of others executed for their involvement in the uprising, ranging from just over one hundred to seven thousand.[16,36,39] The next year saw an order given for the arrest of dissenting priests, who were blamed for stirring up the populace.[42] The nobility and Church saw no need for reform.[44]

The fate of the king was to prove little better. Historian Barbara Tuchman wrote, "Richard developed all the instincts of absolutism except the toughness to quell his opponents."[44] Many years later, he was deposed and executed by his cousin Henry, son of John of Gaunt, who took power as Henry IV. Ironically, Ball and Tyler are most remembered due to the writings of Thomas Walsingham, who was their bitter opponent. Touted for the next 400 years as symbols of disorder and rebellion, they were rehabilitated first by an ardent defense of them by Thomas Paine, whose writings helped drum up support for the cause of American independence in the American Revolution.[43]

Over time the feudal laws were less and less enforced. The economics of fewer laborers could not be suppressed by statutes. In a century, villeinage had practically disappeared. Ironically, it may be most remembered in the word villain, defined as an evil doer. So were the peasants and their leaders seen by the nobility. While the nobles could dictate the histories of the day, history was not on their side. Over the centuries, the power of the nobility declined, while England was to move ever closer to John Ball's ideal of the equality of all.

Chapter 6: Stenka Razin
Russia in Revolt, 1670 CE, Russia

IN THE FALL OF 1941 the German army seemed well on their way to conquering Russia. The retreating Russian troops, defeated and demoralized, fell back. Resting along the road, one of the soldiers, who came from a small village in southern Russia, told his comrades, "We need Stenka Razin." All the soldiers knew of the legend of Razin. It was said that he would return should the Russian people ever need to be delivered from their oppressors. Their lieutenant, a Muscovite intellectual, smiled and answered, "You are right. Do you know that Pushkin, Russia's greatest poet, said that Razin was the one poetic figure in Russian history?"[45] The unit's commissar chimed in saying that Lenin himself had recognized Razin as his forbearer in the fight against slavery and oppression. Who was this Stenka Razin, who so inspired Russians?

Before telling Razin's story, some background is needed. After freeing themselves from weakening Mongol domination in the 1400s, the nation of Russia began to take shape.[45–51] The harsh rule of Tsar Ivan the Terrible (1533–84), greatly expanded the borders of Russia. Yet, the heavy taxes needed to pay for his multiple ongoing wars reduced much of the population to poverty. The taxes and Ivan's reign of terror against his enemies made much of the population flee to the newly conquered, but unoccupied, steppe in the south and southwest.

When Ivan's son and heir, Tsar Fyodor, died in 1598 without heirs, Russia was plunged into what became known as "The Time of Troubles," as one tsar after another seized power only to die or be overthrown. Finally, the nobility chose Michael Romanov as tsar in 1613, initiating the three hundred year rule of the Romanov dynasty. Michael's long reign (1613–45) and that of his successor Alexis (1645–76) saw a centralization of power under the tsar. The rudimentary national assembly and local self-governments were replaced by a stronger autocracy with governors appointed by the tsar. A Russian saying of the time was, "The horse loves oats, the earth manure and the governor tribute."[45] Historian Nicholas Riasanovsky wrote, "The decades that followed the Time of Troubles saw the final and complete establishment of serfdom in Russia and in general a further subjugation of the working masses to the interests of the victorious…gentry."[47]

A rigid social structure was put into place. The Law Code of 1649 divided the Russian population into fixed hereditary occupations. Peasants were tied to their place of residence and townsmen into the occupation of their fathers. It was forbidden to move to a new location on the penalty of death. The state also removed any time limit for the recovery of runaway peasants and imposed heavy penalties on those found to be harboring them. The chief beneficiaries of these rules, besides the state, were the lesser nobility. The increased powers the nobles received over the peasants on their estates reduced the latter to near slavery.[45] While almost 90% of Russia's 7–8 million people were peasants, after 1649 only a minority of these were legally free.[46,48]

Long wars beginning in 1654 under Tsar Alexis with Poland and then Sweden increased the burden of taxes and military service. Despite the harsh penalties for failed attempts, peasants continued to flee, east to Siberia and south and southwest to the Don and Volga river valleys. A peasant saying of the time was, "Don't pay your dues. Run off to the Volga, to the brigands or the boatmen."[45] The government launched massive manhunts into the southern steppes to try to recapture the fugitives.[45]

Discontent was also widespread in the towns, where many people lived on the margin of survival. Even the established merchants and artisans felt the burden of extra taxes, such as the "fifth money," a special tax levied on artisans and traders.[47] Moreover, they had to compete at a disadvantage against merchants favored by the government, who were free of taxes.[45]

Riots broke out in Moscow in 1648 when the salt tax was quadrupled. Riots recurred throughout Russia in 1650 and 1662, resulting in days of violent conflict in the streets with thousands of deaths. When the war with Poland finally ended in 1667, it is estimated that a fifth of the Russian population had died from combat, famine or disease.[45] The stage was set for the great rebellion to come.

The leader of this rebellion, Stenka Razin, was born around 1630 in a Cossack settlement on the lower-middle Don River. At the time the Don Cossacks, such as Razin, prided themselves on their autonomy and self-rule. The Cossacks were governed by a general assembly, the Krug, which gathered periodically in their capital of Cherkassk, located on a large fortified island in the lower Don River. The Krug elected a chieftain, or ataman, as well a body of elected elders to make the day-to-day decisions. Local concerns were dealt with the individual villages, which had their own elected atamans and assemblies.[45]

The Cossacks resented government interference and refused to pay taxes to Moscow. Instead they received an annual subsidy, the zhalovanie, from the Russian state in exchange for providing border defense. The Cossacks were expert horsemen. Gathered together in sections of ten men, their weaponry ranged from lances and swords to muskets and even light cannons.[49] The Cossacks disdained agriculture and prohibited it in areas under their control. They saw it as linked to serfdom and government control. The Cossacks survived by fishing, hunting and herding cattle, horses and sheep. They would also periodically outfit fleets of shallow draft boats with which they raided Tatar, Turkish and Persian settlements on the coasts of the Black and Caspian Seas. The Cossacks also had a strong tradition of not returning runaway peasants. A Cossack slogan was, "From the Don no one is handed over."[45]

While the peasant fugitives who reached the Don were safe from recapture, they were forbidden from pursuing their traditional livelihood of agriculture. Thus, they were forced to work as hired hands for the more established Cossacks. The newcomers were known as the golytha, "the naked ones" since they possessed no property or possessions. To survive many turned to piracy against the Turks and Crimean Tatars. The established Cossacks were willing to supply boats, weapons and supplies in exchange for a share of the loot. However, the government in Moscow, while countenancing such raids in times of war, was opposed to unsanctioned raids and tried to block them.

Stenka Razin was the godson of the supreme chief, the voiskovoi ataman, of the Don Cossacks. He was initially well regarded by the Cossack general assembly, the Krug, which sent him in 1658 as part of the delegation to Moscow to negotiate the Cossacks' annual subsidy from the tsar. In 1661, the Krug entrusted him with negotiating an alliance with the Kalymyks, a neighboring people.[45]

It is unclear what motivated Razin to rebel. At some point in his life he conceived a hatred of men of privilege and authority.[45] Razin reportedly cited the execution of his older brother for going on leave against orders while fighting against the Poles. However, the evidence of this event is lacking. Razin's younger brother, uncle and mother were all to join him in rebellion.[45]

Contemporary accounts describe Razin as a natural leader. Jan Struys, a Dutch seaman who saw Razin in 1669, described him as "a brave man as to his person and well-proportioned in his limbs, tall and straight of body, pock-pitted, but only so as did become rather than disfigure him, of good conduct, but withal severe and cruel."[44]

Another contemporary wrote of Razin's "enormous will and impulsive activity…now stern and gloomy, now working himself up into a fury, now given up to drunken carousing, now ready to suffer any hardship with superhuman endurance. There was something fascinating in his speech; reckless courage was written in his coarse and slightly pock-marked features. The crowd sensed some supernatural strength in him, against which it was useless to struggle."[45]

In April, 1667 Razin launched his first campaign. He recruited a band of about a thousand Cossacks including many of the golytha and fitted out a fleet. His plan was to sail down the Volga to the Caspian Sea. The tsarist government ordered the governors of the downstream towns to block Razin's path. On the Volga Razin intercepted a convoy jointly owned by the tsar, the patriarch of the Russian Orthodox Church and some wealthy merchants. The Cossacks surprised and overwhelmed the guards, seized the merchandise and freed a contingent of political prisoners. The surviving guards were invited to join Razin. Razin reportedly said, "I will not force you to join me, but whoever chooses to come with me will be a free Cossack. I have come to fight only the boyars [the high nobility] and the wealthy lords. As for the poor and plain folk, I shall treat them as brothers."[44] Razin successfully passed the Russian fortresses on the Volga. A series of army detachments were sent after him. The first to overtake him defected to a man. The second mounted an attack, but was easily overcome and its officers killed. Many of the surviving common soldiers joined Razin.[45]

Razin now arrived outside the fortress town of Yaitsk. In the guise of pilgrims, he and forty of his men approached the main gate and asked permission to pray in the town cathedral. Once inside they opened the gates to their comrades and captured the town. Razin overwintered there before sailing in the spring to raid the coast of Persia, where he won a decisive naval victory over the Persians in June 1669. Razin and his men, laden with booty, now sailed back to Russia. Outside Astrakhan, Razin was confronted by a superior Russian fleet. He was offered a pardon if he would give up his ships, booty and prisoners. Razin agreed and made a triumphal entry into Astrakhan where he was feted for his triumph over the Persians. In Astrakhan, Razin gave up his Persian captives, but kept the loot and his ships. Razin returned up the Don River, where he set up a fortified camp on an island.[45]

Historian Paul Avrich described Razin as "A seasoned warrior, whose determination, resourcefulness and restless energy are traits on which all contemporaries agree. He was also a man of strong, at times, ungovernable passions."[44] Razin demonstrated these traits when the tsar sent an emissary to Cherkassk, demanding that the Cossacks restrain Razin. As the Krug met to consider this, Razin burst in. He accused the emissary of being a spy for the aristocracy.

"Who sent you?" Razin demanded, "The Great Sovereign [the tsar] or the Boyars?"[45] The emissary was then thrown into the Don to drown, the traditional Cossack method of execution.

Razin followed the Russian tendency to blame the problems not on the tsar, but on the nobility and bureaucrats who supposedly misled the tsar. In

March 1670, Razin mobilized his army. He proclaimed his goal "to go from the Don to the Volga and from the Volga into Rus [the central part of Russia] against the Sovereign's enemies and betrayers...and to give freedom to the common people."[44] Razin went on to say, "I will not raise my sword against the Great Sovereign. I would rather cut off my own head with it or be drowned in the river."[45]

Razin first captured the city of Tsaritsyn on the Volga from its tsarist defenders. He then defeated an army sent to retake it. At this point Razin summoned a krug, where the decision was made to sail down river to take Astrakhan first rather than immediately marching on Moscow. Razin might have taken Moscow if he had marched there first instead of giving the government a chance to rally its forces.

At the time, the Russian army consisted of about 100,000 men. These were mainly career soldiers called the streltsy, who lived their families in Moscow and in a string of garrison towns. The streltsy were supposed to supplement their low pay with trade and handicraft. The army also included some battle-hardened, Western-trained regiments armed with more modern weapons.

As the rebels approached, the governor of Astrakhan sent a force of 2600 streltsy to intercept Razin. The streltsy, whose low pay was often in arrears, mutinied, arrested their commander and offered to join Razin "to kill the masters, voevodas (governors), officials and other ranks of noblemen."[45] These streltsy now proposed killing their officers. Razin objected that "there must be a few good men who should be pardoned."[45] Avrich wrote, "Razin's leniency was not out of character; except when inflamed by drink he was not as bloodthirsty as his followers."[45]

Astrakhan was a place of great wealth and strategic importance, serving as Russia's chief place of trade with Persia and other areas in the east. Astrakhan boosted strong fortifications with a remaining garrison of 6000 streltsy armed with many cannons. However, the population was sympathetic to Razin. The unpaid streltsy were unreliable. When Razin sent an envoy to demand the city's surrender, the governor beheaded him on the city walls. That night Razin attacked and captured the city. Razin's army seized the treasury and pillaged the houses of the wealthy. Some sixty of the officers and gentry, including the governor, were killed. The toll would have been higher except for Razin's intervention. Ludwig Fabritius, a Hollander serving as a streltsy officer, noted, "Although this brigand (Razin) tyrannized in such an unheard of manner, he nonetheless insisted upon strict order among his men."[45]

On July 20, 1670, Razin began his ascent of the Volga with an army of some 6000 men. Razin promised liberty and deliverance from the noble landowners and tsarist bureaucracy. Emissaries from Razin would arrive in towns with leaflets saying that Razin "was going to Rus to establish the Cossack way…so that all men would be equal."[45] Frequently, the townspeople would then rebel, overthrow the authorities and welcome the Cossacks. Officials were executed, prisons thrown open and taxes abolished. Then the old administration would be replaced by self-rule with a krug and elected ataman.[45,50]

Razin also set messengers to the countryside to rouse the peasantry. The leaflets read, "Whoever wants to serve God and the sovereign and the great host…[should join us]…to eliminate the traitors and bloodsuckers of the peasant communes."[45] Thousands of peasants heeded the Razin's call. Jan Struys, the Dutch sailor, who was in Russia then, wrote, "The peasantry, who indeed were very tyrannically dealt with throughout the Emperor's [the tsar's] domains, here found an occasion to be revenged on their liege lords."[45]

Large numbers of additional recruits came from the non-Russian peoples of the Volga area, whose lands had often been confiscated by the Russian gentry and church. Razin was tolerant of different religions, causing many of different faiths to join him. The Volga boatmen who pulled the barges also joined in large numbers, rebelling against their life of "toil and drudgery till they dig your grave."[45] Women joined the revolt in large numbers, in some cases commanding rebel detachments.

Another important part of Razin's army was its large numbers of the lower clergy. These priests, coming of peasant stock, shared the poverty and grievances of their parishes. Alarmed by this, the chief of the Russian church, the Patriarch Ioasaf, sent a letter to each parish warning the priests "not to be allured by the enticements of the bandit and traitor Stenka Razin and his comrades."[45] The government tortured, banished and executed many priests for writing leaflets for the rebellion.

Revolts in Russia often featured leaders who claimed to be the true tsar, i.e., a son or brother of the former tsar or even the dead former tsar miraculously still alive. For example, Pugachev, who led a huge uprising in 1774, claimed to be the dead Tsar Peter III. Razin never claimed to be other than he was. However, he was not above using this stratagem. The current Tsar Alexis had a son of the same name who had died the year before. Razin presented a boy whom he claimed was the Tsar's son Alexis, miraculously escaped from the violent hands of the nobility.[45,52]

By the summer of 1670, Razin, now widely popular among the people, and his army had advanced northward to control the Volga River region up to 800 miles north of Astrakhan. However, the government had not been idle. It had collected large numbers of troops, veterans of the Polish war now ended, to try to put down the uprising. The troops were armed with the latest weaponry and artillery. The government forces left Moscow at the beginning of September to march south to fight Razin. At this point Razin and his army approached the town of Simbirsk. The town boosted of strong defenses with a moat-surrounded citadel perched high on a hill above the rest of the town. Simbirsk was held by an able commander, Prince Ivan Miloslavsky, who commanded the strong loyalty of his 4000 troops. After an inconclusive battle outside the town, Razin entered the town unopposed and welcomed by the townspeople. The garrison withdrew to the citadel. Three assaults were made on the citadel over the span of a week starting September 15. After desperate hand-to-hand fighting, all were beaten off with heavy losses on both sides.[45]

Razin's army, though outnumbering the government forces, was undisciplined and poorly equipped. Only a small core of Cossacks and ex-streltsy had any military experience. During the month-long siege of Simbirsk, other rebel detachments fanned out across the surrounding countryside and seized other smaller towns. Manor houses were invaded by mobs of peasants and unpopular landlords killed.

On October 1, a relief force of 6000 elite government troops under Prince Yuri Bariatinsky approached Simbirsk. Razin led his army out to meet him. The result was disaster. The rebels rushed in to attack the government forces, but their ranks were torn apart by Bariatinsky's artillery. The rebels broke in the face of this barrage with only the Cossacks offering sustained resistance. Razin himself was wounded in the head and leg and carried off the field by his men. Bariatinsky then overtook the retreating army on the banks of the Sviiaga River. On October 4, the rebels were again decisively defeated. Razin and many of the Cossacks escaped downriver on boats, but hundreds of the rebels were captured. These were quickly executed.[45]

Frolka Razin, Stenka's younger brother, had led another army of rebels up the Don River to the west. However, at the end of September Frolka was also defeated and retreated south along the Don. The tide had turned in favor of the government. In a series of pitched battles, the well-armed and disciplined government troops usually defeated the rebels. The captured rebels, numbering in the thousands, were hanged or beheaded. After one battle, it was reported that "on the fields and roads, horses and wagons could not pass because of all the corpses."[45]

One estimate is that up to 200,000 rebels were killed during the rebellion. Other estimates are lower, but still in the tens of thousands. The government reprisals were brutal and widespread. Avrich wrote, "The violence of the government was a calculated policy ordered by the tsar to terrorize the populace into submission…captured rebels were impaled on stakes, nailed to boards, torn to shreds by flesh hooks and flogged or strangled to death."[45] In the worst-hit districts up to 40% of the population was killed. Thousands of members of the non-Russian tribes of the Volga region were killed and their villages razed.[45]

Meanwhile, Stenka Razin had sailed downriver to his native region in the lower Don. There he recuperated from his wounds even as the rebellion was being crushed. In February 1671, Razin tried to rouse the rank and file of the established Cossacks in Cherkassk to overthrow their traditional leaders and join him in the revolt.

Whether for fear of the tsar or desire to throw in with the winning side, the established Cossacks refused. Razin's godfather Kronilo Yakolev, the chief of the Cossacks, prevented Razin from entering Cherkassk. Razin retreated to his island fort. Approaching this fort under the cover of darkness on April 14, Yakolev and his followers set firewood against the bastion, burning it to the ground. Stenka and Frolka Razin were taken prisoner. In violation of the principles of the Don Cossacks, the Razins were then turned over to the Russian government.[45,51]

The brothers were then taken to Moscow in chains under heavy guard. Stenka Razin was personally interrogated by Tsar Alexis, then subjected to multiple horrible tortures. Asked about his purpose, Razin reportedly said, "We wanted to take Moscow and to thrash to death all you magnates and landowners and the government men."[51] Razin reportedly endured his tortures without a sound. On June 6, 1671, Razin was executed by being torn and quartered in Red Square in Moscow. Razin's mother, uncle and brother Frolka were also executed for their parts in the rebellion. Tsar Alexis received congratulations for crushing the rebellion from rulers as far apart as the Shah of Persia and Charles II of England.[45]

Yakovlev and the other old Cossacks received special rewards at the price of swearing fealty to the tsar, thus sacrificing the Cossacks' traditional independence. The Cossacks were made Russian subjects. Their internal autonomy decreased further over time. The Cossacks became the trusted troops of the tsars, serving as their shock troops to put down political protests.[46,49] They also spearheaded many of the pogroms against the Jews in Russia in the 19th century.[46]

The 17th century in Europe was marked by a trend to more powerful rulers. One of the problems of Razin's revolt was the failure to identify the tsar as the core of the autocratic system. Historian James Billington wrote, "The effect of the heroic rebellions was to strengthen rather than weaken the bureaucratic centralization they were opposing… Even in rebellion, the peasants could not conceive of an alternative political system. They refused to believe that the reigning tsar was responsible for the evils of the time and bureaucrats and foreign elements around him."[52]

Razin, while aiming to keep the tsar as the ruler of Russia, aimed to replace the autocratic top-down government with a decentralized Cossack style regime of popular assemblies and elected leaders. The rebels' biggest problem was their deficiency in arms, discipline and training, which allowed the tsar's Western-trained, well-equipped army to defeat them.[45]

Stenka Razin was long remembered in Russia, becoming the subject of numerous ballads and stories. Russian historian A.V. Arsen'ev wrote that "Razin was the subject of more songs and legends than any other popular hero."[45] Razin was admired for his bravery and daring and his sense of honor and justice. Even after the communists took over in the Russian Revolution in 1917 he remained a source of inspiration. In 1965 the composer Shostakovich created a musical performance, *Kazan Stepana Razina*, celebrating Razin.[52] Razin was not forgotten.

In the West, we regard Russians as a people with a built-in preference for a strong, authoritarian central government. The esteem with which Razin is held rebukes that notion. It suggests that Russians have the same yearnings for liberties and devolution of political power away from an all-powerful ruler as people everywhere.

Chapter 7: Joseph Warren
The Forgotten Founding Father, 1775 CE, Massachusetts

IN 1763 the British Empire in America stood at its zenith. The successful conclusion of the French and Indian War brought the ceding of all of French Canada to Britain. Yet barely twelve years later Great Britain would find itself facing an armed insurrection in the crown jewel of the empire, the thirteen colonies of North America.[53-60]

One of the key American leaders who helped bring about the American Revolution was Dr. Joseph Warren of Boston. Except for fate, Warren would be remembered as one of the founding fathers of the new American republic that was to emerge from the American war for independence.

Joseph Warren was born in Roxbury, at the time a small farming community southwest of Boston, on June 11, 1741. His father was a successful farmer and a selectman for Roxbury, but died when Joseph was only fourteen.[53] Joseph and his three brothers would all go on to successful and prominent careers.[61]

After graduating from Harvard College, Joseph Warren decided on a career in medicine, which meant being apprenticed to a practicing physician. Finishing his apprenticeship, in 1764 Warren married eighteen-year-old Elizabeth Hooton, the only daughter of a successful merchant. He then opened a medical practice in Boston. Warren encountered every layer of Boston society in his work. Historians Ray and Marie Raphael wrote, "He had attended the poor in public clinics and cared for the suffering during a smallpox epidemic. The inoculation hospital he opened then saved countless lives, and ever after he was so widely regarded that diverse Bostonians came to him for doctoring. John Adams and Paul Revere were among them, but also men, such as Thomas Hutchinson, soon to be the Royal governor."[59]

As Warren started his medical practice, conflict between the British government and the colonies began over power and money. The conclusion of the French and Indian War left Britain saddled with debts. The British government looked to the colonies to make up the deficit as well as help pay for Britain's army. To the colonies, the elimination of the French transformed the British military from a necessity to an unwelcome and unnecessary burden. Colonist Ebenezer Fox spoke for many in writing, "The colonies had borne the foremost part in the conflict with very slight assistance from the mother country...[their] men and money had been freely contributed."[53] In contrast, the British government felt that Britain had borne most of the burden while the colonies were the beneficiaries of the successful war.

In Britain, the government consisted of the faction that could gain the most votes in Parliament, with the king retaining major influence through his control of patronage and positions. Most Americans believed that Parliament could legislate over the colonies and even impose so called external taxes, such as duties on imports and exports. However, many colonists did not feel that Parliament could impose internal taxes, taxes within a colony on goods and property, viewing this as the purview of each colony. The Parliament theoretically represented all the citizens in the kingdom, but suffrage was restricted to a tiny minority of landowners in Britain proper.

Why Warren chose to resist the Crown, in contrast to many of the other physicians and members of the colonial elite, can only be seen through his writing, where he decried the British government for suppressing the rights of the colonies. Joseph Warren's closest associate in the politics of resistance to Britain was Sam Adams. While Warren was at the top of his profession in Boston, Adams had failed in almost everything he had tried until he became what would be called a "rabble raiser." From the 1760s onward Adams and Warren were the two main leaders of the protest movement against Britain.[53] Adams wrote later of Warren, "[He was] my intimate friend with whom I lived and conversed with pleasure and advantage. I was animated by [him] in the painful, dangerous course of opposition to the oppression brought upon our country."[61]

In 1765 the conflict began when the British government passed the Stamp Act, a tax on all paper documents, bills of sale, etc. To many colonists, the stamp tax was clearly an internal tax and hence illegitimate. Multiple colonial legislatures, starting in Virginia, protested the Stamp Act.[53] Mob action against Stamp Act officials also occurred in many colonies.

Warren wrote prolifically in both public and private about the Stamp Act. To a friend in England, he wrote, "If the real and only motive of the minister was to raise money from the colonies, that method should have been adopted which was least grievous to the people. Instead of this, the most unpopular that could be imagined is chosen."[53,61] Warren's energy and talents, along with his close relationships with other leaders, elevated him to a leadership role in Massachusetts. Historian Nathaniel Philbrick wrote, "Warren had the rarest of talents: the ability to influence the course of events without appearing to assert his own will□—what one contemporary described at the 'the wisdom to guide and the power to charm.'"[56]

By passing the Stamp Act the British government unwittingly made the thirteen colonies work together, despite their very different histories and societies, for the first time. Forming a Stamp Act Congress comprised of representatives of every colony, the colonies agreed to not import British goods until the tax was lifted. The outcry of the British merchants to Parliament prompted the repeal of the Stamp Act in March 1766. Joseph Warren concluded, "Colonies until now were ever variance and foolishly jealous of each other, [but] they are now…united.[55] While repealing the Stamp Act, Parliament also passed the Declaratory Act, stating that the Parliament had the right to levy whatsoever taxes it deemed fit in the colonies.

The next struggle arose in 1767 with the passage of the Townsend duties. Charles Townsend, the British chancellor of the exchequer, proposed "external taxation" in the form of duties on imports into the colonies of glass, lead, paper, paint and tea. The duties were both to assert the right of taxation and to make up for a tax cut given to British landowners. Again, the colonies erupted in protests. Joseph Warren wrote letters to the *Boston Gazette* under the nom de plume "True Patriot" that helped galvanize the opposition in Massachusetts. Warren also played a leading role in town meetings in Boston.[61] When a mob chased customs officials away from John Hancock's ship *Liberty* in June 1768, the British government decided to send regular army troops to Boston. The troops soon engendered increasing resentment from the populace. Minor conflicts between the soldiers and the people escalated, culminating in the Boston Massacre on March 5, 1770, in which British troops fired on a mob, killing five citizens.[53] Warren and other Boston leaders persuaded the British authorities to withdraw the troops to an island in Boston harbor to avoid further bloodshed. Warren said, "With united efforts, you [the people of Boston] urged an immediate departure of the troops from the town, you urged it with a resolution which insured success; you obtained your wishes; and the removal of the troops was effected without one drop of their blood being shed by the inhabitants."[61]

Large number of colonists reacted to the Townsend duties by again boycotting goods made in Britain. Pressure from British merchants led

Parliament to repeal all the Townsend duties except for the tax on tea. For the next three years, 1770–73, relative calm returned. During this time the Boston radicals, Sam Adams, Joseph Warren and others, created the Boston Committee of Correspondence. The committee drafted a statement of colonial rights which they circulated to other towns in Massachusetts.[53] Those most opposed to British actions were called Patriots while supporters of Britain were called Loyalists. The new governor, Thomas Hutchinson, who had taken office in 1769, recognized the danger posed by the town meetings and other nonofficial links between various other towns and counties. Hutchinson, a patient of Warren, wrote to the British government, "We find, my lord, by experience, that associations and assemblies, pretending to be legal and constitutional, assuming powers that belong only to established authority, prove more fatal to this authority than mobs, riots or the most tumultuous disorders."[61]

In May 1773, Warren's wife Elizabeth died after less than ten years of marriage. Warren gave over his four children to their grandmother to raise. Warren continued his political activities while also pursuing his full-time medical practice, seeing as many as twenty patients a day from the highest to lowest members of society.[56]

The calm was not to last. In 1773 Parliament passed the Tea Act, which eliminated the tax on tea coming into England while taxing tea imported into the colonies. The act bailed out the giant, near-bankrupt East India Company by giving it a monopoly on importing tea into the colonies. The East India Company chose selected American merchants to serve as their agents to handle this importation, cutting out all other merchants from the trade.[60]

Protests erupted over the Tea Act. In Massachusetts, a furor arose when letters from Governor Thomas Hutchinson were made public. In these letters to British officials, Hutchinson had urged strong measures to put down the Boston protests. Pressure from protesters in New York and Philadelphia had forced the tea agents in those cities to resign. In Boston, with support from Hutchinson and the troops based in the city, the five Boston agents refused to resign. Two of the agents in Boston holding this monopoly license to import the tea were Hutchinson's sons. Hutchinson had also invested a huge portion of his money in the East India Company.[53] Warren wrote to Samuel Adams of Hutchinson's desire to ingratiate himself with the British government, noting, "It is probable that [Hutchinson] would have remained in [the people's] interest…had there not been a higher station to which his ambitious mind aspired."[56] Warren added that America needed a government in which "the only road to promotion may be through the affection of the people."[56]

Into Boston harbor sailed the merchant ship *Dartmouth* with 114 chests of tea, followed shortly afterwards by other tea-laden ships. A standoff arose. The patriots in Boston, including the dockworkers and sailors, refused to allow the tea to be unloaded. Hutchinson refused the ship owner's request to allow the ship to leave the city with the tea still aboard. The law held that after twenty days any unloaded tea could be seized by customs and forcibly unloaded. Just before this deadline was reached, the patriots acted. A group of men loosely disguised as Indians boarded the moored tea ships and dumped 342 chests of tea into the harbor in the space of three hours. Nothing else on the ships was touched; a lock that had been broken accidentally was replaced the next day.[53] Historian John Alden wrote of Sam Adams, "it cannot be doubted that he played a large part, with Dr. Warren, in planning the affair."[54]

Britain reacted with outrage. The attorney general and solicitor general were asked if those responsible could be accused of treason. The legal officials replied that the actions in Boston, "do amount to the crime of high treason, namely to the levying of war against His Majesty."[53] Among those named were Sam Adams, Joseph Warren and John Hancock. However, they were not charged as it was felt that no American jury would convict them of treason.

Parliament now responded by passing what the patriots called the Intolerable Acts. The first of these, the Port Act, closed the port of Boston to all trade until the city paid back the East India Company for the dumped tea. A second changed the charter of Massachusetts to greatly increase the power and control of the Crown. A third allowed troops to be quartered in private homes.

The result was further outrage among the colonies. The historian and statesman George Bancroft wrote, "The Port Act had been received on the 10th of May; and, in three weeks, the continent, as one great commonwealth, made the cause of Boston its own."[61] Most Americans still blamed Parliament for the repression and proclaimed their allegiance to the king. The colonies decided to meet, in what was to be called the First Continental Congress, to discuss their response to the Intolerable Acts.

At this point, the king replaced Hutchinson as governor of Massachusetts with the popular and respected General Thomas Gage, who also was the commander in chief of the British army in North America. Gage's popularity dropped he tried to enforce the Parliamentary edicts. Protests grew to the point where Gage dissolved the provincial legislature for its criticism of Britain.[61] Gage wrote to the British government, saying, "I cannot get a worse Council or worse assembly [the two houses of the Massachusetts legislature] who…appeared little more than echoes of the contrivers of all the mischief in the town of Boston."[53] Warren and the other Patriots campaigned for the colonies to halt all trade with Britain until the Port Act was repealed.[60,61] Warren wrote, "We consider a suspension of trade through the continent with Great Britain…as the grand machine that will deliver us."[61]

Parliament had banned the calling of town meetings without the governor's consent. County meetings had not been restricted. Thus, representatives of the counties of Suffolk (which included Boston), Essex, Middlesex and Worcester met together in Faneuil Hall in Boston to consider a unified plan of action. Joseph Warren was elected to chair the meeting. The delegates called for a new government, the Provincial Congress, for the colony of Massachusetts, separate from the old dissolved assembly and the authority of Parliament. The meeting also argued that Parliament had no authority to alter the charter of the colonies, stating, "Every people have an absolute right of meeting together to consult upon common grievances and to petition, remonstrate and use every legal method of their removal."[53]

Sam Adams, John Adams and John Hancock had all gone to the Continental Congress in Philadelphia. Warren now assumed an even larger role in the organized resistance while still carrying on his medical practice. He wrote Sam Adams, saying that he would soon send him an update on developments. Warren wrote, "haste now prevents it as I am constantly busied in helping forward the political machines in all parts of the province."[53]

Gage recognized the impossibility of the situation. He wrote, "Civil government is near its end…[I mean] to avoid any bloody crisis as long as possible."[53] Gage now started preparing for such a conflict, building fortifications around the entry points to Boston. The Patriots also prepared for any conflict, seizing any available public stores of gunpowder and muskets.

Representatives of each of the many towns in Suffolk County, from Boston on down, met to outline their positions regarding the conflict. Joseph Warren was picked to write out the positions of the group. On September 9, 1774, Warren presented the delegates what became known as the Suffolk Resolves. The nineteen resolves outlined the grievances and positions of the people in Suffolk County, views shared by many throughout the colonies. Historian James Nelson wrote, "The Suffolk Resolves were the most radical declaration of rights and determined resistance yet generated in the colonies."[53]

The resolves acknowledged George III as the colony's rightful sovereign. The colonists still blamed Parliament and the government officials, rather than the king, for their oppressions. The resolves argued that it was the duty of the people to uphold their longtime rights and that the acts of Parliament, "were the attempts of a wicked Administration to enslave America."[53] Resolves five and six stated that any judge not appointed according to the original charter was illegal and that those having disputes, in the absence of proper courts, should settle them by arbitration. The resolves called for the halt in the importing or exporting of any goods to Great Britain, the encouragement of American manufacturing and the discouragement of any attacks against Loyalists.

The resolves then called for the militia of each town to select their own officers, as opposed to any appointed by the Crown, and to begin military training. The crucial Twelfth Resolve stated that the people were "determined to act merely upon the defensive so long as such conduct may be vindicated by the reason and the principles of self-preservation, but no longer."[53] This stated that if pushed the people of Suffolk County would fight beyond mere self-defense. A system of couriers was to be set up to spread the alarm if the British threatened action. Finally, the Suffolk Resolves called for the establishment of a Massachusetts Provincial Congress to act as the colony's government while looking toward the Continental Congress for further guidance. After the entire document was read, each paragraph was voted on and unanimously approved.

Warren now turned to his friend Paul Revere to carry the Suffolk Resolves to the Continental Congress in Philadelphia. Philbrick wrote, "The surging rhythms of Warren's prose gave the document an emotional force that succeeded in cutting across the cultural and ideological differences of those gathered in Philadelphia who voted unanimously to endorse the

Suffolk resolves."[56] John Adams called it "one of the happiest days of my life."[53] He wrote to his wife Abigail, "The votes were passed in the full congress with perfect unanimity. The esteem, the affection, the admiration for the people of Boston and…Massachusetts which were expressed yesterday and fixed determination that they should be supported, were enough to melt a heart of stone."[53] In contrast, Joseph Galloway, leader of the Tory faction in the Congress wrote, "By this treasonable vote [on the Suffolk Resolves], the foundation of military resistance throughout America was effectually laid."[53] In London the colonial secretary for America, Lord Dartmouth, wrote in his diary, "In these Resolves, they have declared War against us: they will not suffer any sort of treaty."[53]

Not all Britons saw the American point of view as treasonable. William Pitt was the great prime minister under whose leadership Britain had won the French and Indian War. Though old and sick, Pitt came out of retirement to support the American position and urged compromise. Addressing Parliament, Pitt said, "When your lordships look at the papers transmitted from America, when you consider their decency, firmness and wisdom, you cannot but respect their cause and wish to make it your own."[60] However, Pitt's motions to repeal the Intolerable Acts and withdraw the troops from Boston were defeated in Parliament. Pitt wrote, "We shall be forced ultimately to retract. Let us retract while we can, not when we must."[60] More characteristic of the majority opinion was the comment of Lord Carmarthan, "For what purpose were they [the colonists] suffered to go to that country, unless the profits of their labor should return to their masters here."[61]

Despite this apparent support from the Continental Congress, Sam Adams wrote to Warren urging him to move cautiously to continue to keep this support. Adams wrote, "I have been assured, in private conversations, if you should be driven to the necessity of acting in defense of your lives or liberty, you would be justified…and openly supported by all the means in their power, but whether they will ever be prevailed upon to think it necessary for you to set up another form of government, I very much question."[59]

In October 1774, the Massachusetts Provincial Congress, including Joseph Warren, assembled in Salem, representing the two hundred towns and 350,000 people of Massachusetts.[61] This assembly now wrote to Gage concerning their alarm about the military buildup in Boston, insisting that they did not have "the least intention to do any injury to his Majesty's

Troops."[53] Gage replied, "It is surely highly exasperating, as well as ungenerous, even to hint that the lives, liberties and properties of any persons, except avowed enemies, are in danger from Britons."[53] Gage also castigated the Congress as an illegal body, insisting that they "desist from such illegal and unconstitutional proceedings."[53]

The standoff continued. The Provincial Congress approved the acquisition of military supplies and created a nine-member Committee of Safety, including Warren, to oversee military matters. Warren wrote to his friend Josiah Quincy in England to inquire as to the state of opinion, saying, "I wish to know of you how affairs stand in Great Britain…if the late acts of Parliament are not to be repealed, the wisest step for both countries is fairly to separate, and not spend their blood and treasure in destroying each other."[61] Over the winter Boston appeared quiet, although relations between the troops and inhabitants of the city remained tense. The Boston Port Bill, closing the harbor, had greatly damaged commerce in the city. Warren wrote to a friend on February 20, "It is not too late to accommodate the dispute amicably. But…if once General Gage should lead his troops into the country, with design to enforce the late Acts of Parliament, Great Britain may take her leave…of all America."[57] General Gage, meanwhile, had written to Lord Dartmouth, "It is the opinion of most people, that, if a respectable force is seen in the field, the most obnoxious of the leaders seized, and a pardon proclaimed for all others, [the] Government will come off victorious."[61]

Every March 5 since 1770, Boston had commemorated the Boston Massacre. Joseph Warren was chosen to be the main speaker at the memorial service in 1775, held at the Old South Meeting House. Attendees included Hancock, Sam and John Adams, the aldermen of Boston and some forty British officers who sat conspicuously in the first row. Unknown to the Patriots, a plot had been hatched by the officers to wait for some inflammatory remark by Warren, then hurl an egg at him. This would be the signal to use the ensuing riot as a pretext to seize the American leaders.

Warren, wearing a toga over his clothes for dramatic effect, described the evolution of American and British relations and the Boston Massacre itself before enjoining his listeners to "maintain your rights or perish in the generous struggles."[53] Yet, Warren also said, "An independence from Great Britain is not our aim, No, our wish is, that Britain and the colonies may…grow and increase in strength together.[61] The speech was more moderate than many expected. Lieutenant Frederick Mackenzie, a British officer in attendance, thought that the speech, although disparaging to the troops, "contained nothing as violent as was expected."[53] The officer carrying the egg that was to be thrown had slipped coming in, breaking both the egg and his leg. As such the British officers confined themselves to hissing during Warren's speech.[60]

Sam Adams, speaking next, thanked Warren and noted that another memorial speech would be held the following year marking "the Bloody Massacre." The officers cried, "Fie." People in the back thought they were saying fire. There was a mad scramble for the exits before calm was restored.

As the weather warmed, Gage sent detachments of troops on training exercise through the nearby countryside. Each time the troops would be closely shadowed by large numbers of suspicious American militia from the nearby towns. Gage asked the British government for 20,000 troops to put down the rebellion. The government thought that Gage's 3000 soldiers should be adequate. Lord Dartmouth, writing for the government to Gage, stated, "The first and essential step to be taken toward reestablishing government would be to arrest and imprison the principal actors and abettors in the Provincial Congress."[53] The British government did not want to face the expense of increasing the British army enough to be able to send Gage the forces he had asked for.

The Provincial Congress was meeting in the town of Concord, twenty miles west of Boston. From spies, Gage knew that military supplies were also being collected there. Thus, on the fateful morning of April 19, 1775, Gage sent out a force of some 800 soldiers under Lieutenant Colonel Francis Smith to march to Concord to seize the supplies and American leaders. At this point, Warren was the only major revolutionary leader unafraid enough of arrest to remain in Boston. Word of the British plan reached Warren. To raise the alarm, Warren sent out William Dawes and Paul Revere, later joined by Dr. Samuel Prescott, to warn Hancock and Sam Adams as well as to alert the countryside. Paul Revere later wrote about it, saying, "Dr. Warren sent in great haste for me and begged that I would immediately set out for Lexington, where Messrs. Hancock and Adams were, and acquaint them of the movement, and that it was thought that they were the objects."[58] Adams and Hancock and the militias of several towns were alerted about the British movement.

The British force encountered a group of forty militia arrayed on the town green in the town of Lexington. It is unclear who fired first, but shots rang out, killing eight Americans. The British pushed on further to Concord, only to find that the revolutionary leaders had fled and many of the supplies had been moved. By now the militia was roused and began firing on the British. By noon, when the troops started marching back to Boston, their route was lined by militia men on either side, using the terrain along the route to hide while firing on the British. More militia continued to arrive. Smith's force, batted by incessant fire, was at the breaking point when they were met around 2 PM by a relief force of 1000 men led by Lord Percy. Percy resumed the retreat to Boston, remaining under almost continuous American musketry until the weary British at last straggled back to safety in Boston.

Warren had received word in the early morning of the fighting in Lexington. He directed one of his apprentices to care for the patients he had scheduled and rode off to take the ferry to Charlestown, on the north side of the Charles River from Boston. En route, Warren told a friend, "Keep up a brave heart. They have begun it—that either party can do; and we will end it—that only one can do."[53] Leaving Charlestown, Warren rode up to the rear of Percy's column. Warren was stopped and questioned by two British officers. Fortunately, he was not recognized and was released. Riding on he soon met on William Heath, whom the Committee of Safety had appointed as one of the five generals to command the militia. Nelson wrote, "As the two British columns continued their weary trek back to Boston, Heath and Warren began to organize the American troops into regiments. Heath proved an able leader and kept the militia hanging on the marching British column. Warren moved between functioning as a field officer and as a doctor, one moment directing troops, the next attending as best he could to the wounded."[53] Finally, the British made it back to Boston, suffering three times the number of American casualties. The American casualties came from twenty-three different towns, indicative of the extent of militia participation in the battle. Warren was lionized for his fearlessness in treating the wounded even as musket balls flew about him, grazing his wig.[60,61]

Warren gave up his field command and returned the next day to his role as chair of the Committee of Safety. The committee sent a letter to the other towns in Massachusetts the next day, written largely by Warren, about the fighting. Warren wrote, with exaggerated hyperbole, "The barbarous murders committed on our innocent brethren, on Wednesday the 19th instant, have made it absolutely necessary that we may immediately raise an army to defend our wives and children from the butchering hands of an inhuman soldiery…[which would] take the first opportunity in their power to ravage this devoted country with fire and sword."[53] Warren asked for all available men to come to Cambridge to enlist in an American army. Within days some 20,000 men, the largest military force ever assembled on the continent up to then, had arrived in Cambridge, across the river from Boston. Even after the bloodletting at Lexington and Concord, few in the colonies openly argued for independence at this point. Instead, there was a determination to defend against further British attacks while waiting to see what the British response to the fighting would be. Warren wrote to his friend Arthur Lee, living in Britain, "The next news from England must be conciliatory or the connection between us ends."[59]

Word of the fighting spread quickly across the colonies. Militiamen continued to pour into the rebel camp in Cambridge, first from Massachusetts and then from the other New England colonies. The Committee of Safety tried to organize this mass of militia companies into an army. Warren wrote a friend, "We are in want of everything, but nothing as much as arms and ammunition."[53] The shortage of ammunition was to bedevil the Americans throughout the war. The Committee of Safety under Warren decided to create an army that would remain in the field as opposed to simply militia who would go home after each battle. Warren wrote to the Massachusetts towns, urging them "to hasten and encourage by all possible means the enlistment of men to form the army and send them forward to headquarters at Cambridge."[53] Another letter went to the neighboring colonies, asking for assistance, particularly of military stores and food. At Cambridge, even as new men arrived, other militiamen left to return home. Warren wrote to John Adams in Philadelphia, "As to the Army, it is such a shifting, fluctuating state…they (the soldiers) are continually going and coming."[53] Nevertheless some 10,000 Americans were encamped, over double the size of the British forces.

The Committee of Safety now formed the de facto government of Massachusetts outside British-controlled Boston. Since Hancock and Sam and John Adams were all leaving for the Second Continental Congress in Philadelphia, the work of governance mainly fell to the committee's chairman, Joseph Warren. Philbrick wrote of Warren, "His seemingly limitless capacity for work, along with his unmatched ability to adapt his own actions to meet the demands of the moment meant that…he was inevitably looked to as the person to keep the patriot cause together."[56]

At this point neither the British nor the Americans were strong enough to attack the other. Warren wrote to an associate, "I cannot precisely tell you what will become of General Gage. I imagine he will at least be very closely shut in Boston."[53] The Americans, while numerically superior, lacked the organization and artillery to attack the British and their fortifications in Boston. Gage's numerical inferiority precluded him from attacking the Americans encamped outside Boston despite the urgings of some of his officers.

Warren wrote to Gage seeking an agreement to allow the Patriots in Boston to leave the city and the Loyalists living outside the center enter. Although such an arrangement was reached, Gage slowed the exodus of Patriot sympathizers under pressure from the Loyalists in Boston. Gage wrote to Lord Dartmouth that the Loyalists felt that "none but the ill inclined will go out, and when they are safe with their Effects [property], the Town will be set Afire."[53] Warren wrote to the American governor of Connecticut, "The general [Gage] is perpetually making new conditions and the forming the most miserable pretenses for retarding their removal from the garrison."[53]

Warren wrote to Gage, asking him to stick to his agreement "without hearkening to the mad Advice of Men I know have deceived you."[53] Warren felt that Gage was an honorable man being led astray by his advisors. Warren wrote to Arthur Lee, an American agent in London, about Gage's claim that the Americans had fired the first shot, stating, "My private opinion is that he [Gage] is really deceived in the matter and is led (by his officers and some of the most abandoned villains on earth, who are natives of this Country, and who are now shut up with him in Boston) to believe that our people actually began the fighting."[53] For their part the British often referred to Warren as the "rascally apothecary."[55]

To win support in both the colonies and Britain, the Provincial Congress hurried to collect depositions from eyewitnesses to the fighting. Warren wrote a letter to "The Inhabitants of Great Britain" giving a largely factual account of the events of April 19. He stated, that "the Regulars rushed in with great violence and first began hostilities by firing on said

Lexington company."[53] Warren's letter and the eyewitness depositions was sent by speedy ship to England, arriving 12 days before General Gage's account arrived. Britain was shocked. The king and ministry were so sure that Gage's account would be radically different that they were even more dismayed when his report largely agreed with Warren's, except on the question of who fired first.

Three days after the battles, the Massachusetts Provincial Congress unanimously elected Joseph Warren as president of the Provincial Congress. The Congress called for raising an army of 30,000 men. The Massachusetts Congress also reached out to the other colonies and particularly to the Continental Congress. Warren, writing to his friend Joseph Reed in Philadelphia, stated, "We are all embarked in one bottom; if one colony is enslaved, she will be immediately improved as an engine to subdue the others."[53] Warren had written earlier to the Continental Congress, informing them of events and enclosing the eyewitness testimony about the events of April 19. Warren wrote, "We have the greatest confidence in the wisdom and ability of the Continent to support us, so far as it shall appear necessary for supporting the common cause of the American Colonies."[53]

Warren now managed to combine overseeing the Provincial Congress, the Committee of Safety and a busy medical practice. Philbrick wrote, "Warren appears to have thrived under conditions that most found overwhelming."[56] On May 1 Warren made the decision to send Benedict Arnold, then an ardent Patriot, to capture the British artillery housed at Fort Ticonderoga in New York. Warren let Arnold have 200 pounds of gunpowder, which would be sorely missed, for this expedition.[56]

On May 16, the Provincial Congress asked the Continental Congress to "favor us with your most explicit advice regarding the taking up and exercising the powers of civil government."[53] The Massachusetts body explicitly asked the Continental Congress to take over control of the army, stating, "As the Army now collecting from different colonies is for the general defense of the rights of America, we would leave to suggest for your consideration the propriety of your taking regulation and general direction of it."[53] Eager to get the backing of the large colony of Virginia in confronting the British, Warren and others suggested that George Washington of Virginia be appointed to command the army.

By now no people or goods were coming out of or entering Boston. The Patriots tried to limit the supplies that reached the city. The British meanwhile were sending reinforcements across the ocean. In the British government, there was a feeling that General Gage was not being sufficiently aggressive. King George III, ruler of Britain, after hearing of Lexington and Concord, wrote in a letter, "Once these rebels have felt a smart blow, they will submit."[53]

The next battle occurred on May 27. An American force waded across shallow water to the largely unpopulated Hog and Noddles islands, just offshore of Chelsea to the northeast of Boston. There the Americans removed hay and grazing animals to deprive the British of their use. The British sent the armed schooner *Diana* to drive them off, but the schooner became stuck with the ebbing tide. The Americans, led by General Israel Putnam, a veteran soldier from Connecticut, and accompanied by Joseph Warren, serving as a volunteer, began to fire on the *Diana*. British attempts to free her were unsuccessful and at last she was abandoned. The Americans stripped her of her cannons and other useful items and set her afire.

Gage had received some reinforcements along with three major generals to serve under him. He also received instructions to offer a pardon to all but the top rebels in exchange for their submission. The proclamation, written by Major General John Burgoyne, was notable for its bombastic and condescending tone. It began, "Whereas, the infatuated multitude, who have long suffered themselves to be conducted by certain well known incendiaries and traitors..."[53] The Americans were further antagonized by the message.

The Provincial Congress worried about losing control of the assembled army. The troops were increasingly taking what they needed, particularly in terms of provisions, from the local populace. Warren wrote to Sam Adams, "Unless some authority to restrain the irregularities of the army is established, we shall soon find ourselves in greater difficulties than you can imagine...it is not easy for men, especially when interest and gratification of appetite are considered, to know how far they may continue to tread in the path where there are no landmarks to direct them...if it is with our countrymen as with all other men, when they are in arms, they think the military should be uppermost."[53] Philbrick noted, "Warren came to have a deep sympathy for the men who comprised what was optimistically called the Grand American Army."[56] Warren frequently mingled with the assembled troops. A contemporary observed that he "did wonders in preserving order among the troops...[being] perhaps the man who had the most influence [with them]."[56]

Warren had put himself in harm's way in every battle thus far. On June 2 Warren risked traveling in a small boat to Boston for a secret rendezvous. He tried to recruit a colleague, Dr. John Jeffries, to be the army's surgeon general. Jeffries, a Loyalist, declined the post.[56]

In early June, the Americans learned that the British were planning on seizing and fortifying the high ground around Boston, Dorchester Heights in the south and Bunker Hill on the Charlestown peninsula. If the Americans could get heavy artillery on these heights, they would make the British position in Boston untenable. The British wanted to preclude this. The Committee of Public Safety discussed whether to preempt this by taking Bunker Hill first. Warren and the American generals met in a Council of War to consider this. Israel Putnam was the strongest proponent while the overall commander, General Artemus Ward, and Warren were opposed, noting that they did not have the heavy cannon to make use of the heights to threaten the British. Some officers pointed out that the troops on Bunker Hill could be surrounded. Putnam stated, "[In that case] we shall set for our country an example of which it shall not be ashamed, and show those who seek to oppress us what men can do who are determined to live free or not live at all."[53] Warren replied, "I must still think the project a rash one. Nevertheless, if it should ever be adopted, and the strife becomes hard, you must not be surprised to find me with you in the midst of it."[53] The Council decided to send men to occupy Bunker Hill.

At this point, Warren was no longer a civilian. On June 14, the Provincial Congress, perhaps impressed by his leadership and courage, made him a major general, despite being without any military experience. Warren's rank made him senior to all but Ward and one other general.

On the evening of June 16, an American force of some 1200 men, under the leadership of Colonel William Prescott, a veteran of the French and Indian War, was mustered and ordered to "march to Charlestown and entrench upon that hill."[53] At Putnam's urging they moved past the summit of Bunker Hill to a slightly lower hill, later to be known as Breeds Hill, closer to Charlestown. It was around midnight when the troops arrived and began furiously digging to create a redoubt, a fortification made up of dirt walls. The finished redoubt was roughly five feet tall and about forty yards on either side. Prescott had the troops build an additional entrenchment heading north toward the Mystic River.

When the sun rose early in the morning of June 17, the British discovered the American presence on the hill. The stage was set for the Battle of Bunker Hill. James L. Nelson wrote that the battle "was one of terrific blundering on all sides. For the Americans, [it] took the form of a frightful lack of organization, a failure to think through the objectives of the mission, and an unwillingness to commit the resources needed. The British blundering centered around an arrogant view of the ease with which the Americans could be driven off the hill. They did not employ anything more nuanced than a frontal assault because they felt that they did not need to...they did not even bother to reconnoiter the American redoubt before deciding how to assault it."[53] The British knew that defeat might be irrevocable. General Burgoyne speculated that defeat might mean "a final loss to the British Empire in America."[56]

With daybreak, the British began to bombard the American redoubt with their cannons. Multiple requests were sent to General Ward for reinforcements. At last Ward sent Colonel John Stark with some few hundred New Hampshire men forward as reinforcements. No food, water or extra ammunition was sent throughout that hot June day to the men in the redoubt. Hundreds of Americans milled around atop Bunker Hill in the rear, but did not move forward to reinforce the front-line troops.

On the British side the assault was delayed until the tide was ideal and all the troops could be ferried over to Charlestown. At around 2 PM the first British troops arrived on the peninsula. The delay allowed additional American troops to arrive, enabling them to extend their lines north to the Mystic River. Captain Thomas Knowlton commanded 120 men from Connecticut in a position north of the redoubt while Stark's New Hampshire men held the ground closest to the river. A few men struggled forward throughout the day to join the waiting American troops although not a few of the waiting Americans found reasons to leave their positions to retreat to the rear.

Joseph Warren was in Cambridge where he conducted the business of the Committee of Safety. That morning he went back to bed suffering from a severe migraine headache. When news of the British artillery barrage reached him, Warren rose, reported that his headache was better and that he intended to join the troops on the hill. Many people tried to dissuade him, telling him that his life was too valuable to put at risk. Warren replied to Elbridge Gerry's plea that his life was too valuable to risk by saying that it was impossible for him to remain in Cambridge "while my fellow citizens are shedding their blood for me."[56] Warren rode to the peninsula where he encountered first Putnam and then Prescott. Both, on greeting him, offered to turn over command as he now outranked them. Warren reportedly replied, "I come only as a volunteer. I know nothing of your dispositions, and will not interfere with them; tell me where I can be most useful."[53] Warren joined the men in the redoubt, where the troops greeted him with hurrahs. Nelson wrote, "With that Dr. Joseph Warren, President of the Provincial Congress, Chairman of the Committee of Public Safety, confidant of Sam Adams and John Hancock, took his place at the walls of the redoubt."[53]

The Americans continued to wait as the British brought up their reserves and organized for the attack. The British numbered some 2300 troops, the Americans in the front lines somewhat less. Perhaps a thousand more Americans, enough to have been decisive, waited in the rear, on Bunker Hill proper. Finally, the British advanced. The Americans waited until the British were within some fifty or sixty feet, then let loose a devastating volley. The British fell in droves. In front of Stark's men, some British companies were almost wiped out. In the face of this fire, the British fell back in varying degrees of disorder. A second assault was mounted, but was again driven off with great loss. However, the Americans began to run short of ammunition. It was now that the decision to give Arnold the two hundred pounds of gunpowder may have made the difference. Prescott later stated, "Our ammunition being nearly exhausted, [we] could keep up only a scattering fire. The enemy, being numerous, surrounded our little fort, began to mount our lines and enter the fort with their bayonets."[53] Some Americans tried to run while other swung their muskets like clubs. The British bayonets did deadly execution. The Americans were finally driven from the redoubt. Warren was one of the last to leave the works. The British fired at the retreating Americans. Warren, a conspicuous figure in his fine clothes, was reportedly trying to rally the retreating Americans when he was shot in the head and died instantly.

The Americans retreated, losing many men in the retreat, but continuing to fight until they had been completely driven off the peninsula. By 6 PM, the battle was over. The British lost 226 killed and 828 wounded out of the 2300 soldiers engaged, including a disproportionate number of officers, a casualty rate of almost 50%. The British casualty rate exceeded any battle from the whole of the French and Indian War.[53] General Gage said, "The [American] people show a spirit and conduct against us that they never showed against the French."[55] Most of the British viewed the battle, given their huge losses, more as a defeat than a victory.

The Americans might well have won the battle. Had they had more ammunition or the support of the hundreds of men who loitered far behind the battlefield, the third British assault might have been repulsed. A British defeat, with the catastrophic losses the British suffered, might have resulted in American independence in 1775, rather than was to be an eight-year struggle.

American casualties included 115 dead, 270 wounded and 30 captured. The greatest loss was that of Dr. Joseph Warren. The British exulted in his death. General Howe, surprised that Warren would risk himself in the battle, said, "The victim was worth five hundred of their men."[53] Lord Rawdon, an officer present at the battle, wrote in a letter, "The famous Dr. Warren, the greatest incendiary in all America, was killed on the spot."[58] On the American side, there was great grief over Warren's death. Abigail Adams wrote to her husband, "I wish I could contradict the report of the Doctor's Death, but it is a lamentable truth, and the tears of multitudes pay tribute to his memory."[53] James Nelson wrote, "Joseph Warren was the first great hero and martyr for the cause of liberty and American independence...a man who was at once orator, scribe and soldier for the rights of the colonies. There was no lack of eulogies, orations and essays dedicated to Warren at his death and for years to come."[53] Historian John Alden wrote, "His death deprived them [the Americans] of an ardent, able and generous man who would have been most valuable in war and peace."[54]

Warren is now largely forgotten. He is not included in the pantheon of the Founding Fathers. However, had he not been killed he would have stood high among their ranks. Warren was one of two Patriot leaders who were both political and military leaders. The other, of course, is George Washington. Loyalist Peter Oliver wrote in 1782, "Had [Warren] conquered [at Bunker Hill], Washington [would have] remained in obscurity."[56] Joseph Warren is well worth remembering.

South America 1781 CE

Viceroyalty of New Granada

Guyana

Viceroyalty of Brazil (Portugal)

Cuzco

Viceroyalty of Peru

• La Paz

Viceroyalty of La Plata

• Buenos Aires

Patagonia

Chapter 8: Tupac Amaru
The Great Uprising, 1781 CE, Peru

JOSE GABRIEL TUPAC AMARU is a name unknown to most Americans. Yet almost at the same time the Americans were fighting for their independence, Amaru led a revolt against Spanish rule in South America that spanned the continent, far exceeding in geographical area the American Revolution. What would the world have been like if he had succeeded?

After Christopher Columbus' discovery of the Americas in 1492, the Kingdom of Spain followed up with a lighting conquest, first of the Caribbean, then Mexico and Central America, and finally South America. The dominant power in the western half of South America was the Incas, numbering some 8–10 million people. In 1532, Francisco Pizarro led a small army of Spaniards into Peru and conquered the Incan empire. Within forty years the Spanish had conquered all South America save the Portuguese colony of Brazil.[62-64]

The Spanish tried several approaches to control the native population, who far outnumbered them. Each resulted in high mortality among the Indians. In the encomienda system, a Spaniard would be given an estate, where, with the help of the local Indian leaders, he would be assigned a labor force of Indians, first for one generation and then for up to four generations. Indians on these estates toiled from 2 AM to dark, earning only a handful of pesos in a year.

Indians were made to do forced labor, called the mita.[62,64] Tens of thousands were brought hundreds of miles to work in the mines at Potosi and Huancavelica. There were 1400 mines in Peru, each requiring workers. At the mines, the Indians worked six or seven days a week, often ending up indebted to the mine owners due to fines and other deductions from their minimal pay. One estimate is that over eight million Indians perished in the mines in Peru and the current Bolivia during the colonial period.[62] Don Jose de Armendaris, viceroy from 1724 to 1736, reported, "In the valleys of Runahuana, Huarco, and Chilca, each of which had 13,000 inhabitants...and also in other provinces, there are today scarcely any inhabitants, many villages being utterly deserted."[64]

Other Indians toiled in the obrajes, or factories, from which they were unable to leave. Errors or falling behind one's quota brought swift corporal punishment. The mortality rate among these workers was also high. The end result of these policies was to cut the population of the former Inca empire in half thirty years after its conquest.

The corregidores, the local officials, exploited the Indians, taking the best lands for themselves. They collected the taxes, often keeping two sets of records and thus enabling them to skim money off. If an Indian couldn't pay, everything he owned might be confiscated. The corregidores imposed fines for spurious reasons, pocketing the money.

The repartimiento, enacted in 1751, obligated the Indians to buy a certain amount of goods from Spain. This was an attempt to increase the revenues produced by the colonies.[63] Each corregidor controlled the distribution of goods in their district. The corregidor could arbitrarily select an item for each Indian to buy, whether they wanted it or not, at a price of the official's choosing. When the Indian could not pay, the corregidor seized the Indian's goods, as well as imprisoning them.[62]

Many priests exploited the Indians to make money off of them. They invented various saints' days, then collected large sums from the congregations. Church services would be delayed until everyone had contributed. The priests also charged huge sums for marriages, baptisms and burials. Some priests even were named heirs of the deceased Indians' property.[62]

The corregidores had bought their posts at a high price and expected to make money in the positions. Under the corregidores in each district were the caiques, or chiefs, who were Indians. The caiques enjoyed special privileges, such as exemption from labor and many taxes. As such, most caiques tended to support the existing system and ally with the corregidores rather than the Indians below them.[64] The caiques forced Indians to do work for them or for the Spaniards.

Learning of the widespread corruption in Peru, the reigning Spanish king, Charles III, appointed Jose Antonio de Areche, visitador-general, a position of an inspector general with powers equal to the Viceroy, to investigate. Areche wrote that that the situation was desperate for the Indians. He stated, "The lack of righteous judges, the mita [forced labor] of the Indians and provincial commerce have made a corpse of this America. Corregidores are interested only in themselves… The Indians are very near their tragic end unless a remedy is taken."[62] Nevertheless, Areche was inflexible in insisting on the payment of taxes and complete obedience to Spanish rule.

The revolt that was to follow would be led by Jose Gabriel Tupac Amaru, a descendent of the last Inca kings as well as Spanish nobility. Jose Gabriel was born in 1742 in Peru, where he attended the Jesuit college of San Francisco de Borja in Cuzco, considered the best school in Cuzco.[62–64] Here he learned to read Latin; he could speak both Spanish and his native language, Quechua. He was married at age 16 to Micaela Bastidas Puyacahua, a Spanish woman of good family. They had three children. Tupac Amaru inherited the office of cacique of several locations. In this role, he governed the Indians under him and collected taxes for the Spanish corregidor.[62]

Tupac Amaru dressed and lived like a Spanish nobleman. He was very wealthy by Indian standards, deriving most of his income by transporting merchandise on the back of 350 mules that he had inherited.[64] He was recognized by the governor of his province as the best administrator among the caciques.

Tupac's first political role was in 1777 when he petitioned the viceroy on behalf of the Indians. Tupac Amaru enumerated the abuses of the mita system. He stated, "it is not sensible that the natives suffer bad treatment under the mita when they are considered so useful and necessary."[62] The viceroy told Tupac to go home to await reforms. His uncle, Blas Tupac Amaru, carried some of the Indians' complaints to the Spanish court, where he died suddenly. Speculation is that he may have been poisoned.[64]

The dismissal of his pleas for reform and the death of his uncle may have led Tupac to despair of peaceful reform of the Indians' sufferings. Contemporaries thought his later actions to be motivated by a desire to lift the yoke of oppression from the Indians as well as his exposure to the teachings of the Enlightenment.[62,63] Yet it was to be the 1776 appointment of Antonio de Arriaga, a Spanish military man, as corregidor of the province of Tinta, and thus Tupac Amaru's superior, that would light the fuse of the revolt. Arriaga antagonized people of all classes. Arriaga haughtily dismissed Tupac as the "fraudulent Indian." Tupac Amaru told his friends, "Very soon the corregidor will pay me for this insult."[62] Arriaga also got into a bitter dispute with Bishop Moscono of Cuzco. Arriaga was briefly excommunicated. It seems clear that Moscono then worked with Tupac Amaru to get rid of Arriaga.[62]

On November 4, 1780, Tupac Amaru, with a group of ten men, ambushed Arriaga on his way back from a party. Amaru put Arriaga on trial, which resulted in the death sentence, reportedly at the behest of Bishop Moscono. On November 10, 1780, Arriaga was hanged. Tupac Amaru later wrote that Arriaga had been executed for opposing the Church. Tupac's wife stated that her husband had placed himself in great danger only to please Bishop Moscono, who wrote a letter to Tupac thanking him for Arriaga's death.[62,64] Still Amaru knew that in taking this action, he had made an irrevocable choice to challenge the government.

Immediately following the execution, Tupac Amaru addressed the assembled crowd in the Quechua language. He explained why the corregidor had been executed. He then promised to fight to abolish the mita, the alcabalas (the sales taxes) and the repartimiento. Amaru proclaimed his loyalty to the king and the Church, but also promised to punish those corregidores who oppressed the people. He asked to the people to join his army to aid this campaign. The money taken from the treasury was then distributed among the population. The assembled people proclaimed Tupac Amaru the "liberator of the country "and promised to follow his orders. Amaru then began to collect arms for his forces.[62]

Two days after the execution of Arriata, Tupac Amaru captured Quiquijana, capital of the province of Quispicanchis. He distributed the goods stockpiled there to his followers, which encouraged others to join him. By this time Amaru had an army of some six thousand, although only some three hundred had muskets. Amaru sent out proclamations to the neighboring provinces. One of these read, "Having undertaken…the reform of the corregimientos [the districts], I share it with you… Assemble the inhabitants of the province, seize the corregidores and their adjutants, and place their possessions under strong guard. This order is not against God or King, but against the introduction of bad laws."[62] Tupac Amaru tried to recruit the Creoles, whites born in South America, who often had military experience, into his armies. He gained the support of some, although most remained neutral.[62]

Historian Lillian Fisher wrote, "At no time did Tupac Amaru say that he intended to destroy Spanish institutions… He always showed remarkable loyalty to the Church and Crown, since for the most part these institutions interceded for the Indians."[62] In a letter from Tupac to Areche dated March 5, 1781, Tupac wrote, "Various officials have long acted in disobedience to the expressed will of the crown as regards the treatment to be given to the Indians… The present rebellion is declared not to be directed against the

Crown, rather its purpose is carrying out the king's wishes. Attention is called to the fearful conditions prevailing in mines, obrajes and on farms."[64]

Unpersuaded, the viceroy in Cuzco raised a mixed force of six hundred Spaniards and seven hundred Indians under loyal caciques to suppress the rebellion. This army was camped in the town of Sangarara when, on November 17, 1780, Tupac launched a surprise nighttime attack, routing the Spanish. A portion retreated to the church, firing weapons from there. The enraged Indians then set fire to the church, killing any of the enemy soldiers that tried to escape.[64] Money garnered in the captured towns was distributed among the troops. Tupac took none for himself.[62] The victory at Sangarara caused many Indians to join the revolt, although many powerful chieftains opposed Tupac and took the side of the government.[63]

Tupac now wrote to Bishop Moscono seeking his support.[62] Perhaps fearing that his earlier role in inciting Tupac would come to light, Moscono responded by excommunicating Tupac as a traitor and a revolutionary. The Spanish government tried to reduce support for the rebellion by proclaiming the abolition of the repartimientos, forced labor in workshops and the sales tax.[62]

The Spanish refused to negotiate with Tupac. Tupac now marched south into the basin of Lake Titicaca. In each village and town, he addressed the populace, arguing that he came abolish abuses and punish corregidores. Tupac entered the towns of Ayaviri and Lampa without opposition when their defenders fled in disorder. Hearing news of military preparations in Cuzco against him, Tupac marched back north to his home in Tungasuca.[62]

At this point many provinces were in revolt. While most Indians supported Tupac, Tupac's excommunication reduced his support among the Creoles and the clergy. Although a few priests favored the rebels, most adhered to the Spanish cause. Some priests even raised troops among their parishioners and led them into battle.[62] The Spanish suspected England, with whom Spain was at war, of aiding the rebels, but there is little evidence to support any English role in the revolt.

On December 19, 1780, Tupac led his army, now compromising 25,000 men, although most were untrained and poorly armed, north to capture Cuzco. On December 28 Tupac camped with his troops about six miles away from Cuzco. Tupac now halted to send letters to the authorities in the city, stating that he only wanted to abolish abuses, but that he would take harsh measures if his entrance into the city was resisted. Tupac wrote, "If this is not granted at once, I will not delay for an instant my entrance with fire and sword...I am the only one who remains of the royal blood of the Incas...I have decided to try all means possible that all abuses...may cease. I wish to leave to the King of Spain the direct rule which he has had in his possessions."[62] While Tupac sent these letters and waited, Spanish reinforcements arrived. The royal forces, now numbering some 12,000, attacked Tupac and his army on January 8. After two days of bloody fighting, Tupac and his army withdrew.

Around the same time, Jose Gabriel's brother, Diego Tupac Amaru, commanding a detachment of troops, was defeated and forced to withdraw from the Vilcamayo valley. Despite the twin defeats, the insurrection continued to spread through most of the center, south and west of Peru. On February 23, 1781, the visitidor-general, Areche, arrived in Cuzco with additional forces, bringing the army there up to 15,000 men. The Spanish prepared to launch an offensive to put down the revolt in the outlying provinces. Tupac now wrote to Areche, professing his loyalty to the king and summing up the woes of the Indians. Tupac wrote, "My intention was not to maltreat or disturb the inhabitants of Cuzco...when they [the corregidores] resisted me with great instruments of war, I was compelled to respond. I do not have a heart as cruel or depraved as the tyrannous corregidores and their allies, for I am a good Catholic Christian."[62] Areche refused all negotiations and threatened severe retribution. Areche wrote, "Count with the imagination the many thousands of deaths you have caused...it would have been better to suffer the old evils a little longer...You have filled the provinces with deaths, burnings, insults, robberies, sacrifices and immunities...you pretend that you are trying to free the Indians from the evils they say they suffer, but now their sufferings are doubled."[62] Areche offered only that if Tupac surrendered at once, the method of his execution would be less cruel. The principal army commander, General del Valle, protested that the harshness of the reply made surrender and peace impossible.[62]

Tupac had established a government for the provinces under his control. Although these were generally well administered, Tupac could not always prevent the Indians from killings or destructions. Fisher wrote, "Tupac Amaru did not approve of widespread destruction of property or of an excessive bloodshed...[he] protected his Creole friends, declared himself the liberator of all oppressed races, and was even willing to employ

Europeans who were useful to him. His principal targets were grasping and dishonest corregidores...Unfortunately, his moderate policy could not be enforced on account of the hatred felt by his partisans."[62] Such killing had the counterproductive effect of increasing support for the government.

Tupac's wife, Micaela Bastidas, took over for Tupac at home in his absences. She collected supplies for Tupac's army, corresponded with his generals and tried to recruit officials and priests to support Tupac. She also tried to prevent abuses of prisoners.

While many provinces remained securely under Tupac's controls, others were filled with ongoing battles between Spanish and Indian forces. Usually the superior arms of the Spanish prevailed, but other times the Indians were victorious. The revolt encompassed what is now Peru, Bolivia and the northwestern part of Argentina.

On March 9, General del Valle led an army of some 14,000–16,000 men south from Cuzco to attack Tupac. The Spanish army suffered from snowstorms and lack of food. However, on April 4 they encountered Tupac's army, entrenched on the hills. Tupac's army was also very short of provisions. Tupac attacked the Spanish that night. The superior weapons of the Spanish were decisive. Tupac was defeated, losing all his cannons and much other equipment as well as many men.

Tupac escaped south. His wife and family separately tried to flee, but were captured by the Spanish. Tupac himself fled to the town of Langui. Tupac's commander there betrayed Tupac and turned him over to the Spanish. Tupac and his family were brought as prisoners back to Cuzco on April 14, 1781, to be put on trial. Tupac was charged with almost every possible crime, from plotting rebellion to murder. Tupac refused to confess during the trial. Consequently, he was tortured with the garrucha, a pulley that resulted in the dislocation of his arms.

On May 15, 1781, Tupac was forced to watch the execution of his wife, oldest son, other relatives and lieutenants. Then Tupac's tongue was cut out. His limbs were then tied to four horses which were driven in different directions resulting in his dismemberment. However, the horses proved too weak to effectively pull him apart so his head was then cut off.[62,63] Tupac's younger son, Fernando, age 9, after being forced to watch the death of his parents, was sentenced to life imprisonment in Africa. Reportedly King Charles III of Spain, horrified by the grisly sentences imposed by Areche, spoke to his confessor, "I fear to speak of it...to kill successors of the kings of Peru."⁶² Areche banned the speaking of the local language, Quechua, and ordered the destruction of all folklore and writings about the days before the Spanish conquest.⁶⁴

The revolt did not end with Jose Gabriel Tupac Amaru's death. The continued fighting claimed many lives on both side, including thousands of noncombatants. The widespread revolt proved difficult for Spain to suppress, even after Tupac's death.

Battles continued through 1781, particularly around the huge Lake Titicaca high in the Andes. The city of Sorata was besieged for ninety days by a force of almost 20,000 Indians, led by Andres Tupac Amaru, a relative of Tupac. After the Spanish garrison refused to surrender, Andres Tupac Amaru built a dam on the nearby snow-covered Ancoma Mountain. On August 4, 1781, he broke the dam, releasing the water to wipe out the Spanish trenches defending the town. The Indians killed some 10,000 people in Sorata and burned down the town.⁶²

Further south, the city of La Paz underwent two sieges by rebels lasting 109 and 75 days respectively. By the time the first siege was broken at the end of June, one-third of the population of La Paz had died from hunger, from illness or in the fighting. The relieving force, plagued by desertions, withdrew from La Paz on August 1, promising to return with reinforcements. The renewed siege wasn't broken in mid-October. Some 60,000 people died during the sieges, two-thirds of them Indians.⁶²

Battles continued through the spring of 1782 as the revolt spread through the present-day nations of Ecuador, Columbia, Venezuela and Panama. The Spanish put down these uprisings with significant bloodshed.

Tupac's brother Diego still held out. To end the rebellion the Viceroy of Peru extended a pardon to him and his relatives. Diego finally agreed and laid down his arms in December 1781. The viceroy wrote to Diego, "You, your nephews, and dependents shall be entirely free of cares, since you are admitted under royal protection, the pardons shall be kept in good faith, if you remain faithful and obedient to the King."⁶²

There were many among the Spanish who felt that he had been treated too leniently. On April 15, 1783, Diego was arrested along with sixty-three of his relatives. The charges against them were trifling and without supporting evidence. Fisher wrote, "Diego was accused of being deceitful, of corresponding with the natives…that he wanted to keep his ancestral name, Tupac Amaru, that he lived in a manner unbecoming to a pardoned rebel, and that he had conducted funeral rites for his brother."[62] Diego, his mother and other relatives were sentenced to be dismembered and executed. Diego was tortured before being killed by having pieces of flesh torn out with red hot pincers.

Bishop Moscono was accused of being sympathetic to the rebels. He successfully answered the charges in Madrid and was promoted to become archbishop. Vistador General Areche was removed from his position in 1782 for misconduct. It would be many years before he could reenter government service.[62]

The revolt did result in some important reforms. The repartimientos, the forced purchase of goods, was abolished. The mita, the involuntary service, was modified to limit the term of service. In 1785 Viceroy Teodoro de Croix abolished the system of corregidores. A smaller number of governors of a generally higher quality were appointed to oversee the provinces of Peru. Croix was vigorous in removing officials who committed abuses.[62] These reforms kept the Spanish in control for a few more decades, but it wasn't long before the South American provinces obtained their independence.

In geographical and human terms, the revolt led by Jose Gabriel Tupac Amaru was the greatest ever seen in South America. Despite Tupac's defeat, it showed that even oppression could not last forever. The revolts that led to independence largely were led by Creoles, people of European descent born in the Americas. In recent years, however, more and more leaders of Native American heritage have emerged. They are the heirs of Tupac Amaru.

IRELAND

Chapter 9: Wolfe Tone
The Battle for Irish Independence, 1798, Ireland

THERE IS A SIMPLE GRAVE in a tiny cemetery in County Kildare in Ireland. The man resting in the grave is venerated by all sides in Irish politics, from Protestant loyalists to the hard men of the Irish Republican Army. The man buried there, Wolfe Tone, lived only thirty-five years, but it was long enough to make him beloved throughout Ireland ever since.

The history of Ireland has invariably been linked to its larger neighbor to the east, Britain.[65-69] The English first conquered Ireland barely a hundred years after the Norman conquest of England in 1066.

When King Henry VIII of England broke away from the Catholic Church to create the Protestant Anglican Church with himself at the top, the Irish largely refused to follow, remaining staunch Catholics. Thus, a religious component was added to the conflict between British and Irish. When a revolt under the Catholic Huge O'Neill was crushed in 1601, his supporters in the province of Ulster in northern Ireland fled into exile. Their lands were seized to be settled by English and Scottish Protestants.[66]

In 1690, the Protestants, under William of Orange, who had seized the English throne, won a decisive victory over the deposed King James II and his largely Catholic forces at the Battle of the Boyne. Protestant supremacy in Ireland thus was assured for centuries to come. In the aftermath of the war, what was known as "The Laws in Ireland for Suppression of Popery," were passed. The laws treated Catholics harshly. Only Protestant schools were allowed. Intermarriage between Catholics and Protestants was forbidden. If it occurred, any property would go to the Protestant side. Catholics were barred from the army, the civil service, the legal profession and any elected positions. A couplet summed this up, "Catholics could not read nor teach, plead nor preach."[66] Catholics, most of the population, owned only 14% of the land, a percentage that dropped to less than 5% within 50 years.[66] During the 18th century, Ireland was hit by four major famines. Oppressed by poverty, hundreds of thousands of Irish, both Protestant and Catholics, emigrated and settled in America.

It was into this environment that Theobald Wolfe Tone was born in Dublin in 1763. He was the oldest of sixteen children in a middle-class Protestant family. Tone entered a preparatory school where he learned Greek and Latin and formed a debating society. When Tone was thirteen or fourteen, his father suffered a head injury and gave up his business. The family moved to property they held in rural Kildare, leaving Tone alone to lodge in Dublin. At seventeen he decided to join the British army. Tone wrote, "Being at this time approaching to seventeen years of age, it will not be thought incredible that woman began to appear lovely in my eyes, and I very wisely thought that a red coat [the army uniform]...would aid me considerably in my approaches to the objects of my adoration."[68] Tone was dissuaded by his father, who told him that he would not assist him in this ambition.[66,68]

In 1781 Tone started Trinity College, one of the elite institutions of Ireland. Many of his classmates were from the highest strata of society and would rise later to high positions in the Irish government.[68] While in college, Tone, age 22, met the 16-year-old Matilda Witherington. After a courtship of a few months they eloped and were married on July 21, 1785.

Deciding on a career in law, Tone began his legal training in London in January 1787, leaving his wife and daughter in Ireland. During his two years in London, Tone continually worried about money, unlike many of his wealthier peers. In 1789 Tone passed the bar and became a barrister or lawyer in Dublin. Tone was not a success, finding the law dominated by those with elite connections or money.

Following the end of the American Revolution in 1783, the British government tried to assuage Irish unhappiness with British rule by offering the Irish more power. Restrictions on the powers of the Irish parliament were removed. The British parliament officially renounced its claim to legislate for Ireland in 1782. In theory, Ireland was now an independent kingdom sharing a monarch with Great Britain. Several of the restrictions on Catholics were repealed, most notably in the relief act of 1778 that effectively allowed Catholics to own land.[67]

In practice, Britain retained effective control in Ireland. The lord lieutenant, nominated by the British government, ran the executive branch of government and chose the judges in Ireland. Moreover, the ability to vote for the members of parliament was restricted exclusively to wealthier Protestants, principally the great Anglican landowners. Neither Catholics nor the bulk of Protestants, who were mainly Presbyterians of Scottish origin, had significant political power. In addition, the lord lieutenant controlled patronage and pensions that could be given or withheld to members of Parliament, thus effectively controlling many of the members.[67]

The Presbyterians made up the majority of the population in the north in Ulster while the rest of Ireland was mainly Catholic.

Tone, after having mingled with elite society at Trinity College, increasingly felt estranged from the wealthier members of Irish society. His relative poverty may have contributed to his increasing criticism of this society. Tone was unimpressed by his observations of the Irish Parliament, seeing it as tool of British rather than Irish interests. Tone began writing political pamphlets or essays.

In 1790 Britain went to the brink of war with Spain. Tone now wrote an essay arguing that Ireland should not automatically enter Britain's wars as the benefits of the war largely would accrue to England while Ireland would suffer disproportionate costs and casualties. While Tone accepted the rule of "our King," he also wrote, "we should spurn the idea of moving, a humble satellite round any power, however great, and claim…our rank among the primary nations of the earth."[68] Here Tone argued that Ireland should be an independent kingdom under the same king as Britain.

Tone's views continued to evolve over time. He began to question the Irish elite's view that Protestants must dominate Ireland. Historian Mariane Elliot wrote, "It is not republican separatism that Tone considered his most important contribution to the history of Ireland, but his effort to heal its religious divisions."[68] The minority Protestants feared giving power to the Catholics. Many Protestants believed that Catholics' greatest loyalty was to the pope.[68]

In August 1791, Tone's third and most famous essay, titled "An Argument on Behalf of the Catholics in Ireland," was published. Tone stated that Ireland should be "free of Britain and free of religious oppression." He wrote, "No reform can ever be obtained which shall not comprehensively embrace Irishmen of all denominations."[68] Tone wrote that the Irish Protestants must "put away our childish fears, look our situation in the face like men…[and] speak to this ghostly spectre of our distempered imagination…Irish Catholicity."[68] Tone also argued that the French Revolution showed that a very Catholic country could be turned into a secular republic. Tone wrote, "Look at France…where is the intolerance of popish bigotry?"[65] Tone argued that the reform could never succeed if the government could play off the Catholics against the Protestants. He proposed that Irish Protestants and Catholics should work together for the goals of reform.[66] Tone's pamphlet was an immediate best seller. It helped reduce Protestant and Catholic fears and antipathy.[69]

Tone now escalated his political activity in hopes of bringing about reforms. In October 1791 Tone, along with others, formed the Society of United Irishmen. The goal of the society was to reform Parliament to give an equal representation to all Irish and decrease British control over Irish affairs. In Dublin, the society was a mixture of Catholics and Protestants, while the latter dominated in Belfast in northern Ireland.[66] Sympathizers in Belfast started a newspaper, the *Northern Star*, which helped lay out the views of the United Irishmen. At its height, its readership of 4000 made it the largest of any contemporary Irish newspaper. Tone was impressed by the anti-aristocratic and anti-English views of the Belfast Protestants. Tone wrote, "The Dissenters of the north…[are] sincere and enlightened Republicans, they have among them, but few great landed proprietors…they have ever, in a degree, opposed the usurpations of England whose protection…they did not, like the Protestant aristocracy, feel necessary for their protection."[68] In early 1792, the Anglican-elite-dominated Irish Parliament rejected reforms giving Catholics even a limited vote, even though the British government urged concessions to the Catholics to prevent the formation of an anti-British Catholic–Presbyterian alliance.[65] Tone seemed to be succeeding in uniting poor and middle-class Protestants and Catholics in opposition to the pro British Anglican landowners who dominated the Irish parliament. The administration of the lord lieutenant in Dublin saw the United Irishmen as secret revolutionaries, whose demand for parliamentary reform was a ruse to cover their real goal of independence for Ireland.[65]

Tone's arguments earned him a very favorable reputation among the Catholics. In April 1792 the chairman of the Catholic committee thanked Tone for "his exertions in the cause of emancipating the Catholics."[68] In July 1792 Tone was made chief publicist and agent of the Catholic Committee.[68] Tone, along with others, went to London to petition for increased rights for Catholics. The petition led to the Catholic Relief Law of 1793, repealing some of the Penal Laws.[66,67] Catholics remained excluded from Parliament and higher offices.[67] Disappointment over the limited reforms led to riots that were forcibly suppressed. Declaring at least partial victory, the Catholic Committee disbanded.[68]

It was left to the United Irishmen to continue the fight. In 1794 the Dublin society of the United Irishmen put forth a plan for parliamentary reform in Ireland that would create suffrage for all Protestants and Catholics. The Irish Parliament ignored the proposal.[67]

The French Revolution that began in 1789 led to the fall of the French monarchy and its replacement by a radical republic. By February 1793, Britain was at war with France, a situation that would continue, except for one short truce, for over twenty years. The French, looking for ways to weaken Britain, saw Ireland as Britain's Achilles heel. The British tried to anticipate this by cracking down on potential allies of French in Ireland, including the United Irishmen. The Irish lord chancellor, John Fitzgibbon, singled out Tone, although few others at the time thought him dangerous. Fitzgibbon, a cousin of Tone's wife Matilda, wrote that Tone, who first proposed an alliance between the Puritans and Catholics, "is the son of a bankrupt tradesman, and has had the merit of being the founder of the Society of United Irishmen. He was the original projector of the Catholic Convention…and composes most of the seditious and treasonable libel which are put forth by the Society of United Irishmen."[68]

The French, contemplating an invasion of Ireland, sent two agents to Dublin to help assess Irish sentiment. The first was William Jackson, an Irish-born Anglican clergyman turned radical. His companion, John Cockayne, was a secret spy for the British. The two joined the United Irishmen. They began visiting Hamilton Rowan, a prominent member of the United Irishmen, who was in Newgate Prison, but allowed to receive frequent visitors. In his cell, Jackson and Cockayne met a fellow visitor, Wolfe Tone. Tone and Rowan thought that the people in Ireland would welcome a French invasion launched to remove British control of Ireland. Rowan and Jackson asked Tone to draw up a paper outlining the pros and cons of such an invasion and showing that there was support for it. Tone wrote, "In Ireland, a conquered and oppressed and insulted country, the name of England and her powers is universally odious, save to those who have an interest in maintaining it."[68] Tone also argued that the French must clearly proclaim in advance that they were there to support Irish independence and disclaim any idea of conquest to win the support of the Irish populace. Tone wrote the report, but then, realizing the danger of putting these thoughts to paper, asked for it back. Rowan, however, had already made copies. Cockayne reported all this back to the British government, who arrested everyone involved.[66]

Rowan somehow escaped prison and fled to the United States in May 1794. After a long imprisonment and conviction for treason, Jackson killed himself on April 30, 1795.[67] The evidence against Tone was weak as Cockayne refused to testify against him, whether due to guilt over his role or perhaps feeling that Tone had been lured into the plot. In return for a statement outlining his involvement, Tone received immunity from prosecution. However, he also had to agree to leave Ireland.[68,69] The Society of the United Irishmen was suppressed and its papers seized in May 1794.[68] It reemerged, however, as a secret society.[65]

In the summer of 1794, the British government tried conciliation, appointing a reformist lord lieutenant, Earl Fitzwilliam. Fitzwilliam proposed total repeal of the remaining anti-Catholic Penal Laws. In response, the government dismissed Fitzwilliam from office in February 1795. The result was widespread disappointment among the Catholics and further popular alienation from the government.[68]

Tone's exile had been delayed while this struggle had been going on. Now, however, he had to go into exile. On June 3, 1795, Wolfe Tone, his wife Matilda, his children and a younger brother set sail for America.

Arriving in Philadelphia in August, Tone found the Americans divided between two factions: those partial to the British, the Federalists, and those leaning towards France, the Democratic Republicans. The American president, George Washington, tried to maintain American neutrality in the conflict even as many of his countrymen tried to push him into supporting one side or the other.

Tone was unhappy in America. He found the weather in the summer too hot and humid and the cost of living in Philadelphia high. Tone wrote that the Americans seemed, "not to be amiable; they seem selfish and interested, and they do fleece us emigres, at a most unmerciful rate."[68] Tone's unhappiness in America increased his sense of loss at his exile from Ireland.

Before leaving Ireland, Tone had agreed to become the United Irishmen's emissary to France. Meeting the French ambassador, Pierre Adet, in Philadelphia, Tone proposed that the French invade Ireland. Tone argued that 90% of the population would support such an invasion. Adet arranged for Tone to travel to France under the alias James Smith. On January 1, 1796, Tone sailed to France.[66]

In France Tone was warmly received by the Francophile American ambassador James Monroe. Monroe went so far as to act as a translator for Tone in his meetings with French officials.[66]

Tone was finally able to convince the French government to mount an invasion of Ireland. France's most famous general at the time, General Louis Hoche, was named to command the invasion. On July 12, Tone met Hoche, who questioned him closely about the situation in Ireland. Tone told him that the French needed to send a large enough army to help the doubters in Ireland come out in support. Hoche replied, "Undoubtedly, men will not sacrifice themselves when they do not see a reasonable prospect of support; but if I go, you may be sure that I will go in sufficient force."[68] Tone was appointed a colonel in the French army. Unfortunately, the plans for the invasion kept changing, delaying the start. While the French delayed, in November 1796 the British arrested many of the most prominent United Irishmen in Ulster, in the north of Ireland. At last, on December 15, 1796, a French armada of forty-three warships and almost 15,000 men under Hoche, accompanied by Wolfe Tone, set sail from the port of Brest in France for Ireland.[68]

Adverse weather and poor seamanship resulted in the ships becoming widely separated. General Hoche's ship was blown far out into the Atlantic Ocean away from the others. Many of the former captains and officers of the French navy had been casualties of the revolution, leading to a decline in competence. The storms were a consequence of delaying the invasion until the winter. Finally, thirty-six ships arrived at their destination, Bantry Bay in Ireland, on December 21. Another large storm arose that night, scattering the fleet. Continued poor weather prevented those ships that were left from landing any troops. Tone wrote, "I see nothing before me, unless a miracle be wrought in our favor, but the ruin of the expedition, the slavery of my country and my own destruction…I have a merry Christmas of it today."[68] Finally, the remaining ships set sail back to France. Tone's ship was one of only fifteen that returned safely.

At the time, the British had just over 15,000 widely scattered regular troops in Ireland, of a quality far inferior to the French. It is likely that the French would have been able to conquer all of Ireland had they been able to land as planned. The French were surprised that their mere presence offshore had not caused the Irish to revolt. Elliot wrote, "French perceptions of Irish willingness to revolt were indeed inflated, and most of the warnings by Tone, O'Connor and others that the response of the Irish would depend on the strength of the French forces and their initial actions upon landing, were conveniently forgotten."[68] The British government had been totally surprised both by the idea of the invasion and its near success.[68,69]

Hoche was now transferred to a command along the Rhine River. Tone was made an adjutant general in the French army and accompanied Hoche to the east of France. Tone's family settled in Hamburg. Tone continued to try to persuade the French to consider another invasion. The French, particularly General Hoche, began planning such a campaign. However, Hoche soon died of tuberculosis at the age of 29.[68]

The near success of the French invasion frightened the British government, which increased its defenses in Ireland and further cracked down on potential supporters of the French. The United Irishmen had signed up thousands of members in the preceding year, including many members of the Irish milita. In 1797, the government passed an Insurrection Act, which allowed imposition of curfews and gave the government extensive powers to search for arms. It suspended habeas corpus and made the swearing of oaths (to the United Irishmen or other underground groups) a crime punishable by death or involuntary exile to Australia.[65,67] The British government was particularly harsh on any potential disaffected soldiers, executing over twenty in 1797 for having joined the United Irishmen. Others were flogged, sent to Australia or drafted into the British navy.[65]

British spies had infiltrated the ranks of the United Irishmen.[65,70] The British arrested many members. Those arrested were tortured to inform on others, notably by being tied to large triangular wooden frames. Here they would be flogged without mercy, sometimes with salt rubbed into the wounds.[70] In March 1798 the British arrested many of the key leaders of the United Irishmen, including its military leader, Lord Edward FitzGerald.[69]

Nevertheless, in May and June 1798, roughly a year and a half after the first French expedition, revolts broke out throughout Ireland. The British, under General Lake, crushed these revolts with great ferocity. An estimated 30,000 Irishmen were reported to have died in the fighting.[66,69] Ulster, a center of the United Irishmen, had been so sapped by intercommunal violence and government crackdowns and arrests that the risings that occurred there were easily put down.[65,69] The revolts were also notable for who did not support them. For example, the Catholic hierarchy was almost uniformly supportive of the government.[65]

If the French had invaded in sufficient force at the time, the revolt may well have succeeded. However, the second French invasion wasn't launched until September 1798. This force included 2291 men under General Hardy. Tone accompanied this force, although his expectations were low. Tone's son later wrote, "At the period of this expedition, he was hopeless of its success. He had all along deprecated the idea of these attempts on a small scale. But he had also declared repeatedly that if the [French] Government sent only a corporal's guard, he felt his duty to go along with them."[68]

Again, the fleet was thrown into turmoil by foul weather and poor French seamanship. Moreover, the British navy was waiting. The British inflicted an overwhelming defeat on the French, capturing all the French ships on October 12, 1798. Tone had sailed as a French officer in the ship *Hoche* under the name James Smith. The *Hoche* fought a stubborn battle against the British, losing some 200 men killed or wounded, before surrendering. Tone was at first unrecognized. However, when Tone disembarked as a prisoner, he was recognized by a lawyer loyal to Britain, Sir George Hill, against whom Tone had argued in court. Hill wrote, "This morning some hundreds of the prisoners are just landed…the first man who stepped out of the boat…was T. W. Tone; he recognized and addressed me instantly."[68]

Tone was taken in chains to Dublin, the most prominent prisoner captured by the British. The French commander, General Hardy, wrote to General Cornwallis, the current lord lieutenant, protesting this treatment, saying, "I will not touch on the question of grievances you may have against this officer, but he is a French citizen, member of the French army, prisoner of war and for each of these reasons he should be treated with consideration and respect."[68] Cornwallis' secretary answered for him, replying, "Theobold Wolfe Tone is known only to his Excellency as a traitor…who at last is about to receive the punishment due to the crimes he had been guilty of committing against his King and country."[68]

Despite never having served in the British army, Tone was tried by an army court martial on November 10. Tone read out an explanation of his actions. Tone stated, "The great object of my life has been the independence of my country. Looking upon the connection with England to have been her bane I have endeavored by every means in my power to break that connection...to create a people in Ireland...by uniting the Catholics and the Dissenters [non-Anglican Protestants]. For a fair and open war I was prepared; if that has degenerated into a system of assassination, massacre and plunder I do...most sincerely lament it...I have attempted to establish the independence of my country; I have failed in the attempt; my life is in consequence forfeit and I submit; the Court will do their duty and I shall endeavor to do mine."[68] Tone asked to be shot as befitting an officer.

Tone was convicted of treason and sentenced to be hanged on November 12. Tone spent the day of November 11 writing letters to the French government, arranging financial assistance for his wife and family and writing to old friends, his father and his wife.

On the night of November 11 Tone cut his throat with a penknife, severing his windpipe. He wanted to deny the British the satisfaction of hanging him. Four surgeons successfully kept him alive and stitched up his wound to allow him to be hung the next day. Ironically the next day his friends' challenge to the military court and its sentence was accepted. The judge ordered Tone brought to the court, but Tone's attempted suicide had weakened him enough that he could not be moved. In this era before antiseptic conditions for surgery and antibiotics, it is not surprising that his wound became infected.

Tone's surgeon ordered him not to move his head in a certain way lest it instantly kill him. Tone reportedly thanked the doctor for his kind words and moved his head in that exact manner, resulting in his death. Tone died November 19, 1798, and was buried in a family plot in an unmarked grave on November 21 in County Kildare.[66]

Tone's wife, Matilda, helped ensure that Tone's martyrdom would be remembered. She and her son carefully edited his memoir, which became standard reading for both Protestant and Catholic Irish leaders. In time, Wolfe Tone became synonymous with the justice and virtue of the fight for Irish freedom.[66] Tone would become a symbol for many of those fighting for Irish independence in the next two centuries.

Chapter 10: Toussaint L'Ouverture
The Greatest Slave Revolt, 1801 CE, Haiti

THE SLAVE was named Francois Dominique Toussaint a Breda. He had just seen his master's wife and children safely to a ship to avoid being killed. He had sent his own wife and children to safety in the Spanish colony to the east. Now at last this small and quiet man rode to join the slave rebellion in St. Domingue (modern Haiti). Speaking of his decision to fight to abolish slavery, Toussaint later said, "Those first moments were of beautiful delirium, born of a great love of freedom."[70,71] No one would have predicted that his future would be as ruler of the whole large island of Hispaniola.

Discovered by Christopher Columbus on his first voyage, Hispaniola is one of the largest islands in the Caribbean, about the size of Ireland. In 1492, it was covered with thick vegetation and inhabited by about half to one million largely peaceful Indians called Tainos.[70-72] Disease and harsh treatment by the Spanish wiped out the Indians. Forty years after Columbus's initial visit only some 200 Indians survived. To replace the Indians as a labor force, the Spanish imported slaves from Africa. In 1695 by the Treaty of Ryswick the western half of the island of Hispaniola was ceded from Spain to France to become the French colony of St. Domingue.[70–76]

The late-17th-century introduction of sugar cane into St. Domingue transformed the colony. The initial small landholdings were converted rapidly into massive sugar plantations, for the sugar crop was immensely profitable. The growing and harvesting of sugar cane was very labor intensive, requiring an enormous number of workers. The cheapest source was slaves imported from Africa. It is estimated that 300 slave ships sailed to St. Domingue every year bringing 20,000 slaves annually.[71,74] More slaves were brought to the colony than to the whole United States.[72]

The slaves were treated harshly. On arrival at the plantation, all slaves would be branded with hot irons bearing the mark of their new owners. On the plantations, the slaves labored from dawn until late in the evening six days a week. The average slave population on a large plantation might exceed 1000 people. An estimated 5–10% of the slave population died every year.[72–74] Harsh punishments and tortures were used to control the slaves.

By 1788 the population of St. Domingue had grown to 42,000 whites and some 500,000 black slaves. Given the high mortality rate among the black slaves, new slaves had to be constantly imported. Of the half million slaves in the colony in 1789, more than two-thirds had been born in Africa.[75] There were also 38,000 mulattos, product of unions between the white slave owners and their black slaves. The mulattos were frequently not slaves and ranged in economic status from poor to wealthy. The late 1700s saw passage of increasingly discriminatory laws that placed the mulattos far below the whites, although above the slaves.[71,73]

Saint Domingue, by 1790, was France's richest colony. Known as the "Pearl of the Antilles" it supplied more than a third of France's foreign trade, 40% of Europe's sugar consumption and 60% of its coffee.[70] The colony was also notorious for the degeneracy of the plantation owners. One observer wrote, "No white man did any work that he could get a Negro to do for him."[75]

This status quo was disturbed first by the American and then the French Revolution. The Declaration of the Rights of Man passed by the French National Assembly in 1790 stated that "men are born and remain equal in rights."[74] The proclamations of liberty and equality by the French revolutionaries raised hope for freedom and improved status among the mulattos and blacks on St. Domingue. Members of the French National Assembly pushed to grant political equality to the mulattos. This was grievously resented by the white slave owners on St. Domingue, who refused to implement this reform. The whites on the island took advantage of the French Revolution to set up white-only colonial assemblies in the colony, which agreed on little except maintaining the superiority of the whites. The year 1791 was marked by fighting between pro-revolutionary and royalist factions among the whites.[74] Yet while the whites squabbled, the black slaves decided to break the chains of slavery. Before discussing the great slave revolt that followed, we shall return to the slave who became its leader.

Toussaint a Breda was born around 1743–46 on the planation of Breda on St. Domingue. Like his father before him, Toussaint was granted unusual privileges by his owner, the Comte de Noe, who had a reputation for humanity unusual on the island. Toussaint was taught to read by his godfather, Pierre Baptiste. Toussaint read all the books on the estate, including those on Roman history, philosophy and military strategy. His most read book was by the stoic Epictetus. Toussaint believed, like Epictetus, that endurance, abstinence and discipline were the foundations of character.[71] Toussaint also read a history of the West Indies by the Abbot Raynal, who predicted that one day a leader would rise from slavery to free the slaves on one of the Caribbean islands.[76] Toussaint was made steward of the animals on the estate, giving him administrative experience.

In Toussaint's late twenties, a cousin of the Comte, Bayon de Libertas, took over running the estate. Again, Toussaint became a favorite, taking charge of the stables. Recent research suggests that Toussaint was freed around age 25, although his wife Suzanne and children remained slaves.[70] While Toussaint was well treated at the Breda plantation, he heard about the miserable treatment of slaves on other estates. Thus, when the great slave revolt began, he knew that he must fight against slavery.

On August 14, 1791, a group of some 200 slaves met in secret to plan the revolt. The leader was an escaped slave named Boukman.[76] The group pledged in blood, "We swear to destroy the whites and all they possess. Let us die rather than fail to keep this vow."[71] On August 22, slaves across the northern plains of the colony erupted in revolt. They massacred any whites they could find, man, woman and child, sparing only a few known for their kindness. A few white survivors fled to the town of Le Cap. The whites in Le Cap turned on the free blacks and mulattos in the town, killing them by the score. The slave army attacked Le Cap, but was driven off by the garrison and Boukman killed. In a single month, some 2000 whites and 10,000 blacks died.[71] By the end of September, the insurgent slaves numbered in the tens of thousands. Over 200 sugar plantations and some 1200 smaller coffee plantations had been destroyed.[74]

The army of the escaped slaves was now commanded by an ex-slave named Jean Francois. Upon joining them, Toussaint used his knowledge of plants and herbs to treat the sick in the camp and was named chief physician of the army. Soon after Toussaint's arrival the worst excesses of the slave army were checked. Toussaint worked to assure a food supply for the army. He also acted to improve the treatment of prisoners. Impressed by his leadership, Jean François named Toussaint a field commander over a portion of the army.

Under Toussaint's command the rebels now advanced toward Le Cap, capturing outlying forts. A Frenchman wrote of Toussaint's troops that "they did not expose themselves on masse with their former fury; they formed groups hiding in the thickets before falling on their enemy. They even withdrew swiftly into the undergrowth…it was a new type of warfare more dangerous because it was unknown."[71] This would later be called guerrilla warfare.

Toussaint's troops were also known for their rigorous discipline. A French general, Pamphile Lacroix, wrote, "No European army was subjected to a severer discipline than Toussaint's…[his] officers have the power of life and death over those under their commands."[71] Toussaint punished any soldiers who committed acts of cruelty.

Toussaint was noted for living with his men and sharing their hardships. Once he had his hand crushed helping his troops move a cannon.[75] Toussaint later estimated that he was wounded seventeen times during his years of battle.[70]

While Toussaint rose in status among the rebels, fighting broke out in Le Cap between royalist and revolutionary sympathizers among the whites. The mulattos rose in the west of the colony, quickly defeating the whites there. In the south, it was the whites who attacked, first the mulattos and then the revolting blacks. The barbarity committed by the whites in this area rivaled the worst excesses of the revolting slaves in the north. The colony of St. Domingue was riven by bloodshed.[71]

Threatened by famine, the slave army offered to negotiate, asking for limited freedom and amnesty for the insurgents. The colony's white assembly refused, demanding that the blacks surrender unconditionally to their authority.

The French National Assembly appointed three commissioners, accompanied by 6000 troops, to go to the island to try to resolve the conflict. The whites on the island were infuriated by the commissioners' rumored intention to end slavery. The president of the island assembly said, "The colonists have not imported half a million Negroes into St. Domingue in order to make them French citizens."[71]

The French troops, led by Etienne Bizefrance, Comte of Laveaux, defeated the rebel army, inflicting one of Toussaint's only defeats. Toussaint led his surviving 600 men up into the mountains to regroup.

The already confused situation got more complicated. The slaves now made an agreement with the Spanish in the eastern half of Hispaniola, who promised them arms, ammunition, land and Spanish citizenship. Facing threats from French royalists and the Spanish, the French commissioners promised the blacks freedom in exchange for their assistance. Commissioner Sonthonax took the ultimate step of proclaiming the end of slavery in the colony on August 29, 1793.[74] Toussaint sent out his own proclamation, saying, "Having been the first to champion liberty, it is my duty to continue to work for it...Join me and you will enjoy the rights of free men sooner than by any other means."[71] In another proclamation a few days later he signed for the first time as Toussaint L'Ouverture, a name he would use for the rest of his life.[71]

The slaves rebuffed the French republic's offer of freedom in exchange for their loyalty. Toussaint wrote to Laveaux saying, "The Spanish have offered me their protection and liberty for all who fight for the King and having always fought for that same liberty I adhere to their offer." Toussaint may not have immediately gone over to French Republic as it appeared headed for defeat. Nor was it clear that the French government would ratify Sonthonax's abolition of slavery.[74]

Under Toussaint, the slave army, now well equipped, swept across the northern province, capturing town after town. Toussaint prevented any looting or massacres, which made others more willing to surrender. By early 1794 Toussaint's forces had grown from 600 to 5000 and through him the Spanish controlled the entire north except for Le Cap.

Toussaint became disillusioned with the Spanish, who made no effort to abolish slavery. When the government in France confirmed the abolishment of slavery, Toussaint decided to change allegiance. After extracting his family from the Spanish colony of San Domingo in the eastern half of Hispaniola, Toussaint wrote on May 18, 1794, to General Laveaux, commander of the French army in St. Domingue, proposing an alliance. Toussaint wrote, "It is true, general, that I was deceived by the enemies of the Republic, but what man can boast of being able to escape every pitfall...I have seen the decree of the National Convention dated 4 February, 1794 declaring the abolition of slavery; this is the most comforting news for all friends of the human race. Let us occupy ourselves solely with the defeating of our enemies."[71]

Once France abolished slavery, Toussaint thought of himself as a French citizen for the rest of his life. Allying with the French forces on St. Domingue, Toussaint now proceeded to throw the Spanish back. Meanwhile a close and lifelong friendship grew between Toussaint and Laveaux.[71]

While Toussaint fought with the Spanish in the north, the British, at war with France, seized the south and west of the island. The British restored slavery in the areas under their control.

Laveaux took over as governor of the colony. He appointed Toussaint commander in chief of the French forces. The British quickly came to respect Toussaint. A British officer wrote that Toussaint's forces were "infinitely the most formidable enemy the British arms have to encounter with…[their tactics consist] entirely of ambuscades for which the face of the country is particularly calculated."[70] Toussaint proceeded to defeat a combined force of British, Spanish and 800 French royalist emigres in the Mirebelais Valley in the south. After the commander of the royalist emigres told Toussaint that the emigres would die fighting rather than be killed after surrendering, Toussaint replied, "I don't shoot my prisoners." Toussaint kept his word after their surrender despite urgings that he do otherwise. During these years of confused fighting the black masses learned to trust and follow Toussaint, while the whites recognized that Toussaint protected them against reprisals from the former slaves.[75]

After emancipation, the French commissioners on the island passed laws obligating the former slaves to work on their plantations as "cultivars" who would receive 25% of what they produced with another 25% going as taxes to the state.[73] Toussaint had to deal with unhappy former slaves who did not want to have to continue to work on the plantations, even for wages. Toussaint was firm that the former slaves could not live a life of idleness as the prosperity of the island depended on its agriculture. Toussaint proclaimed, "Work is a virtue. It is a necessity. All vagrant and idle men will be arrested and punished under the law."[71] Toussaint's policy generated significant resentment among the former slaves.[76] Toussaint felt that France would stick to emancipation of the slaves only if St. Domingue continued to produce the sugar and coffee that the mother country demanded.[74] Toussaint said, "The liberty of the blacks can be consolidated only through the prosperity of agriculture."[74]

In early 1795, the Spain gave up trying to take over St. Domingue. The British army still outnumbered Toussaint's forces, but was stretched over a protracted line of territory. On February 3, 1795, Toussaint concentrated his forces to attack at strategic points along this line, routing the enemy at these spots, then moving quickly on to another point of attack. In a week, Toussaint won seven victories, destroying most of the British army on the island. The British asked for terms and agreed to evacuate from all but two ports on the island. The historian Fortescue wrote, "The British campaign in the West Indies…cost England in army and navy little fewer than 100,000 men. The secret of England's impotence for the six years of the war [against France] may be said in the two fatal words St. Domingue."[71] A British diplomat of the time wrote, "Toussaint with a greatness of mind which was remarkable agreed to allow those French colonists who had sided with us to remain and promised to respect their properties; as it was known that this magnanimous black ever kept his word, no important exodus followed our retreat."[71] One of the terms of the agreement with Britain was that Toussaint would not support attempts to liberate the slaves on the other islands. Toussaint kept that agreement, informing the British of plans to launch a revolt on their colony of Jamaica in 1799.[72]

There were many in the colony, particularly among the mulattos, who resented Toussaint's prominence and his close relationship with Governor Laveaux. On March 20, 1796, a group of mulattos attempted a coup, seizing Laveaux and throwing him in prison. They planned to replace Laveaux with a mulatto governor. Toussaint responded by sending 6000 troops to the capital, proclaiming, "in disrespecting the Governor you have disrespected France."[71] Laveaux was released and the conspirators went into hiding. In a ceremony Laveaux now named Toussaint the lieutenant governor, saying, "There stands this black Spartacus, the Negro…prophesized [to] avenge his race." Toussaint drew and sword and replied, "After God—Laveaux."[71]

Appointed one of the island's representatives to the French Assembly, Laveaux sailed to France in October 1796, never to return. He and Toussaint continued to write to each other regularly, but never met again. Toussaint accepted the French government's invitation to send his sons to be educated in France.

In France, representatives of the planters tried to reverse emancipation of the slaves. Laveaux took the lead in passing a law giving citizenship to all who had been brought to St. Domingue as slaves. He argued that this was the best way to preserve the colony, stating that in war the black citizens would be "soldiers, and valiant because they will be defending their rights and their country."[74] Laveaux, in his speech, said that under the rule of Toussaint, the colony would soon "be as prosperous as it was in 1788…cultivated by hands forever freed from slavery."[74]

The French government sent a new governor, Comte Hedouville, to the colony. Before he departed, General Kerverseau said to him about Toussaint, "He is a man of great good sense whose attachment to France cannot be doubted…who enjoys the confidence of all colors. With him you can do all; without him you can do nothing."[75] However, those sympathetic to the former slave owners disparaged Toussaint to Hedouville.

Toussaint had negotiated a treaty removing the last British troops. Arriving in St. Domingue, Hedouville was enraged to have been left out of the negotiations. He was angry that Toussaint had reached an agreement with the British while France remained at war with Britain, as well as by Toussaint offering amnesty to the emigres. Toussaint heard about how he was being continually attacked and belittled by Hedouville and his aides. Toussaint resigned as commander in chief of the army, writing, "If I have asked your permission to resign, it is because having served my country honorably, having wrested it from the hands of its powerful enemies, having put out the fires of civil war…I wish now in my old age to save the honor of my name from insult for the sake of my children.[71]

Hedouville acted to abolish the post of commander in chief and to disband the black regiments. Hedouville dismissed Toussaint's adopted nephew Moise from command of his regiment. Moise refused to give up his command. Hedouville then ordered Rigaud, commander of the mulatto troops, to come to the capital to solidify his control. At this Toussaint acted, ordering his troops to march on the capital. Hedouville fled to a warship and sailed to France. However, before leaving he incited Rigaud and his mulattos to break with Toussaint, appointing Rigaud commander in chief. Hedouville wrote to the French government, saying that "it is important to embitter the hate which exists between the mulattos and the blacks and to oppose Rigaud to Toussaint."[71] Toussaint told Moise, "Hedouville has spread it that he is going to France to seek forces to come back…I do not want to fight with France. I have saved this country for her up to the present, but if she comes to attack me I shall defend myself."[75]

A meeting between Toussaint and Rigaud failed to resolve the conflict over control in the colony. Historian Laurent Dubois argued that it was less a racial quarrel than a battle over power.[74] Shortly thereafter Rigaud began massacring the blacks in the south, causing open war to break out between the mulattos and blacks. Toussaint responded by besieging the city of Jacnel, a mulatto stronghold. After a prolonged siege, the commander of the garrison sent the starving noncombatants, the old men, women and children, out of the two city gates. Those who faced Toussaint were taken in and cared for. However, those who went out the other gate faced the forces commanded by Toussaint's lieutenant Christophe. Christophe ordered his men to shoot down all the refugees.⁷¹ This was one of the first occasions where Toussaint did not punish a subordinate for cruelty. Perhaps the task of imposing harsh discipline on his supporters in the face of continuing conflicts had become too difficult.

Toussaint's forces swept through the south, defeating Rigaud. While Toussaint defeated Rigaud on land, the American president, John Adams, an admirer of Toussaint, ordered the US Navy to blockade the southern ports, cutting off Rigaud from resupply.⁷⁴ Rigaud fled to France. While Toussaint continued to treat prisoners and his enemies humanely, his principal subordinates, Christophe and Dessalines were much more ruthless. When Toussaint appointed Dessalines to command the region in the south, Dessalines responded by killing every mulatto officer and official that he could find. When Toussaint heard of this, he was reportedly ashamed and said, "I only asked him to prune the tree, not to pull it out by the roots."⁷¹ However, Toussaint did not remove Dessalines from his position.

Toussaint now invaded the Spanish colony, Santo Domingo, on Hispaniola. Toussaint conquered this colony and ended slavery there. For the first time in years, peace reigned over the whole island. After twelve years of war there were only 10,000 whites and perhaps 350,000 blacks left in St. Domingue, down from some 40,000 whites and 500,000 blacks at the onset of the revolt.

Toussaint began a vigorous program to rebuild St. Domingue as a multiracial colony where all could live in harmony. He reorganized the courts, pruned the civil service, cut taxes and imposed severe penalties for corruption. Toussaint invited priests in to set up schools throughout the country. He worked to rebuild the roads and the towns. Toussaint rode tirelessly across the island to check on the progress and on the actions of the local officials. Toussaint also encouraged the spread of painting and the theatre, and supported trade with the United States. President Adams encouraged this trade.⁷⁶ Most of the arms and ammunition of the Toussaint's army were purchased from the United States.⁷³ Under Toussaint, coffee production had reached nearly pre-revolt levels while sugar production also rapidly rose.⁷³ Toussaint also applied military discipline to plantation laborers who failed to do their work and restricted their ability to abandon the plantations.⁷⁴

Toussaint seemed to be everywhere, checking up on administrators, officials and ordinary people across the island. The military continued to be the most powerful element in the society. High-ranking military officers often leased or bought the former plantations. Work was enforced as a duty for everyone, which was not popular. Toussaint argued that he was trying to increase, "the general happiness of the island… [allowing people] to taste liberty without license."[74] Wenda Parkinson wrote, "No one was penalized in any way for their color. The equilibrium between the races remained steady. It was only under Toussaint that this happy and rational balance was achieved."[71] Toussaint would mix a few white seeds with more black seeds in a bottle to demonstrate his idea of a multiracial state to people.[76]

While the wars raged on St. Domingue, France had gone through a variety of leaders. By 1800, based on his military victories, Napoleon Bonaparte had become the dominant leader in France. In 1800 Napoleon pushed through a new constitution that allowed for the reintroduction of slavery in the colonies. On a pragmatic basis, given Toussaint's army, Napoleon promised to respect the abolition of slavery in St. Domingue. Toussaint stated, "It is not a circumstantial liberty conceded only to us that we want, it is the absolute acceptance of the principle that no man, whether born red, black or white, can be the property of another."[74]

Toussaint decided to act rather than waiting for new laws for St. Domingue to be imposed by Napoleon. Toussaint created a constituent assembly, which promulgated a new constitution in July 1801 for the island and included self-government. The constitution declared that the colony was part of France, governed by its own set of laws and that "all men within it are born, live and die free and French."[74] Slavery was abolished forever. Toussaint would be governor for life, able to sign and make all laws, all government appointments and enforce all laws. The constitution, written by a commission made up largely of white planters, also established stronger restrictions upon the agricultural workers. The constitution even allowed the importation of Africans as farm workers, although not as slaves.[73] While many of the island's whites saw it as severing the ties with France, Toussaint's generals, who were ambitious men, were also angry at the terms of the constitution giving Toussaint lifetime rule. His nephew Moise, with whom he had been close, called Toussaint "an old fool…who does he think he is, King of Haiti."[71]

Toussaint ignored the insults, but when Moise let his troops go on a rampage, killing whites and looting towns, Toussaint acted. He quickly defeated Moise. Toussaint insisted on the execution of Moise, who had been his most trusted officer for many years. Almost immediately Toussaint felt great remorse, exhibiting sadness and tears whenever Moise's name was mentioned.[71,75] Toussaint followed this up by threatening any officers who did not enforce his decrees. Toussaint later claimed that in early 1802 the colony was "enjoying its greatest tranquility…that commerce and cultivation were flourishing."[74]

Angry at Toussaint's effrontery in not deferring to him, Napoleon flew into a rage upon receiving the new constitution. He reportedly cursed Toussaint as "this gilded African." Napoleon continued, "I will not rest until I have torn the epaulettes off every nigger in the Colony."[71] General Vincent, who had served as Napoleon's emissary to St. Domingue, pleaded for him to reconsider, writing, "Sire, leave it alone! It is an island of content within your dominion. God destined this man to govern. Races melt beneath his hand. For you he has saved the island from the British."[71] Napoleon reacted by banishing Vincent to exile on the island of Elba.

Napoleon instead decided to invade St. Domingue. He sent forth a fleet of 86 ships carrying 30,000 troops under the command of his brother in law, Charles Leclerc. Rigaud and several other mulatto generals accompanied the force. Napoleon secretly instructed Leclerc that Toussaint and his principal officers would either be shipped to France as prisoners or shot. Slavery would be reinstated and education of blacks abolished on St. Domingue. On hearing about the French expedition, Toussaint began expanding his military even while publicly expressing disbelief that France would attack.[74]

The French expedition arrived off Le Cap on January 29, 1802. They ordered Toussaint and his generals to submit to and welcome the French forces. Toussaint now decided to withdraw his forces into the interior rather than fight the overwhelming French force in the open. Toussaint ordered his troops, "to tear up the roads with shot, throw corpses and horses into all the fountains, burn and annihilate everything, so that those who have come to return us to slavery will always find in front of them the image of hell they deserve."[70] Christophe, in command in Le Cap, evacuated the population and burned the city to the ground.

Toussaint was dismayed how many of the people he had treated so well, particularly among the whites, defected to the French. Historian C.L.R. James wrote that Toussaint made the mistake of not explaining the situation and his plan clearly. James wrote, "He should have declared that a powerful expedition [Leclerc's army] could have no other aim than the restoration of slavery, [and] summoned the population to resist…[Toussaint] left even his generals in the dark…He gave orders and expected them to be obeyed."[75] Toussaint refused to surrender despite his discouragement. Leclerc then issued a new proclamation, saying, "I come to restore prosperity and abundance, everyone must see what an insensible monster Toussaint is."[71]

Toussaint now began a guerrilla war against the French in the hills. The overconfident French forces suffered heavy losses, often launching frontal attacks against fortified positions. With the onset of the rainy season in April increasing numbers of the French soldiers fell victim to malaria and yellow fever. By April, Leclerc had only 11,000 of his original 30,000 troops left, along with a force of 9000 blacks of dubious loyalty.

Yet the French had other tricks to play. Leclerc tried to suborn some of Toussaint's generals, promising them wealth and high positions. Christophe defected to the French in April, handing over 1200 soldiers, 100 cannons and 2000 white prisoners. Toussaint was shocked by the treachery.

Toussaint now tried to reach a peace agreement. Parkinson wrote, "Toussaint's one major weakness as a general was that he abhorred any unnecessary loss of life, even that of his enemies…he was sickened by the suffering, by the destruction of the land, by the starving children. He wanted peace, but also the guarantee of freedom."[71]

Toussaint now agreed to meet Leclerc face to face. Toussaint agreed to terms on May 6, 1802. In exchange for stopping fighting against the French, Toussaint and others would receive a general pardon and immunity from any prosecution. Slavery would not be restored. Many of Toussaint's generals, including Dessalines, would remain in command of their troops, but Toussaint must agree to retire.[75,76] Toussaint now dismissed his personal bodyguard of ninety dragoons and returned to his plantation at Ennery. Leclerc wrote, "I gave him my word of honor that he would be free to go where he wished."[75] Dessalines, known for his hatred of whites, quickly adapted to his new loyalties, turning rapidly from murdering whites to murdering recalcitrant blacks.[72]

Toussaint embraced a quiet life at his plantation, where he would often go to work in the fields wearing his oldest clothes. This was not enough for Leclerc. He wrote to Napoleon, "I informed you in one of my last dispatches of the pardon I had been induced to grant General Toussaint. This ambitious man from the moment of his pardon has not ceased to plot in secret."[71]

Leclerc decided to arrest Toussaint, saying it "is necessary because I must show some form of strength."[71]

A French general wrote Toussaint, asking him to come visit him for a discussion. After Toussaint arrived, he was seized and taken aboard a French warship. Leclerc then arrested Toussaint's wife, children and other family members. His wife and children were brought out to the same warship where Toussaint was imprisoned, but they were not allowed to see him. Leclerc later produced forged documents reporting to show Toussaint plotting to overthrow the French government on the island. Leclerc wrote to Napoleon saying, "You cannot keep Toussaint at too great a distance…this man has raised the country to such a pitch of fanaticism that his presence would send it up again in flames."[75]

Toussaint was never allowed to see his wife, who was imprisoned separately. He was taken to the Fort de Joux high in the Jura Mountains neighboring Switzerland. On August 25, 1802, Toussaint entered the prison and was placed in solitary confinement in a tiny cell. He was stripped of his uniform, given old clothes, and never allowed to leave his cell, even to exercise. He complained of being cold all the time.

Toussaint wrote to Napoleon, saying, "My wife and children were seized without respect for their station, their sex without humanity or charity. They have done nothing, they are blameless, they must be returned…I demand again to stand trial before a tribunal or court martial…without a doubt I have received this treatment because of my color. But my color did not prevent me from serving my country faithfully and zealously."[71] Napoleon did not reply, but Toussaint's treatment was made even harsher. All his remaining possessions were removed. All doctor visits were stopped. He was not allowed pen or paper. A new jailor was appointed who harassed Toussaint continuously, waking him constantly at night for searches of his cell. Finally, for four days he received no food. When the jailor returned on April 7, 1803, Toussaint L'Overture was found dead.

Toussaint had declared, when the French had arrived, "In overthrowing me, you have cut down only the trunk of the tree of liberty of the blacks; it will grow back from its roots because they are deep and numerous."[73] The insurrection against French rule in St. Domingue erupted again and grew stronger with the reinstatement of slavery on islands of Martinique and Guadeloupe as well as the reopening of the trans-Atlantic slave trade.[72,74–75]

The forcible disarmament of many black troops led to rumors that slavery would be reinstituted in the colony. The French, alarmed by defections of black troops to the rebels, accelerated the process by arresting and killing many of the black troops that had remained loyal to them.[74] Leclerc himself died of yellow fever on October 22, 1802. After another year of brutal fighting that alienated the populace, the French gave up.

The declaration of independence of St. Domingue, renamed Haiti, was proclaimed on November 29, 1803, followed soon after by the massacre of most of the remaining whites by General Dessalines.[72] Historian Phillipe Girard wrote, "Haiti proved that masters…could be vanquished. If successful, the Haitian experiment could have proven all the racists, imperialists, and slavery advocates wrong. Unfortunately, Haiti failed to live up to the hopes its independence had raised. The Haitian government's first act of self-governance could have been to outlaw slavery in the New World, to welcome runaways or to launch a program to educate its illiterate population: it chose massacre instead…For years people of African descent paid the price of Dessalines' folly, as their calls for racial equality and self-rule were met by memories of the 1804 massacre."[72]

Dessalines proclaimed himself Emperor Jacques I of Haiti. He died a violent death not long afterward.[76] Haiti spiraled downward as leader followed leader, almost all devoted self-aggrandizement. Other factors contributed to this decline. For many decades, few of the major powers recognized Haitian independence, forcing Haiti's leaders to spend disproportionate amounts on its military. The island's rich soil was worn out by the sugar crops. The ongoing deforestation contributed to further soil loss, helping to ruin the agricultural productivity of Haiti.[73] Today what was once the richest colony in the West Indies is now one of the poorest countries on earth.

Toussaint was ultimately successful in his fight to bring independence for the island. Haiti was the first free black republic in the world and the second free country in the western hemisphere.[72] Toussaint had led the world's largest and most successful slave revolt.[74] However, Toussaint's dream of a successful, prosperous multiracial republic was to die with him. The new republic sorely missed his leadership. Ironically, Napoleon was to have said on his deathbed that targeting Toussaint had been one of the great mistakes of his career.[73]

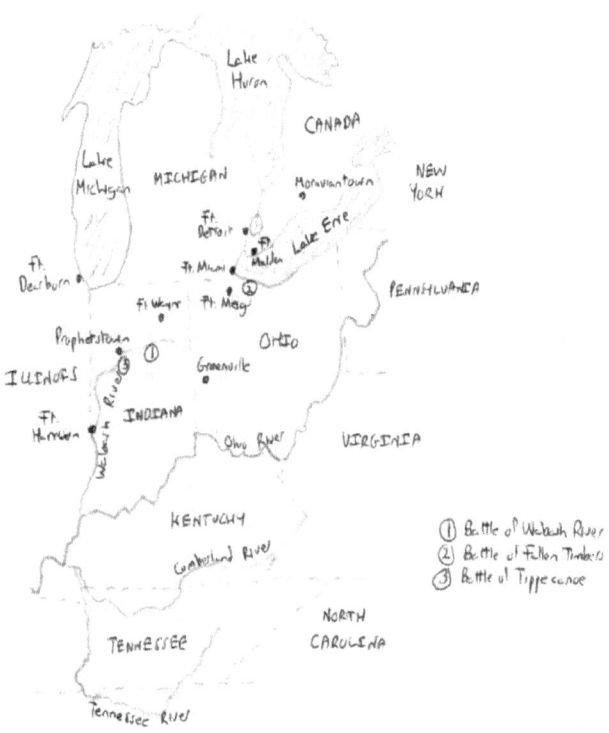

Chapter 11: Tecumseh
Holding Back the Tide, 1813 CE, United States

THE WOMAN SHOWED their newborn son to her husband, Pukeshinwau. Pukeshinwau was a chief among the Shawnee tribe, who lived in the eastern forests of North America. Looking at the newborn, Pukeshinwau said, "We shall name him Panther passing over the Sky...Tecumseh." Pukeshinwau frowned as he thought about the future his son would face. Increasingly the white settlers had been crossing the Appalachian Mountains to the lands of the Shawnee. This was despite a treaty with the British in 1764, four years before, that forbid the settlers from crossing the mountains. Pukeshinwau could understand why they would want to live here, for the land was good for crops, particularly the Shawnee staples of corn, beans and squash, and the forests were full of animals. Pukeshinwau did not know that it was to be Tecumseh's fate to have to try to save the lands west of the mountains for the Indians. [77-84]

In 1775, Pukeshinwau was killed in the battle against Virginia militia, leaving four children and a pregnant wife. Soon after this battle the American Revolution broke out. The Shawnees initially tried to stay neutral, but the increasing number of settlers in Kentucky led them to ally with the British. The Kentucky militia responded by attacking the Shawnee villages. Tecumseh and his family were forced to move several times to try to get farther from this militia. Tecumseh's older brother Cheeseekau played a vital role in raising his younger sibling, teaching him skills and the principles of proper conduct among the Shawnee.

In the Treaty of Paris that gave America independence in 1783 the British forgot their promises to their Indian allies and gave all the lands west of the Appalachians to the United States.[81] War between the United States and the trans-Appalachia Indians broke out in 1786. Tecumseh took part in his first battle at the Mad River, although he ending up fleeing and hiding until the battle was done. Tecumseh redeemed himself in subsequent fighting along the Ohio River.

The Shawnees often attacked settlers attempting to raft down the Ohio River.[77] After one engagement Tecumseh watched his companions torture their prisoners. Tecumseh said to the other Indians, "What we have done is wrong. It is one thing to kill an enemy in battle. It is another to torture him when he is helpless...The Big Knives [the Americans] suffering does no justice to our cause. Let us fight like men and leave the dead on the field of battle."[77] Tecumseh persuaded those with him to stop the torture. Tecumseh refrained from it in the future.

Tecumseh's closest friend, Sinnamatha, was a white boy originally named Stephen Ruddell, who had been captured at age 12 in 1780 and chose to remain with the Shawnees for many years afterwards. Ruddell wrote of Tecumseh that "when prisoners fell into his hands he always treated them with…humanity… neither did he tolerate the killing of women and children."[77] Another relative, Anthony Shane, wrote, "Tecumseh was remarkable for his hospitality and generosity…He was particularly attentive to the aged and infirm. This course of conduct was not confined to the rich or those of influence and reputation."[77]

While the war of the Shawnees and other tribes against the Americans continued, Tecumseh's family moved into present-day Missouri in 1788. When Tecumseh returned to the Ohio River in 1791, he had a reputation as a minor war leader and boasted ten followers. Among the Shawnee the power of a chief was based on his leadership and the respect in which he was held. Immense importance was placed on being able to speak well before an audience.[79]

Around this time, a force of Shawnees and other tribes under their chief Blue Jacket inflicted the most one-sided defeat ever suffered by an American army from Indians. The Indians defeated an American force under General Arthur St. Clair at the Battle of the Wabash River, killing 650 Americans with only 61 Indian deaths.[77]

In September 1792, Tecumseh's older brother and mentor, Cheeseekau, was killed in a battle in the present-day state of Tennessee. Tecumseh stayed in the South for two more years, attacking American settlements.[80] While Tecumseh was in the South, in 1793 American forces under General Anthony Wayne took revenge for the defeat at the Wabash River by decisively defeating a coalition of Indian tribes at the Battle of the Fallen Timbers. Tecumseh's last older brother, Savawaseeku, was killed in the battle. Some of the Indian survivors had fled to the British Fort Miami, but the commander refused to allow them entry.

In 1795, the war ended when Wayne and many of the Indian tribes signed the Treaty of Greenville, ceding most of Ohio and Indiana to the United States. In exchange the Indians received annual payments of money. Ninety-one chiefs from twelve tribes in the Ohio River Valley and the

Lower Great Lakes signed the treaty. The Indians were also asked to settle near American forts in these areas.[77]

Tecumseh's reputation as a war leader had grown during the long conflict, expanding the number of Shawnees who chose to follow him. Tecumseh was also famed as a hunter, known for his ability to keep his people fed. Tecumseh, now leader of a band of some 250 Shawnees, refused to attend or sign the Treaty of Greenville. Tecumseh opposed the land cessations. He also felt that living near the forts would reduce the Indians to dependency on the Americans. Tecumseh led his band into south and central Ohio, trying to live in areas apart from the Americans.

In 1800, the United States established the Indiana Territory, covering land west to the Mississippi and north to Canada. William Henry Harrison, a veteran of the Battle of the Fallen Timbers, was appointed governor. Harrison was to become Tecumseh's nemesis. Harrison was initially sympathetic to the Indians. He wrote, "The Indian chiefs all profess, and I believe most of them feel, a friendship for the United States…but they have made heavy complaints of ill treatment on the part of our Citizens. They say that their people have been killed—lands settled on—their game wantonly destroyed and their young men made drunk…Of the truth of these charges I am well convinced."[77] Harrison continued, "A great many of the Inhabitants of the Frontiers consider the murdering of the Indians in the highest degree meritorious."[83] With the French ruling the adjacent Louisiana Territory, President Jefferson ordered Harrison to buy as much Indian land as possible lest it be acquired by the French. Shrewdly negotiating with one Indian tribe at a time, Harrison acquired for the United States some 70 million acres of Indian land in the present day states of Indiana, Wisconsin, Illinois and Missouri, paying an average of two cents an acre.[77]

In November, 1805, Tecumseh's younger brother Lalawe'thika underwent a major transformation. Previously considered a lazy drunkard by the Shawnee, Lalawe'thika had a series of visions that led him to urge the Indians to reject all white influence, including the alcohol, food, clothing and weapons of the whites.[83] Tecumseh followed his brother's lead in rejecting white clothing, food and drink, but kept his musket and other European innovations that he found useful. Lalawe'thika became known as the Prophet. He declared that his "sole object was to reclaim the Indians from bad habits and to cause them to live in peace with all mankind."[83]

The Prophet preached against Christianity and against witches, leading his followers to slaughter many Christian Indians and supposed witches. Tecumseh stepped in to end these killings, but not before hundreds had been killed.[80] The witch hunts shocked Harrison, who wrote to the Delaware tribe, "Let your poor old men and women sleep in quietness, and banish from their minds the dreadful idea of being burnt alive by their own friends and countrymen."[83]

Governor Harrison tried to undermine the Prophet's influence. He told other Indians, "Who is this pretended prophet who dares to speak in the name of the Great Creator…If he is really a prophet, ask him to cause the sun to stand still or the dead to rise from their grave."[77] The Prophet took up the challenge. On June 16, 1806, the Prophet held up his arms and the sun disappeared. It was, of course, a solar eclipse, but the episode caused the Prophet's influence to soar. So many Indians came to the Shawnee village at Greenville where Tecumseh and the Prophet lived that Tecumseh had to turn them away.

Not all Shawnees accepted either the brothers' preeminence or the idea that rejecting all European influence was optimal, leading to serious dissension within the tribe.[81] Many of the older chiefs viewed Tecumseh and his small band as recalcitrant troublemakers.

It was during these years that Tecumseh started to push the idea of a pan-Indian confederacy. Originally put forth in 1783 by the Mohawk Iroquois Joseph Brant, the idea was that the land belonged to all Indians and could not be sold off by individual tribes or groups. The land was likened to a common meal from which everyone ate, or "a dish with one spoon."[81] This concept was not accepted by all Indians or tribes who viewed their individual territories as theirs to do with as they pleased.[81] Tecumseh traveled widely, visiting many other tribes, to push his vision.

Tecumseh argued that he wanted to reduce white influence among their people, but by self-imposed separation rather than war. Tecumseh spent many evenings in settler communities trying to reassure them of the Shawnees' peaceful intentions. In September 1807 Tecumseh met with Thomas Kirker, acting governor of Ohio, who was seeking information about his goals. John McDonald, an eyewitness, reported, "When Tecumseh rose to speak, he appeared one of the most dignified men I ever beheld…He spoke confidently about the Indians intention to adhere to the treaty and live in peace and friendship with their white brethren, and by doing so, he dispelled as if by magic the apprehensions of the whites."[76,81] Tecumseh spoke for three hours, declaring that no chief or individual Indian had the right to sell Indian lands since Indian land belonged to all Indians rather than individuals or tribes.[80] Governor Kirker subsequently wrote to President Jefferson, supporting the Indians' complaints about the settlers.

Game animals had become scarce around Tecumseh's village. Later that autumn Tecumseh moved his people farther west to where the game was more plentiful. In the spring of 1809, Tecumseh and the Prophet established the village of Prophetstown on the bank of the Tippecanoe River. Soon thereafter an influenza epidemic swept through the town, killing many and weakening support for Tecumseh and the Prophet.

Tecumseh also spent his time traveling from tribe to tribe, campaigning for the idea of a confederacy of the tribes. Meeting with British officials at Fort Malden in Canada, Tecumseh outlined his aim of creating an Indian nation that would limit further American expansion.[80] Tecumseh told them that while he would fight the Americans if necessary, he had no desire to do so at the present. The lieutenant governor of Upper Canada, Francis Gore, met with Tecumseh and called him "a very shrewd, intelligent man."[77] The British sent food, arms and ammunition to Tecumseh and other Indians, but also urged the Indians to avoid fighting the Americans prematurely.[83]

In 1809, Governor Harrison seized the opportunity provided by Tecumseh's absence to negotiate the Fort Wayne Treaty. He ignored President Madison's stipulation that the treaty should only go ahead if "it will excite no disagreeable apprehensions, and produce no undesirable effects" among the Indians.[81] In this treaty, the Delaware, Miami and Potawatomi tribes ceded three million more acres of land to the United States. Tecumseh was incensed by the treaty, which undermined his efforts to unify the tribes. Tecumseh proclaimed it invalid because it was not agreed to by all the Indians of the region. Tecumseh said, "The land belongs to all Natives and none it should be ceded by one tribe without the consent of all."[77] Tecumseh then threatened to kill the chiefs who signed the treaty and any settlers trying to settle on the land involved.[77]

Harrison and Tecumseh met on August 12, 1810, to discuss the issues. After Harrison spoke, Tecumseh replied. Tecumseh started by listing all the treaties where the Americans had broken the terms. Tecumseh looked at Harrison and said, "Brother, after such bitter events, can you blame me for placing little confidence in the promises of Americans…the only way to stop this evil [of further Indian land sales] is for all tribes to unite in claiming an equal right to the land…Sell a country! Why not sell the air, the clouds and the great sea, as well as the earth?"[79] Tecumseh finished by demanding the return of land sold in the Fort Wayne treaty. Harrison replied, "The United States has been fair in dealing with the Indian tribes. We have negotiated legal treaties signed by chiefs."[80] Tecumseh cried out, "We will kill these chiefs." One of the chiefs who signed the treaty leaped to his feet and drew his tomahawk. Tecumseh drew his. Harrison stepped between them and said, "Tecumseh, you must realize that this chief made a fair deal with the United States."[80] "Liar," Tecumseh shouted. Now Harrison drew his sword. The surrounding Indians and soldiers raised their weapons as well. Finally, Harrison lowered his sword, followed by Tecumseh putting away his tomahawk. The next day Tecumseh formally apologized to Harrison for his behavior. Tecumseh told Harrison that while the Indians would fight to the death to protect their lands, they would prefer to live in peace with the Americans. Harrison promised to forward Tecumseh's words to the president.

During the fall of 1810, the Americans held two councils with Indian tribes in the region, trying to get the chiefs to pledge loyalty to the United States and reject any British alliance. Agreements between individual tribes and the Americans would effectively limit the power of Tecumseh's proposed confederacy. Many chiefs there were critical of Tecumseh and the Prophet and jealous of their influence. The brothers did not attend either conference.[79]

The growth from 1796 to 1810 of the American population in Ohio from 5000 to over 230,000 worsened the odds against the Indians.[82] Irritated by the burgeoning American population, the number of Indian raids against settlers by young warriors increased over the winter of 1810–1811.

Governor Harrison met again with Tecumseh in July of 1811. Tecumseh outlined his plans for a peaceful Indian confederacy. Harrison replied, "Last year you declared that the Treaty of Fort Wayne, fairly negotiated with the representative tribes, was somehow underhanded and deceitful. You declared as much on behalf of all the tribes on the continent. The matter has been taken to the President…I can offer you safe keeping should you and your brother wish to travel to Washington to address the matter directly with the President."[77]

Tecumseh answered, "I have meetings of mine own to attend to and cannot meet with the great father. After much trouble and difficulty, I have united the northern tribes. When the council is concluded, I will go south to unite those tribes. Do not be alarmed. I look to your own country as an example of uniting all the fires that compose your confederacy."[77]

"Will you try to stop the settlement of the new purchase?" asked Harrison.[77]

Tecumseh replied, "I hope that no attempts will be made to settle it until I return in the spring. I expect the Wyandot and the Iroquois to arrive this fall. They must occupy that tract as a hunting ground…I wish everything to remain in the present state until I return. I will then go and see the Great Father and settle everything with him. The affairs of all the tribes in this quarter are in my hands and nothing can be done without me."[77]

Harrison said, "The moon which we behold…will sooner fall to earth than the President will suffer his people to be murdered with impunity. I will put my warriors in petticoats sooner than I will give up a country that I have fairly acquired from its rightful owners."[77] After five days, the council ended on that note of disagreement. Tecumseh headed south to meet with the tribes there.

Harrison wrote down his thoughts on Tecumseh afterward, stating, "The implicit obedience and respect which the followers of Tecumseh pay him is really astonishing, and more any other circumstances bespeaks him as one of those uncommon geniuses which spring up occasionally to produce revolutions and overturn the established order of things. If were not for the vicinity of the United States, he would, perhaps, be the founder of an empire that would rival in glory that of Mexico or Peru. His activity and industry supply the want of letters. For four years he has been in constant motion…and wherever he goes he makes an impression favorable to his purposes."[77]

Despite his admiration for Tecumseh as a person, Harrison recognized his absence at the best opportunity to eliminate the threat the Indians posed to the newly bought territories. He decided to preempt Indian occupation of the lands ceded in the Fort Wayne Treaty by marching to Prophetstown while Tecumseh was absent.

Harrison now gave the Prophet an ultimatum demanding that non-Shawnee Indians must leave Prophetstown. The Prophet ignored this ultimatum.[84] Before departing, Tecumseh told his brother to abandon the town rather than get in a battle if Harrison attacked. At the end of September Governor Harrison led a force of about 1000 soldiers and militia toward Prophetstown. By early November the soldiers were camped a mile away from the town. The Prophet asked to meet with Harrison the following day. The Prophet had fewer than 500 Indian warriors with him. At dawn, the Prophet sent his warriors to attack the American force, urging them to kill Harrison. He had told the Indians that he would protect them, saying, "Do not fear bullets. My magic will make them useless."[77] The Indians lost the advantage of surprise when the sentries roused the American camp. The Indian warriors lost confidence when it was clear that the American bullets remained lethal. The Indians retreated and abandoned Prophetstown, which the Americans burned to the ground. The Prophet had been thoroughly discredited.[77] Harrison reported that he always believed that "the Prophet was a rash and presumptuous man, but he has exceeded my expectations. He has not contented himself with throwing the gauntlet, but has absolutely commenced the war."[83]

Tecumseh returned shortly afterwards. He said, "I stand on the ashes of my own home…I swore once more eternal hatred—the hatred of an avenger."[77] Tecumseh was incensed at his brother, whose rashness had undone much of Tecumseh's efforts. Tecumseh put his knife to the Prophet's throat, but stopped, saying that death was too good for him.[77]

Tecumseh's visits to the South did not persuade many chiefs to submit to his leadership, but many Indian warriors joined him. At a meeting with the Creek tribe, Tecumseh said, "Brothers, we all belong to one family; we are all children of the Great Spirit…the white men are not friends to the Indians. At first, they only asked for land sufficient for a wigwam; no, nothing will satisfy them, but the whole of our hunting grounds, from the rising to the setting sun…Brothers, we must be united; we must smoke the same pipe; we must fight each other's battles."[79] Still, unwilling to risk a potentially disastrous war with the United States, the Creek, Choctaw and Chickasaw tribes decided to maintain their neutrality. When Tecumseh's oratory in the village of Tuckhabatchee failed to convince a chief named Big Warrior to join him, Tecumseh angrily cried out that he would go back north. Tecumseh said, "Once there, I will stamp my foot and shake down every house in Tuckhabatchee."[79]

Now the earth itself intervened. On December 16, a series of powerful earthquakes began, centered at New Madrid at the Tennessee–Missouri border. This seemed to suggest to many Indians that Tecumseh's words had come true.[79] By June 1812, Tecumseh claimed that his confederacy was backed by 3500 warriors from at least ten different tribes, mainly in the north.[77] Efforts had been made to reconcile with the United States during the preceding winter, although it is unclear if this was in earnest or to buy time. At a council, Tecumseh told assembled chiefs, "Governor Harrison made war on my people in my absence...We hope that it will please God that the white people may let us live in peace. We will not disturb then, neither have we done it, except when they come to our village with the intention of destroying us...I will further state that had I been at home there would have been no blood shed at that time."[81]

For most of the prior decade relations between Britain and the United States had been tense. The United States was angered by the British blockade of the Europe that limited American commerce as well as the British impressment of sailors from American ships into the British navy. Finally, on June 18, 1812, the United States declared war on Great Britain.

Tecumseh saw this conflict as the best opportunity to defeat the Americans and establish an Indian confederacy. To garner British support for this objective, Tecumseh returned to Fort Malden, the closest British fort to the American border, situated at the western end of Lake Erie. There Tecumseh met Isaac Brock, the British commander of their forces in the west. Brock had only 1600 soldiers under his command for the whole province of Upper Canada. He was far outnumbered by the Americans, 2200 of whom were approaching under the command of elderly Revolutionary War veteran General William Hull. Hull had advanced to with five miles of Fort Malden, when he suddenly pulled back, fearing the size of the enemy forces. An attempt by the Americans to approach again by crossing the Aux Canard, a river near Fort Malden, was beaten back by Tecumseh and his warriors. Hull then retreated to Fort Detroit, at the site of the current city.

In early August Tecumseh led a force of 24 Indians and 40 British soldiers that defeated a 150-man detachment bringing supplies to Fort Detroit. Hull had abandoned his invasion of Canada and focused on securing his supply line south. Here, on August 9 a column including American regular troops drove away a mixed force of British and Indians, but the blockade of Fort Detroit was unbroken. Tecumseh was lightly wounded. His reputation rose with each battle. The British and Indian successes brought hundreds of Indian warriors in to join them. The Potawatomis captured Fort

Dearborn, site of present-day Chicago, on August 15. Fort Michilimackinac, at the straits between Lake Michigan and Lake Huron, had fallen earlier.

At this point, Brock arrived with reinforcements. Brock, although still outnumbered, decided to attack Fort Detroit. When Brock finished describing his plans to a gathering of soldiers and Indians, Tecumseh turned to the Indians and said, "Hoo-ye! This is a man."[77] Brock and Tecumseh led 700 soldiers and 600 Indians to besiege Fort Detroit. Hull had 2200 troops. Hull at first refused Brock's demand that he surrender. Tecumseh then led his Indians multiple times across a clearing in view of the fort, convincing Hull that he was surrounded by thousands of Indians. Hull then surrendered his troops and substantial amounts of munitions and supplies.[77]

Brock credited Tecumseh with his role in the victory, calling him "the Wellington of the Natives." Brock wrote of Tecumseh in a letter to Lord Liverpool, the British Prime Minister, stating, "A more sagacious or a more gallant warrior does not, I believe, exist. He has the admiration of everyone who conversed with him."[77] By the end of the summer the British and Indians had taken every American fort on the Great Lakes west of Cleveland. Brock and Tecumseh now planned to move south to attack Forts Wayne and Harrison, which would give them control over the present-day state of Indiana. However, Brock was hurriedly summoned east to defend the border near Niagara.

Colonel Henry Proctor became the temporary British commander in the west. On orders from Britain, he delayed the attacks to see if diplomacy could end the war. When this failed to occur, Proctor and Tecumseh moved south with 800 Indians and 250 British troops and militia. The delay had allowed the Americans to raise fresh troops, under the command of the now General William Henry Harrison. Attacks on Fort Wayne and Fort Harrison had to be abandoned. Even more disastrous for Tecumseh, Brock was killed in a battle near the Niagara River. Proctor became the permanent British commander in the west.[77] The importance of Brock's death was masked for a time when the Indians and British had another victory, defeating a force of militia at the battle of Rum Raisin on January 22, 1813, killing or capturing almost another 900 troops.[81]

Harrison began building a new base, Fort Meigs, close to the British position at Fort Malden. Proctor announced that he was going to attack before the fort was completed. Tecumseh joined his 1200 Indians with Proctor's 800 British soldiers to lay siege to Fort Meigs on April 28.

However, the British and Indians were unable to penetrate the fort's defenses. A lengthy British bombardment was largely ineffective. When reinforcements arrived, Harrison launched a counterattack. The American attackers under Colonel William Dudley captured the British artillery and then pursued the Indians into the woods. There the British and Indians turned upon the pursuers, killing or capturing all of Dudley's 800 soldiers.

The battle was barely over when Tecumseh received word that the Indians at Fort Miami were torturing and killing their American prisoners. Tecumseh rode into the fort and persuaded the Indians to stop, saving the remaining Americans. One of the surviving American prisoners present at the fort wrote, "Never did Tecumseh shine more truly than on this occasion."[79] Nevertheless, the British and Indian campaign was ultimately unsuccessful. Although the British lost only 100 men in the siege compared to 1000 American casualties, they could not take the fort. The siege was abandoned on May 8 and the British and Indians retreated.

A subsequent attack on Fort Meigs, involving a force of some 2500 Indians under Tecumseh, in July was unsuccessful. A British attack on Fort Stephenson was also defeated, leading many of the western Indians to desert.[81] The Indians strength was not in taking fortified positions, and the British, lacking sufficient artillery, were no more successful.

On September 10, 1813, American Oliver Perry defeated the British on a naval battle on Lake Erie, giving Americans naval supremacy on the lake. Proctor ordered the evacuation of Fort Malden without informing Tecumseh. Learning of Proctor's plans, Tecumseh demanded a council of war with Proctor. They met at Fort Malden on September 18 along with their chief lieutenants. Tecumseh reminded Proctor of British promises, saying, "Listen! When war was declared, our Father [the British king] stood up and gave us the tomahawk and told us he was now ready to strike the Americans; that he wanted our assistance, and that he certainly would get us our lands back. We are astonished to see our Father [Proctor] preparing to run...without letting his red children know what his intentions are...we must compare our Father's conduct to a fat animal that arrives with its tail upon its back, but when affrighted, it drops between its legs and runs off."[77] Tecumseh concluded, "You have got the arms and ammunition which our Great White Father set for his red children. If you have an idea of going away, give them to us...We are determined to defend our lands."[77]

135

Proctor now revealed the British naval defeat and told Tecumseh that he planned to retreat to Chatham, where he would fortify the lower Thames River to make a stand. Tecumseh covered the British retreat, arriving three weeks later with 1200 warriors at Chatham only to discover that the British had fled further to Moraviantown. Tecumseh retreated further, followed closely by Harrison with an army of 3500 Americans. In vain Tecumseh attacked Harrison, trying to delay him, and suffered a slight wound in the battle. As the retreat continued Tecumseh's warriors melted away in the face of impending defeat. Tecumseh arrived at Moraviantown with only 500 men. He found even fewer poorly positioned, discouraged British soldiers under Proctor. Soon both were faced by Harrison's larger force. Tecumseh told Proctor, "Father, tell your men to be firm, and all will be well. Father, have a brave heart."[77] Tecumseh rode along the British and Indian lines before the battle, offering encouragement. Inwardly more pessimistic, Tecumseh told his men to give his sword to his son Paukeesa should he die.[77]

On October 5, 1813, the Americans began the battle by launching an attack on the British line. Proctor responded by retreating, leaving the Indians alone to bear the brunt of the attack. Tecumseh and his warriors did not retreat. Tecumseh was leading a counterattack when he was hit by a bullet in the chest. He fell off his horse, dead upon the ground. With his death, the Indians retreated, ending the battle. It was a decisive American victory. Six hundred British soldiers surrendered afterwards. Tecumseh's body was given to the British. His burial site remains unknown.[77]

The Prophet stayed in Canada for a decade before being invited back to the United States in 1824, where he eventually settled with his followers in the new Shawnee reservation in Kansas. In 1831, the last Shawnee in Ohio were forced to move to reservations in Kansas and Oklahoma.[82]

The Americans' decisive victory at Moraviantown doomed any chance the Indians had of emerging from the eventual peace treaty at Ghent in 1814 with guaranteed lands. Tecumseh's idea of a pan-Indian confederacy was to die with him. Although other Indian leaders were to try to unify the tribes, none came closer than this Shawnee leader. Over time Tecumseh's legend grew. Historian John Sugden wrote, "Tecumseh may have been unsuccessful, but he bequeathed to Indian people something of great importance; from his memory they have drawn pride and self respect…Tecumseh's ambition to be a national Indian leader; rather than a merely a local one, and his vison of a pan Indian brotherhood have powerful appeal for the Indians of today."[81] Tecumseh was also remembered by Canadians as a patriot, for he had indeed helped save Canada from American conquest. Americans too remembered Tecumseh with a high opinion. Months after Moraviantown, the *Dayton Republican*, an Ohio newspaper, praised Tecumseh as, "perhaps the greatest Indian general that ever lifted a tomahawk."[81] Multiple American historians proclaimed Tecumseh the greatest of all Indians.[81] Such views have helped keep Tecumseh's memory alive.

United States 1824

Chapter 12: Henry Clay
Thrice- or Six-Time-Defeated Presidential Candidate, 1824 CE, United States

WHEN HENRY CLAY was born on April 12, 1777, the United States was less than a year old and still battling with Britain for its independence. Few noted the birth of the man that was to be one of America's greatest, yet most unsuccessful, leaders of the next century. Clay later quipped that his memory was limited about the event, saying, "I was very young at my birth."[85]

At age 4, Henry watched as British dragoons ransacked his house, later writing, "I recollect in 1781 or '82 a visit made by Tarleton's troops and of their running their swords into the newly made graves of my father and grandfather, thinking they contained hidden treasures."[86] Henry grew up in a relative comfort, but had a limited formal education, spending only three years at a school in a one-room log cabin.[85]

In 1791, when Clay's family moved to Kentucky, Henry, age 14, remained in Virginia. A year later he became an assistant clerk In the Virginia Court of Chancery, the highest court in Virginia. Henry's neat handwriting led to his hiring as a stenographer, and eventually private secretary, for Virginia Chief Justice George Wythe, a signer of the Declaration of Independence.[85] Clay was to say, "To no man was I more indebted by his instructions, his advice and his example."[86] Wythe was unusual in freeing his slaves during his lifetime after making sure that they had been taught a trade beforehand. Inspired by this example, Clay was to argue throughout his life that slaves needed to learn skills before being freed lest their situation become even worse.

In 1796, Wythe asked Robert Brooks, the attorney general of Virginia, to teach Clay the law. Within a year, Clay, now age 20, was found competent to practice law. Since Virginia was full of lawyers, Clay decided to move west to Lexington, Kentucky, in 1797.

Lexington, with about a thousand people, was the largest town west of the Alleghenies. Clay developed a successful law practice involving both civil and criminal cases. Historian Merrill Peterson wrote, "The incredible confusion over land titles made Kentucky a paradise for lawyers."[87] Clay's courtroom oratory and manner helped give him a reputation as a defender of the little man.[85] Ironically, an early client was Andrew Jackson, later to become Clay's bitter enemy. Clay became famed as a speaker. Historians Daniel and Jeanette Heidler wrote, "Even those of Clay's speeches that do not read well were stunning when he spoke them. In person, listeners hung on his friendly, colloquial cadence that gave the peculiar impression that he was speaking directly to each of them."[85]

Clay wrote in the *Kentucky Gazette*, under the pen name Scaevola, an essay advocating gradual abolition of slavery in Kentucky, asking, "Can any humane man be happy or contented when he sees near 30,000 of his fellow beings around him deprived of all the rights which make life desirable, transferred like cattle from the possession of one to another?"[85] Ignoring this, the delegates to the state's constitutional convention left slavery unmentioned. Although Clay remained a slave-owner during his life, he always viewed slavery as an evil.[85] Clay made the case for gradual, rather than immediate, emancipation a year later in another Scaevola letter, when he wrote, "Thirty thousand slaves, without preparation for enjoying the rights of a free man, without property, without principle, set loose upon society, would be wretched themselves and render others miserable."[88]

On April 11, 1799, Henry Clay, age 22, married Lucretia Hart, age 18, daughter of a wealthy merchant in Lexington. Between his marriage and his successful law practice, Clay's wealth increased. By 1805 he owned eight slaves, more than 6500 acres of land and eight horses.

Politically Clay stood with most Kentuckians in supporting the Democratic-Republican Party, which stood for the common people and a weak central government, over the rival Federalists who favored a strong central government able to protect the interests of the wealthy. Clay's first political address, in 1798, was an attack on the Federalist Alien and Sedition laws aiming at silencing dissent against Federalist policies. Witness reported the surrounding crowd in Lexington was so electrified by his words that "the people took Clay…upon their shoulders…through (the) streets amid shouts and applause."[86]

In 1803 Henry Clay was elected to the Kentucky House of Representatives, where he quickly rose to a position of leadership, eventually becoming Speaker. Clay became adept at fashioning compromises between different factions. The Heidlers wrote, "He became wedded to the idea that the key to political success was to promote the possible and avoid the unattainable ideal."[85]

Kentucky elected Clay to the United States Senate in 1809. Clay campaigned for greater military preparedness given the continuing insults to American shipping from the French and British, locked in the long struggle of the Napoleonic wars. Clay suggested support for domestic manufacturing to allow America to be independent of the need of goods from Europe. Clay urged resistance against British pressure, saying, "Is the time never to come when we may manage our affairs without the fear of insulting his Britannic majesty?"[85] Deciding that he preferred the House of Representatives to the Senate, Clay left the Senate and was elected to the United States House of Representatives in the fall of 1811.

On November 3, 1811, Clay was elected Speaker of the House. At age 34 he was the only freshman congressman ever elected as Speaker.[86] Clay was celebrated as "the greatest natural orator" of the age. Clay did not write out or even make notes before speaking. As such, his speeches are only known to the extent that they were reported.[87] Historian George Bancroft, a contemporary, wrote, "[Clay's] voice was music itself, penetrating and far reaching, enchanting the listener."[86] As Speaker, Clay appointed the chairman and members of the House committees. Clay also controlled who could speak on the floor about each bill and for how long. One veteran congressman, protesting when Clay cut his time short, said, "I speak to posterity." Clay answered." Yes, and you seem resolved to continue speaking until the arrival of your audience."[86] Unlike prior Speakers, Clay would temporarily leave the Speaker's chair to join in debate when the House debated issues as the "Committee of the Whole."

One of Clay's strongest opponents was John Randolph of Virginia. Randolph regularly brought his dogs into the House chamber, letting them roam free and caning another representative who complained. Clay ordered the doorkeeper to remove the dog. Randolph waited for Clay to leave, the blocked the way, snarling, "I never sidestep skunks," to which Clay replied, "I always do," before walking past Randolph.[86] Randolph never brought a dog again, but was to harbor a bitter hated of Clay.[85]

Henry Clay was to be the strongest Speaker seen during the fifty years that followed. Initially, Congress was viewed as the predominant branch of government. President James Madison shared the view of Clay and the other founders of the Constitution that the legislature should take the initiative in most matters. Clay and Madison shared a belief that the nation's military needed to be strengthened in the face of Britain's arrogant behavior. Britain had restricted America from trading with France, with whom Britain was at war. Clay addressed the issue in the House, acting as a Committee of the Whole, saying, "We are called upon to submit to debasement, dishonor and disgrace. It was not by submission that our fathers achieved our independence."[85] Clay persuaded the Congress to approve 100,000 six-month volunteers as well as new taxes and loans to pay for them.

Clay has been blamed for pushing the nation into the War of 1812. However, President Madison and Secretary of State James Monroe shared his viewpoint that the United States could no longer accept British limits on American trade. When Britain failed to rescind its restrictions on American shipping, on June 1, 1812, Madison asked Congress for a declaration of war. Within two weeks Congress declared war.

The war started with a series of disastrous defeats for the Americans. The Federalists, who largely had opposed the war, intensified their criticism of the Madison and his administration. Although Clay privately admitted that "Mr. Madison is wholly unfit for the storms of war," Clay publicly defended the administration.[87]

By the start of 1814 British and Americans agreed to start peace negotiations. Clay was asked by Madison to serve on the negotiating team. Clay reluctantly resigned as Speaker and sailed to Europe, arriving in June 1814 in Ghent, Belgium, for the talks. Napoleon's abdication freed Britain to concentrate its resources against the United States. Consequently, Britain intended to impose much harsher terms.

However, British defeats at Baltimore and Plattsburgh led the British to eventually agree to peace with the return of all territories to their prewar status in December 1814. The delay in transmitting the news across the Atlantic led to one final battle, the rout of the British by General Andrew Jackson at the Battle of New Orleans.

Clay was reelected to the House and chosen again as Speaker. Clay now pushed President Madison's program of internal improvements, protection of American industry and increased military improvements through Congress. Clay argued that Congress had implied powers beyond those listed in the Constitution. Clay said, "The Constitution vests in Congress all powers 'necessary and proper'…to put into motion and activity the machinery of government which it constructs. The powers that may be so necessary…are not defined in the Constitution."[86]

Clay found himself frequently in disagreement with Madison's successor as president, James Monroe, who argued that federal construction of local roads was unconstitutional.[86] Clay continued to argue for what he called "The American system," which included internal improvements and tariffs to protect infant American industries from being overwhelmed by more established European competitors. While focusing on the needs of the United States, Clay argued that the United States should give at least moral support to those in South America rebelling against Spanish rule. Clay's support won him the deep gratitude of the leaders of the new independent nations of South America.One final event occurred during Monroe's presidency that would hugely impact Clay's future. When General Andrew Jackson exceeded his instructions to attack Spanish forts in Florida, Clay attacked Jackson, stating that Congress had a duty to prevent "a triumph of military over civil authority."[85] However, Jackson became a hero when the Spanish ended up selling Florida to the United States. Jackson now considered Clay a personal enemy.

Slavery was to be the issue that would most consume Clay's life. Clay helped found the American Colonization Society, which aimed to find a home for freed slaves in Africa, for he did not believe that they would be tolerated by white society. Clay was unusual at that time in not believing blacks to be inherently inferior. Clay stated that freed slaves were "the most corrupt, depraved and abandoned class of people in the nation…it is not so much their fault as the consequences of their anomalous condition. Place ourselves, place any men, in the like predicament and similar effects would follow…prejudices, more powerful than any laws, deny them the privileges of free men."[85] Clay never wavered from his expressed desire to see the gradual end of slavery in the United States.

The national political struggle over slavery first heated up in 1819, when Missouri, a slave-owning territory, applied for statehood. By this time slavery had disappeared in most northern states while growing stronger in the southern states. New York Congressman James Tallmadge proposed an amendment forbidding the imposition of more slaves into Missouri and providing for gradual emancipation for existing slaves. Anger now broke between the North and South over slavery. Clay told a friend, "The words, civil war and disunion, are uttered almost without emotion."[89] Clay supported what became known as the Missouri Compromise, allowing Missouri to be admitted as a slave state and Maine as a free state, while prohibiting slavery north of the southern border of Missouri. Shortly, afterward, controversy again erupted when Missouri wrote a constitution forbidding free blacks from entering the state. Clay engineered a compromise essentially negating this provision.[89] Ironically Clay is remembered falsely as the author of the First Missouri Compromise while the equally important Second Missouri Compromise, which he did engineer, is forgotten.[87] Clay was hailed for his role in enacting these compromises. Senator Thomas Hart Benton of Missouri, later an enemy of Clay, lauded Clay as "The Pacificator of ten millions of Brothers."[87]

In 1823 Clay was again elected Speaker of the House. Clay argued that the United States would be better served by becoming self-sufficient rather than dependent on imports from Europe, particularly Britain. Clay said, "Encourage fabrication at home, and there would instantly arise animation and a healthful circulation throughout all parts of the Republic."[87] He continued, "No country on earth…contains within its own limits more abundant facilities for supplying our national wants than ours does."[87] Under Clay's leadership, the House passed a protective tariff and money for internal improvements such as roads and canals in 1824.

Clay decided to run for President in 1824, facing four other strong candidates, Secretary of State John Quincy Adams, Secretary of the Treasury William Crawford, Secretary of War John Calhoun, and General Andrew Jackson. Clay's dominance of the House would become particularly important if no candidate won an Electoral College majority in the 1824 race, since the Constitution said that the House of Representatives would then pick between the three candidates with the most electoral votes. As the election approached, Calhoun dropped out to become Jackson's vice-presidential candidate. Crawford then suffered a stroke from an excessive dose of the drug digitalis. His condition was kept secret.

When the electoral votes were counted the top three vote getters were Jackson, Adams and Crawford. Both the Adams and Jackson camps had maneuvered to give enough votes to Crawford to eliminate Clay from the race.

The decision was thrown into the House of Representatives to choose the next president. Clay, reelected as speaker, was now courted heavily by the remaining candidates. Crawford was too ill and near death for Clay to support. Clay viewed Jackson as dangerous, noting that he would not support "the election of a military chieftain."[85]

Clay declared for Adams, who was chosen president on the first ballot in the House. Jackson was furious. He became even more enraged when Henry Clay accepted the position of secretary of state. Jackson's supporters alleged that Clay had only supported Adams in exchange for this job, dubbing the appointment "The Corrupt Bargain."[87] Jackson told a friend, "The Judas of the West has closed the contract and will receive the thirty pieces of silver. His end will be the same."[85] Jackson was unforgiving, holding Clay and Adams responsible for charges of bigamy against Jackson's wife Rachel during the campaign. Jackson described Clay as "the basest, meanest scoundrel that ever disgraced the image of his god."[87] Jackson and his supporters determined to destroy the Adams administration in any way possible.

Buffeted by these vicious attacks and the sudden deaths of two daughters within five weeks, Clay tried to throw himself into his work. However, attempts at reaching an agreement with Britain on trade and with France on its debts both proved elusive. Clay was frequently ill during his term as secretary of state. Clay admitted later, "It would have been wiser and more politic to have declined the office of secretary of state."[86] The continued attacks on the Adams administration and its lack of success in foreign or domestic affairs greatly lowered its popularity.

The Presidential election of 1828 was a sweeping victory for Jackson over Adams. After being briefly depressed by Adams' defeat and his loss of office, Clay's spirits and health began to improve once he returned to Kentucky. Clay continued to champion his "American System" of internal improvements and tariffs to protect industries.

Elected to the United States Senate in 1831, Clay returned to Washington. Clay took over the leadership of those opposed to Jackson. President Jackson and Vice President Calhoun had fallen out, leading to the resignation of Calhoun and most of the cabinet. Clay felt that Jackson was politically vulnerable in his bid for reelection in 1832.

The old Democratic-Republican Party of Jefferson and Madison gradually split between those favoring a stronger central government and another faction that emphasized states' rights. Clay was nominated to run for president against Jackson in 1832 by those favoring a stronger central government. Clay underestimated Jackson's popularity, and overestimated any negative effect on Jackson of the Bank of the United States controversy.[90] The result was a landslide victory for Jackson over Clay.

Although crushed at the polls, Clay once more found himself indispensable. The election was soon followed by the Nullification Crisis. South Carolina, an agricultural state, angered by the high Tariff of 1828, had passed a law claiming that the national tariffs did not apply in the state. South Carolina now threatened to secede from the nation unless the tariffs were abolished. President Jackson threatened to prevent this by force, saying, "I consider the power to annul a law of the United States assumed by one state, incompatible with the existence of the Union [and] contradicted expressly by the letter of the Constitution."[86] In the face of imminent civil war, people looked to Clay for answers. Even Clay's bitter opponent John Randolph said, "There is one man, and one man only, who can save the Union—that man is Henry Clay."[85]

Clay now proposed a compromise. The northern manufacturers would receive nine years of protection against imported goods while the southerners gained the promise that the tariff would eventually be abolished. Clay gained Jackson's tacit support by passing a bill allowing Jackson to use force against South Carolina if necessary. The compromise made the use of force unnecessary. Clay stated that his plan "was founded on that great principle of compromise and concession which lies at the bottoms of our institutions."[89] The passage of what was called the Compromise of 1833 restored Clay's national stature. Clay said of the adoption of the compromise, "was the most proud and triumphant day of his life."[89]

Grief stricken by the death of his last surviving daughter in December 1835, Clay chose not to run for President in 1836. Jackson's vice president, Martin Van Buren, was elected to succeed him as president.

Soon after the election, the economy crashed in what was called the Panic of 1837. As the downturn dragged on, it seemed likely that the opponents of Jackson, who called themselves Whigs, would have a good chance of winning the presidency in 1840. For the first time, the Whigs decided that their candidate be chosen by national convention.

The years running up to the convention saw John Calhoun and Clay offer competing visions for the country. Calhoun campaigned to protect slavery, arguing that the Congress must positively support slavery or risk disunion. In contrast, Clay remained convinced that slavery was an evil, but that no obvious path existed to abolish it without a national catastrophe. Clay answered that he did not "believe that it is prudent or wise to be so often alluding to separation of the Union. We ought not to be perpetually crying wolf, wolf, wolf." In the end, Clay persuaded the Senate to agree that the government should "neither protect nor interfere with slavery."[85] Clay also blocked an attempt by southerners to pass a gag rule in the Senate, as had passed in the House, to prohibit the reading of petitions against slavery. Clay stated, "The Constitution requires the Senate to accept petitions and the constitutional right of petition to abolish slavery clearly exists."[86] Clay was attacked from both North and South for his views on slavery. Calhoun remarked, "He [Clay] ought to have seen that it was impossible for him to take [the] middle ground on the abolition question."[85] Clay consistently argued that slavery was immoral, but that the abolitionists had no practical plan to deal with the results of eliminating slavery. Clay felt that the increasing belligerence of the abolitionists delayed progress on the issue and threatened national harmony. His position cost him support from both ends of the political spectrum.

When the Whig Convention opened on December 4, 1839, Clay was warned that his sentiments were hurting his presidential chances. Clay reportedly said, "I had rather be right than be President."[85] Clay received the most votes on the first ballot at 103, with 128 needed for the nomination. Opponents of Clay whispered that he could not win the general election. The party leaders in New York and Pennsylvania favored William Henry Harrison, who eventually won the nomination. Despite his disappointment, Clay actively campaigned for Harrison and the Whig ticket in 1840.

Harrison won the election while a Whig majority was also elected to Congress. Clay was the acknowledged leader of this group. A capital reporter, T.N. Parmelee, said of Clay, "His is the ascendency of a powerful intellect and a bold determined spirit over lesser minds and fainter hearts…Never was there more cheerful submission and more unhesitating devotion. If he was to intimate a wish that the majority of the Senate should go to [hell]…they would immediately raise a committee to ascertain the most direct and eligible route."[87] A month after his inauguration, Harrison, age 61, died suddenly. His vice president, John Tyler of Virginia, took his place.

Tyler, whose views were little known when chosen to be vice president, was opposed to most of the Whig program, most notably the creation of another Bank of the United States to replace that killed by Jackson. Tyler wanted to be elected president in his own right in 1844 and viewed Clay as his major competitor. The Whigs in Congress passed a bill creating a bank, which Tyler vetoed as unconstitutional. The Whig legislators then changed the bill to the form Tyler said that he could accept, but Tyler vetoed this as well. Tyler said that the incorporation of a national bank was "the original sin against the Constitution."[87] Clay complained, "The second [bank bill] charter was prepared according to his wishes…How is he to be justified for his breech of good faith?"[86] At this, most of the Cabinet resigned. Two days later the enraged Whig members of Congress voted to expel President Tyler from the party. Tyler's new cabinet, with the important exception of Daniel Webster, was largely made up of men dedicated to states' rights rather than national powers and of enemies of Henry Clay.

The debacle in Washington resulted in the rout of the Whigs in the off-year elections. Clay, approaching age 65, decided to resign from the Senate on March 31, 1842. Clay spent much of the next year traveling to address Whig gatherings. Once again, Clay was the clear Whig favorite as a candidate for president in the 1844 elections. In the North, an abolitionist petitioned Clay to free his own slaves. Clay answered, "I look upon it [slavery] as a great evil and deeply lament that we have derived it…from our ancestors…In my opinion, the evils of slavery are…nothing in comparison with the far greater evils…from a sudden…indiscriminate emancipation…I believe that gradual emancipation is the only method of liberation that has ever been thought safe or wise."[86]

In 1844, the country was divided over whether to annex Texas, which had won its independence in 1836, which would create another slave state. There were also cries to annex Oregon, i.e., the Pacific Northwest, whose ownership was disputed with Britain. Clay counselled caution and delay on both issues. The Democrats nominated James Polk, a Jackson ally, who argued for annexing both Texas and the Pacific Northwest.

The Democrats hammered at Clay over the Texas issue. The Democrats also attacked Clay as an elitist. Polk defeated Clay by a margin of 38,000 votes out of the 2.7 million cast. Clay lost support from both North and South for trying to reach a middle ground on slavery and on Texas. Clay said, "If anyone desires to know the leading and paramount object of my public life, the preservation of the Union will furnish him the key."[86]

Personal tragedy was not finished with Henry Clay. After negotiating a peaceful division of the Pacific Northwest with Britain, President Polk decided to fight against Mexico, which disputed the border with the United

States. Clay opposed the war. However, his favorite son, Henry Clay, Junior, enlisted in the American army. In a battle, Henry, Junior, was killed. The news stunned Clay.

As the 1848 election approached many Whigs again touted Clay as their best candidate for president. Clay, now 70 years old, was initially silent on whether he wanted the nomination. Unknown to all, Clay had tuberculosis, a disease rampant at the time.[85] Finally, Clay announced that he was running for president, basing his candidacy on his opposition to the Mexican War. Clay told an audience, "Of all the dangers and misfortunes which could befall this nation, I should regard that of it becoming a warlike and conquering power the most direful."[91] However, when a successful peace treaty was signed that transferred huge territories to the United States, Clay lost his major issue. The Whig convention chose Zachary Taylor, a successful general in the Mexican war, as their nominee rather than chance the oft-defeated Clay. Taylor was elected President in 1848.[85]

Slavery became more and more the dominant issue of the day. Congress became locked in a bitter dispute over whether to admit new territories with or without slavery. The House, dominated by the more populous North, repeatedly passed the Wilmot Proviso, outlawing slavery in any territory acquired from Mexico. The Proviso was repeatedly blocked in the Senate, where the South had at least equal power. Tensions between the two regions of the country continued to rise.

Clay continued to own slaves while he condemned slavery as an evil. Clay arranged that all his slaves would be freed in his will. He was dismayed when Indiana, a free state, barred the entry of free blacks. Clay remarked, "What is to become of these poor creatures? In the name of humanity, I ask what is to become of them—where are they to go?"[85] Clay saw the lack of any plan for the slaves once freed as the biggest barrier to the abolition of slavery. Clay was attacked by both abolitionists and slave owners when he called for the "gradual and ultimate extinction of slavery" in Kentucky.[89]

For a while Clay resisted entreaties that he return to politics, but by February 1849 he relented, being elected easily to the Senate. Clay had said, "If I could be persuaded that I could materially contribute to the proper adjustment of the momentous question which has grown out of the acquisition of New Mexico and California, I should cease to feel any repugnance to the resumption of a seat in the Senate."[89] Clay's overall health seemed to improve, but he continued to have a nagging cough.

It was clear that many Americans viewed Clay as the best hope for avoiding sectional conflict, possible disunion or civil war.[89] Clay told audiences that he would do anything in his power to prevent "the dissolution of the union and all the horrors of civil war."[89] A young representative from Illinois, Abraham Lincoln, observed at the time that Clay was "my beau ideal of a statesman, the man for whom I fought all my humble life."[89]

The clash over slavery worsened. Northerners wanted to outlaw the slave trade in the nation's capital, while Southerners, dismayed by the escape of slaves to the North with the assistance of abolitionists, demanded a stronger fugitive slave law. When gold was discovered in California in 1849, the sudden population rush to California led to its application for statehood with a constitution prohibiting slavery. Southerners saw that California's admission as a free state would deprive them of their power in the Senate to block anti-slavery measures. New Mexico wished to organize as a territory barring slavery while Texas, burdened by huge debts, claimed ownership over most of the New Mexico territory and threatened to seize it by force. Southerners under John Calhoun had organized a convention of southern states to be held in June 1850. Many expected that the southern states might try to secede at that time.[89]

Clay began his last and greatest legislative endeavor. The opening of the Congress betrayed the violent antagonism on both sides about slavery. It took the House of Representatives 63 ballots to even elect a Speaker. In January, southern senators openly talked about dissolution of the Union unless their demands were met. Clay visited Senator Daniel Webster, trying to win his support for a compromise plan. Webster observed that he thought "Mr. Clay's objects were great and highly patriotic…perhaps Providence had designed the return of Mr. Clay to the Senate to afford the means and the way of averting a great evil from the country."[89] On January 29, 1850, Clay submitted his proposals to the Congress. The eight-part plan included admission of California as a free state, New Mexico as a state where slavery would be decided by its population, the settlement of Texas' boundary and assumption of its debts by the federal government, abolition of the slave trade in the District of Columbia, a stronger fugitive slave law and the declaration that Congress would not regulate the slave trade within the slave owning states.[89] Warning of the risk of disintegration of the union, Clay begged his fellow senators "to pause at the edge of the precipice before the fearful and disastrous leap is taken into the yawning abyss beyond."[91] While many applauded the plan, there were those both North and South who denounced it. The *New York Herald* editorialized, "Henry Clay may never reap the reward of his devotion to the United States, to the Union and to constitution, but posterity will do him justice, if the present generation do not."[89] Abolitionist and former slave Frederick Douglas called Clay a "moral monster" for supporting a stronger Fugitive Slave Act while from the other extreme South Carolina Senator Andrew Pickens Butler roared, "Compromise? Its name is frailty—its consequences treachery."[91] Clay threw himself into a campaign to reach a peaceful compromise on an issue that seemed likely to lead to the splitting up of the union. Clay said, "I go for honorable compromises whenever it can be made…All legislation, all government, all society is formed upon the principle of mutual concession."[86] Clay was to be on his feet in debate seventy-two times from January 29 to August 1, 1850. Clay worked diligently to stir up public support for the compromise. He convened a daily caucus of Whigs and Democrats who were committed to the Union.

Clay's proposal also extended the Missouri Compromise to the Pacific, excluding slavery above the line. Clay stated, "No earthly power could induce me to vote for a specific measure for the introduction of slavery where it has not existed before."[85] Clay argued for compromise, describing the horrors of war that would result from Southern secession over these issues. When Mississippi Senator Henry Foote accused Clay of betraying the South, Clay answered, "I know no South, no North, no East, no West to which I owe my allegiance…My allegiance is to this Union and my own state."[89] The terminally ill John Calhoun, now so weak that his speech had to be spoken for him, replied, vowing resistance against any additional Southern concessions. Three days later, on March 7, Daniel Webster answered him. Webster started, "I wish to speak today, not as a Massachusetts man, not as a northern man, but as an American…I speak for the preservation of the Union. Hear me for my cause."[89] Webster continued, extolling the union of the states and condemning extremists on both sides. Agreement on the compromise remained elusive. Then on March 31 Calhoun died.

On May 8, Clay proposed a revised compromise. Congressional agreement could not be achieved. Members trying to defeat it offered repeated amendments that threatened to derail its support. The Southern convention met at Nashville, but decided to not act until they saw what happened in Congress.[89]

More worrisome to Clay, President Taylor opposed the plan as well. Suddenly Taylor became ill with a gastrointestinal illness on July 4. Taylor died five days later, to be succeeded by Millard Fillmore, who promised to sign any compromise.

On July 22, 1850, Clay gave what turned out to be his last major address. Clay attacked the idea of the South seceding to form a Southern confederacy, declaiming, "Never! Never will we who occupy the broad waters of the Mississippi and its tributaries consent that any foreign flag shall float [over them]." Clay also said that he believed that the omnibus bill "is the reunion of this Union. I believe it is the dove of peace, taking its aerial flight…[carrying] the glad tidings of peace and restored harmony to all the remotest extremities of this distracted land."[89] At last the compromise was agreed to. A Senate vote was imminent when a supporter of the compromise proposed changes. Rapidly the whole deal fell apart as others proposed widespread changes. Clay, increasingly weak from his tuberculosis, said, "I think I am angry at everyone. Here is our country on the very verge of civil war which everyone pretends to be anxious to avoid, yet everyone wants his own way, irrespective of the interests and wishes of others."[91] Clay, in a last bid for compromise, said, "I was willing to take the measures united. I am now willing to see them pass as separate and distinct."[87]

Discouraged and weakening, Clay left Washington for the cooler climate of Newport, Rhode Island. Yet his efforts at persuading seemingly irreconcilable factions to compromise were not in vain. In August, shortly after Clay's departure, Stephen Douglas succeeded in getting the components of the Compromise of 1850 passed as a series of separate bills in the Senate followed in September with passage by the House, largely upon the lines that Clay had proposed.[89]

The Compromise of 1850 did not solve the slavery issue. However, it kept the United States together for another crucial ten years during which the forces supporting the Union gained in material power. It is unlikely if the South could have been kept from successfully seceding in 1850.[87] Twenty-five years later, Senator Foote was to say, "had there been one such man in the Congress of the United States as Henry Clay in 1860–61, there would, I feel sure, been no civil war."[89]

Clay returned to Washington at the very end of 1850. Clay now began to cough up blood and rapidly lose weight, both hallmarks of tuberculosis. He became significantly weaker. When his physician mistakenly told him that the cough was the result of a digestive disorder, Clay answered, "Be that as it may, I must get rid of the cough or it will dispose of me."[85] Too weak to leave his room at the National Hotel, Clay lingered there for several months before dying on June 29, 1851.

Henry Clay became the first American to lie in state at the Capitol. Not even any president had had that honor. In his eulogy, Lincoln said of Clay, "He loved his country…He gave the death blow to fraternal strife…and peace to a distracted land."[86]

Henry Clay was nominated three times as a candidate for president and lost all three elections. He failed in his campaign to be his party's nominee at least three other times. Yet he is remembered as a great statesman and symbol of the Union, creating compromises that prevented his country's demise. Some historians have attributed the decision by Kentucky, a slave state, to stay in the Union during the civil war to the influence of Henry Clay.[87]

Clay's politics were more centrist than many of the others in this book. Yet he was never simply in the favor of the status quo. He fought passionately for his causes of American independence and self-sufficiency, the gradual abolition of slavery and the preservation of the Union.

Other nations did not forget Henry Clay. Remarkably, the ministers of twenty Latin American republics assembled In Washington on the 150th anniversary of his birth to pay tribute to Clay for his support.[87] Clay is remembered for what he accomplished, not where he failed. If he was not able to give the death blow to fraternal strife, he fought with all his might to prevent it.

Habsburg Empire, 1848 CE

Chapter 13: Louis Kossuth
Liberal Nationalism, 1848 CE, Hungary

"Felix, how are you?" Count K____ asked.

"Well, Istavan. Will you join me for coffee?" his friend Count T____ answered him. The two nobles were in their comfortable club in Buda, the fashionable part of Budapest, in Hungary. The year was 1833.

"Gladly," Istavan replied, sitting down. "What are you reading?"

"It's a report about what's happening in the Diet, you know, the parliament here in Hungary."

"I am more inclined to the hunt than politics," Istavan answered. "Enlighten me please. I didn't think the Diet publicized their discussions."

"They don't. This is put together by a clever fellow named Louis Kossuth. He's sitting in as a deputy in the Diet for Count M____, who couldn't be bothered," Felix replied.

"Tell me about this Kossuth."

"He's from a family of minor nobles up near the northern border. He's a lawyer and apparently speaks six languages. He ran into some problems and has sworn off gambling and drinking forever."

"What an odd fellow," Istavan replied. "So what does he have to say?"

"Well, you know that Hungary had been an independent country where the king was elected by the nobility. In 1526, we elected a Habsburg as a monarch and then in 1687 made it hereditary. We have been under the thumb of Habsburg emperors and Austrians, in the form of the Austrian Empire, ever since. Kossuth has apparently become quite well known reporting on the doings of the legislature so the whole nation would know what is going on."

"The Hungarian nation is the high aristocracy, like us, represented in the upper House of the Diet, and the lesser nobility which makes up the lower House," Istavan snorted. "The peasants and townspeople and the ethnic minorities—the Slovaks, Croats, Serbs, Rumanians, Germans and Jews—they don't matter."

Felix answered, "It's true that they don't have the same rights as us. Since 1222 we nobles don't pay taxes or tolls and owe service and allegiance only to the king. The commoners pay the taxes, do military service and often are our subjects. Still, folks like Count Széchenyi and this Kossuth are agitating for change. It's 1833. Things don't stay unchanged forever." Felix was more right than he imagined. After centuries as one of the most backward parts of Europe, Hungary, largely due to Louis Kossuth, was suddenly to change dramatically.[92-96]

Louis Kossuth was born September 19, 1802, in northern Hungary. He went to Budapest for his legal training before returning home. He lived simply, having to provide for himself, his parents and four sisters. In 1832 Kossuth was chosen by several of his aristocratic clients to serve as their representative to the Diet in their absence, a customary practice of the day.[92]

Hungary had some limited powers in the vast Austrian Empire, which included the modern-day nations of Austria, Hungary, the Czech Republic, Slovakia, Slovenia, Croatia, northern Italy and much of Romania. This power, such as it was, was found in the Hungarian Diet, the national legislature.

The Diet of 1832 was agitated by the writings of Count István Széchenyi, which laid out the ills of Hungary, including serfdom and lack of rights for most population. Széchenyi in vain argued for at least moderate reforms.[92] Kossuth began writing daily reports about the meetings of the Lower House where he sat, which he mailed out all over Hungary. Kossuth's reports were eagerly snapped up by people all over Hungary. Kossuth sent out multiple copies of 334 handwritten reports over the next four years, becoming nationally known.[92]

When the Diet session ended in 1836, Kossuth then launched a new journal, called *Municipal Reports*, a biweekly account of developments in the different counties throughout Hungary. Friends would forward information to Kossuth, who would edit and distribute it. Due to his criticism of imperial absolutism and corruption, the mail service refused to deliver Kossuth's correspondence. Kossuth had to rely on a system of friends and couriers to deliver the journal.[92]

Shortly thereafter the imperial government cracked down on the Hungarians. Kossuth was arrested in May 1837 on the charge of sedition. Kossuth conducted his own defense at his trial, which further bolstered his reputation. He was sentenced to prison, but had the freedom to read and write during his imprisonment. He was set free in May 1840, three years after his arrest, as part of a general amnesty. Historian István Deák wrote, "Imprisonment had worked to Kossuth's advantage: he was now a national martyr and hero: he had had time to read; he had proven himself supremely able to resist the stress of isolation, to work under duress, to prepare plans, and to develop trust in himself as well as in his many friends."[92]

In 1841 Kossuth, a Lutheran, married Terez Meszlenyi, who was Catholic. Such mixed marriages were forbidden. Kossuth appealed to the Pest County assembly, the local government, who allowed the marriage to proceed. Their marriage would prove lasting and harmonious.[92]

Around the same time, Kossuth started a newspaper, *Pest Hilo* (*Pest News*). Kossuth saw that conditions in Hungary were centuries behind much of the rest of Europe. Kossuth was determined to modernize Hungary and reduce the inequality which he saw contributing to this backwardness. *Pest Hilo* was dedicated to a radical reform agenda, particularly focusing on the feudal status and plight of the peasants. With all land owned by the nobility, the peasants had to deliver unpaid labor on the noble's personal plot while paying cash for the plots they cultivated. Services and dues were also extracted from the peasants by the villages, counties, churches and nation. Peasants drafted into the military faced years, sometimes even a lifetime, of military service. The lack of capital and technological know-how meant that agricultural productivity remained very low.[92] The abysmal roads led to starvation in some districts even while others had a glut of crops.

Kossuth demanded the landowners free the peasants from the requirement of unpaid labor. He also argued that the nobles' immunity from taxation should be ended. Kossuth advocated for improved prison conditions, an institute for the blind, orphanages and a children's hospital. Kossuth also began the innovation of including editorials in his newspaper issues.[92]

By its peak, his paper's circulation was over 5000, an enormous number at a time when most Hungarian papers had two to three hundred readers and most Hungarians were illiterate.[92] Kossuth's radicalism finally succeeded in irritating the government enough that he was forced out as editor and the paper closed in 1844.[92]

In 1846, the Austrian imperial government under its longtime leader, Prince Metternich, tried a different approach to undercut the Hungarian reformers. A Conservative Party was organized, with an agenda of modest reforms that Metternich hoped would foreclose more radical steps. During the months before the Diet of 1847 opened, the opposition joined together to create its own party, the Party of United Opposition, with Kossuth as its strongest leader. In June,1847 the party laid out all the liberal demands, including freedom of the press and religion, the extension of suffrage, equality under the law and the abolishment of peasant servitude. When the government forbade the printing of this declaration, it was printed clandestinely. Importantly, the declaration called for these reforms, not simply in Hungary, but in all the parts of the Habsburg Empire.[92] Kossuth argued that Hungary could not count on its freedom under an emperor who had absolute rule in the rest of his domain, thus arguing that Austria should have a constitution as well.[94]

Kossuth now ran for the Diet in Pest County, the most important territorial unit in Hungary. Pest, the more populous part of Budapest, had a population of some 110,000 in 1848, although only the 14,000 adult nobles could vote. It contained Hungary's only university, its important newspapers and journals, and the biggest collection of factories in the country. The Conservative Party, the Catholic prelates and the big landowners heavily campaigned against Kossuth, who was elected by a two to one margin. A government official from Pest observed, "Kossuth is an agitator…He is of the kind who alone will cause more trouble than the rest of the Diet combined."[92]

Developments elsewhere in Europe now drove events in Hungary. In January,1848 a revolution broke out in Sicily, which soon spread to Italy proper. Protests in France led to the abdication of the king. Each revolt encouraged those looking at the increased freedoms in other countries in Europe to consider striking out for these liberties at home. One of the precipitants may have a major economic crisis that occurred in Europe in 1845–47 when many harvests failed, leading to hunger and unemployment among the poor. The revolutionary movements, however, were usually led by middle-class intellectuals.[93]

On March 3, Kossuth set forth his proposals in the Diet, calling for modernization, liberalization and an increase in Hungarian self-rule within the Austrian Empire. Kossuth proposed a Hungarian financial system separate from Austria, elimination of feudal dues and required services from the peasants, taxation of the nobility, a Hungarian military answering to the Diet and a revision of Hungary's relations with the other Habsburg territories. Kossuth also argued that expanded liberties would be needed for all the inhabitants of the empire to secure Hungarian enjoyment of their liberties. Kossuth concluded, "The dynasty must choose between its own welfare and the preservation of a rotten system."[95] The Lower House of the

Diet, composed almost exclusively of the nobility, passed this radical program. However, the Upper House, made up of the wealthiest nobles, refused to consider the program. The Lower House now threatened to send this proposal, called the Address to the Throne, directly to the Emperor.[92]

Before this could happen, on March 13 a revolution broke out in Vienna, the Habsburg capital. Inspired by uprisings elsewhere in Europe, students from Vienna University invaded a meeting of the Austrian parliament. Factory workers joined the protest. Imperial troops clashed with demonstrators, leaving 45 of them dead on the streets of Vienna. Seeking to mollify the population, the emperor dismissed Metternich and the arch-conservative Hungarian Chancellor Apponyi. The next day the Viennese obtained arms for the middle-class–dominated national guard. Censorship was abolished.[92] The Austrian ministers tried to blame, without any evidence, the unrest on Kossuth and the other Hungarian liberals.[96]

In Hungary, the Upper House, frightened by the revolution in the capital, now accepted Kossuth's proposals on March 14. The next day the Diet, at Kossuth's suggestion, asked for the immediate appointment of a Hungarian prime minister. In Austria, further unrest led the emperor to promise a constitution soon. The Czechs, who dominated the northern part of the Habsburg Empire, now demanded their own constitution and self-government.

While the intellectuals of Pest admired Kossuth, many advocated even more radical reforms. Their spokesman was Sándor Peton, a lyricist and political radical. On March 11, Peton's followers, called "Young Hungary" presented its "Twelve Demands." They included Kossuth's proposals plus freedom of the press, complete civil and religious equality, trial by jury, a Hungarian national army and a popularly elected Hungarian parliament. When word of the Vienna revolution arrived, the radicals decided to act. They gathered large numbers of students and other residents, marched to City Hall and forced the city council to set up a Committee of Public Safety. On March 15, 20,000 demonstrators crossed the bridge over the Danube River from Pest to Buda and invaded the Vice Regal Council, which represented the central government. The Council effectively surrendered to the crowd, ordering the garrison not to interfere and abolishing censorship.[92]

The same day the Hungarian Diet sent a delegation, including Kossuth, to Vienna to meet with the imperial government. They arrived in Vienna to be greeted by a cheering crowd of 100,000 people. Women rushed forward to touch Kossuth's cloak. He was forced to stop his carriage frequently to give a speech. Deák wrote, "Kossuth was not only a brilliant speaker, alternatively majestic, dignified, fearsome, mellow, flattering and humble, refined and direct in simplicity—but his voice carried farther than that of any one else, an indispensable attribute for someone constantly addressing crowds."[92]

The next day Archduke Stephen, the emperor's nephew and the royal representative to Hungary, informed the emperor and the government that unless they gave in to Hungarian demands, the country might secede and form a republic. One day later, on March 17, the imperial government gave in to all the demands, appointing Kossuth's associate Count Batthyány as the Hungarian prime minister.[92]

The turmoil in the Habsburg Empire continued. Revolution broke out in the imperial city of Venice on March 17, followed by an uprising in Milan. The uprising in Milan was marked by bitter street battles between the populace and the Imperial Army.[95] On March 21, the Austrian commander in Venice capitulated to the revolutionaries, who proclaimed a republic. The king of the northern Italian kingdom of Piedmont-Sardinia had been forced by protests to agree to a constitutional monarchy on March 4. Sensing opportunity, Piedmont-Sardinia now declared war, sending its army into the Austrian-governed portion of northern Italy.[92] Turmoil also rocked the north of the empire. Bowing to Czech demands, the emperor on April 8 agreed to separate assemblies for the two Czech provinces of Bohemia and Moravia.[95]

Hungary was stunned and elated by the complete triumph of the Hungarian delegation. Széchenyi, who had opposed Kossuth, wrote to a friend, "We have lived through miracles…Act One of the Drama was a magnificent success…I shall serve Batthyány and Kossuth most sincerely…My policy was certain, but slow. Kossuth staked everything on one card and has already won as much for the nation as my policy could have produced over perhaps twenty years."[92] The Diet now rushed to enact further reforms. On March 18 Kossuth won passage of equal voting rights for the hitherto politically weak representatives of the towns. Feudal dues and services were abolished. The practice of mandatory tithes, where 10% of all income was given the Church, was ended.

The reforms of the Diet continued. On March 20, it voted to meet annually, created a national bank and abolished censorship, although with only a limited freedom of the press. On March 21, a law was passed giving municipal voting rights to every qualified city inhabitant regardless of religion. However, the measure produced rioting in Pressburg with beating of Jews and looting of their shops. Kossuth condemned the pogrom, but the Diet had no forces available to control the mob. Over Kossuth's lukewarm objections, the law was modified to withdraw suffrage from the Jews.[92]

On March 22, the Diet created a national guard to give it a military force. On March 23 seven major laws were passed. The same day Prime Minister Batthyány submitted his proposed cabinet list to the Lower House. Kossuth was appointed minister of finance. The imperial government would not accept him in a more critical position, while the Diet and people would have turned against Batthyány if Kossuth had not entered the government. Ironically, the emperor's advisors saw Batthyány as a radical puppet of Kossuth while the Pest radicals saw him as a conservative. Batthyány, one of Hungary's richest landowners, actually had views similar to those of Kossuth. All the other ministers save Kossuth were titled landowners.[95]

On March 28, the imperial government tried to reassert its power, stating in a royal reply that the emperor would retain control over all tax revenues and the army. The Diet erupted in outrage. Kossuth persuaded the deputies to reject this reply. Kossuth hinted at revolution, stating, "It seems that God will not grant us the joy and pleasure of realizing our transformation without our citizens having to shed their blood."[92] At the same time, Kossuth urged that negotiations with the Imperial Court be continued. The Buda-Pest Committee of Public Safety then held a mass meeting where Peton and others demanded the proclamation of an independent republic. March 29 saw a massive march on the Pest City Hall to demand arms for the populace and the setting up of barricades against any imperial counterattack. The next day the imperial government met with Hungarian leaders and, after an all-night debate, dropped almost all the restrictions on Hungarian self-government, finances and the military. The emperor would maintain a monopoly on the commissioning of military officers and use of Hungarian troops abroad. Kossuth accepted these terms. The amended royal reply was greeted in the Diet on March 31 with cheers and elation. The next day the Diet expanded suffrage to the middle class and professionals, while continuing to exclude the poor and Jews.[92] Kossuth supported the widening of the franchise. Historian Priscilla Richardson wrote that Kossuth "believed that this nation of noblemen could never be great until it was turned into a real democracy."[94]

Hungary now had its own government, responsible to a parliament meeting regularly, along with its own army, administration and judiciary. Kossuth proved to be a diligent and innovative finance minister. He persuaded Hungarians to accept new banknotes as currency, thus financing the Hungarian government and military. Serfdom, along with other feudal restrictions on the free flow of labor and goods, was abolished. The new government had to face several major challenges almost immediately. The spring was marked by widespread strikes by factory workers demanding better conditions. The government met enough of their demands, such as the limit of an eleven-hour day, to quiet the workers.

Now a series of further pogroms against the Jews broke out. Anti-Semitism was widespread in Hungary. The guild workers had been incited by their employers to view the Jews as unfair competitors. To the old prejudices was added the view of Jews as revolutionary radicals. A Hungarian-born Jewish doctor, Adolf Fischer, was one of the leaders of the Vienna revolt while Jewish journalists in Pest were among the foremost radicals.[92] The Hungarian government finally deployed troops, allowing it to suppress the riots.

The new Hungarian government also had to deal with unrest among the peasantry, confused over the meaning of the new reforms. A state of siege was proclaimed on June 21 as the government cracked down on rioters, and was eventually able to restore calm to the countryside, at least among the ethnically Hungarian peasants.[92]

The biggest problem facing the Hungarian government was that of national minorities. The administrative unit of Hungary under the Habsburg Empire included multiple non-Hungarian minorities who together made up 60% of the population.[91] These minorities were initially supportive of the liberal reforms. However, to different degrees they demanded their own autonomy within Hungary, including in some cases separate governments and armies. The Hungarian government attempted to satisfy these demands, but ultimately the Croats, Serbs and Romanians were to turn into opponents of the Hungarian state. These minorities were supported by the imperial government, who saw them as counterweights to Hungary.[93]

Kossuth tried to accommodate the minorities, opposing forced assimilation of minorities and favoring allowing them to use their own language in private life. Kossuth told a group of Serbs on April 8 that "the true meaning of freedom is that it recognizes the inhabitants of the fatherland only as a whole, and not as castes of privileged groups, and that it extends the blessings of collective liberty to all; without distinction of language or religion."[95] However, he added that the unity of the kingdom required the official language to be Hungarian.

The issue of allegiance was very confusing for many of the minorities within the empire. In June, the first open battle between the Hungarians and the minorities occurred, with the Serbians successfully fighting off Hungarian forces in the province of the Banat.[95] The Croatian assembly voted to secede from Hungary to join the Austrian part of the empire.

The Hungarian government also struggled to reach an accommodation with the imperial government, itself made up of different factions and viewpoints. The servicing of the state debt and the military command structure remained issues. The Hungarian government was also split on the issue of sending Hungarian troops to aid the imperial forces in their war with the Italians. Many Hungarians sympathized with the Italians.

Hungary elected its new House of Representatives, replacing the Diet, in June. The Conservative Party had disappeared and there were few deputies representing any of the national minorities in Hungary. Kossuth's influence was increased. Kossuth spoke to the House on July 11 asking that the Hungarian army be increased to 200,000 men and that taxes be raised to pay for it. The deputies rose to their feet to roar their approval even before he finished. Kossuth concluded in response, "You have risen to a man, and I prostate myself before the nation's greatness. If your energy in execution equals the patriotism with which you made this offer, I will make bold to say that even the gates of hell shall not prevail against Hungary."[92]

By the summer the revolts across Europe were dying down. The French revolt has been smashed in June. Disturbances in Prague and Berlin had been suppressed. In July, the Habsburg army in Italy inflicted an overwhelming defeat on Piedmont, which sued for peace. Meanwhile there was a reaction against the revolution in Vienna. Worker strikes were put down by the middle-class, moderate-conservative national guard. The revolutionary Committee of Security was forced to disband. The Imperial Court, which had earlier fled the city, returned to the city in triumph in August.[92]

As the imperial government regained control in other parts of the empire, it took a harder stance against the Hungarians. Batthyány, usually with Kossuth's backing, continued, unsuccessfully, to try to reach an accommodation with the imperial government. Batthyány was prevented from seeing the emperor.[94] On August 31, the imperial government, bolstered by the improving situation in Vienna and in Italy, accused the Hungarians of acting in bad faith and ordered Hungary to surrender her independent finances and army. Hungarian delegations traveled to Vienna, but could not reach an agreement.[92] An American diplomat assigned to Vienna during 1848–49, William Stiles, writing in 1852, noted, "The opposition of the Austrian cabinet to the late concessions, and which displayed itself only months after the concessions were made, resulted…not from any constitutional scruples…but from the altered condition of the empire, consequent upon the late triumphs of the imperial arms in Italy."[96]

On September 11, Jelačić, leader of the Croats, invaded Hungary with an army of 50,000 men, claiming that his goal was to restore the unity of the empire. Stiles wrote, "that the imperial family encouraged the insurrections against Hungary was generally believed."[96] The imperial government named Jelačić civil and military governor of Hungary. He ordered the Diet dissolved and imposed martial law.[94] The Croats alienated the local peasantry with their looting, but advanced against weak Hungarian resistance.[92] By September 15 they were forty miles from Budapest.

Kossuth dominated the government. Kossuth spoke in the House two to three times a day, while pushing into law a series of measure to build up the country's defenses. On September 21 Kossuth persuaded the Assembly to elect a committee, called the National Defense Committee, to assist the prime minister. Kossuth, one other liberal and six radicals made up the initial membership of the committee.[92] Batthyány, frustrated by his inability to reach agreement with the imperial government, resigned on October 1.

On September 29, the Croatians were defeated at Pákozd. They then withdrew to Austria. On October 7, another Croatian army was forced to surrender. Kossuth had spent much of the month traveling through central Hungary to help spur support for the Hungarian nation. Deák wrote, "For the first time, the peasants had laid eyes on their already legendary liberator. The magic of his oratory, his charm and sincerity roused the customarily dour and suspicious peasants of the Great Plain to paroxysms of enthusiasm that was to last a century."[92]

On October 3, the emperor, at the direction of his ministers, had announced the dissolution of the Hungarian National Assembly and the proclamation of martial law in Hungary. A few days later the National

Assembly, at Kossuth's urging, unanimously rejected the imperial decrees. Deák wrote that the liberal deputies "gave him [Kossuth] full authority because he alone could tame the radicals without resort to arms, and because he alone could mobilize the lower classes in defense of the country."[92] On October 8, the deputies voted to vest all executive authority in the National Defense Committee and elected Kossuth its president.[92]

The Hungarians expected an immediate attack by the Imperial Army. The attack was delayed by another revolt in Vienna on October 6, which drove the Imperial Army out of the city. The emperor and the court fled as well. The Austrian Diet, taking power in Vienna, said, "The Constitutional Diet declares that there reigns in Vienna neither anarchy nor brutal force. The Diet and the ministry are laboring to maintain legal order and the people are sustaining them."[96] The Diet invited the emperor to return to his palace, but the Imperial Court was determined to crush the revolt. The Hungarian army now advanced to support the Viennese rebels, but was reluctant to enter Austria uninvited. While the Austrian Diet hesitated to ask for Hungarian support, the Imperial Army under General Windisch-Graetz, stormed Vienna after a massive bombardment and recaptured the city. Stiles concluded, "Thus ends the last siege of Vienna...[conducted] by the civilized Austrians...against their own beautiful and justly admired capital."[96]

The conflict forced the officers and troops of the Habsburg army, made up of the multiple nationalities of the empire, to choose who to support. Of the 400,000-man army, about 50,000 chose to fight for Hungary. The Hungarians recruited tens of thousands of new recruits to the national guard, which by September numbered some 150,000 troops with arms or at least partial training. Kossuth also built an arms industry almost from nothing in Hungary while importing large numbers of arms from abroad.[92]

On November 1, Kossuth promoted Arthur Gorgey, a thirty-year-old former officer in the Imperial army, to command the Hungarian army facing the Austrians. Kossuth and Gorgey soon clashed over Kossuth's preference for a large citizen army versus Gorgey's preference for a small professional force.[92] Richardson write of Gorgey, "Contemptuousness was outstanding among his expressed feelings. He sneered openly or privately at Kossuth and the government of Hungary, at the common people, at the militias, at his own soldiers and even at himself."[94]

Kossuth attempted to negotiate an armistice with Austria through the offices of the American diplomat, William Stiles. Stiles was told that the Hungarians had to surrender unconditionally. He was to later write that the struggle was "a long continued and systematic effort on the part of Austria to subdue Hungary, break down the constitutional privileges and place her on a footing with the other provinces of the empire."[96]

In mid-December, the main Austrian army under Windisch-Graetz crossed the Hungarian border. The smaller Hungarian army retreated. On December 31 Kossuth, the Hungarian National Assembly and their families, the press for printing Hungarian money, and the arsenal and armaments industry left Budapest for the town of Debrecen, 140 miles to the east. When Kossuth arrived on January 7, the gatekeeper's log noted the arrival of "Kossuth, the Moses of the Hungarians."[92] The Austrians had meanwhile occupied Budapest. They arrested Batthyány, the former prime minister, and heavily fined the Jewish community, for the Jews had been notable for their service in the Hungarian army.[94]

By this time many of the prewar leaders were no longer involved in the government, leaving almost all decisions to Kossuth. Richardson wrote, "Only Kossuth could have kept the nation together at all during that winter for the Austrian armies kept advancing."[94] In the National Assembly, both the "Peace Party" that favored a compromise with Austria, and the radicals, who favored complete independence, tried to sway Kossuth to their side. Kossuth reviewed and replied to some thirty to forty lengthy documents a day, ran the government, and managed to keep an army of some 200,000 men supplied and in the field. Kossuth appointed some eighty-plus commissioners who reported to him. Some ran districts in Hungary while others were assigned to army units or went on special missions. The commissioners helped mobilize the population and supervise the army. The region of unoccupied Hungary had minimal industry. Kossuth had the arms factories reassembled and up to their prior production by February.[92] Kossuth lived plainly, allotting one hour a day to play with his children and the rest to work and seeing visitors of every rank.[94] Waxing poetic, the diplomat Stiles wrote, "The labors of Kossuth were Herculean; and assisted by the most gallant people of Europe no contest more worthy of the poet and the historian has ever been waged between the opposing spirits of freedom and tyranny."[96]

The Austrians, having taken Budapest and much of northern Hungary, were in a position in early January to take Debrecen, which was weakly defended. However, they did not advance further. Gorgey now defeated the northern Austrian army, which evacuated northeastern Hungary.[92]

Kossuth continued to have political problems with the army, whose officers rebelled against Kossuth's chosen commanders in chief in favor of Gorgey. Gorgey stated that the army would not obey Kossuth or the National Defense Committee. Richardson wrote, "His officers adored him [Gorgey]. By refusing to serve under anyone else they made him practically independent of the government."[94] At last, in March, Kossuth, willing to subordinate any differences to achieve victory, made Gorgey commander in chief of the Hungarian army. Gorgey now launched a series of attacks on the Austrians, defeating them in battles in April.[92]

The Austrian emperor Franz Joseph now proclaimed a new constitution, changing Hungary to one of the many imperial provinces rather than a sovereign kingdom. In the face of the new constitution and bolstered by the recent victories, the National Assembly, at Kossuth's urging, now proclaimed Hungary independent and the Habsburgs no longer its rulers. The Hungarian Declaration of Independence was modelled on the American one. Kossuth was chosen unanimously as the governor-president. He promised to serve only till victory was achieved, stating, "I swear to God Eternal, and by my honor, that after that moment, I shall become a modest and poor private citizen again."[92] Kossuth chose an energetic cabinet, including Gorgey as minister of war. The future government of Hungary was left open. Over the following months, Kossuth was to offer the crown several times to different foreign princes who rejected it.

On April 23, the Austrians, facing encirclement, withdrew from Budapest while leaving four battalions entrenched in a fortress on Castle Hill in the center of the city. By late April almost all of Hungary had been liberated. Gorgey then decided to attack the Austrians on Castle Hill rather than pursuing the main Austrian army. It took three crucial weeks to capture the fortress. By then the main Austrian army had been reinforced and was now commanded by General Haynu.[92]

Historian Deák wrote, "By May Kossuth had more confidence in Gorgey than the general had in him…winning the war with a disciplined army was more important for Kossuth than his memories of a rebellious Gorgey."[91] Gorgey, meanwhile, had been convinced that a large faction of the Assembly opposed dethronement of the Habsburgs and was hostile to Kossuth. Gorgey met with some of these deputies in late May and allegedly proposed a military coup. The deputies refused to agree, saying, "We want no rule of the sword."[92]

Far worse for Hungary, Russia had decided to intervene in the war on the Austrian side. Russia and Austria had been allied ever since the fall of Napoleon in 1815, working together to suppress any revolts or challenges to the established order. On May 1, Emperor Franz Joseph put in a plea to the tsar for armed assistance in "the holy struggle against anarchy."[92] Tsar Nicholas told his general that while he was reluctant to get entangled in Hungary, he saw in the "rascals in Hungary…the enemies of order and tranquility in the entire world…whom we must destroy for the sake of our own tranquility."[95]

Hungary unsuccessfully appealed for help from the other European countries. While the British public was sympathetic, the government was committed to the integrity and unity of the Habsburg Empire. Britain counselled the Ottoman Empire against intervening to help the Hungarians against the Ottomans' traditional enemies of Austria and Russia.

Even while the war continued, Kossuth persuaded the Assembly to continue reforms. On June 28, the Assembly passed a law granting widespread rights to all the national minorities. At the same time the Assembly passed a measure giving equal rights to the Jews. The Hungarian Jews had been staunch supporters of the revolution, enlisting in large numbers in the national guard and army.[92]

On June 17, the Russians entered northern Hungary while the rejuvenated Austrian army advanced from the west. The allies far outnumbered the Hungarian armies. The Russians advanced slowly, but almost unhindered. The Hungarians repeatedly battled the Austrians, but the battles ended either as Austrian victories or at best a draw. The Austrian army entered Buda on July 13 while across the Danube the Russians later occupied Pest. The Hungarian government, along with the treasury and weapons factories, had again fled the city, this time to the southeast. Sándor Peton was killed in battle on July 29. The Hungarian armies continued to suffer defeats. On August 9, Haynu decisively defeated the Hungarians at Temesvar, destroying an entire army.

Gorgey now had the only sizeable army left in Hungary. On August 11 Gorgey met with Kossuth in the fortress of Arad. Gorgey forced Kossuth to resign and appoint Gorgey as commander in chief and dictator of Hungary. The details of this astonishing turn of events were never made public. It is possible that Gorgey threatened to turn Kossuth over to the Austrians for execution or he could have threatened to surrender the army if Kossuth did not turn over power to him. The National Assembly met for the last time that day. The remaining deputies fled into exile or prepared to face imprisonment.

Two days later, Gorgey unconditionally surrendered his army to the Russians. Of all the Hungarian officers, only Gorgey received an amnesty from the Austrian emperor. The unanswered question is whether Gorgey received this pardon in exchange for surrendering the Hungarian army. The last Hungarian fortress, Komáron, surrendered in September.[92] Historians have attributed the Hungarian defeat to a combination of Austrian military superiority, particularly in logistics; the ethnic conflicts that drew off Hungarian forces to the south and east; and the Russian intervention.[95]

The Austrian commander, General Haynu wrote, "I shall make order here and I shall have hundreds shot with the best of conscience."[92] The Austrians executed thirteen Hungarian generals along with another hundred other Hungarians, including former Prime Minister Batthyány. Fifteen hundred more were sentenced to long imprisonment. Women were stripped and flogged for allegedly supporting the rebels.[96] Haynu announced that he would burn whole towns at the first sign of protest.[94,96]

Kossuth had crossed the border into the neutral Ottoman Empire on August 17. Kossuth and other prominent exiles were sentenced to death in absentia.[92] The Austrians and Russians pressed for the extradition of Kossuth, but the Ottomans, with British support, refused. An Austrian plot to kidnap Kossuth was foiled. Tired of the pressure for extradition, the Ottomans were delighted when the American government invited Kossuth to come to the United States. On September 18, 1851, Kossuth, his wife and a few aides boarded the US Navy frigate *Mississippi*. When the ship docked en route in France and Britain, Kossuth was hailed by the populace as a hero. Ordinary people saw him as a great leader who had stood up to Austrian tyranny.

When Kossuth arrived in America in December 1851 he was celebrated by the American people at countless meetings, dinners and parades. Richardson wrote, "Kossuth's gift for language was so great that he was later able to enthrall audiences in England and America with the English he had learned by reading Shakespeare in prison."[94] Kossuth addressed a congressional banquet on January 7, 1852, saying, "And where kings and Caesars never will be hailed for their power, might and wealth, there the persecuted chief of a down trodden nation is welcomed as your great Republic's guest, precisely because he is persecuted, helpless and poor."[92] Kossuth left for England, arriving in July 1852. Here he was again lionized. He supported himself giving speeches and writing.

Kossuth was to spend the next decades trying to win the support of the large European powers for Hungarian independence. In 1859, French Emperor Napoleon III formed an anti-Austrian alliance with the Italian kingdom of Sardinia-Piedmont. Kossuth met several times with the emperor, who promised Hungarian independence in exchange for his support. Kossuth joined a Hungarian government in exile in Genoa, Italy, and recruited a Hungarian force to fight the Austrians. However, after the French and Italians defeated the Austrian army in the summer of 1859, Napoleon III abandoned the Hungarians, agreeing to a separate peace with Austria. In 1866, the Prussian chancellor Bismarck talked to Kossuth as the Prussians prepared for war against Austria. Prussia allowed the formation of a legion of Hungarian troops in Prussia. Defeated, Austria surrendered to Prussia, but Hungarian independence was not included in the terms of capitulation.[92] To the other European powers, Hungary was not a priority.

Kossuth was idolized by many Hungarians, his portrait a fixture in many households. Kossuth was one of the few Hungarian exiles who remained abroad. He lived in Turin, Italy, writing and meeting official delegations and private visitors alike.

In 1879, the Habsburg Empire passed a law, nicknamed the "Lex Kossuth," requiring all Hungarian citizens living abroad to renew their citizenship every ten years, including an oath of loyalty. In 1890 Kossuth was deprived of this citizenship for refusing this oath. He was elected in absentia again and again to the Hungarian parliament. Dozens of Hungarian cities made him an honorary citizen. Kossuth refused to take an oath of allegiance to the Habsburgs and the emperor never forgave him. Kossuth died peacefully on March 20, 1894, at age 92. His body was brought back to Budapest for burial. The emperor forbid any official notice, resulting in violent street demonstrations in Hungary.[92]

Kossuth was unsuccessful in achieving Hungarian independence. Yet, many of the reforms he helped push through remained in place. Serfdom and feudalism remained abolished. His rise was marked by some of the first conflict between liberalism and nationalism, for the Hungarians' reformers were, in general, unwilling to recognize the rights of the country's minorities even as they fought for its independence. Hungary was not to achieve independence until after World War I, as a rump of its former size. Kossuth remains as one of Hungary's greatest heroes, remembered for what he did and what he tried to do.

Chapter 14: Elizabeth Cady Stanton
Fighter for Women's Rights, 1848 CE, United States

THE MID-NINETEENTH CENTURY in America was a time of great ferment and upheaval. Hard on the heels of the movement to abolish slavery was the fight for equality and freedom for women. One of its greatest champions was Elizabeth Cady Stanton.

Elizabeth Cady was born in 1815 in Johnstown, New York, to a prosperous family. Her father, Daniel Cady, was a successful lawyer, landowner, state legislator and judge. The Cadys were strict and devoted to family, tradition and the conservative Federalist Party. Elizabeth Cady was to comment on her upbringing that the church, family and school taught only that "everything we like to do is a sin, and…everything we dislike is commanded by God or someone on earth."[97] Elizabeth Cady told of spending her childhood trying to impress her learned father.

Elizabeth attended the Johnstown Academy. She was the only girl in the higher classes of mathematics and languages. Upon graduating at age 16, she entered the Troy Female Seminary, complaining about not being able to go to the same colleges as boys. Elizabeth graduated and returned home, where she enjoyed "the most pleasant years of my girlhood."[97]

In the fall of 1839, Elizabeth became engaged to Henry Brewster Stanton, a thirty-four-year-old anti-slavery lecturer. They were married May

1, 1840, sailing soon afterward to London. There they attended the World Anti-Slavery Convention, where the women delegates were not permitted to sit with the men. The women's exclusion, along with Elizabeth's conversations with many of the female abolitionists, led to Elizabeth feeling that "no question [was as] important as the emancipation of women from the dogmas of the past."[97] Elizabeth was greatly influenced by the abolitionist and women's rights advocate Lucretia Mott, who helped crystalize Elizabeth's thoughts about women's inequality. Two years later Elizabeth wrote to Mott, "The more I think of the present condition of women, the more I am oppressed with the reality of her degradation."[98]

At Judge Cady's urging, Henry studied and passed the bar. In 1847, the Stantons moved to Seneca Falls, New York, a town of some 4000, where they lived in a house bought by Judge Cady. The couple, who now had three young sons, were to have four more children in the next twelve years. Elizabeth met other women who advocated for women's rights. On June 9, 1848, Elizabeth and several other women met with Lucretia Mott, visiting from Philadelphia. Ignoring many supporters of women's rights who thought that ending slavery should take priority, the women decided to call a meeting "to discuss the social, civil and religious condition and rights of women."[97]

Some three hundred women and men, virtually all abolitionists and many of them Quakers, met in Seneca Falls. The women met alone on July 19, and were joined by the men the next day. At the end of the meeting, the delegates published a Declaration of Sentiments. It began, "We hold these truths to be self-evident that all men and women are created equal."[97] Historian Lori Ginzberg wrote, "Adopting the language of the Declaration of Independence was an inspired move. It made the document instantly recognizable and, because of that, repeatable."[97] The Declaration went on to assert that "the history of mankind is a history of repeated injuries and usurpations on the part of men toward women."[97]

At a time when suffrage was limited only to white male property owners, the document's ninth and most controversial resolution declared, "It is the duty of the women of the country to secure to themselves their sacred right to the elective franchise."[97] The language demanding women's suffrage noted that women should be given a right, "which is given to the most ignorant and degraded men—both natives and foreigners."[97]

The Declaration of Sentiments eloquently explained how American society defined women entirely as dependent members of families, rather than individuals.[97] Elizabeth Cady Stanton consistently fought for the notion that women should be judged as individuals rather than members of a class.

Elizabeth Cady Stanton began to write and give speeches in support of women's rights. Her first speech was at the Waterloo Quaker Meeting House in the fall of 1848. Stanton argued that women themselves must demand their rights, stating that "women alone can understand the height and the depth, the length and breadth of her own degradation and woe."[97] Stanton argued that "the only happy households we now see are those in which husband and wife share equally in counsel and government."[97] She wrote to the Ohio Women's Convention in 1850, "A married woman has no legal existence; she has no more absolute rights than a slave on a Southern plantation. She takes the name of her master, holds nothing, owns nothing, can bring no action in her own name."[99] Stanton combined her writing and speechmaking with running her household and raising her increasing number of children.

In May 1851, Elizabeth Stanton met Susan B. Anthony, a Quaker who was also an abolitionist and a temperance proponent, at an anti-slavery meeting in Seneca Falls. The two were to become very close friends and collaborators for the rest of the century. Ginzberg wrote, "Stanton was more intellectually courageous [and] had a remarkable fluency with writing…Anthony had a prodigious talent for organizational detail, strategic planning, and plain old hard work."[97] Anthony organized the Women's New York State Temperance Society, recruiting Elizabeth to write a lecture and serve as president. At the society's first convention on April 20, 1852, Elizabeth argued that women should be allowed to divorce drunkards, at a time was divorce was largely taboo, and should shift their support from missionary work in other countries to the "poor and suffering around us."[98] Stanton continued to stress the legal disability of women, telling the women's rights convention in Albany in 1854 that "We are persons, native, free-born citizens; property holders, tax payers; yet we are denied the exercise of our rights to the elective franchise."[97]

Elizabeth continued managing her household while campaigning for women's rights. She wrote, "While I am about the house, surrounded by my children, washing dishes, baking, sewing, I can think up many points, but I cannot search books."[97] Elizabeth's domestic responsibilities precluded her from going to many of the many women's rights gatherings in other locations. Susan B. Anthony frequently visited, and brought letters from Elizabeth to such meetings. Anthony, who was unmarried, was irked by Stanton's continued childbearing, writing, "Alas Mrs. Stanton...For a moment's pleasure to herself or her husband, she should thus increase the load of cares under which she already groans."[97]

Stanton emphasized the importance of suffrage, writing, "The grant to you [women] of that right will secure all others, and the granting of every other right, while this is denied, is a mockery."[99] Despite her words, Elizabeth campaigned to expand other rights for women. In February 1860 she addressed the New York legislature. In the wake of her address, the legislature expanded the Married Women's Property Act, giving women expanded rights to their property and wages, and over their children.

In 1860, Stanton shocked her audience at the Tenth National Women's Rights Convention in New York City by continuing to demand reform of the divorce laws. At the time marriage was considered a permanent arrangement with exceptions only for adultery, abandonment and cruelty.[99] Stanton stated, "Any covenant between human beings, that failed to produce or promote human happiness, could not be of any force or authority; and it would be only a right, but a duty to abolish it."[99] Stanton combined the issue of temperance with that of divorce, arguing, "Let no woman remain in the position of wife to the confirmed drunkard."[99]

In November 1860 Abraham Lincoln was elected president. The Civil War began in 1861 after the secession of the southern states. Both Stantons thought the war would result in the abolition of slavery in the United States. Elizabeth Cady Stanton declared, "The war is music in my ears."

In August 1861, Henry Stanton, now a prominent member of the governing Republican party, accepted the prominent position of deputy collector of the New York Custom House. The Stantons moved to New York City in 1862.

The enthusiasm of the abolitionists for the war was increased by the Emancipation Proclamation freeing many of the slaves. Elizabeth Stanton and Anthony proceeded to organize the Women's Loyal National League in May 1863 to support the government. The group passed Anthony's resolution that "There can never be a true peace in this Republic until the civil and political rights of all citizens of African descent and all women are practically established."[97] Stanton mentioned the plight of women slaves, noting, "Are not two millions of native-born American women, at this very hour, doomed to the foulest slavery that angels ever wept to witness?"[99] Stanton became president and Anthony secretary of the League. Anthony was to spend much of her time living with the Stantons. Elizabeth noted that she and Anthony tried to resolve their political differences in private, writing, "We have indulged freely in criticism of each other when alone, and hotly contested whenever we have differed. To the world we always seem to agree and uniformly reflect each other."[98] The League was to gather 300,000 signatures on a petition to Congress to abolish slavery.

Henry had gotten their eldest son Neil a clerkship in the Customs House. In the fall of 1863, Neil was implicated in a scandal. An inquiry found no evidence that Henry was involved. While his contacts prevented Neil's prosecution, Henry was forced to resign. His political career was over. He was to find work as a political reporter for different New York newspapers.

The passage of the Thirteenth Amendment ended slavery. However, the end of the war shortly afterward saw harsh and often violent mistreatment of the freed blacks in the South. Abolitionist Frederick Douglas and other leaders felt that "without the elective franchise, the Negro will still be practically a slave."[97] In 1865 only a handful of northern states permitted blacks to vote. The Republican Party was divided over the issue of black suffrage. Many abolitionists considered, as Henry Ward Beecher proclaimed, "The question of black men's and all women's rights are one and the same."[97] However, there was not enough support in the Congress to pass increased rights for both. In reaction to the abuse of the freed slaves, congressional Republicans proposed the Fourteenth Amendment, offering equality under the law to all male citizens, and the Fifteenth Amendment, allowing suffrage for all men regardless of race.

The exclusion of women from these amendments enraged Stanton. She argued, "Some tell us that this is not the time for women to make demands, that this is the negro's hour. No, my friends…this is the Nation's hour. This is the hour to settle what are rights of citizens of the Republic."[97] In 1866 Anthony and Stanton and others established the American Equal Rights Association (AERA) to campaign for women's suffrage. Stanton declared herself a candidate for Congress, the first women to do so, although she garnered few votes. In 1867 Stanton and Anthony unsuccessfully urged New York to give women the vote. They enraged the publisher Horace Greeley, who was pushing for black suffrage, but not that for women, by presenting a petition for women's suffrage signed by his wife. Meeting them later, Greeley told them that he had given orders to his newspaper that any mention of women's rights was to be taboo.[98]

Stanton now argued that suffrage, if not universal, should be based on "worth." She argued that women were more qualified that blacks to vote. Stanton contrasted the freed slaves, "incoming pauperism, ignorance and degradation with the wealth, education and refinement of the women of the Republic."[97] Asked if she was willing, "to have colored men enfranchised before the women, "she answered, "No, I would not trust him…degraded, oppressed himself, he would be more despotic with the governing power than even our Saxon rulers."[97] Stanton was blind to the effect her negative rhetoric would have on the reputation of the women's movement.

The news from the South continued to be of murders and lynchings of former slaves. Stanton's attacks were very hurtful to black abolitionists such as Frederick Douglas, a long-time friend. Douglas, who strongly supported women's suffrage and said, "I do not see how anyone can pretend that there is same urgency in giving the ballot to women as to the negro…when women, because they are women, are hunted down…when they are dragged from their houses and hung upon lamp posts…when they are in danger of having their homes burnt down over their heads, when their children are not allowed to enter schools, then they will have an urgency to obtain the ballot equal to our own."[97] Stanton instead saw the Fifteenth Amendment as a battle between the sexes in which all men had joined forces to keep women down. In May 1869, Stanton and Anthony left the AERA over its support for the Fifteenth Amendment.

In 1867, the Kansas legislature placed on the ballot two referenda, one for black suffrage and the other for women's suffrage. Angered by Republican leaders' focus on black suffrage, Elizabeth and Anthony joined forces with George Train, a racist Democratic merchant who opposed black, but supported women's suffrage. Many abolitionists were appalled that the two women would align with Train. The women replied that it was "the action of the Republican party that created a hostile feeling between women and colored people."[97] Stanton also said, "Women generally awoke to their duties to themselves…if the leaders in the Republican and abolition camps could deceive us, who could we trust?"[99] Both referenda were defeated.

In 1868 Elizabeth Stanton, with funding from Train, founded and edited a newspaper called *The Revolution*, which argued strongly for women's rights, but was disparaging to minorities and immigrants. One article warned against allowing "the Jews and Chinese" into the country, saying of the Jews that "as a race…they are a useless portion of society."[97] Train soon absconded to Europe. *The Revolution*, facing financial collapse, was sold in 1870, with Stanton and Anthony no longer having a role at the paper.

In 1869, shortly after leaving the AERA, Stanton and Anthony founded and led the National Woman Suffrage Association (NWSA). Another group of women, who supported the Fifteenth Amendment as a step forward, had formed the rival American Woman Suffrage Association. The Sixteenth Amendment, giving women the vote, had been introduced in Congress, but had gone nowhere. Stanton had pushed the NWSA to campaign for reform of the divorce laws. However, as the organization increasingly focused on the one issue of suffrage instead, Stanton began to distance herself from the NWSA.[99]

In 1869, Stanton signed up with the James Redpath Lyceum Bureau, which organized speaking engagements for her. Stanton found that people would pay to hear her speak. Stanton said, "So long as people will pay me $75 or $100 every night to speak on my own hook, there is no need of my talking in Conventions…I have done working for nothing."[97] Behind this lay in part Stanton's desire to maintain a comfortable lifestyle. Although the Stantons still had money inherited from Elizabeth's father, they had the expenses of several children in college and law school. Elizabeth spoke frequently across the country during the 1870s, making the modern equivalent of over $100,000 a year.[97]

The relationship between Henry and Elizabeth had become distant. When Elizabeth purchased a house in Tenafly, New Jersey, Henry rented rooms in New York, crossing over to New Jersey only on weekends. Henry died in 1887. Elizabeth claimed that their relations were like that of other couples married for fifty years, but admitted, "we should be nearer and dearer if he was as accepting as her of their differences."[97]

By the end of the 1870s, Stanton had gotten tired, despite the money and applause, of the lecturing and being on the road. Stanton and Anthony began writing a history of the women's movement. It would take them a decade to produce the massive three-volume *History of Women's Suffrage*.

Three more volumes would be added later. The history, the major primary source of materials on the nineteenth-century women's movement, has been criticized for ignoring the role of women who were political opponents.[97]

Stanton felt discouraged about the lack of progress toward suffrage, noting in 1886, "It is humiliating for a woman of my years to stand up before men twenty years younger, and ask them for the privilege of enjoying my rights as a citizen."[100] In 1890, the two women's suffrage organizations merged to form the National American Women's Suffrage Association (NAWSA). Although Stanton, on Anthony's insistence, was elected the first president, the organization was more conservative than Stanton, preferring to focus on suffrage alone while she urged trying to make progress on other aspects of women's lives.[99,100] Stanton wrote Anthony in 1899, "To my mind our Association cannot be too broad…it is therefore germane to our platform to discuss every invidious distinction of sex."[99]

Stanton had originally argued for suffrage as a universal right. After the failure of women to gain the vote in the 1860s, Elizabeth Stanton increasingly suggested that education could be a criterion for suffrage in place of gender or race. In 1868 she said, "Educated women first, ignorant men afterward."[97] Ten years later she supported a constitutional amendment to limit the vote to those who could read and write the English language. Stanton declared that an educational qualification "in no way conflicts with the popular theory that suffrage is a natural right [because it] does not abolish the suffrage for any class."[97] Over the next decade and a half, Stanton's arguments were challenged by other women's suffrage proponents, including her daughter Harriet Stanton Blatch. In 1894 Harriet wrote a letter to "my Honored Mother" attacking the doctrine of suffrage based on knowledge of English. Harriet wrote, "You go further and call every American citizen who was born in Europe and who cannot read or write the English language, an ignorant foreigner."[97] Replying, Elizabeth informed Harriet, "I am opposed to the admission of another man, either foreigner or native, to the polling booth, until women, the greatest factor in civilization, is first enfranchised."[97] Stanton stated, without citing any evidence, that "foreigners are opposed to the enfranchisement of women."[97] This attitude was to convince many immigrants that the movement for women's suffrage was primarily concerned with gaining rights for white, middle-class women.

While Susan B. Anthony focused intensely on the suffrage issue, Elizabeth's interests were broader. She would, "amuse myself shocking people with all manner of heresies, political, religious, social."[97] In 1892 Stanton spoke to the NAWSA convention, saying, "The point I wish plainly to bring before you…is the individuality of each human soul…the strongest reason why we ask for women a voice…[is] because, as an individual she must rely on herself."[97]

Stanton's views reflected her long hostility to organized religion. She felt that it was the biggest obstacle to women's rights, stating, "We can make no impression on men who accept the theological views of women as the author of sin."[100] Stanton had said of the Bible, "A book that makes [woman] the author of sin and a mere afterthought in creation and baptizes all this as the word of God cannot be said to be a great blessing to the sex."[97] Stanton also wrote, in 1886, that "Most of the women in our movement today care more about their religion, the salvation of their souls, than they do about enfranchisement. To concentrate their interest [and] enthusiasm on their own emancipation, their faith in the old theological superstitions must be unsettled."[100]

Stanton embarked on an ambitious project to reinterpret the biblical texts. Many women opposed her project, viewing it as an attack on their own faith and a diversion. The last two decades of the century were a time of increased religiosity, with exponential growth of the Protestant denominations and religious publishing.[100] Anthony argued, "You say women must be emancipated from their superstitions before enfranchisement will be of any benefit and I say just the reverse."[97] Stanton replied, "Let us remember that all reforms are interdependent…the object of the individual life is not to carry one fragmentary measure, but to utter the highest truth."[97] Stanton's cousin, Elizabeth Smith Miller, wrote to her that none of "your great reforms has been dependent on the Bible…the cause of women is rapidly advancing…[it] does not require the proposed work and would probably derive no benefit from it."[100]

The first volume of the *Women's Bible* was published in 1895 and the second in 1898. Stanton and her coauthors offered a harsh critique of biblical teaching and a reinterpretation of the Bible's treatment of women. The book presented biblical passages pertaining to women and then offered interpretative commentaries. Stanton herself wrote over 50% of the commentaries.[100] The book also implicitly indicated a preference for

Protestantism. Stanton admitted looking forward to when "robust Saxon sense has flung away Jewish superstition and Eastern prejudice."[97]

The *Women's Bible* evoked a strong negative reaction and not just from the conservative clergy. Many in the women's movement saw it as a threat that would draw condemnation upon the movement. The next winter, in January 1896, the NAWSA moved to censure Stanton, the organization's founding president. The Association voted to have "no official connection with the *Women's Bible* or any theological publication."[97] Stanton was further hurt that Anthony did not resign as president of the organization following the vote. Stanton wrote in a letter "to have a majority pass such a resolution was indeed humiliating."[100]

Stanton appeared to recover quickly, writing her son Theodore, "Whenever there is a lull in the sales of the *Women's Bible*, some convention denounces it…the bigots promote the sale every time."[97] Yet, there was long-term cost as Stanton was increasingly marginalized by the NAWSA and other suffrage organizations.[100] Harriet Stanton Blatch wrote that the younger suffrage leaders, in the wake of the *Women's Bible*, had proceeded, "to bury her [Elizabeth Stanton] alive."[100]

As the 1890s came near a close, Stanton's goal of women's suffrage seemed no closer. As late as 1887 the US Senate rejected an amendment for women's suffrage by a two-thirds majority. Stanton's vision declined, forcing her to dictate her writing. Her obesity limited her ability to walk. Stanton's weakness prevented her from attending the 50th anniversary of the Seneca Falls meeting. In 1891 Elizabeth published her autobiography, called *Eighty Years and More*. Stanton wrote in 1898, "I begin to feel discouraged…all my fifty years work seem to have borne little fruit."[100] She was bitter than the women's movement had not helped her publish a compendium of her writings, noting, "They have given Susan thousands of dollars, jewels, laces, silks and satins and me criticism for my radical ideas."[99] Stanton continued to write even as her health deteriorated further over the next four years.

On October 26, 1902, Elizabeth Cady Stanton died. She had dictated so many articles in her final days that the newspapers were still printing them for weeks afterward. At the time of her death women's suffrage had not been achieved. The Nineteenth Amendment, granting suffrage to women, would finally be passed in 1920.

Many women's rights advocates saw Susan B. Anthony as having been the main leader in the cause of women's rights. Ginzberg wrote, "Within a few years of her death, Stanton had been largely superseded by her friend in movement legend, her reputation damaged by the *Women's Bible* controversy and by her insistence on being remembered as an intellectual radical."[97] Nevertheless, the ideas of Stanton of the essential equality of men and women, often rejected during her lifetime, became more and more the reality of a changing world in the years that followed.

Chapter 15: Oliver Otis Howard
The Freedmen's Bureau, 1866 CE, United States

THE CIVIL WAR brought the abolition of slavery in the United States. After the war, against strident opposition from the defeated South, an attempt was made to bring the freed blacks into Southern society as equal citizens. Leading this fight was the Freedmen's Bureau, under a Union general named Oliver Otis Howard.

Oliver Howard was born in 1830 in the isolated farm hamlet of Leeds, Maine. He spent his summers working on the family farm and became friends with a black youth, Edward Johnson, who had been hired to work on the farm. Howard wrote that his friendship with Johnson, "relieved me from the feelings of prejudice which would have hindered me from doing the work for the freedmen."[101] During the school year Howard attended school in various parts of Maine.

Howard graduated from Bowdoin College, a liberal arts college in Maine, but was unsure what he should do for a living. His uncle, Congressman John Otis, secured for Howard admission to the United States Military Academy at West Point, giving him the opportunity for a career in the military. Howard graduated from West Point in June 1854 and was commissioned a lieutenant. Howard admitted to doubts about his career, noting, "If I believe from my heart a war to be unjust, I would have difficulty to ask the blessing of God to rest upon me in its prosecution. The army officer, even here in America, is not his own master."[101]

The election of Abraham Lincoln in 1860 caused the secession of the southern states into the Confederacy and the outbreak of the Civil War when the Confederates fired on Fort Sumter. At Lincoln's call, each state remaining in the Union formed volunteer regiments to put down the rebellion. Howard was appointed to command the Third Maine regiment.

By the time of the first major battle, Bull Run, Howard commanded a brigade. At the Battle of Fair Oaks April 31–May 1, 1862, Howard received a severe wound in his right arm, necessitating its amputation. Howard returned to the army in time to lead a brigade at the Battle of Antietam in September 1862 and a division at the Battle of Fredericksburg on December 11, 1862. Explaining Howard's rise in rank, historian John Carpenter wrote, "He was attentive to duty, strict in obedience to orders, thorough in their execution. He also had the happy trait of being able to get along well with others...He never was a member or a clique nor participated in intrigue...early in the war he acquired the reputation of being absolutely fearless under fire."[102]

Howard was promoted to take command of the 11th Corps, but his first battle as corps commander ended with disaster when the corps was routed by Confederate General Stonewall Jackson at the Battle of Chancellorsville. After a better performance at the Battle of Gettysburg, Howard and the 11th Corps were shipped west to become part of the army of Union General William Tecumseh Sherman that marched south to capture Atlanta.

After the battlefield death of Major General James McPherson in July 1864, Sherman promoted Howard to succeed McPherson. Historian Bruce Catton wrote, "McPherson's old job went to Oliver Otis Howard...who for some inexplicable reason was doing a much better job...than when he led troops in the more sedate Army of the Potomac; he never drank and never swore...He was never brilliant, but he was reliable and Sherman...had come to trust him."[103]

Two days after taking command, Howard found himself under attack by the Confederates under General John B. Hood at the Battle of Ezra Church. Howard's troops threw back the attacking Confederates, inflicting 5000 Confederate casualties for a loss of 600 Union troops. Three days later Howard again defeated the Confederates south of Atlanta at the Battle of Jonesboro. Carpenter wrote, "The principal reason that Howard became a successful commander in the last year and a half of the war is that he had learned."[102] Howard, commanding the Army of the Tennessee, remained part of Sherman's forces for the duration of the war. Howard noted that his army was accompanied by "throngs of escaping slaves, from the baby in arms to the old negro hobbling painfully along the line of march."[104]

Following the Emancipation Proclamation, President Lincoln created the Freemen's Inquiry Commission on March 16, 1863, to plan for the slaves' future after the war. The commission called for a federal agency to protect the ex-slaves and assist them in making a living. In March 1865 Congress created the Bureau of Refugees, Freedmen and Abandoned Lands, which became known at the Freedmen's Bureau, to assist the freed slaves and manage the lands confiscated from the Confederacy. For the first time, the federal government would be administering charity to the needy. Based on his successful record in the war, Secretary of War Edwin Stanton picked Howard to run the Freedmen's Bureau.

The Bureau was to distribute food, clothing and fuel to the freed slaves and destitute white refugees. Howard, as commissioner, was given jurisdiction over all lands in the South commandeered during the war. The law specifically directed that these lands be broken up into forty-acre plots to be leased to the freedmen for three years for a rent equal to 6% of land's prewar value.

Howard started on May 25, 1865. His ten assistant commissioners were all army officers, many of them his wartime friends. Howard considered sympathy with the freedmen's plight a prerequisite for service in the bureau. Before the war had ended, Howard had visited the Sea Islands off the South Carolina coast. Here, under General Rufus Saxton, land had been distributed to the freedmen and schools established. Many hoped that this would be a model for the whole program.

Prior to starting, Howard met with his commander, General Sherman. Sherman cautioned Howard against radical steps, writing that having the freedmen vote would bring on another war while even redistributing land to the freedmen would require large numbers of troops to maintain their possession of this land. Sherman, speaking of Howard's assignment, said that he had "not known whether to congratulate him or not…I cannot imagine that, what may involve the future of four million slaves, could be put in more charitable or more conscientious hands."[101]

Congress had not provided any money to pay bureau employees. As such, Howard had to rely on army officers, who received their usual army pay, as staff. Many of Howard's favorite assistant commissioners were men who had served under him in the Army of Tennessee. The assistant commissioners were given leeway in how they ran their states. Howard emphasized the importance of caring for both the freed slaves and the poor whites. Almost immediately those commissioners who were most sympathetic to the freedmen engendered complaints from the Southern whites.

Howard's greatest battle was to be against President Andrew Johnson, who had been vice president when Abraham Lincoln was assassinated. Johnson, the former pro-Union governor of Tennessee, was determined to win support among the whites of the South and cared little about the former slaves.

The freed slaves were being mistreated throughout the South, but nowhere worse than in Texas. Bureau Inspector General William Strong, wrote that the blacks "were frequently beaten and shot down like wild beasts, without provocation,...and maltreated in every possible way."[101] Bureau agent Samuel Sloan observed, "White Texans would not accept the fact that the blacks had to be paid for their labor and had rights under the law."[105]

To run the Freedmen's Bureau in Texas, Howard picked General Edward Gregory, who had a reputation as an abolitionist. Howard said that Gregory "was so fearless that I sent him to Texas."[101] Gregory moved cautiously, suggesting to the former slaves that they contract their labor to their former owners as the bureau had no land to give them. Nevertheless, former Texas president David Burnett complained to President Johnson that Gregory was "inspiring the freedmen to hate their former masters."[101] By January 1868 Johnson insisted that Gregory be replaced by someone more acceptable to the white Texans.

In Mississippi Assistant Commissioner Samuel Thomas campaigned to allow the freedmen to own farms, saying, "The freedmen will never be thoroughly emancipated until they are allowed to own lands."[101] The reconstituted Mississippi legislature passed laws prohibiting blacks from owning farmland. The white Mississippians complained about Thomas until President Johnson ordered him replaced. Howard was aware of Johnson's sympathy for the white Southerners rather than the freed slaves. Howard wrote, "The President...musters out all my officers...Measures are on foot...which are doubtless intended to utterly defeat reconstruction."[101]

This measure came on May 29, 1865, when President Johnson announced his Amnesty Proclamation, pardoning all Confederates except their top leaders and restoring to them any lands that had been confiscated. Howard appealed to the president that the removal of the confiscated lands from the jurisdiction of the Freedmen's Bureau removed the bureau's only source of funds. At the time the bureau only controlled some 800,000 acres of farmland, insufficient to provide farms to more than a handful of the four million freed slaves. On June 28 Howard sent out Circular 13 to the bureau staff, instructing them, "to set apart the lands for the freedmen by actually distributing the land to the Negroes in forty acre plots."[101] Howard added, "The pardon of the President will not be understood to extend to the surrender of abandoned or confiscated properties."[101] Howard wanted to confront Johnson with a completed action that the president could not undo.[101]

Howard then traveled to Maine to visit his family and friends, his first leave since his injury at Fair Oaks three years earlier. In his absence, his adjutant general, James Fullerton, worked to undo Howard's circular by advising the commissioners not to act hastily to implement it. President Johnson received a request from a pardoned Confederate landowner in Tennessee for the return of his land, which had been confiscated. Johnson ordered the bureau to return this land, adding, "The same action will be had in all similar cases."[101] Fullerton tried to ingratiate himself with the president by attacking those commissioners who were considered too sympathetic to the freed blacks. One of these was General Rufus Saxton, the commissioner in South Carolina, who protested the return of lands to the pardoned Confederates at the expense of the slaves. Saxton wrote to Howard, "On this soil have they [the freed slaves] and their ancestors passed 200 years of unremitting toil. Could a just government drive out all these loyal men who held firm and loyal in her cause in all her darkest days?"[101]

Howard returned to Washington. He appealed to President Johnson, suggesting that "all men of property to whom he was offering pardon should be conditioned to provide a small homestead…to each head of family of his former slaves."[101] Howard noted that "President Johnson was amused and gave no heed to this recommendation."[101] Howard wrote to Saxton, "I do not feel secure in the possession of either confiscated or abandoned property and hence wish to stimulate the purchase of land by freedmen and secure new titles from [the] owners just as far as possible."[101] Howard wrote his wife on September 13, 1865, "I have had more frequent interviews with the President and am quite apprehensive that the freedmen's rights will not be cared for as much as I could wish."[102] Howard was forced by Johnson to rescind Circular 13. Historian George Bentley wrote, "Johnson had prevented what had promised—or threatened—to be the most revolutionary feature of Reconstruction…If it had been applied it might have broken up the plantations and given the land to the freed slaves and poor Unionist whites."[106]

The president now sent Howard to tour the South. He was to meet with white Southerners to increase their support of the President. Howard could only plead with the local whites to be kind to the freed slaves. Howard went first to South Carolina, where he met with the blacks farming on the Sea Islands. Howard admitted that he could not ensure their continued possession of the land, but committed to fight for them. Howard wired

Secretary of War Stanton that he was "convinced that something must be done to give these people and others the prospects of homesteads."[101] Howard also urged that Saxton be retained as assistant commissioner despite the complaints of the white South Carolinians. Finally, under pressure from Johnson he removed Saxton in January 1866.

Howard ended his tour in New Orleans. There the assistant commissioner, Thomas Conway, had tried to protect the freed slaves from having to work for the former masters lest they face a charge of vagrancy. Conway complained to the mayor about a black jailed unfairly for vagrancy. Conway's actions brought complaints from white Louisianans to President Johnson, who passed on the complaints to the Freedmen's Bureau. Fullerton wrote to Howard on August 20, saying, "I fear Conway will bring us into trouble."[101] The final straw for Johnson was Conway's support of black suffrage. Conway was removed in September 1865. Fullerton took over as his temporary replacement. Fullerton began a massive restoration of lands to the planters and enforcement of the vagrancy laws to help President Johnson's preferred candidate win the state gubernatorial election. Howard, arriving in New Orleans the day before the election, could offer little concrete support to the freedmen. The New Orleans *Tribune*, the black newspaper of the city, noted that "people were thoroughly satisfied by the sincerity and good intentions of General Howard."[101]

Privately, Howard doubted whether President Johnson's program, later called the Presidential Reconstruction, was in the interest of the freedmen. He later wrote in his autobiography that "The freedmen were left outside of all proper citizenship. They had no voice directly or indirectly in the new governments over them, and soon, worse than that, vicious laws were passed that made their actual conditions deplorable. They were indeed, but for military protection, which still lingered in the South, worse off than under slavery."[101] By the fall of 1865 most of the former Confederate states had passed "Black Codes" placing restrictions on the freedom of blacks that were not imposed on whites. Carpenter wrote that Southern whites "were determined to retain as much control over the Negro population as was possible and inevitably they saw the Freedmen's Bureau as an obstacle in their path."[102] Bentley wrote, "Most white people in the ex-Confederate states were bitterly opposed to the Freedmen's Bureau...[they saw it as] the enemy's agent. It was a denial of state's rights and self-government."[106]

Returning to Washington, Howard, along with Stanton, went to the White House to try to persuade Johnson to protect the freedmen. Howard directed the new assistant commissioner in Louisiana, Absalom Baird, to discontinue the worst of Fullerton's anti-black policies. In his annual report about the bureau, Howard laid responsibility for his actions on "the Executive under whose express orders I was acting."[101] In his report, Howard also recommended that Congress be asked to purchase lands "with a view to the rental and subsequent sale to the Freedmen."[101] The bureau was aware that their agents often faced severe hostility from the Southern whites. A bureau report about one Virginia agent noted that he was, "violently assaulted on the streets of Lexington in one or two instances, annoyed and insulted on many occasions by gangs of rowdies gathering around his office after nightfall...the position of this officer, alone and unaided, has been anything, but...agreeable."[105]

Congress was scheduled to meet in December for the first time since the bureau had started. Howard wrote to Senator Henry Wilson, chair of the Senate's Committee on Military Affairs arguing that the bureau must be "continued at least a year longer for the settlement of questions of national importance."[101] Howard noted that he was "sorry for the policy [Johnson] adopted of restoring lands...without affixing conditions."[101]

When the Congress met, the governing Republicans acted to continue and enlarge the powers of the bureau. Many in Congress were outraged over the reports of the attacks on the freed blacks in the South, some of which were connected to the bureau's efforts to assist them. For example, a colonel stationed in North Carolina wrote, "An old church which was being prepared for a freedmen's school was burnt and some discharged negro soldiers cruelly beaten."[107] One of the factors that allowed for the spread of this violence was the rapidly diminishing numbers of Union soldiers stationed in the South from 1865 to 1866.[107]

Illinois Senator Lyman Trumbull introduced a bill, Senate 60, to extend the Freedmen's Bureau indefinitely with money to hire civilian staff. The bill also extended the mandate of the bureau to be able to help the freedmen in every state. Trumbull and Howard, who had both grown up on small farms, believed that owning land was essential for the freedmen to prosper. Trumbull stated, "a homestead is worth more to these people than almost anything else...if it were in our power to secure a homestead to every family that had been made free...we would do more for the colored race than by any other act we could do."[101] The third section of Senate 60, in Howard's words, would allow the government, "to purchase [the lands] and allot them for rental and subsequent purchase by Negroes."[101] It provided for the giving of three million acres of public lands to the freedmen and loyal refugees. Finally, Senate 60 would also transfer jurisdiction of civil rights cases from state to federal courts "until the state courts in the south were ready to grant equal rights to the Negroes."[101] Trumbull had discussed the bill with President Johnson, who originally raised no objections.[107] Senate 60 had sufficient support to be formally passed by both houses of Congress on February 13, 1866.

The bill was sent to President Johnson, who vetoed it. For Johnson, the biggest factor was the opposition of white Southerners to anything that would raise the status of the freedmen. In his veto message Johnson decried the bureau as unconstitutional, unaffordable, and a vast patronage scheme that would encourage blacks to live a "life of indolence."[108] Johnson had James Fullerton write a twenty-page letter attacking the agency he worked for. Fullerton argued that the freedmen would fare better under the authority of the restored state governments in the South than under the bureau. The governor of Kentucky supported Johnson, arguing, "we are not willing to take…a Freedmen's Bureau which places a Northern fanatic as overseer over white and black."[101] Southern editor James Debow summed up white Southern sentiment when he testified before Congress, "I think if the whole regulation of the negroes…were left to the people of the communities in which they live, it will be administered for the best interest of the negroes…I think there is a kindly feeling on the part of the planters toward the freedmen…The Freedmen's Bureau, or any other agency to interfere between the freedman and his former master, is only productive of mischief."[109] Republicans in Congress, unmoved by this argument, moved to override the veto. However, the override failed, securing thirty votes for override against eighteen votes against, thus failing to secure the two-thirds needed. Howard, as part of the administration, could say nothing about what he felt about Johnson's action.

Following the veto, Johnson sent Fullerton and a like-minded officer, General Steedman, to do an inspection tour of the South in hopes of discrediting the Freedmen's Bureau, thus justifying the veto. Their report was so negative that Howard wrote President Johnson, "I suspect the object of this inspection, as they understood it, was to bring the Freedmen's Bureau into contempt before the country."[102] Steedman admitted as such, writing to Johnson that they would be successful in disillusioning the Northern public about the Freedman's Bureau "by exposing the abuses and frauds and peculations of its officers, then by attacking the system."[106] In fact they could make very few specific accusations against bureau officers.[106] During their tour, blacks rallied to support the bureau. One speaker, among the eight hundred blacks who crowded into a Wilmington church to meet Steedman and Fullerton, stated, "If the Freedmen's Bureau was removed, a colored man would have better sense than to speak a word on behalf of the colored man's rights for fear of his life."[108] Black audiences also told them that if they had to choose one, the presence of the Freedmen's Bureau was more important to them in the South than that of the army.[108] By now Johnson wanted to get rid of Howard, whom he saw as "a thorough radical," but was afraid of arousing more opposition. In 1867 Johnson offered the job of bureau commissioner first to Frederick Douglas and then to John Langston, two leading black figures in the North. Johnson expected to wreck the bureau by driving out many officers who would not have served under a black. Both Douglas and Langston, recognizing this cynical maneuver, refused the appointment.[106]

To protect the freed slaves against the attacks of white Southerners, Congress passed Senate 61, the Civil Rights Bill of 1866. The bill declared, "that all persons born in the United States…are hereby declared to be citizens of the United States."[109] The bill authorized bureau agents, along with US attorneys and marshals, to institute proceedings against civil rights violators. Johnson vetoed the bill, but this time Congress successfully overrode Johnson's veto.

Congress also defied Johnson by passing a law extending the life of the bureau on July 16, 1866. The cost of passage of the revised bill was removal of the provision for giving public lands to the freedmen.[106]

Howard formally defended the bureau, writing to President Johnson in April 23, 1866, "Could the Freedmen's Bureau be now administered with your full and hearty cooperation it would fulfill the objects of its creation in a short time…if the Government would keep good faith with its new made citizens, some sort of United States agency must be maintained in the Southern states."[101]

The Bureau at its peak included some 900 agents, including a handful who were black, scattered through the South. The necessary reliance on army officers, due to the lack of any budget for other employees, led to frequent turnover in agents as the officers were transferred or left the service. There were too few agents to do all the tasks required of them. One lone agent in South Carolina found himself responsible for 40,000 freedmen.[108]

During this time, the bureau continued its efforts in many spheres. Following the end of the war and for several years many freedmen faced severe hunger. The bureau tried to provide food and clothes for the freed slaves as well as poor whites. Howard had persuaded Commissary General Amos Eaton to provide the bureau with food.[106] In the summer of 1865 the bureau supplied 150,000 people with daily food rations, one-third of whom were white refugees.[107,109] The assistant commissioner for North Carolina wrote on June 22, 1865, upon arriving in Raleigh that he found "Hundreds of white refugees and thousands of blacks were collected about this and other towns, occupying every hovel and shanty, living upon government rations, without employment and without comfort, many dying for want of proper food and medical supplies."[109] During its life, the bureau was to dispense some 21 million rations of food, clothing, medicine and fuel.[105] Southern newspapers complained that giving food to the blacks, "has induced idleness, if not vice."[106]

The bureau tried to take advantage of the Southern Homestead Act, passed on June 21, 1866, which authorized the bureau to give wild, undeveloped land to freedmen willing to settle on it. The law proved ineffective as the land was generally of inadequate quality for agriculture. Nor did the freedmen have the basic equipment for farming or the resource to survive until they could bring in their first crop. Only 4000 freedmen ended up creating farms through this program.[108]

The bureau also established schools and hospitals for the freedmen. The bureau treated some 450,000 patients at its hospitals over its tenure.[105] Although many of the schools were operated by Northern charitable organizations, the bureau played a key role in supervising the schools, renting buildings for classrooms, buying books and providing military protection for students and teachers.[109] By 1870 the bureau had helped maintain over 4300 schools enrolling 247,000 students.[105] Despite bureau efforts, few poor whites were willing to have their children educated with blacks. Whites comprised only 1300 of the students.[107] Howard tried, often unsuccessfully, to get local governments in the South to provide medical care and education to the freedmen, so that they would see the freedmen as part of the population for whom they were responsible.[108]

The teachers, more and more of whom were black, and the agents of the bureau were increasingly targets of violence. One Southern publication wrote that "besides teaching the freedman…his a,b,c's, these teachers from abroad put foolish notions in his head."[106] In Mississippi, Lieutenant J.B. Billings, a bureau agent, was murdered while out on a stroll. The next day a "committee" of white citizens visited his superior, warning him that "the teachers [of the freed slaves] must leave, and that if he himself did not leave he would be killed next."[107] One bureau teacher in Alabama reported that so many teachers were threatened that the schools had to close.[107] Burning of bureau schools was a frequent occurrence. Howard sympathized with these teachers, writing, "Despised, misrepresented, called mercenary, ostracized by persons of less culture than themselves, these teachers…[have] demonstrated by their success, the true nature of their mission."[107]

The bureau also created, through the purchase of land, the erection of building or outrights gifts, several colleges designed to be open to people of all races including the Hampton Institute, Atlanta University, Fisk University, Lincoln University and Howard University.[102] One key aim was to foster the develop of teacher training schools.

Howard helped found Howard University in the District of Columbia. Originally conceived of as a theological training school, it was expanded to include other subjects and graduate programs in law and medicine. The founders decided on the name over Howard's protests. The bureau helped pay for the land and for the construction of some of the buildings. Howard became president of the university in 1868 while remaining head of the Freedmen's Bureau, and remained as president for five years, expanding the physical plant and trying to maintain high academic standards.[102]

The bureau also tried to mediate labor agreements between the white landowners and the former slaves. Bentley wrote that Howard "frequently emphasized the idea that the Negroes must work. But he also stressed that the planters must pay them for their labor and treat them as a free people…the chief device of the Freedmen's Bureau for combatting this tendency toward reenslavement, or continued slavery, was the labor contract."[106] Historian Eric Foner wrote, "justice to the laborer formed the basis of a free labor economy—this was the unwelcome message the bureau brought to Southern planters."[108] Howard decided not to stipulate a minimum wage, arguing that conditions varied too much between localities. One bureau agent concluded that "the present contract system may be regarded as half successful and half failure—it has succeeded in making the Freedman work and in rendering labor secure and stable—but it has failed to secure to the Freedman his just dues or compensation for his labor."[106]

Howard and the bureau tried to make use of the Civil Rights Bill of 1866, which had declared that the freedmen "shall have same right, in every state…to make and enforce contracts, to sue…and to the full and equal benefit of all laws."[101] Howard ordered his assistant commissioners, "to adjudicate all difficulties arising between Negroes and whites in places where the civil courts were interrupted or where they do not admit Negro testimony."[106] Howard estimated that the bureau courts heard over 10,000 cases a year, most dealing with disputes over contracts and wages, but some over criminal matters.[106]

The Civil Rights Act had also set up bureau tribunals wherever conditions of "rebellion" existed. In December 1866, Assistant Commissioner General John Schoefield remanded to a military tribunal a white man, Dr. James Watson, acquitted by a white jury in the murder of a black. Howard supported this action, writing to Schoefield, "It is better to test the law now, and if it is not sound Congress will make it so."[101] President Johnson responded by issuing an executive order dismissing the tribunal and freeing Watson.

Bureau agents also tried to be available in the courts to serve as advocates for the freed slaves or at least watch for overt racial discrimination. Occasionally the bureau would hire lawyers to represent the freedmen, but it did not have the resources to do this regularly. Even the most conservative assistant commissioners, such as Davis Tillson in Georgia, were skeptical about these local courts. Tillson wrote that he had "no hope or belief whatsoever that justice would be done the freed people by the civil authorities."[106] Assistant Commissioner Thomas in Mississippi wrote that local court decisions, "with reference to the freedmen are a disgrace to any tribunal."[106]

The bureau's budget of $6.9 million dollars for the period July 1866–June 1867 was spent as follows: $4.7 million for relief supplies and hospital costs, $1.3 million to transport some 29,000 destitute freedmen to reunite them with their families and $.5 million for rental and repair of schools. A mere $326,000 was spent on administration and staff costs.[101] In 1867, new laws authorized the registration of blacks as voters. Bureau agents played a role registering blacks and poor whites as new voters. Southerners accused the bureau of favoring the Republican Party in this registration efforts.[106] The bureau also created and initially administered the Freedmen's Saving Bank. The ex-slaves were encouraged to put aside as much money as possible. The Bank grew to include some 34 branches.

The year 1866 was marked by two large outbreaks of racial violence against blacks. On May 1, black soldiers in Memphis helped free a black arrested by police. White Memphis residents, including many policemen, responded by rampaging in the black part of the city, stealing, raping, burning and killing. When the blacks protested, they were told, "tell the Freedmen's Bureau in the morning."[101] The next day hundreds of blacks came to the headquarters of the Freedmen's Bureau seeking protection. The white mob's cry was, "Now let's clean out that damned Freedmen's Bureau."[101] The riot was in finally put down on May 3 when the local Union Army commander sent troops into the city and declared martial law. The local newspaper, the *Memphis Avalanche*, concluded, "Thank Heaven the white race are once more rulers in Memphis."[101]

In July in Louisiana a coalition of white and blacks had succeeded in calling a convention to amend the state's constitution to give more rights to blacks. Outside the meeting in New Orleans on July 30 blacks demonstrating for the vote were interrupted by a crowd of white opponents. The white crowd and police attacked the meeting itself, killing the delegates as tried to flee. The official toll was 48 dead and 166 wounded.[101] Major General Phillip Sheridan, after reviewing the violence, concluded that the New Orleans violence "was no riot; it was an absolute massacre by the police."[107]

These and other attacks on blacks and liberal whites throughout the South persuaded Congress to pass, on March 2, 1867, the Military Reconstruction Act, dividing the rebel states into military districts until they ratified the Fourteenth Amendment giving blacks equal rights. The act greatly increased the power to the local military commanders. Increasingly these local commanders became the assistant commissioners for their states. Howard reported in 1867, "All officers and agents [of the Freedmen's Bureau] have been to some extent under the military supervision and control of these district commanders."[101] The support given the freedmen varied widely depending on the local army commander.

Ironically, as the military rule grew Congress declared the bureau unnecessary in states reorganized under military control. This action, on July 25, 1868, led to the shrinkage of the bureau. Historian Bentley wrote, "Some of the Bureau's early supporters felt that Military Reconstruction offered the Negroes sufficient protection and many of them assumed that federal aid would no longer be either necessary or proper in states reconstructed on the Congressional plan."[106] By the end of 1868 the bureau had dwindled to 159 men, responsible only for limited supervision of education and payment of veterans' claims. The bureau officially closed on June 30, 1872.

The Freedmen's Saving Bank continued, but its control was shifted to outside financiers, notably Henry Cooke, brother of the financier Jay Cooke. The economic crash of 1873, precipitated by the failure of Jay Cooke and company, resulted in the collapse of the Freedmen's Saving Bank in 1874. Some 60,000 depositors, mainly freed slaves, lost their savings.[101]

Howard continued to advocate for the freedmen outside his work in the bureau. Howard helped organize the purchase of some 375 acres in the District of Columbia, which was divided into one-acre farms that were sold to the freedmen to show that blacks could be successful farmers and landowners. Howard was also very involved in the formation of the First Congregational Church in Washington, where he successfully argued to allow black members.

In 1870 Howard was attacked by Democratic Congressman Fernando Wood, a Southern sympathizer, for alleged financial improprieties at the bureau. A committee, which was set up to investigate, cleared Howard of all charges.

In February 1872, as the bureau was being wound down, Howard was sent to Arizona to try reach a peaceful settlement with the Apache chief Cochise, a fierce foe of white settlers. Howard, accompanied by only a single aide, was guided into Cochise's territory. Impressed by his bravery, Cochise signed a treaty with Howard. Cochise and his followers could stay where they were in exchange for peace, an agreement that Cochise kept for the rest of his life. Carpenter wrote, "By a bold maneuver Howard accomplished in a few days what no one else had been able to do in thirteen years."[102] Howard acknowledged that the Indians had legitimate issues, later writing, "The Indian has a complaint against us because we can and do punish him, but do not and cannot punish white men who steal the Indian's property and take life."[110]

Howard would be again attacked for alleged financial improprieties in the bureau. A Special Army Court of Inquiry from March–May 1874 completely exonerated Howard, writing that Howard had "not violated any law of Congress, regulation of the Army or rule of morals."[102]

Howard took command of the Department of the Columbia in the Pacific Northwest in 1874. In 1877, the Nez Perce War broke out when the Indian Bureau tried to push the Nez Perce to live on designated reservations. Howard had urged the government to leave the Nez Perce where they were. He wrote later, "If I had the power and management entirely in my hands, I believe I could have…established peace and amity with Joseph's Indians…But this power I did not have."[110] In May 1877, Howard met with Chief Joseph, leader of those Nez Perce who had refused to move onto a reservation. Joseph had reportedly agreed to move to the reservation when some younger Nez Perce attacked and killed some white settlers. The Nez Perce fled, followed by the US Army.

Finally, after a circuitous trek of over 1500 miles, on October 5 Howard and his troops caught up with the Nez Perce just 40 miles shy of the Canadian border. Chief Joseph surrendered to Howard, saying, "Tell General Howard I know his heart…I am tired, my heart is sick and sad. From where the sun now stands I will fight no more forever."[102]

The rest of Howard's army career was spent in routine assignments before he retired at age 64 in 1892. He occasionally expressed unorthodox opinions, stating his opposition to the exclusion of Chinese immigrants and his support for women's suffrage. Howard also continued to argue, in opposition to the prevalent theory of the day, that blacks were the intellectual equals of whites and had as much capacity for learning.

After retirement, Howard lectured frequently and wrote, including his autobiography. He helped create the Lincoln Memorial University for the poor inhabitants of eastern Tennessee and served as its president. Howard was still active and alert at age 91 when he died, of what was probably a heart attack, on October 22, 1909. Howard wrote, "My glory, if I ever have any, consists in results achieved; and the results in the case of the Freedmen's Bureau, are, for me, more marked than those of war."[102]

The great black historian W.E.B. DuBois wrote, "The Freedmen's Bureau was the most extraordinary and far reaching institution of social uplift that America has ever attempted…the most fortunate thing that Lincoln gave the bureau was its head, Oliver Howard…He was sympathetic and human and tried with endless application and desperate sacrifice to do a hard, thankless duty."[105] The forces opposing the Freedmen's Bureau were very powerful. DuBois continued, "Nothing is more convenient than to heap on the Freedmen's Bureau all the evils of that evil day and damn it utterly for every mistake or blunder that was made."[105] The Freedmen's Bureau and Oliver Howard's goal of elevating the freed slaves to a position of at least legal equality with whites would not happen for almost another century. Nevertheless, the essential equality of the races has become an accepted tenet of the modern world, even as American blacks today continue to try to surmount the harsh legacy of slavery.

Chapter 16 Giuseppe Garibaldi
Soldier for Humanity, 1882 CE, Italy

GIUSEPPE GARIBALDI was one of the most celebrated figures of the 19th century. He was famous for his role in the unification of Italy. Yet in his battles against tyranny, he lost more often than he triumphed.[70,111–115]

Garibaldi was born in 1807 in the city of Nice, which at the time of his birth was part of France before later being transferred to the Italian Kingdom of Piedmont-Sardinia. Garibaldi always viewed himself as an Italian. His father was a fisherman. Garibaldi grew up fluent in both French and Italian, but with a limited formal education. Garibaldi later wrote, "There was nothing odd about my youth…my childhood went by with mixture of play, happiness and misery."[111] He did admit to "a propensity to a life of adventure."[111]

At age 16 Garibaldi went to sea as a cabin boy. He spent the next ten years as a merchant sailor in the Mediterranean, rising eventually to become a ship's captain. Historian Alfonso Scirocco wrote, "[Garibaldi] read a great deal during the hours of inactivity imposed by long sea voyages and during his moments of solitude. He studied various disciplines in such depth that when he happened on hard times, he was able to make a living teaching them."[111] He spent the years 1828–31 in Constantinople teaching Italian, French and mathematics as a tutor. A friend later wrote of Garibaldi, "He knew how to swim, ride, climb, shoot a rifle, fence with a saber, and if necessary use a knife, without anyone having taught him how to do it."[111]

In the 1830s, Italy was divided into multiple states, with much under the direct control of the pope and the Austrian Empire. In March 1833, Garibaldi's outlook was altered forever when his ship carried a group of French passengers, followers of Count Saint Simon, who taught that society should promote social justice and peace, leading to the unification of all peoples.[111] Garibaldi wrote of being struck by the idea "that a man who, by becoming cosmopolitan, adopts humanity as his country and, by offering his sword and his blood to every people that struggles against tyranny becomes something more than a soldier; he becomes a hero."[111] Garibaldi was to spend his life fighting for humanity against tyranny.

Following this voyage, at age 26, Garibaldi was introduced to Young Italy, a secret society aimed at creating a democratic, unified Italy. This was to be the second of the great ideals that guided Garibaldi's life. Giovan

Cuneo, who was to be one of his closest friends and first biographer, introduced Garibaldi to Young Italy.[112] Garibaldi wrote, "Columbus was not as happy at the discovery of America as I at finding a man actually engaged in the redemption of his country."[112]

Young Italy had been founded in 1831 by Giuseppe Mazzini, who viewed a unified Italy as a first step toward a European union of democratic nations. Prince Metternich, the power behind the throne in Austria, called Mazzini "the most dangerous man in Europe."[70] Mazzini argued that that only a war of an aroused populace could topple the powerful states dominating the Italian peninsula, writing, "Insurrection by means of guerrilla bands is the true method of warfare for all nations desirous of emancipating themselves from a foreign yoke."[70] Mazzini argued that even failed uprisings were useful because, "ideas rise quickly when nourished by the blood of martyrs."[95] Garibaldi whole heartedly embraced the cause of Italian unification, never forgetting it even when circumstances took him far away.

At age 27, Garibaldi was serving in the Royal Sardinian Navy when Mazzini asked him to incite a mutiny among the other sailors in Genoa. On February 11, 1834, Garibaldi went to the Piazza Sarzona, where the insurrectionists were supposed to meet. Garibaldi wrote, "I heard that the affair had failed, that arrests had been made and that the republicans had fled."[113] Friends helped him flee to France. The kingdom sentenced Garibaldi to death in absentia.[111]

Garibaldi initially lived in Marseilles, where he volunteered to treat those affected by a cholera epidemic. Finally, in the summer of 1833 he sailed as a boatswain on a ship to Rio de Janeiro. Economic circumstances had compelled many Italians to emigrate to Brazil, Argentina and Uruguay. Working a variety of jobs, Garibaldi also tried to organize a section of Young Italy in Rio.[115] Garibaldi wrote to Cuneo, "I am tired of being a merchant seaman. Be sure of one thing, we are destined for greater things."[111]

Garibaldi remained inspired by the notion of fighting for people's liberties against tyranny. When the Brazilian province of Rio Grande do Sol tried to become independent, Garibaldi joined the fight in 1837. He started out as a privateer, attacking enemy shipping. With his first ship, which he named the *Mazzini*, and a crew of twelve he captured two ships. However, later while battling a larger enemy ship, Garibaldi was wounded in the neck.

Escaping the larger pursuer, Garibaldi sailed to neutral Argentina, where his ship was confiscated. While recovering from his wound he learned Spanish and how to ride a horse. Trying unsuccessfully to escape Argentinian custody, he was recaptured, flogged and tortured. Finally, in February 1838 the Argentinians released him. Scirocco wrote of Garibaldi, "He had discovered an aptitude for command, coolness in the face of danger and an ability to put up with privation and sacrifice."[111]

Garibaldi returned to fight for Rio Grande do Sol. Although outnumbered he frequently found success against the Brazilian ships while capturing the city of Laguna from the sea. Garibaldi first commanded forces on land in 1839. However, he became disenchanted with the infighting within the province and left the war in April 1841. He was no longer convinced that he was fighting for the cause of liberty against tyranny.

Garibaldi soon found a more inspiring cause. In 1842 Garibaldi joined the forces of Uruguay, fighting for its liberal government against an Argentinian dictator and a deposed Uruguayan ruler. Garibaldi fought for Uruguay from 1842–48. He was often outnumbered, but would still attack at times despite this disadvantage. He was known for his humane treatment of prisoners, a rarity at the time, releasing them if he did not have a place to hold them rather than killing them. He also trained his soldiers not to mistreat civilians.[70] Garibaldi organized an Italian Legion from among fellow immigrants in Uruguay. This eight-hundred-man force was known for their guerrilla tactics and red shirts. Historian Max Boot described Garibaldi as, "Stocky, bearded and long haired, with a serene expression and eyes steadfast and piercing, wearing a red tunic, black felt hat, gaudy handkerchief around his collar, a cavalry sword dangling from his waist and a pair of pistols in a saddle holster."[70] His enemies, first the Brazilians and then the Argentinians scorned him as a pirate and bandit.

In 1839 Garibaldi had met Anita Maria Riberio da Silva, an 18-year-old Brazilian. On meeting her, Garibaldi immediately said, "Thou oughtest to be mine."[70] She was equally smitten with him. Garibaldi wrote, "I had discovered a hidden treasure, a treasure of incredible value to be sure…I embarked accompanied by Anita, who from now on never left me on my campaigns."[113] Garibaldi and Anita moved to Montevideo, capital of Uruguay, after the birth of their son Menotti so that Garibaldi could ensure the safety of his family. They lived in poverty as Garibaldi gave away most of his money.[112] Garibaldi wrote later, "What did I care that I owned no other clothes than those I had on my back? What did I care that I served a poor republic which could not pay? I had nothing, but a sabre and a carbine which I carried over my saddle. My treasure was my Anita, who was aflame no less than I for the holy cause of the people."[113]

The Argentinians marched on Montevideo, a city of some 42,000, and put it under siege. Garibaldi divided his time between the Italian Legion and rebuilding the Uruguayan fleet. Hi drove off the besieging Argentinian fleet on September 18, 1844. The Uruguayan commander now offered the legion a large area of land as a reward. Garibaldi replied that the legionnaires were "persuaded that it was the duty of every freeman to fight for liberty wherever tyranny raises its head…[they were not] desiring distinctions or rewards of any kind."[111] Following the defeat of this general, Garibaldi took over the task of defending the capital in April, 1845. The British historian G.M. Trevelyan wrote, "The Italian Legion saved Montevideo. They took the leading part in the battles close round the capital."[112] The siege of Montevideo was to last nine years. Garibaldi took the offensive with captured Argentinian ships, capturing several Argentinian towns. In his most famous battle of the campaign, the Battle of San Antonio, Garibaldi successfully fought off a force that outnumbered him six to one before successfully retreating.[115] However, by 1848 Garibaldi was discouraged by the factional strife that was raging in Uruguay, writing, "The disagreements encouraged by the selfishness and ambition of a few competing individuals have resulted in immense catastrophe…today it is a sluggish and pointless war."[111] Garibaldi was willing to fight for a people's freedom, but would not persevere so that individuals could gain selfish advantage.

Garibaldi's conduct earned him acclaim in Europe. Reporting to the British House of Lords in 1849, Lord Howden stated that Garibaldi was, "the only unselfish man among a crowd of individuals who sought their own personal aggrandizement."[111] Mazzini also had helped publicize Garibaldi's exploits.

In 1848 revolutions erupted across Europe against established kingdoms and empires. Uprisings had forced Austria to retreat from the cities of Milan and Venice. The people had also revolted against the despotic Kingdom of Naples and in the Papal States, forcing the rulers to agree to the establishment of legislatures.[95]

It was time to return home. Garibaldi returned to Nice in June, 1848, accompanied by sixty-three of his legionnaires. Garibaldi wrote, "We had fought gloriously to defend the oppressed in other countries, now we were hastening to take up arms for our beloved motherland."[70] In Nice, Garibaldi first met Mazzini. However, they quarreled over priorities. Mazzini argued for establishing a republic in Italy while Garibaldi thought the priority should be liberating Italy from Austrian domination.[111] At a rally in Genoa, Garibaldi said, "The great, and only, question at the moment is the expulsion of the foreigner and the war of independence."[115]

The Kingdom of Piedmont-Sardinia had declared war against Austria, hoping to take advantage of the revolts to seize territory in northern Italy and preempt the republicanism being urged in Milan and Venice. Piedmont rejected Garibaldi's offer of service. Garibaldi wrote of meeting King Charles Albert of Piedmont, noting, "I met him and saw the distrust with which he received me; the hesitancy and indecision of the man to whom Italy's destiny had been entrusted made me grieve. I would have obeyed the King's orders as readily as I would have done in a republic.[95]

Rebuffed by Piedmont, Garibaldi entered the fight on behalf of the revolutionary forces in Milan. He led 1500 volunteers to attack Austrian forces in Lombardy. He wrote that he had hoped to rouse "his fellow countrymen in a guerrilla war which…would lead to the liberation of Italy."[70] However, the Austrians effectively discouraged the local populace from joining the revolt, destroying utterly villages from which the inhabitants had been expelled. Garibaldi wrote, "For the first time I saw how little the national cause inspired the local inhabitants of the countryside."[95] Garibaldi added, "Almost every night we had to change positions in order to elude and deceive the enemy."[70] Meanwhile the Austrians decisively defeated the army of Piedmont, forcing the kingdom to sue for peace. After three weeks of battles, Garibaldi was forced to retreat into Switzerland to seek refuge, from where he rejoined his family in Nice. Garibaldi began to be troubled by arthritis that would worsen over the years. Recognizing his service, a constituency in Piedmont elected him to parliament while he also remained a member of the Uruguayan legislature.

The revolutions in Italy were not over. Most of central Italy was ruled directly by the pope. Papal rule was marked by discouragement of education and harsh treatment of suspected liberals. Trevelyan wrote, "The life, freedom and property of no one who was not a friend to the government had no real security in the Papal States."[112] The populace of the Papal States was dismayed at the pope's decision to not aid the other Italian states against

Austria. On November 15, 1848, the moderate prime minister, Count Pellegrino Rossi, was murdered. Crowds marched on the papal residences demanding a constitutional assembly and war against Austria. On November 24 Pope Pius fled to Naples, where the reactionary government had regained control. The pope excommunicated in advance anyone participating in the new Roman constituent assembly. Garibaldi was elected to this assembly. At the swearing-in ceremony, Garibaldi said, "Shall we waste time discussing formalities? I firmly believe that as the former system of government has come to an end, the most suitable form for Rome today would be the Republic."[115] On February 9, 1849, the assembly proclaimed the Roman Republic. Mazzini was selected as one of the three leaders of an emergency government. The republic abolished the Inquisition, censorship and the death penalty, but church property was largely protected.[95] The pope wrote in April, "The city of Rome, the principal seat of the church, has now become, alas, a forest of roaring beasts, overflowing with…apostates, or heretics or leaders of communism and socialism."[112]

Garibaldi had arrived on April 17, 1849, at the head of some 1300 volunteers to fight for the republic. Opposed to the Romans were the armies of the Catholic monarchies of Austria, Spain, Naples and France, who all sought to restore papal rule over Rome. Garibaldi, fighting against the pope and his foreign supporters, denounced the pope as the "Antichrist" and his supporters as, "the pestilent scum of humanity, the prop of every vice, despotism and corruption to be found on this earth."[70] An initial French assault on the city was defeated on April 30, when Garibaldi led a bayonet charge, attacking the French from behind. Trevelyan wrote, "Above the tide of shouting youths, drunk with their first hot drought of war, rose Garibaldi on his horse, majestic and calm."[112] Garibaldi, shot in the side, ignored the wound and had it treated privately that night. The French lost 500 killed or wounded and 365 prisoners.[112] Garibaldi followed this success by taking 2300 men to rout 10,000 Neapolitans at Velletri, south of Rome, on May 19. While sparing his captured enemies, Garibaldi enforced strict discipline on his own men, sometimes shooting those who plundered from the local population.[113]

After their initial defeat, the French had signed a truce with the Roman Republic. They now announced that they would resume hostilities on June 4. Treacherously, the French launched a surprise attack on June 3, capturing the key hill positions of the Villas Pamfili and Corsini overlooking Rome.[112]

Desperate counterattacks led by Garibaldi the next day were unsuccessful. The French, outnumbering the Roman forces two to one, bombarded the city from the captured heights. The French still could make only slow progress against desperate resistance. Trevelyan wrote that Garibaldi "constantly went the rounds, visiting the places where the fire was hottest, and restoring the enthusiasm of the defenders, now by a word of personal sympathy, now by standing like a statue above his prostate companions."[112] Garibaldi and the Romans slowly were forced back by superior numbers. On June 30 Garibaldi was summoned to the Constituent Assembly. Trevelyan wrote that Garibaldi "galloped up to the Capitol, dismounted, and entered the assembly as he was, his red shirt covered with dust and blood, his face still moist with the sweat of battle, his sword so bent that it stuck halfway out of the scabbard. The members deeply moved, rose to their feet and cheered."[112] Against Mazzini's advice, the assembly voted to surrender. Mazzini sailed into exile. Garibaldi had been wounded, but refused an offer from an American diplomat to evacuate him on an American warship, for he was determined to keep fighting.

Garibaldi decided to wage a guerrilla campaign in the surrounding countryside on behalf of the Roman Republic. Garibaldi called for volunteers, saying, "This is what I have to offer to those who wish to follow me: hunger, cold, the heat of the sun, no wages, no barracks, no ammunition, but continual skirmishes, forced marches and bayonet-fights. Those of you who love your country and love glory, follow me."[70] Four thousand volunteers marched out of Rome with Garibaldi at nightfall on July 2, 1849. Anna, pregnant with their fifth child, was among them despite Garibaldi's plea that she stay behind. Tens of thousands of enemy soldiers pursued them.

Garibaldi was disappointed that so few of the peasants joined him, while many of his troops deserted. Garibaldi cursed, "the timidity and effeminacy of my fellow Italians...who were incapable of keeping the field a month without their three meals a day."[70] Garibaldi constantly marched and countermarched in ways his enemies did not expect, evading their superior forces. On July 31, having reached the neutral Republic of Sam Marino, Garibaldi freed his remaining men from any obligation and acknowledged that "the Roman war for Italian independence" was over.[111,112]

Garibaldi, with a small cadre, now tried to reach Venice, still in revolt against the Austrians, by sailing up the Adriatic coast, but Austrian ships forced him ashore while capturing or scattering his companions. Garibaldi carried his feverish and ailing wife ashore, along with only one other companion. She could not recover. Anita died on August 4, just short of Ravenna. Garibaldi, weeping, had to be dragged away from her fallen body. The Austrians, desperate to capture him, proclaimed death to anyone who gave him or his followers, bread, water or shelter.[112] Garibaldi managed to escape capture, aided by many sympathizers, at last reaching Genoa in Piedmont. After a brief imprisonment, Piedmont sent him into exile. The papal government restored the Inquisition and the death penalty and forced the Jews, who had been given full rights under the republic, back into the ghetto.[95] Trevelyan concluded, "Although as a military operation, the retreat [from Rome] was foreordained to failure, it served as a mission of political propaganda in the highest sense of the word."[112]

In June 1850, Garibaldi sailed to the United States. He told the New York *Daily Tribune* in August that he hoped to become a, "citizen of this great Republic of Free Men, sail under its flag, follow a career that will allow me to earn my living, and await a more favorable occasion to free my country from its domestic and foreign oppressors."[111] Garibaldi remained in exile until 1856. He traveled widely, supporting himself and his family with jobs ranging from a candle maker to a ship's captain.

In 1856, Garibaldi used an inheritance from his brother to buy a portion of the tiny island of Caprera, near Sardinia. Here he built, with his own hands, a four-room stone cottage. Scirocco wrote, "He introduced fruit trees, cereals, vegetables and silage and kept horses, cattle, sheep and bees."[111] In 1866 Garibaldi began a relationship with his children's nanny, who bore him three children. He finally married her in 1880.[70]

Garibaldi had concluded that Italian independence would only result from the support of major countries. In 1854 Garibaldi told the Russian revolutionary Alexander Herzen, "I have been a republican all my life, but now it is not a question of having a republic…For the masses, for the Italian people, there is only one flag to which they will rally; that of unification and the expulsion of the foreigner. And how can you achieve thus if you antagonize the only strong Italian monarchy [Piedmont-Sardinia]."[111]

In 1858 Garibaldi was recruited by the prime minister of Piedmont, Count Camillio di Cavour, to join in a war between Piedmont and France on one side and Austria on the other. Garibaldi met the new king of Piedmont, Victor Emanuel on March 2, 1859. Garibaldi wrote in his memoirs, "From the moment I was convinced that Italy had to march with Victor Emanuel to free itself from foreign domination, I have believed it my duty to follow his orders at any cost, even if it meant quieting my republican conscience."[111] When war broke out in 1859 Garibaldi was commissioned a major general in the royal army of Piedmont, and waged a guerrilla campaign against the Austrians. He won a series of victories against the more numerous and better equipped Austrians. Scirocco wrote, "Austrian soldiers feared him and called him "the red devil" because of his unpredictable maneuvers and ability to escape numerically superior forces."[111] The war ended with the defeat of Austria, but France agreed to a peace with Austria that limited the Italian gains. Lombardy was ceded to Piedmont, but Garibaldi was dismayed to find out that Piedmont gave Nice and the surrounding region to France.

On April 4, 1860, a revolution broke out in Sicily, then part of the Bourbon Kingdom of Naples. Garibaldi wrote, "the Sicilian insurrection carries the destinies of our nation. In the end I will find myself in my element: action in the service of a noble idea."[111] Garibaldi sailed from Genoa with a force of 1089 volunteers, mainly from the cities of northern Italy, as well as his son Menotti. They became known as "the Thousand" or "the Redshirts." Garibaldi managed to avoid the Neapolitan navy and land at the Sicilian port of Marsala on May 11. Four days later Garibaldi ran into a force of 3000 Neapolitan troops. Outnumbered three to one and equipped with antiquated rifles, Garibaldi said, "Here we either create Italy or we die."[111] He ordered the Redshirts to fix bayonets and charge up the hill at the enemy. After desperate fighting, the Neapolitans fled. Garibaldi wrote that the battle "had an immeasurable moral result in encouraging the population and demoralizing the hostile army."[70]

Garibaldi now advanced on Palermo, a city of 160,000, with a garrison of some 20,000 troops. Although Garibaldi had picked up local recruits, he remained vastly outnumbered. He avoided battle with the numerically superior Bourbon troops. Garibaldi instead repeatedly feinted. He then sent his wounded and artillery marching away from the city. A strong Neapolitan force pursued them. Then Garibaldi and the rest of his army, some 2000 men, quietly slipped into Palermo at 2 AM on May 27, catching the garrison by surprise. The Neapolitans began bombarding the areas of town containing the Redshirts with artillery. This angered the populace, who joined Garibaldi. Garibaldi wrote, "Many joined us with daggers, knives, roasting spits and iron utensils of all kinds since they didn't have rifles. Every balcony and loggia was covered with mattresses for defense and heaped with stones and projectiles of every description."[70] Garibaldi personally led counterattacks to fight off the Neapolitan troops. The Bourbon commander finally agreed to a truce that allowed him to withdraw his troops from the city.

Europe was astonished at Garibaldi's success. Victor Hugo wrote, "He is a man, nothing more. But a man in all the sublime meaning of the term."[111] Friedrich Engels, writing as a correspondent for the New York *Daily Tribune*, wrote, "Garibaldi has masterfully demonstrated that he is a general capable not only of partisan warfare, but also of much more important operations."[111] Historian Jasper Ridley wrote, "Neither before nor after 1860 has any foreign leader aroused the enthusiasm of the British people as Garibaldi did during the Sicilian expedition."[115] The Neapolitan army still overwhelmingly outnumbered Garibaldi in the rest of Sicily. Receiving reinforcements of volunteers and arms from northern Italy, Garibaldi continued his campaign, defeating the rest of the Neapolitan troops in Sicily. Yet the Bourbon King of Naples still boasted of 80,000 troops and a large navy.

Avoiding this navy, on August 19, 1860, Garibaldi and his army crossed over to land unexpectedly at Calabria in the south of Italy. He seized the city of Regio in a night attack. Garibaldi, with some 3600 men, defeated the Neapolitan troops sent to meet him. Many of the Bourbon soldiers surrendered or deserted. Garibaldi told the captured men, "Soldiers, you as well as my companions are the sons of Italy; remember that. You are at liberty…whoever wishes may go home."[114]

On September 5, Francis II, the Bourbon king, abandoned the capital of Naples to concentrate his remaining forces in the north of his kingdom. Garibaldi now marched north toward Naples. Trevelyan wrote, "All along the road the people and the local authorities vied with each other in the frenzy of their enthusiasm…One Garibaldi legend, seriously told and believed a few years later was…[that] once when his army was in need of water, Garibaldi fired a cannon at a rock and water gushed out."[114] Fearing disorder, the mayor of Naples urged Garibaldi to hasten his arrival. Leaving the army to follow, Garibaldi with a handful of aides, entered Naples in triumph. Six thousand Neapolitan troops still in the capital took no action. Garibaldi addressed a huge crowd of citizens from the central balcony of the royal palace, thanking them "in the name of all Italians and all humanity."[111] Characteristically, Garibaldi chose a small room in the palace to stay in. Garibaldi was now ruler of Sicily and much of the Italian kingdom of Naples. Garibaldi put the 1848 constitution of Piedmont into place as the law, often commenting that he was ruling on behalf of Victor Emanuel.[111] As the effective ruler, Garibaldi was lobbied constantly by the Mazzini's supporters, who wanted a republic, and Cavour's supporters, who favored an immediate plebiscite and annexation by Piedmont.[115]

The Neapolitan army gathered for a counteroffensive north of the city. On October 1–2, Garibaldi, with a force of 30,000, defeated 50,000 Neapolitans at the Battle of the Volturno, effectively ending the war. Garibaldi had planned then to advance north to free Rome, hoping to crown Victor Emmanuel king of Italy on the Capitol in Rome.[114] However, the Piedmontese army forestalled that, seizing much of the Papal States, leaving the pope in control of Rome, and then advancing into the Kingdom of Naples to prevent Garibaldi from advancing northward. Meeting the Piedmontese King Victor Emanuel on October 26, Garibaldi said, "I hail the first King of Italy."[114]

Garibaldi then organized a plebiscite in which the people of Sicily and Naples agreed to accept union with Piedmont under the rule of King Victor Emmanuel II, forming the Kingdom of Italy. Garibaldi handed power over to the king and, disdaining rewards and power, retired to Caprera. An English naval officer who knew Garibaldi commented, "The irresistible spell which enables him to usurp all hearts may be traced to the simple fact that he is…a honest man."[70]

Garibaldi was very disappointed in the Kingdom of Italy's treatment of his volunteers. Scirocco wrote, "Garibaldi was alone in displaying his gratitude to the volunteers. Garibaldi's request to remain as the King's representative in southern Italy for a year was refused as was his request that his army not be disbanded."[111] Garibaldi confided to a naval officer on leaving for Caprera, "Men are treated like oranges; once all the juice has been squeezed out of them, the skin is thrown away." Scirocco noted, "of all the riches of the Kingdom of the Two Sicilies, he [Garibaldi] took with him…a few packets of coffee and sugar, a sack of pulses, a sack of seed and bale of dried cod."[111] Louis Kossuth, who admired Garibaldi, on hearing that

Garibaldi had returned to Caprera without any reward, commented that such an action was unprecedented in the history of mankind.[111]

Garibaldi lived with a son and daughter and a few other friends in Caprera. Ridley wrote of Garibaldi, "As soon as he had finished dictating his letters, he went out and worked in the orchards and fields…Garibaldi firmly believed in the virtues of labor, particularly of physical labor."[115]

In 1861 Garibaldi was offered a command in the Union army in the American Civil War. Garibaldi refused any position because America at this point had not agreed to the abolition of slavery.[111]

Garibaldi and Mazzini helped form the Italian Emancipation Association, which proposed that Rome should be the capital of Italy and "that armed citizens should be rallied to promote and ensure the country's unity and liberty."[111] Garibaldi was greeted by vast admiring crowds wherever he traveled. In Sicily, the crowds hailed him and shouted, "Rome or death."[111] Garibaldi began to plan an expedition to free Rome from papal rule despite opposition from the Italian government. In August 1862, Garibaldi sailed with 2000 volunteers from Sicily and landed in southern Italy. Troops from the Kingdom of Italy were sent to block his advance. When Garibaldi encountered them, he ordered his men not to open fire. The royal troops fired on Garibaldi and his men. Garibaldi was hit by bullets in the thigh and right ankle. His troops laid down their arms. Disabled by the ankle wound, Garibaldi was carried in a stretcher to prison. Doctors finally extracted the bullet in November 1862. Eventually Victor Emanuel declared amnesty, freeing Garibaldi to return to Caprera.

Garibaldi was unable even to get up on crutches until January 1863, and remained dependent on them for most of the year. Garibaldi later wrote of about the debilitating nature of the wound, saying, "Until '66 I led an inactive and useless life."[111] In December 1863, Garibaldi resigned from the Italian parliament, citing the transfer of Nice to the French and the martial law that had been imposed on Sicily to suppress disturbances.[111]

By 1866 the government of Italy needed Garibaldi again. Italy had joined with Prussia in a war against Austria. The government decided to form a Corps of Volunteers under Garibaldi, figuring that his popularity would help rally support. In place of the 15,000 expected, over 30,000 volunteers turned up. Garibaldi took his Corps of Volunteers, now numbering 38,000, wearing the red shirts, to the area of Trentino. Garibaldi defeated the Austrians in several battles, while suffering yet another wound.[111] Although the regular Italian army was defeated, the Prussian victories against Austria led to the cessation of Venice to Italy.

Garibaldi, once more an ordinary citizen, campaigned for candidates of democratic, left-wing groups on an anti-clerical platform. Garibaldi again agitated for action to liberate Rome from papal rule and reunite it with Italy. As enthusiasm for the idea grew in the country, the government arrested Garibaldi in September 1867 and exiled him to Caprera where Italian warships patrolled offshore to make sure that he would not leave. Garibaldi said, "The Romans have the right of slaves to revolt against their tyrants, the priests. The Italians have the duty to help them, and I hope they will do so, even if the government imprisons fifty Garibaldis."[115] Planning for the campaign went forward. Garibaldi, age 60, now escaped, singlehandedly rowing a small boat under the cover of fog to a neighboring island and then taking a fishing boat to the mainland. Garibaldi reached Florence to be greeted by a joyous crowd. Garibaldi now led a force of 4500 volunteers south toward Rome, where they were confronted by a superior force of French and papal troops. Although Garibaldi led a charge that scattered the papal troops, the superior firepower of the French troops, boosting the newest rifles, defeated the volunteers. Garibaldi withdrew north and disbanded his force. Garibaldi was again arrested and sent into exile on Caprera in November.

Garibaldi's health continued to worsen with his increasing arthritis. A visitor in December 1869 reported, "The old man's health is already broken and the doctors cannot assure him of a long stay among the living."[111]

In 1870 the French emperor, Louis Napoleon, was defeated and captured in a war between France and Prussia. Italy took advantage of his defeat to enter and capture Rome. France now declared itself a republic, but remained besieged by the Prussian army. Garibaldi volunteered to help, saying, "Whenever an oppressed people struggles against its oppressors, whenever an enslaved people combats for its liberty, my place is in their midst."[70] Garibaldi telegraphed the new republic, saying, "What remains of me is at your service. Give me instructions."[111]

Landing in Marseilles in October 1870, Garibaldi was given command of an irregular force, the Army of the Vosges, in eastern France. Garibaldi declined a request to serve as commander in chief of the radical Paris commune on the grounds of age and ill health.[115] Instead, Garibaldi conducted guerrilla war against the Prussians, tying down some 100,000 troops. Nevertheless, the war ended with French defeat and the surrender of Paris in January 1871.

After the war, Garibaldi was elected to the new French Republican Constituent Assembly by five different departments. Conservative delegates were extremely hostile, given Garibaldi's hostility to the papacy, and said that his election was invalid because he was not a French citizen. Scirocco wrote, "Victor Hugo replied that no king and no nation had come to France's aid: just one man was the exception: Garibaldi."[111] Garibaldi left France and returned to Caprera.

Like Mazzini, Garibaldi long argued for a peaceful and united Europe. After the final defeat of the Neapolitans in October 1860, Garibaldi had sent a memorandum to the European powers arguing for a single united Europe, saying, "There would be no more armies…the immense riches…squandered in the services of slaughter, would be redirected to the advantage of the people."[111] In 1867 Garibaldi joined with worker associations in Paris and Berlin which had voted resolutions condemning war, saying, "The time has come for nations to understand each other without recourse to war."[111] An International Congress for Peace and Freedom was held in Geneva in September 1867. Garibaldi, named honorary chairman, proposed that all disputes between nations be judged by a Congress of Nations and that the republic was the only worthy form of government.[111] Garibaldi also proposed that "The Papacy shall be declared to have ceased because it is the most harmful of sects…the priesthood of revelations and ignorance shall be replaced with the priesthood of science and intelligence."[111] Conservative Catholics in Europe were shocked by Garibaldi's attack on the papacy and redoubled their hostility to him.

Garibaldi continued to campaign for democracy and a republic. In 1879 Garibaldi, by now semi-paralyzed by arthritis, went to Rome for the last time to campaign for universal suffrage as "the main and fundamental reform."[111] He announced creation of a League of Democracy to fight for suffrage, social justice and freedom. Garibaldi was elected to the Italian parliament in 1874 and again in 1880. By 1880 King Victor Emanuel had died. Garibaldi now argued that Italy should become a republic, saying that while the monarchy had been a rallying point during Italian unification, afterward it had "trampled on the people's rights and reduced them to poverty."[111] Garibaldi resigned from the parliament when his son-in-law was arrested in Genoa after a republican demonstration.

Garibaldi spent most of his final decade on Caprera, facing declining health and marked immobility. Garibaldi turned to writing to provide more financial security for his wife Francesca, finishing his memoirs in 1871–72 and writing historical novels. Garibaldi died at his home on June 2, 1882. Italy announced two months of official mourning. Victor Hugo said, "It is not Italy that is mourning, nor is it France; it is all humanity."[111]

The British historian A.J.P. Taylor called him "the one wholly admirable figure in modern history."[70] Max Boot concluded, "He consistently displayed humanity and restraint in his war making and never sought power or riches for himself."[70] More than any other man, Garibaldi made a unified Italy a reality.

Yet, Garibaldi's battles for humanity often ended in defeat. It would take another sixty years after his death and two world wars before a democratic Italian republic would take its place among the nations of Europe.

Chapter 17: Eugene Debs
The Rights of Labor, 1894 CE, United States

AMONG THE PEOPLE who fought for justice at the end of the 19th century and the beginning of the 20th was Eugene Debs, leader of the Pullman Strike, founder of the Industrial Workers of the World, five-time Socialist candidate for president and Woodrow Wilson's most famous political prisoner.[116-127]

Eugene Victor Debs was born on November 5, 1855, in Terre Haute, Indiana, to parents who had emigrated from France following the collapse of the European revolts of 1848. Eugene grew up listening to his father reading to him the works of liberal European writers such as Hugo and Goethe. He was most inspired by Hugo's *Les Miserables*. The generosity of the book's main character, Jean Valjean, would be matched and exceeded by Eugene Debs during his life. Eugene spent much of his time helping in the family store. Bored, at age 14 Eugene Debs quit school, but he continued to try to read and educate himself though his life.

A friend of his father helped him get a job working for the railroad. On May 23, 1870, Debs began cleaning grease from freight engines, earning 50 cents a day. In December 1871, Debs was promoted to be a fireman, shoveling coal into the train engines. His wages topped 1 dollar a day.

In the fall of 1873, a depression struck the country. Debs was laid off. Since there were no open railroad jobs in Terre Haute, Debs traveled to St. Louis where he found a job as a locomotive fireman. In this larger city, Debs saw firsthand the poverty of the workers in a way that he had not seen at home. When a worker lost his job, it would mean that his family often would be expelled from their home and forced to live in a cardboard shanty.[116] Debs wrote to his parents, "It makes a person's heart ache to go along some of the main streets in the city and see men, women and children begging for something to eat."[121]

The railroads skimped on equipment and repairs to save money. When one of Eugene's friends was fatally injured in a railroad accident, Eugene heeded his mother's plea to return home. Debs later wrote, "As a locomotive fireman, I learned of the hardships of the rail in snow, sleet or hail, of the ceaseless danger that lurks along the iron highway, the uncertainty of employment, scant wages and altogether trying lot of the working man, so that from my very boyhood I was made to feel the wrongs of labor."[116] The Interstate Commerce Commission records of 1880 showed that one out of every 115 railroad workers were killed and one out of ten injured in that year.[124]

In Terre Haute Debs took a job as a billing clerk for a wholesale grocer, but did not like the work. Debs wrote, "There are too many things in business that I cannot tolerate. Business means grabbing for yourself."[116] One evening in 1874, Debs went to hear Joshua Leach, the Grand Master of the Brotherhood of Locomotive Firemen (BLF), who had come to Terre Haute to speak. Debs wrote, "Old Josh Leach, a typical locomotive fireman of his day, founded the brotherhood and I was instantly attracted by his rugged honesty, simple manner and homely speech."[124] Afterwards, Debs persuaded Leach to let him join the local chapter or lodge, where he soon rose to become secretary and eventually master of the lodge.

Debs spoke at the Occidental Literary Club in August 1878, championing the poor and the Democratic Party. Debs attracted the notice of party leaders, and the next year he was elected on the Democratic ticket as city clerk in Terre Haute, where he served two terms.

In the evenings, Debs worked on his duties for the BLF. Membership had declined as hard times made many firemen doubt the benefits of membership. In 1878 Debs was named assistant editor of the *Brotherhood* magazine, becoming editor as well as secretary-treasurer of the BLF in 1880.[116] The BLF was saddled with debt. Debs first worked to pay off these debts, paying off much of it from his own pocket. Yet, doubting the benefits of the Brotherhood, when the BLF national convention met in September 1880, many of the delegates were ready to dissolve the union. Debs persuaded them to give it another year.

Over the next year, the BLF membership began to grow even as the railroads plotted to destroy the union, discharging workers on the mere suspicion of union membership.[116] When a BLF official told Debs that he had been thrown out of the office of a vice president of the Pennsylvania Railroad, Debs went and confronted the railroad official. The story of how Debs had stood up to the vice president was repeated frequently among railroad workers. Debs was often on the road setting up new lodges. He depended on rides from friendly train crews, sleeping on the floors of the caboose. By 1881 the BLF membership had doubled and by 1882 it had doubled again to 5000. The Brotherhood still argued against strikes in favor of arbitration for labor-management disputes.

In 1881, the Federated Trades and Labor Council, soon to become the American Federation of Labor (AFL), was founded in Pittsburgh. The principal leader was Samuel Gompers, leader of the cigar makers union. Ironically, Debs saw the AFL as too radical, saying, "Some have gone so far as to say there is a natural, a necessary conflict between labor and capital. These are very shallow thinkers."[116] Gompers defended strikes to increase the wages for workers, but eschewed union involvement in politics. Debs, in contrast, felt that politics offered a key route for workers to secure justice. In 1884 Debs urged workers to elect candidates to repeal those laws that "permit money capital…to extract dividends from labor capital and leave it to starve in sight of the wealth it creates."[121]

In 1884 Debs was elected as a Democrat to the Indiana House of Representatives. Debs managed to get the House to pass a bill forcing the railroads to compensate their employees for on-the-job injuries, but the bill was gutted in the state Senate. Debs was also on the losing side on his votes to abolish all distinctions of race in the laws of Indiana and to extend suffrage to women. Disillusioned by his inability to implement reform, Debs decided not to run for reelection.[116] Debs later wrote, "There was a time in my life, before I became a Socialist, when I permitted myself as a Democrat to be elected to the state legislature. I have been trying to live it down. I am as much ashamed of that as I am proud of having gone to jail."[124] Debs took time in June 1885 to marry Kate Metzel, a friend of his older sister Marie.

In 1885, the delegates to the BLF convention eliminated the no-strike policy of the BLF, and removed the more conservative leadership. Debs, popular among all factions, kept his post. Debs now tried to persuade the Brotherhood of Locomotive Engineers to work together nationally with the BLF, but the leadership of the engineers refused. Nevertheless, on a local level the engineers and fireman worked together to win two disputes with railroads. Debs wrote in the BLF magazine, "The incident supplies abundant proof that the two great Brotherhoods are necessary to each other."[116]

In February 1888, the engineers and firemen, after months of fruitless negotiations, called a joint walkout against the Chicago, Burlington and Quincy Railroad. Debs had abandoned his earlier opposition to strikes, writing, "The strike is the weapon of the oppressed, of men capable of appreciating justice and having the courage to resist wrong and contend for principle."[116] Debs persuaded the switchmen to join the strike. The walkout continued through the spring, costing the company millions of dollars. Debs worked tirelessly to raise money for the strikers and their families, borrowing money for the strike fund on his personal guarantee. Finally, the company decided to go to court to ask for an injunction against the strike. This was a frequent tactic of the day, for the courts usually agreed with the railroads' contention that unions were an illegal restraint of trade. The chief of the Brotherhood of Engineers, P.M. Arthur, advised that an injunction might make the strike leaders liable for jail if they continued the strike, ordered the engineers back to work. Arthur told the joint strike committee, "I want to say here that I would not go to jail for 24 hours for your whole Brotherhood."[116] The strike failed.

The failure of the strike helped persuade Debs that the railroad employees needed to work together to win the battle. Debs wrote and lobbied among the other brotherhoods to win their support. In 1889 the Brotherhoods of Firemen, Brakemen and Switchmen, later joined by the Brotherhood of Conductors, joined to create the Supreme Council of the United Orders of Railway Employees. They agreed that a strike must include all the workers of a railroad rather than a single craft. Historian Ray Ginger wrote, "The Supreme Council won every battle during its first year and it did not order a single strike."[116] Debs seemed triumphant, having taken an organization of 2000 members up to 20,000. Subscriptions to the BLF magazine that he edited had gone up ten-fold. Suddenly, despite this success, a bitter factional battle erupted between two of the member brotherhoods. Since they would not agree to compromise, the Supreme Council dissolved in June 1892.

The year 1892 was marked by two epic labor conflicts. At the Carnegie Steel Homestead plant, Carnegie's lieutenant Henry Frick locked out the workers to try to smash their union. He hired 300 Pinkerton private security guards who fought a pitched battle with striking workers. The strike was finally put down by 8000 state troops. A strike by silver miners in Idaho was put down by federal troops. At the end of the year, Debs wrote, "If the year 1892 has taught the workingmen any lesson of heed, it was that the capitalist class, like a devilfish, has grasped them with their tentacles and was dragging them down to fathomless depths of degradation."[116]

The members of the BLF appreciated Debs's brilliance as a leader as well as his willingness to sacrifice his own comforts to serve the union. Debs answered their accolades by saying, "When I see suffering around me, I myself suffer, and so when I put forth my efforts to relieve others, I am simply working for myself."[122] Yet, Debs decided to resign as secretary-treasurer of the BLF, telling the members, "A life purpose of mine has been the federation of railroad employees...I don't believe it can be done on the present lines [of railroad workers divided by their craft]."[116] He wrote in the BLF magazine, "the old year bears away in its archives the switchmen's strike at Buffalo, where organized labor was struck down because organized labor was deaf to the appeals of organized labor for help."[116] Debs resigned from the leadership of the BLF. Historian Nick Salvatore wrote that Debs "intended to create an organization that would replace the brotherhoods, abolish craft distinctions and unify all railroad workers."[121]

The year 1893 was marked by another severe economic downturn. The railroads responded by cutting the wages of their employees. On June 20, 1893, fifty railroad workers, including Debs, from various crafts met in Chicago. That evening Debs announced the formation of the American Railroad Union (ARU), open to any white railroad worker. Debs was forced to accept the other members' insistence of banning blacks from membership, but became a fervent opponent of racism. Debs was chosen as president of the ARU. In January, 1892 Debs had said, "If organized labor has any mission in this world, it is to help those who cannot help themselves."[121] Debs also commented, "If all employers had always treated their employees fairly, there would never have been a single labor union in the world."[124]

The railroad craft brotherhoods, threatened by the popularity of the new union, were united in their opposition. However, there was a stampede of railroad workers into the ARU. Those previously unorganized or who were unable to afford the high dues of the brotherhoods joined at a rate of two to four hundred new members a day. Within two months, 87 lodges had formed. Debs worked tirelessly for the new union. Debs's friend, the poet James Riley, said in 1893, "God was feelin' mighty good when he made Gene Debs."[116]

The first strike for the new union was on the Great Northern Railroad following multiple pay cuts. The owner of the Great Northern, James J. Hill, ordered anyone known to be sympathetic to the union to be fired. Yet when the strike started the 9000 workers of the Great Northern to a man stopped working. The railroad brotherhoods either condemned the strike or were neutral. It didn't matter. All the Great Northern trains were stopped except those trains carrying the US mail, which Debs ordered should keep running.

After trying several unsuccessful tactics, Hill met with Debs, who told him, "All the men are united in this action. It will be to no avail to attempt to divide us into factions. If wages are not restored, you can not have the services of the men."[121] Finally, Hill arranged for Debs to address the St. Paul Chamber of Commerce, feeling that the business community would react with opposition to the ARU.[116] Walking into a hostile audience, Debs talked about the lives of the railroad workers. When Debs finished, the chamber surprised Hill by urging that the dispute be submitted to arbitration.

Eighteen days later the arbitration panel found for the workers, giving them almost all their demands. Debs later wrote, "The Great Northern strike was the only clear cut victory of any consequence ever won by a railway union in America."[116] Debs also said, "One of the remarkable features of this victory is that the great ideal of arbitration has been firmly established in America. Arbitration means mutual concessions; it means peaceful adjustment of all difficulties between the employee and employers."[124] Four thousand neighbors hailed Debs on his return to Terre Haute, where he told them, "I hope to see the time when there will be mutual justice between employers and employees."[121] James Hill later wrote, "Gene Debs is the squarest labor leader I have ever known. He cannot be bought, bribed or intimidated…his spoken word is as good as his bond or signed contract."[124] By 1894 the ARU membership had reached 150,000 compared to a combined total of 90,000 in all the railway brotherhoods and 175,000 in whole American Federation of Labor.

1894 was to be the year of the great Pullman strike. The Pullman Company, which made the sleeping cars for all the trains in the country, was the only employer and the only landlord in the company town of Pullman, Illinois. The town of Pullman was designed to represent the workplace hierarchy, with free-standing houses for the executives, row houses for skilled and senior workers, and tenements and rooming houses for the unskilled workers.[123] George Pullman, owner of the company, barred unions from his factory. With the onset of an economic depression in 1893, Pullman cut employees' wages by 20–80% while keeping rents in Pullman unchanged. Consequently, many Pullman employees joined the ARU in early 1894. On May 10, a committee of Pullman employees tried to talk to management about the situation, but they were put off. After a second meeting, three members of the committee were fired. With that, the Pullman workers voted to strike. On May 11, 1894, 3000 Pullman workers left their jobs. Pullman asserted, "The condition of the men was better than that of any body of workingmen in this or any country."[123]

The strike was initially peaceful. Debs hurried to Pullman to investigate the situation. After talking to hundreds of employees and their families, Debs told a meeting of Pullman workers, "The paternalism of Pullman is the same as the self-interest of a slave holder in his human chattels. You are striking to avert slavery and degradation."[116] Nevertheless, Debs looked for ways to reach a settlement. Debs told the workers on May 14, "As a general thing, I am against a strike, but when the only alternative to a strike is the sacrifice of rights, then I prefer to strike."[123] The mayor and city council of Chicago along with the Civic Federation, a group of high-ranking businessmen, recommended arbitration, but Pullman refused to consider compromise.[123]

Shortly thereafter, the ARU, now including 465 locals, held its first national convention in nearby Chicago on June 12. Debs told the convention, "The forces of labor must unite…then labor's hosts, marshalled under one conquering banner, shall march together, vote together and fight together until working men shall receive and enjoy all the fruit of their toil."[116] Debs appointed a committee to meet with the Pullman Company, hoping to settle the dispute peacefully through arbitration. The company refused to negotiate with either this committee or another made up solely of Pullman employees, arguing that wages and conditions were solely an issue for management to decide. The ARU convention voted to boycott all Pullman cars effective July 26. Debs was skeptical about the chance for victory, but he followed the delegates' decision.[116]

On June 26, the ARU ordered the railway workers to remove all the Pullman sleeping cars from trains. At this point, the railroads joined in on the side of Pullman, leading the workers to go on strike. The Chicago-based General Managers Association, representing twenty-four railroads with capital of over $800 million, looked forward to the opportunity of breaking the union. The railroad brotherhoods refused to cooperate with the ARU.

Nevertheless, by June 28, 130,000 railroad workers had left their jobs. The railroads were largely shut down across the West and Midwest due to the lack of workers. The railroads were losing millions of dollars. Debs was careful to urge that the strikers avoid violence and avoid stopping any trains. The railroads began to recruit strikebreakers, promising them permanent jobs in place of the strikers. The US district attorney in Chicago, Thomas

Milchrist, hired special deputies to protect the companies' property. The railroads wrote false reports of damage done to trains and interference with the trains carrying the mail. Historian David Papke wrote, "The railroads intentionally disrupted their own schedules to irritate the public at the union's expense. The railroads attached Pullman [sleeping] cars to freight trains, suburban carriers and—most important—mail trains."[123] The railroads blamed the disruption on the union.[121]

Newspapers sympathetic to the railroads, led by the Chicago *Tribune*, claimed that Chicago was ruled by mobs. The *Tribune* reported, "Through the lawless acts of Dictator Debs' strikers the lives of thousands of Chicago citizens were endangered yesterday."[116]

The railroads persuaded Attorney General Richard Olney, himself a corporate lawyer who had represented the railroads, to appoint an attorney of the local railroads as the government's representative to the conflict. The boycott was affecting two of Olney's client railroads as well as the interests of several business associates, including George Pullman.[123] Two local judges sympathetic to the railroads issued a broad injunction, prepared by the railroads, prohibiting the strike leaders from any action to aid the boycott, including even the right to speak to the strikers. A month earlier one of these judges, in a speech, had attacked labor federations as a threat to civilization.[123] The ARU executive board decided to ignore the injunction even at the risk of jail. Debs said, "The crime of the American Railway Union was the practical exhibition of sympathy for the Pullman employees."[116] Debs persuaded Clarence Darrow, then an unknown railroad attorney, to become special counsel for the ARU. By now, a quarter million railroad employees were striking in twenty-seven states, especially in the Midwest and West.[125] The *New York Times* wrote that the conflict was "a struggle between the greatest and most important labor organization and the entire railroad capital."[123]

The railroads escalated their tactics, telegraphing Olney and President Grover Cleveland that widespread violence was occurring and that troops were needed to protect the mails. Cleveland now sent in 8000 federal troops to Chicago, telling a friend, "If it takes every dollar in the Treasury and every soldier in the US Army to deliver a postal card in Chicago, that postal card shall be delivered."[116] Even worse, the government hired an army of 5000 special marshals in Chicago, not bothering to exclude criminals and gangsters from their ranks.[116,126] The Chicago chief of police stated, "There was no violence where there were no troops. In all cases where the police were left to themselves, peace was preserved, property was kept uninjured and interference with non-union workers was trifling."[124] In vain the governor of Illinois, John Altgeld, protested that there was minimal violence, that the mail was being delivered without problems, and that the introduction of troops, without a request from either the Illinois legislature or executive, was unconstitutional. The governors of Kansas, Colorado, Texas and Oregon made similar protests.[116]

The special marshals now proceeded to initiate violence against strikers while sometimes damaging railroad equipment to discredit the strike. The police chief of Chicago complained that the marshals fired into crowds of innocent people for no reason. Debs continued to counsel the strikers against violence, saying, "I appeal to you to be men, orderly and law abiding."[116] Debs had the enormous tasks of running the overall strike while giving advice and assistance to locals across the country.

The Chicago newspapers continued to misrepresent the situation, running headlines such as, "Thirsty for Blood, Frenzied Mobs Still Bent on Death and Destruction. Violence at Every Hand."[116] Conservatives labelled the strike "The Debs Rebellion." The *New York Times* called Debs "an enemy of the human race."[119] Seeing that the government intervention had doomed the strike, Debs offered to call it off if the railroads would take back their striking employees. The railroads refused. Debs then suggested a general strike to get the railroads to agree to rehiring the strikers.[121] While many workers supported the strike, the AFL refused to back it, ordering all AFL workers striking in sympathy to return to work. Gompers argued, "To recommend to various labor organizations to strike in sympathy with the ARU movement was unfair to those wage earners, as the ARU confessed failure and the strike was a lost cause."[121]

On July 17, Debs and the other leaders of the ARU were arrested for violating the injunction. Initially they refused bail as a matter of principle with Debs commenting, "The poor striker who is arrested would be thrown in prison. We are no better than he."[123] While Debs and the other union officials were in jail, federal authorities ransacked the ARU offices, even opening personal mail. Similar injunctions in other cities were used to jail other local union leaders. Debs commented, "The rapid-fire injunction is a great improvement on the Gatling gun. Nothing can get beyond its range and it never misses fire."[116] Deprived of its leadership, the strike at last was beaten. Thirty strikers had been killed, sixty injured, and over 700 arrested.[126]

President Cleveland appointed a commission to investigate the strike. The commission's report, released in November, was very favorable to the ARU. Yet this did not change anything. Pro-business newspapers continued to vilify the union. The *Daily Inter Ocean* wrote that Debs was "as much a criminal as are the outlaws who hold up trains."[123]

Debs and the other strike leaders were sentenced to six- and three-month jail terms respectively, for violation of a civil action, the injunction. A trial on more serious criminal charges of interfering with the mails was held. The government, in their opening remarks, said, "Men have a right to strike."[122] Debs replied, "If this is so, it ends the case, for no one but the evil genius that directs the prosecution believes these men did anything else."[122] The government attorney admitted that "the union leadership had itself neither engaged in violence or stopped a single train."[123] The defense, led by Clarence Darrow, was aided by Debs's impressive testimony and by the minutes of the General Managers Association railroad meetings, which showed how the railroads had colluded to create a crisis. It appeared likely that the defendants would be acquitted when the trial was stopped on February 8, 1895, when a juror fell seriously ill. The government declined to retry the case.

Former US Senator Lyman Trumbull, the author of the Thirteenth Amendment, outlawing slavery, tried unsuccessfully to persuade the Supreme Court to free the union leaders from imprisonment for violation of the injunction. Most of the Supreme Court had earlier in their careers represented railroads.[123] The court ruled against the union leaders. Trumbull said, "This decision carried to its logical conclusion means that any federal judge can imprison any citizen at his will."[122] Commenting on this and the court's earlier finding that an income tax was unconstitutional, Debs said, "Both decisions are absolutely in the interests of the corporations, syndicates and trusts, which dominate every department of the Federal Government."[123]

After serving six months in jail, Debs was released on November 22, 1895. He later wrote, "The Chicago jail sentences were followed by six months [in jail] at Woodstock and it was here that socialism gradually laid hold of me in its own irresistible fashion."[123] On his release, a train took him to Chicago, where 100,000 workers crowded to meet him and hoist him on their shoulders. The pro-business Chicago *Chronicle* reported, "Never did men strive and struggle to demonstrate their love for a fellowman just released from a convict's cell."[124] Debs told them, "I am here to declare that if the American Railway Union erred, it has been on the side of sympathy, mercy and humanity."[122] Another huge crowd welcomed him home to Terre Haute.

Debs now began to travel and lecture to try to raise money to pay off the ARU debts. However, the workers were now too afraid to remain part of the union. Historian Ginger wrote, "On railroad after railroad the ARU members were blacklisted, driven from their jobs…any railroader who was caught at a Debs' meeting was fired."[116] The Pullman workers were forced to sign yellow-dog contracts, promising not to join a union, as the price of employment. Debs wrote, "The General Managers Association pursued the American Railway Union with fiendish ferocity, determined to stamp out the last sparks of its life."[122] The ARU finally disbanded in June 1897.

In the following years, the railroad brotherhoods and AFL moved to appease the corporate world lest they be destroyed. They continued to ban blacks from membership and ignore less skilled workers, in exchange for certain wage and other concessions.[121,123] On the other hand, Debs and other labor leaders were outraged by the blatant favoritism shown the railroads and other businesses by the courts and the government, leading them to increasingly believe that capitalism was at the root of the problem.

The 1896 Democratic convention in Chicago saw a repudiation of the conservative, pro-business Cleveland. Led by Illinois Governor Altgeld the reformers set forth a liberal platform that denounced "government by injunction as a new and highly dangerous form of oppression."[116] The Democrats nominated William Jennings Bryan for president.

Two weeks later the People's Party, or Populists, held their convention. The Populists were a farmer-based party that sought to tame the excessive power of the railroads and banks. The Populist delegates favored Debs as their presidential candidate. After thinking it over, Debs telegraphed, "Please do not permit use of my name for nomination. E.V. Debs."[116] The Populists decided to endorse Bryan as well.

Debs spent the fall campaigning for Bryan and other progressive candidates. Debs wrote Bryan, "In the great uprising of the masses against the classes, you are at this hour the hope of the Republic…"[121] Debs made seventy-seven speeches for Bryan in the campaign.[124]

The Republicans raised vast sums of money from business while warning of catastrophe should Bryan be elected. The result was a Republican landslide. Ginger wrote, "If Bryan had been elected President in 1896, Eugene Debs might never have become a socialist."[116]

By the start of 1897 Debs began to make the case for socialism. In January 1897, Debs wrote in the *Railway Times*, "The issue is Socialism versus capitalism. I am for Socialism because I am for humanity… Money constitutes no proper basis of civilization."[116] Debs continued, "The time has come to regenerate society—we are on the eve of universal change."[126] Debs was more interested in achieving positive reforms than the manner in which this was accomplished, having little interest in Marxist theory.[118]

In July Debs went to West Virginia in support of striking coal miners. Finding that many miners owed more in the company stores than they earned, he stated, "The only way to get even is to quit. I wish every foe of labor agitation could see the poverty I have seen in the last week."[124]

Debs helped form the Social Democratic Party in October 1898, which later renamed itself the Socialist Party. The party grew rapidly. Modest about his role, Debs reluctantly agreed to run as the party's candidate for president of the United States at the urging of most of the party. The Social Democrats campaigned for public ownership of factories, railroads and banks. The platform also urged equal civil and political rights for women, abolition of war and use of international arbitration in its place. Debs stated, "The one vital issue in the present campaign springs from the private ownership of the means of production and it involves the whole question of political equality, economic freedom and social progress."[124] Debs received 96,878 votes in November 1900, up from the party's 12,000 votes in 1898.

Debs consistently opposed war, and argued against war with Spain, stating, "There are thousands who are not swept off their feet by the war craze. They realize that war is national murder [and] the poor furnish the victims."[116] After its victory over Spain, the United States took over possession of the Philippines, deploying the army there to put down a movement for independence. Debs opposed this, telling an audience in Indianapolis in 1898, "We are making a market over there in the Orient for the products of half paid labor in this country; making the market by force of arms and at the expense of the lives of a people whose only offense has been their love of freedom and self control."[116]

Debs continued his lecturing, which formed his major source of income. Debs traveled endlessly, giving seven speeches of two hours in length each week. Remembering the epic train strike, Debs would sleep upright on his long train trips, refusing to use a Pullman berth.[121] In 1903, speaking in Rochester, Debs spotted Susan B. Anthony sitting in the audience. The two talked afterwards. "Give us suffrage and we'll give you socialism," Anthony said. Debs replied, "Give us socialism and we'll give you suffrage."[116] Asked what socialism was, Debs replied, "Merely Christianity in action. It recognizes the equality in men."[118]

Debs was again chosen as the Socialist nominee for president in 1904. Debs argued that socialism was in the American tradition of resistance to unfair conditions, saying, "Socialism is the evolution of Jeffersonian democracy."[124] Debs also persuaded the Socialists to adopt a resolution in January 1903 specifically welcoming blacks to "membership and fellowship" in the party.[124] Debs quadrupled his vote to 420,000 in the 1904 election. Debs wrote, "Only when our economic interest becomes mutual, when socially we own what we socially need and use…only then can we develop and express the best that is in us."[119]

Debs and many other labor leaders felt that a new labor federation was necessary to help organize the unskilled workers and advocate a more radical political position than the conservative AFL. Under Debs leadership, the Industrial Workers of the World (IWW) was founded in June 1905. The IWW was the first national American union to be open to all workers regardless of skill, race, gender or nationality. Debs stated, "There is but one hope, and that is in the economic and political solidarity of the working class; one revolutionary union and one revolutionary party."[122] The IWW, supportive of the Socialists, was attacked by the major newspapers as too radical. On the other side, many in the Socialist Party argued that they instead should try to capture control of existing unions in the AFL. Debs tried to persuade both the IWW organizers and the other Socialist leaders that their best hope was to work together.

On December 30, 1905, the anti-union former governor of Idaho, Frank Steunenberg, was killed by a bomb in his home. A member of the Western Federation of Miners, Harry Orchard, confessed to the crime, claiming that he had been hired by the leaders of the Western Federation of Miners, Bill Haywood and Charles Moyer, as well as businessman George Pettibone, to carry out the killing. The trio was arrested in Colorado on a Saturday night and put on a special sealed train that brought them to Idaho. The three were indicted for murder on March 6, 1906. James McParlan, the Pinkerton detective who had extracted the confession, told a reporter that the men "will never leave Idaho alive."[116]

Convinced of their innocence, Debs gave hundreds of speeches in defense of the accused men. In support of the defendants he was joined by the more conservative craft unions of the AFL and the Socialist Party.

The jury trial of Moyer, Haywood and Pettibone started in Boise. Large rallies across the country protested the prosecution. Clarence Darrow, conducting the defense, forced the key prosecution witness Harry Orchard to admit to being a paid informant for the Mine Owners Association.[118] Finally, the jury found all three defendants innocent.

The victory was costly. During their imprisonment, rivals of Haywood and Moyer took the Western Federation of Miners out of the IWW, which lost its biggest union. The leaders of the IWW now advocated labor action only, while deciding to avoid political participation. Ginger wrote, "It was inevitable that Eugene Debs, who insisted on both industrial unions and the Socialist Party as the cornerstones of sound policy, would resign from the IWW."[116] Debs, unwilling to attack the IWW, simply let his membership expire.

Debs took a firm stand against racial prejudice, refusing to speak to segregated audiences in the South. He was rare among labor leaders in attacking such anti-black propaganda such as the movie *Birth of a Nation*.[116,121] Debs' sympathy for blacks and his recognition of the special troubles they faced grew over time. Debs was to state, "Never do I see a Negro, but my heart goes out to him…my Black brother for the crimes perpetuated upon his race by the race to which I belong."[124]

The 1908 presidential campaign pitted William Jennings Bryan for the Democrats against William Howard Taft of the Republicans. Debs was again chosen to be the Socialist candidate. The Socialists rented a locomotive and sleeping car to carry Debs around the country on a speaking tour, dubbing it the Red Special. Debs was to speak five to twenty times a day, giving speeches up to one to two hours long, for sixty-five consecutive days. The poet Carl Sandburg joined the Red Special in Wisconsin, writing of Debs, "Such a light as shines from him—and such a fire as burns in him—he is of a poet breed, hardened for war."[124] Historian Ernest Freeberg wrote, "The Socialists charged admission to hear their candidate, funding their national campaign not with donations from wealthy industrialists, but from the nickels and dimes of workers. And still, as reporters often noted with surprise, Debs spoke to overflowing crowds."[119] One self-described cynical Socialist told a reporter, "When Debs says 'comrade', it's all right. He means it. That old man with the burning eyes actually believes that there can be such a thing as the brotherhood of man. And that's not the funniest part of it. As long as he's around I believe it myself."[116] The results were disappointing to the Socialists. Debs won only 420,000 votes, no more than in 1904. Debs was exhausted after the campaign, suffering from arthritis and recurring severe headaches.[116] He returned home to Terre Haute and tried not to get involved in the internal conflicts within the Socialists that followed.

The Socialists continued to be wracked by conflict between those who believed in allying with other reformers and trying to win over existing unions and those who saw this as an abandonment of principles. Debs, while leaning more to the latter viewpoint, tried to avoid the party conflicts, usually choosing to skip the party conventions. The party had increasing electoral success, electing fifty-six mayors, one congressman and over 300 aldermen and city councilmen in 1911.[118] From a mere 10,000 in 1900, party membership had risen to 150,000 in 1911.[119,121]

The Socialists again nominated Debs to be their presidential candidate in the 1912 election, which saw both Theodore Roosevelt and Woodrow Wilson trying to run as progressives. Debs questioned the progressive credentials of both men. Of Wilson, Debs said, "He has as rotten a labor record as any man possibly could have."[118] Debs campaigned widely for the Socialist ticket and ideals, and stated, "All the votes of the people would do no good if our party ceased to be a revolutionary party…yielding more and more to the pressure to modify the principle and program of the party."[118] Debs conceded that he would be a terrible president, telling Lincoln Steffens, "When Socialism is on the verge of success, the party will nominate an able executive and a clear headed administrator…not Debs."[119] In the 1912 presidential election, Debs won nearly 900,00 votes, almost 6% of the total cast.

Debs delivered an estimated 6000 speeches during his life.[124] Historian Arthur Schlesinger, Junior, wrote that when Debs spoke, he showed his "sweetness of temper, his generosity and kindness, his perfect sincerity, his warm and sad smile and his candid gray eyes."[118] Debs fought aggressively against the idea of idolizing any leader; rather, he emphasized the potential of every individual, telling workers, "I would have you understand that within yourselves there is all that is necessary to develop a real man."[121] In a famous statement, Debs told listeners, "I do not want you to follow me or anyone else. I would not lead you into the promised land if I could, because if I could lead you in, someone else would lead you out. You must use your heads as well as your hands and get yourselves out of your present condition."[121]

Debs' listeners also appreciated that he tried to support all workers, regardless of background. The editor of the *Forward*, New York's Socialist Yiddish daily, explaining why pictures of Debs plastered the walls of Jewish immigrant workers, commented, "Debs was the liberator, the first who had come from the ranks of the American workers, holding out his hand and saying, "I am your brother."[121]

In June 1913, Debs received headlines after the daughter of an old friend was arrested for prostitution. As city clerk, Debs had refused to fine the prostitutes who had been arrested. He now persuaded the authorities to appoint him as temporary probation officer and took the girl back into his own home, Debs stated, "Why not war on the immoral people in high life instead of prosecuting this penniless girl?"[116] Debs eventually found the girl a new job in a new city.

Debs continued to campaign for workers, for example going to West Virginia in May 1913 to try to aid striking coal workers. After 18 years, Debs also succeeded in paying off the $22,000 debt of the American Railway Union, which he had taken on a personal obligation.

Debs consistently remained a fierce opponent of war, calling it, "the supreme crime of twentieth century civilization."[116] In 1913 President Wilson sent the US Marines into Mexico at Veracruz, ostensibly to protect American lives and property. Debs viewed this as mainly aiming at protecting the property of the Rockefellers' Standard Oil Company. Debs argued that the troops should be withdrawn rather than crushing the peons, "into hopeless slavery and degradation."[116] Describing the American intervention, Debs said, "It is one thing, ye uniformed slaves, to fight for your country and another thing to fight for the Rockefellers' oil derricks…Let the capitalists do their own fighting and furnish their own corpses."[116] The same month World War I broke out in Europe.

Debs called for complete American neutrality. He stated that the war had been precipitated by the ruling classes in each country and that the workers had no interest in the conflict. Debs denounced the socialists in Europe who had rallied to their country's side, saying, "We socialists are not wanting in genuine patriotism, but we are deadly hostile to the fraudulent species...which prompts every crook and grafter and every blood sucking vampire to wrap his reeking carcass in the folds of the national flag."[116] The sinking of the *Lusitania* with the loss of many American lives led to many turning against Germany. Debs, while calling the sinking "a fiendish crime," praised Wilson's restraint in not going to war after the episode.[119] Debs said, "Must we send the workers of one country against another because a citizen has been torpedoed on the high seas?"[119]

Wilson supported a limited rebuilding of the American military. Debs disagreed with those on the left who had begun to support war preparedness and possible intervention, noting, "I do not know of any foreign buccaneers that could come nearer to skinning the American workers than is now being done by the Rockefellers and their pirate pals."[116]

Debs rejected all attempts to nominate him again as the presidential candidate of the Socialist Party, feeling that the Socialists were too reliant on his personal popularity. However, when the Socialists in Terre Haute nominated him to be their congressional candidate, he felt honor bound to run, knowing that he would lose. Debs campaigned through his district on a platform of opposition to war. Debs said, "Mr. Wilson, who had all his life been opposed to militarism, has now become the avowed champion of plutocratic preparedness and today he stands before the country pleading in the name of Wall Street and its interests for the largest standing army and most powerful navy in the world."[120] Debs beat the Democratic incumbent, but fell way behind the Republican candidate. Debs commented, "Blessed are they who expect nothing, for they shall not be disappointed."[116]

In February 1917, Germany announced unrestricted submarine warfare, prompting the United States to break off diplomatic relations. Debs began touring the country, arguing against going to war. In New York, Debs proposed a nationwide general strike if Congress declared war, but the AFL and railroad brotherhoods vowed to support the government should war be declared.[116] On April 6, 1917, the United States declared war on Germany. Almost alone, the Socialist Party responded by proclaiming "its unalterable opposition to the war just declared by the government of the United States."[116]

Congress passed the Espionage Act in June 1917. Under its provisions, many opposed to the war, including many Socialists, were arrested. A popular backlash also led to beatings of anti-war protesters. While Debs denounced such atrocities, he did not criticize those who left the Socialist Party to support the war, being unwilling to attack many long-time friends and collaborators. Debs was in poor health, and was bedridden for much of the war. He was diagnosed with a dilated heart and advised by his doctor to keep "free of excitement."[119] His wife and brother also may have been trying to dissuade him from saying anything that could be deemed criminal.[116]

The Bolshevik takeover in Russia in November 1917 led to increased fear of socialism in America. In early 1918, waves of Socialists, members of the IWW and other radicals were arrested. The Socialist press, short of resources to begin with, had been widely suppressed or stripped of their mailing permits.[117]

By May 1918, Debs had recovered enough to start a limited speaking schedule. It is unclear if Debs was determined to force the government to arrest him or was trying to avoid such a fate.[116,119] On June 16, 1918, Debs defended those imprisoned, saying, "Many of us have [realized] that it is entirely dangerous to exercise the constitutional right of free speech in a country fighting to make democracy safe in the world."[116]

Debs was arrested two weeks later on the charge of encouraging men to avoid conscription due to his criticism of the war. The trial began on September 9. Debs argued that under the First Amendment, his speech was not criminal. Debs said, "I can yet look the court in the face…for my conscience, in my soul, there is festering no accusation of guilt… I wish to admit the truth of all that has been testified to in this proceeding…I admit being opposed to the present form of government. I admit being opposed to the present social system…the time has come for a better form of government, an improved system, a higher social order, a nobler humanity and a grander civilization."[116] Debs defended his right to oppose a war he thought unjust, saying, "The Mexican War was bitterly condemned by Abraham Lincoln, by Charles Sumner, by Daniel Webster and by Henry Clay."[116] Debs continued, "I believe in free speech, in war as well as in peace. I would not, under any circumstances, gag the lips of my bitterest enemy."[119] Debs commented, "I have never advocated violence in any form."[121] After speaking for two hours, Debs concluded, "I cannot tell what may be, nor does it matter much, so far I am concerned. Gentlemen, I am the smallest part of this trial...American institutions are on trial here before a court of American citizens."[121] While the judge dismissed the counts against Debs for ridiculing the government, the jury found Debs guilty on the charge of obstructing the conscription act by his speeches against the war.

At sentencing Debs spoke again. Debs said, "Your Honor, years ago, I recognized my kinship with all living things, and I made up my mind that I was not one bit better than the meanest of the earth. I said then, I say now, that while there is a lower class, I am in it; while there is a criminal element, I am of it; while there is a soul in prison, I am not free."[116] Debs was sentenced to ten years in prison.

Debs, now age 62, reported to the state prison in Moundsville, West Virginia. He quickly tried to help the other prisoners, giving advice and writing letters for them. When Debs was transferred two months later to the federal prison in Atlanta, the warden of Moundsville wrote to the warden in Atlanta about Debs, saying, "I never in my life met a kinder man. He is forever thinking of others, trying to serve them and never thinking of himself."[116]

In Atlanta Debs refused special privileges other than being able to receive more visitors. He continued trying to help the other prisoners with their problems. He gave away the contents of the packages he received to the other inmates. Ginger wrote, "When he had been in prison less than a month the other inmates began calling him little Jesus."[116] Debs became very ill. He was transferred to the prison hospital, where he slowly improved.

In 1920, the Socialist Party nominated Debs again as their presidential candidate. The government allowed him to send out one press release a week from the prison during the campaign. Debs reserved most of his attacks during the campaign against the incumbent President Woodrow Wilson. Debs, an inmate of Atlanta Prison, received nearly a million votes for president, many from non-Socialists opposed to his imprisonment. The Republican Warren Harding won a landslide victory. Debs commented, "The people can have anything they want. The truth is they do not want anything. At least they vote that way on election day."[116]

Immediately after the armistice, many liberals urged Wilson to give a general amnesty to all political opponents of the war. While Wilson was initially sympathetic, he had changed his mind by the summer of 1919, saying at a cabinet meeting, "Suppose every man in America had taken the same position Debs did. We would have lost the war and America would have been destroyed."[119] Many unions and others petitioned Wilson to grant amnesty to Debs. Clarence Darrow, leading the campaign, visited Debs in prison, remarking that Debs was "loved and idealized by all the inmates."[116] Wilson maintained, "Once the Congress of the United States declared war, silence on his part would have been the proper course."[120] In the last months of the Wilson administration Attorney General Palmer recommended that Debs' sentence be commuted, freeing him in another year. He noted that Debs was age 65, in poor health and might die in prison. Wilson denied this recommendation, telling an aide, "This man was a traitor to his country and he will never be pardoned during my administration."[116] Debs replied, "I understand perfectly the feelings of Woodrow Wilson…No man in public life in America ever retired so thoroughly discredited, so scathingly rebuked, so overwhelmingly impeached and repudiated as Woodrow Wilson."[116] After this was published, the Department of Justice suspended all of Debs's ability to write or receive visitors."[116]

One of the first acts of the new President, Warren Harding, was to instruct Attorney General Harry Daugherty to review the Debs case. On March 24, 1921, Debs, alone and unguarded, took a train to Washington for a three-hour interview with the attorney general. Daugherty later told Clarence Darrow, "He spent a large part of the day in my office, and I never met a man I liked better."[116] After this meeting, many conservatives attacked the administration for even considering freeing Debs. "If the American Legion is unanimous in just one thing," its commander Alan Owsley told Daugherty, "it is opposition to the pardoning or releasing of Gene Debs."[119] On the other side, Upton Sinclair published a book, *Debs and the Poets*, containing contributions from famous writers from Carl Sandburg to H.G. Wells and George Bernard Shaw, speaking for Debs. The poet Siegfried Sassoon wrote of Debs, "I honor his name and loathe the system which has persecuted him."[119] Harriet Stanton Blatch, daughter of Elizabeth Stanton, joined the Socialist Party to work a full-time lobbyist for amnesty. In November, a petition with 300,000 signatures calling for Debs's release was delivered to Washington. Finally, on December 23, 1921, it was announced that Debs and twenty-three other political prisoners would be released on Christmas Day. When Debs left the prison, the warden let the 2300 inmates join in saying goodbye. They repeatedly cheered and called Debs's name. Debs wrote that "This was the most deeply touching and impressive moment and the most profoundly dramatic incident in my life."[119]

More than 25,000 people met Eugene Debs when he returned to Terre Haute. He was in poor health, with recurrent headaches, severe arthritis, kidney and stomach problems and difficulty sleeping. A continuous stream of visitors, endless phone calls and piles of mail made it hard for him to rest. In March 1922 Debs told a visitor, "You cannot seem to understand that I am sick and worn and have not had the ghost of a chance to rest since I got out of the penitentiary."[121]

Debs's poor health led him to spend time in a sanitarium near Chicago. In collaboration with David Karsner, the Sunday editor of the *New York Call*, Debs wrote a series of articles about prison conditions. However, most of the articles were felt to be too inflammatory to be published until after his death. Debs spent the next few years trying to write and give lectures, but his health frequently broke down.

During Debs's time in prison, the Communists had split off from the Socialist Party. Refusing to join the Communist Party, Debs told a group of Communists, "I am not a Communist and I don't want to be one. I do not believe in minority rule."[119] Despite disagreeing with aspects of the Socialist Party, Debs decided to remain a member, writing, "I have spent the better part of my active life in its service and why should I now turn upon it and rend it."[116] Salvatore wrote, "The continued sniping between Socialists and Communists in the post war years provided a false sense of vitality for each side."[121]

On October 15, 1926, Debs had a heart attack. Lapsing into a coma, he died five days later. By the time of his death the Socialist Party had dwindled to fewer than 10,000 members.[119] Upton Sinclair, who had maintained his friendship with Debs, summarized him, saying, "Gene was one of the noblest and kindest men I have had the good fortune to meet. He was a tireless fighter for social justice. He was one friend of the poor and lowly who stood by his principles and never wavered."[127] Clarence Darrow stated, "There may have lived sometime, somewhere, a kindlier, gentler, more generous man than Debs, but I have never met him. He was the bravest man I ever knew."[124]

The industrial unionism that Debs championed hardly existed at his death. Socialism in the United States had failed. However, the next decade saw the creation of the Congress of Industrial Organizations (CIO), an alliance of unions organized to include all the workers in an industry. The CIO successfully organized the auto, steel and other industries in the 1930s, at long last giving these workers a voice. Yet, in recent years the workers' gains have been reversed, as manufacturers moved factories and jobs to non-union states or overseas or replaced workers with automation. The battle to provide economic justice continues.

Chapter 18: William Jennings Bryan
The Great Commoner, 1896 CE, United States

FARMERS REMAINED the largest part of the population in the United States at the end of the 19th century, although they had seen their incomes decline relative to the rest of the population. Moreover, farmers felt increasingly in thrall to the railroads and the other middlemen involved in getting their crops to market. The great champion of the farmers and the other less powerful residents of America was to be William Jennings Bryan, who would be the only man nominated as the Democratic candidate for president three times without success.[128–131]

William Jennings Bryan was born in Salem, Illinois, on March 19, 1860, the eldest son among eight children. His father, Silas Bryan, was a lifelong Democrat who had been elected as a judge on the state circuit court, as county superintendent of schools and to the Illinois State Senate. The Bryan family's strong active Christian faith was shaped by the teachings of Charles G. Finney in what was called "The Second Great Awakening."[127] One aspect of this was the belief that any man or woman could achieve salvation through faith. A second tenet was post-millennialism, the idea that the reform of society would hasten the return of Jesus Christ and the heavenly kingdom.[128] These two ideas would motivate William Jennings Bryan throughout his life.

Bryan's faith led him to focus on improving the lives of people, particularly the poor and oppressed. Historian Michael Kazin wrote, "Bryan's gospel of collective good works avoided debates about the particulars of his faith…Both his personality and politics made him a tacit ally of the liberal optimists for whom Jesus was a benevolent figure and hell an anachronistic abstraction."[129]

At age 21 Bryan graduated from Illinois College in Jacksonville, where he was the valedictorian of his class of eleven men. After graduation, Bryan read law for two years at the Union College of Law in Chicago. In Chicago, he then worked as law clerk, earning $5 a week, for former United States Senator Lyman Trumbull, an old political friend of his father. Bryan and Trumbull remained friends and political allies. Historian Raymond Coletta wrote, "Bryan's belief in the need for reform was strengthened by Trumbull. He told Bryan to speak out against injustice, whether racial, political or economic."[130]

Bryan married Mary Baird, daughter of a successful merchant in Jacksonville. He had written Mary from law school that he prayed that "I may develop powers that exert a great influence for good."[130] William was later to help Mary become a lawyer in her own right.[128]

Seeking a place with more opportunities for a young lawyer, in 1887 Bryan moved to Lincoln, Nebraska. He opened a law office and became active in local Democratic politics. Bryan became law partners with Adolphus Talbot, a friend from law school and a Republican. This partnership lasted almost ten years.[129] Bryan earned a paltry $9.60 in his first month of practice, but by 1890 he was making $2000 a year, a good income for that time.[130]

William Jennings Bryan made a speech at the Nebraska Democratic Party convention that impressed the party leaders with his oratory. Consequently, Bryan accepted the party's nomination for Congress in July 1890.

The national Democratic Party in 1890 favored states' rights and limited federal government. While conservatives in the party were suspicious of any reforms, the liberal portion of the party increasingly argued that something should be done for the farmers and workers who were suffering in the great surge of industrialization and business consolidation. Bryan, along with many in the South and West, was squarely in the latter camp.

Nebraska, which was considered part of the West, faced economic hard times in 1890. Wheat that had sold for $1.19 a bushel in 1881 now sold for 49 cents.[130] The Republican incumbent accepted Bryan's challenge to a series of eleven debates. Kazin wrote, "[Bryan] spoke fluently without either text or notes. His voice rang out with a clarity that pleased everyone who heard it, whatever they thought of his views."[129] Bryan won every debate. Bryan stated, "The Democratic party has always claimed to represent the mass of the people. The Republican party has long since ceased to do so."[130] Running in a traditionally Republican district, Bryan won by a margin of 6713 votes, the second Democrat ever elected to Congress from Nebraska. Nationally, the Democrats seized control of the House of Representatives.

Bryan was given a seat on the key Ways and Means Committee in exchange for supporting the successful candidate for Speaker of the House.[130] In March 1892, Bryan stunned Congress with a masterful speech arguing for lowering the tariff on imported goods. The high tariffs helped protect American manufacturers, but made goods much more expensive for farmers and other citizens. He derided the Republicans for arguing simultaneously that protection didn't raise prices and that removing the tariff would flood the nation with cheaper goods from abroad.[129] Alluding to the recent Homestead steel strike, Bryan commented that manufacturers asked for high tariffs on the grounds that they could then pay higher wages, but "when the employee asks for the high wage promised him…you find Pinkerton detectives scheduled to keep him off and foreigners brought in to supply his place."[130] Bryan spoke for three hours, concluding with Thomas Jefferson's admonition that government "shall not take from the mouth of labor the bread it has earned."[129] The speech brought Bryan into national prominence.

Bryan ran for reelection in a district whose boundaries had been changed to increase the proportion of Republicans in 1892. Bryan's campaign emphasized the need of the poorer farmers. Consequently, conservative Democrats gave Bryan only lukewarm support.[129] Bryan had earlier commented that "They call that man a statesman whose ears are attuned to the slightest pulsation of the pocket book, and they describe as a demagogue anyone who dares listen to the heartbeat of humanity."[130] Bryan was reelected by a narrow margin of 140 votes.

In 1892, there were only as many paper dollars as there was gold to back them in the United States Treasury. By using silver as backing for paper dollars, additional dollars could be printed, thus increasing the money supply. Farmers and other workers, particularly in the South and West, wanted an increase in the available money supply, which would raise the prices of crops and devalue the debts they owed to banks. The banks and many industrialists, whose capital would be worth more if the supply of money was limited, opposed adding silver to gold as backing for paper currency. When the country fell into a depression in 1893 with hundreds of bank closings, President Cleveland, a supporter of gold as the only backing for the currency, proposed repeal of the Silver Purchase Act, which had allowed for the use of a limited amount of silver to back up the currency. Cleveland accepted the prevailing theory that restoring business confidence, by insuring a "sound currency" was the key to recovery.

Bryan argued instead for more, not less, use of silver, thus increasing the money supply. When repeal of the Silver Act failed to help the economy, Bryan commented, "Cleveland might be honest, but so were Indian mothers who with misguided zeal threw their children into the Ganges."[132] Denouncing the president's policies in a three-hour speech in Congress, Bryan argued, "The poor man is called a socialist if he believes that the wealth of the rich should be divided among the poor, but the rich man is called a financier if he develops a plan by which the pittance of the poor is converted to his use."[129]

Bryan sought other means as well to help what he saw as the underdogs, the poor and oppressed. Bryan spoke out for a graduated income tax, federal insurance for bank deposits and the right of workers to join a union and go on strike. Bryan denounced the use of court injunctions and Cleveland's intervention in the Pullman strike.[129] Bryan also argued for direct election of United States senators and a strengthened Interstate Commerce Commission to better regulate huge businesses.[130] Bryan said in a speech in the House, "Today the Democratic party stands between two great forces, each inviting its support. On one side stands the corporate interests of the nation, its moneyed institutions, its aggregations of wealth and capital, imperious, arrogant and compassionless. They demand special legislation, favors, privileges…On the other side stands the unnumbered throng which gave a name to the Democratic party…Work-worn and dust-begrimed they make their sad appeal."[132] To help alleviate the depression, Bryan argued that the government should print paper money to increase the money supply and pay for public works projects.

In 1894 Bryan gave up his House seat to run for the United States Senate in Nebraska. In 1894, senators were chosen by the state legislature, although Nebraska allowed an advisory vote by the population first. Bryan received 75% of the popular vote, but the Republican-controlled state legislature ignored this to pick Republican John Thurston, chief counsel of the Union Pacific Railroad, who had received 2% of the vote.[129]

Bryan now accepted the editorship of the *Omaha World-Herald*, the state's most popular daily newspaper. He published many pro-silver editorials. In February 1896, Bryan wrote, "The Democratic party cannot serve God and Mammon; it cannot serve plutocracy and at the same time defend the rights of the masses."[129]

Bryan also toured the country advocating the increased use of silver. He earned up to $100 a speech, which enabled him to give up his law practice. He became a popular speaker, able to win the affection of his audiences.[128,129]

In 1896, the Democratic Party held its convention in Chicago. The depression that began in 1893 was still ravaging the nation. The party lacked a clear frontrunner for president and was badly split between its liberal and conservative wings. The convention repudiated the position of the conservative incumbent Grover Cleveland in its platform. The conservative and liberal wings put together a competing roster of speakers, including Bryan for the liberals, to present their positions on July 9, the third day of the convention. The night before, Bryan told his wife and a friend at dinner, "These people don't know it, but they will be cheering for me just this way tomorrow night. I will make the greatest speech of my life tomorrow."[130]

Bryan began, "I come to speak to you in defense of a cause as holy as the cause of liberty—the cause of humanity."[129] Bryan defended the income tax, then continued to say, "You come before us and tell us that we are about to disturb your business interests. The man who is employed for wages is as much a businessman as his employer. The farmer, who goes forth in the morning and toils all day is much a businessman as the man who goes upon the board of trade and bets upon the price of grain."[129] Bryan concluded, "Having behind us the producing masses of this nation and the world, supported by the commercial interests, the laboring interests, and toilers everywhere, we will answer their demand for a gold standard by saying to them: You shall not press down upon the brow of labor this crown of thorns, you shall not crucify mankind upon this cross of gold."[129]

After Bryan's speech, the convention went silent for a few minutes as Bryan left the stage, then erupted with applause. The *New York World* reported, "Everybody seemed to go mad at once…the whole face of the convention was broken by the tumult—hills and valleys of shrieking men and women."[129] Historian Paul Waibel wrote, "Bryan's speech was an eloquent defense of the Jeffersonian vision and Jacksonian democracy. He portrayed America locked in a desperate struggle of right against wrong, the South and West against the East, silver against gold, the noble and righteous farmer against the greedy industrialist and corrupt politician…Bryan condemned the notion that what was good for the industrialist was good for all Americans."[128]

The next day the balloting for the party's presidential candidate began. Bryan, second initially, gained enough votes over the next two ballots to be chosen as the Democratic nominee for president, the youngest presidential candidate at age 36. The party's liberals were overjoyed by his selection

In contrast, conservatives were outraged by the choice. The *New York Times* headline ran, "The Silver Fanatics are Invincible: Wild, Raging, Irresistible Mob Which Nothing Can Turn from Its Abominable Foolishness."[129] The *New York World* commented, "Lunacy having dictated the platform it was perhaps natural that hysteria should evolve the candidate."[130]

Accepting the nomination, Bryan said, "There are those who believe that, if you will only legislate to make the well to do prosperous, their prosperity will leak through on those below. The Democratic idea, however, has been that if you legislate to make the masses prosperous, their prosperity will find its way up through every class that rests on them."[129] When representatives of the railroads offered Bryan a private car for his trip home, a supporter objected, saying, "Mr. Bryan, you should not accept this offer. You are the Great Commoner, the people's candidate, and it wouldn't do to accept favors from the great railroad corporations."[130] Skipping use of the private car, Bryan was to carry the moniker the Great Commoner for the rest of his career.

Hurrying to distance themselves from Bryan, conservative pro-gold standard Democrats held a convention in Indianapolis, nominating their own candidates as the National Democratic Party, where Bryan was attacked as someone who would "deliver the safety of the nation into the hands of socialism, zealotry, fanaticism and dishonesty."[130] Scores of formerly pro-Democratic papers, such as the *New York World*, announced that they would ask their readers to vote against Bryan. While conservatives abandoned Bryan, he subsequently received the nominations of the Populist Party and the National Silver Party as well as that of the Democrats.

Bryan was to campaign ceaselessly throughout the fall of 1896. He traveled 18,000 miles during the campaign, giving more than 600 speeches. Often speaking from the rear platform of a train, Bryan spoke to an estimated five million people, mostly around the Great Lakes region. Kazin wrote, "Rarely did Bryan give a campaign speech devoid of biblical invocations and metaphors."[129] Speaking to a meeting of Jewish Democrats in Chicago, Bryan said that the Republicans were like the pharaoh, who "lives on the toil of others and always tries to silence complaints by making the load heavier."[129] William Allen White, a Republican editor in Kansas, remarked, "It was the first time in my life and in the life of a generation in which any man large enough to lead a national party had boldly and unashamedly made his cause that of the poor and oppressed."[129]

In addition to silver, Bryan campaigned for higher wages for workers, a graduated income tax and mortgage relief. Bryan attacked the use of injunctions and troops against strikers.[128] His attack on the ruling classes and advocacy of silver meant that he received little financial support from eastern financiers, the Democrats' usual source of campaign funds. Bryan quipped, "Probably the only passage in the Bible read by some financiers is that about the wise men of the east. They seem to think that wise men have been coming from that direction ever since."[130] Eugene Debs was the only major labor leader to support Bryan, wiring Bryan, "Under your administration the rule of the money power will be broken."[130]

The Republican candidate, William McKinley, remained at home at Canton, Ohio, receiving those few visitors who came to see him. McKinley said, "I might as well put a trapeze on my front lawn and compete with some professional athlete as go out speaking against Bryan."[129] McKinley's campaign manager, the industrialist Mark Hanna, raised millions from bankers and the captains of industry, threatening that Bryan's election would be disastrous for them. Large employers warned their employees that Bryan's election would mean factory closings and widespread layoffs. Coletta wrote, "Eastern insurance companies, which held many Western mortgages, sent agents to contact every borrower to offer a five year extension of loans at low interest rates if McKinley was elected."[130] For the first time, corporations made political contributions directly from their corporate treasuries.[132] Kazin wrote, "Hanna organized the most sophisticated campaign to that point in US history…he hired 1400 speakers to stump in doubtful states and oversaw the printing of more than 120 million pieces of literature."[129] When someone told Hanna that Bryan might win, Hanna replied, "Do you think we'd let that damned lunatic get into the White House? You know you can hire half of the people of the United States to shoot down the other half if necessary, and we've got the money to hire them."[132] The Populists and Democrats together only had one-tenth the money of the Republicans.

Bryan was called a demagogue, a fraud, a communist, a socialist and a revolutionary.[128] *Harpers Weekly* commented, "Beyond his feeble and ignorant presentation of this money heresy lies the deep abyss of socialism, into which…he is inviting the American people to plunge."[130] Conservatives called the Democratic platform, with its call for a graduated income tax and increased regulation of the railroads, "the concrete creed of the mob."[132]

When the ballots were cast, McKinley received 7,108,480 votes and 271 electoral votes to Bryan's 6,511,495 and 176 electoral votes. Bryan carried most western states in addition to the South, winning 26 states to McKinley's 21. A difference of 19,000 votes in five close states would have given him the election.[130] Referring to the effect of the economic depression on popular support for the Democratic Party, Bryan commented, "I have borne the sins of Grover Cleveland."[130]

Despite his defeat, Bryan remained the most popular figure in the Democratic Party. He received some 2000 letters a day. From these letters, Bryan's brother Charles started a huge card file of supporters, to whom he sent regular mailings. Bryan, with his wife's help, assembled a collection of speeches and a short biography which they published as *The First Battle*. It sold 200,000 copies in the first eight months after publication.[129]

Bryan continued to fight for the common man, urging state legislatures to pass legislation increasing control over trusts and railroads and banning campaign contributions by corporations. He pushed cooperation between the Democrats, Populists and the National Silver Party, emphasizing bimetallism, the income tax and the settling of labor disputes through arbitration.[130]

In 1898, America declared war against Spain, in large part over Spanish treatment of rebels seeking an independent Cuba. Bryan, although sympathizing with the rebels, initially opposed the decision to go to war. Once war was declared in April 1898, Bryan volunteered for active duty. He was appointed a colonel by the Populist governor of Nebraska and began to raise and train a regiment of volunteers. Thousands wrote to Bryan, asking to serve under him. Bryan served only five months, mainly fighting disease among his troops in Florida. When a peace treaty with Spain was signed, he resigned his commission the same day.[128] Bryan quipped, "I had five months of peace in the army and resigned to take part in a fight."[129]

While Bryan saw the war with Spain as a moral crusade to free Cuba from Spanish despotism, he strongly opposed the idea that America should keep and govern any of the lands acquired from Spain in the war. Before leaving for Florida, Bryan had said, "Is our national character so weak that we cannot withstand the temptation to appropriate the first piece of land that comes within our reach?"[129] Bryan supported the peace treaty with Spain despite the part that granted the United States control of the Philippines. While many Democrats opposed the treaty, Bryan argued that Congress, especially if the Democrats were triumphant in the 1900 election, could grant independence afterward. Many opposed to annexation thought that Bryan should have opposed the peace treaty, which passed by a mere two votes over the two-thirds required.

In February 1899, six months of tension between US Army and the Filipino forces turned to open conflict. Initially defeated in conventional battles, the Filipinos hoped that an election victory by Bryan and the Democrats would lead to independence.

At the Democratic convention in 1900, the party kept the pro-silver platform and again nominated Bryan. Some advisors suggested that he could carry the eastern states if he avoided the silver issue, but he refused to hide his views.[130] In his acceptance speech, Bryan, discussing the Philippines, said, "A war of conquest would…leave its legacy of perpetual hatred, for it was God Himself who planted in every human heart the love of liberty."[129] He continued, "We cannot set a high and honorable example for the emulation of mankind while we roam the world like beasts of prey seeking whom we may devour."[130]

In addition to opposing imperialism and favoring an expanded money supply, Bryan urged regulation of the railroads and trusts. He quipped, "There can be no good monopoly in private hands until the Almighty sends us angels to preside over the monopoly."[129] Bryan campaigned for direct elections of senators, the income tax and the settling of international disputes by arbitration rather than war. Bryan's faith and idealism led to a belief in the eventual triumph of justice.[130]

In response, McKinley's running mate, Theodore Roosevelt, attacked Bryan as a purveyor of "communistic and socialistic doctrines."[129] Bryan had a challenging time unifying those who opposed imperialism with those supporters of "free silver." McKinley, basking in the glow of a successful war and increased prosperity, won a bigger majority against Bryan in 1900.[128]

After his defeat, Bryan returned to the newspaper business, founding *The Commoner*, a national newspaper that first appeared on January 23, 1901. Bryan served as publisher, editor and was the main writer until he entered Woodrow Wilson's cabinet in 1913. *The Commoner* then continued as a monthly from 1913 until April 1923.[128] It was printed on a union press and refused to take ads from big corporations or liquor or tobacco companies.[129]

In the paper, Bryan's positions broke with the Democrats' prior stance advocating limited government to advocate an expanded, stronger government that would help protect the interests of ordinary people. Bryan advocated a federal income tax, use of initiatives and referenda to pass laws, passage of pure food and drug laws, and municipal ownership of utilities and streetcars. He argued for the prohibition of corporate campaign contributions, a limit on profits from new patents, infrastructure improvements, and reformation of criminals, and against child labor. He advocated constitutional amendments to elect senators by popular vote and to limit presidents to a single term.[130] Bryan also urged limiting the hours of workers and prohibiting sweatshops and child labor.[130]

After Bryan's two defeats, the 1904 convention saw conservative, pro-gold standard Democrats nominate a conservative New York judge, Alton B. Parker, for president. Bryan forced the conservatives to accept a more progressive platform than they wanted. He spoke for the rights of labor and farmers at the convention, giving another memorable speech where he said, "You may dispute whether I have fought a good fight, you may dispute whether I have finished my course, but you cannot deny that I have kept the faith."[130] H.L. Mencken, who disliked Bryan, wrote that Bryan's speech in 1904 was the best he ever heard, writing, "What a speech, my masters! What a speech! Like all great art, it was fundamentally simple."[129] During the ensuing campaign, Bryan was to do more speaking for a ticket he disliked than the Democratic nominee.[129] Parker lost in a landslide to Theodore Roosevelt.

Bryan continued his advocacy for liberal causes after the election. He urged states to create old age pensions and suggested that a permanent board of arbitration be established for labor issues. He continued to argue for freedom for the Philippines. Bryan also argued for a stronger central government, stating, "Government should be for the governed and communities should do for themselves what they are now permitting individuals or corporations to do."[130] Bryan went even further when he argued for "The law of just rewards…the principle that compensation should be commensurate with service, each one drawing from society in proportion as he contributes to the welfare of society."[130]

Over time, particularly after the winning election in his own right in 1904, President Roosevelt took increasingly liberal positions. Bryan publicly supported Theodore Roosevelt's progressive statements and policies, saying, "In President Roosevelt himself there have been symptoms of reform that I for one had no suspicion of…[the Democrats] should help the President carry out whatever is good."[130] Coletta wrote, "Roosevelt adopted Bryan's demands for licensing of interstate businesses, the federal control of railroads, the physical valuation of railroad property, the prohibition of corporations from contributing to political campaigns, the arbitration of industrial disputes, the regulation of the procedures by which courts issued injunctions, the federal control of corporation securities, an inheritance tax and pure food and drug legislation."[130] The breath of their agreement led the press to comment on the "Roosevelt–Bryan Merger."[130]

In 1907, Bryan, Mary, and two of their children, both teenagers, embarked on an around the world tour. They returned in August 1908 after visiting eighteen countries. In Russia, Bryan visited the aging Leo Tolstoy at his estate. Kazin wrote, "Twelve hours of uninterrupted conversation persuaded each man that he had found a kindred spirit."[129] Bryan found much to emulate in terms of public policy in Europe and Japan, while criticizing many of the colonial policies he witnessed, particularly those of the British in India.

By the time Bryan returned home, even conservative Democrats talked about supporting him in the 1908 election. This was not to last. Bryan was consistent in his belief that the public should own the utilities on which they depended. On his return, Bryan surprised a large audience at the Madison Square Garden by saying late in the speech that railroads, then the most powerful industry in America, "must ultimately become public property and be managed by public officials in the interest of the whole community."[129] Conservatives were outraged.

While Bryan publicly denounced lynchings of blacks in his 1896 and 1900 campaigns, he did not speak out against southern Democrats' suppression of black rights. This would have been political suicide. In 1906, Bryan denounced President Roosevelt for his handling of an incident in Brownsville, Texas, where the killing of a white civilian by an unknown assailant led to the dishonorable discharge of 167 black soldiers. This stand led black leader W.E.B. DuBois to endorse Bryan for president in 1908.[128]

The economy again deteriorated in what was called the Panic of 1907, with widespread business failures and unemployment. Bryan urged the federal government to provide aid and jobs for the unemployed, while also advocating government-sponsored insurance of bank deposits to protect depositors against bank failures.[128] Bryan advocated that speculation in securities be separated from routine banking business. He suggested that the government should lease, rather than sell—often for a pittance—land containing minerals and oil. Bryan also proposed that corporations be limited from controlling more than 50% of the US market in any product. This would have resulted in the breakup of some huge trusts, such as Andrew Carnegie's US Steel and John D. Rockefeller's Standard Oil.[130]

Bryan's religious faith led him to see social reform as the best way to change people's attitudes to each other. He called for a "moral awakening" so that men "would love another instead of running riot after money."[130]

Nominated again by the Democrats for president in 1908, Bryan campaigned explicitly as the champion of workers. William Howard Taft, Roosevelt's handpicked successor, had commented during the Pullman strike, "They have killed only six of the mob as yet. This is hardly enough to make an impression."[129] For the first time the American Federation of Labor endorsed a presidential candidate, enthusiastically supporting Bryan. This started the trend of labor backing Democrats. On the other side, James Van Cleve, the president of the National Association of Manufacturers told members that they should, "bury Bryan and Bryanism under such an avalanche of votes that neither man or movement could rise again."[129] Claiming that he would continue Roosevelt's reforms, Taft beat Bryan by 1.2 million votes.

In 1910 Bryan came out for women's suffrage and prohibition. Prohibitionists tended to be largely liberal reformers at the time, for saloons were seen of robbing workers of both their wages and the hope for change.

In place of running for president in 1912, Bryan instead authored most of the Democratic platform. To his wife's entreaties that he run, Bryan answered, "I have had this nomination three times. It is not fair to others for me to take it again. I believe another man would be better for the party."[131]

Bryan supported Woodrow Wilson as the best candidate among those running. While president of Princeton, Wilson, viewing Bryan as too radical, had refused to let him speak at the college. Wilson became more progressive after being elected governor of New Jersey in 1910, passing substantial reforms. Wilson invited Bryan to dinner in 1911. Afterwards Wilson commented, "He has an extraordinary force of personality and it seems the force of sincerity and conviction…a truly captivating man, I must admit."[120] Believing him to be the most liberal of the candidates, Bryan ignored Wilson's prior hostility. His support was instrumental in Wilson being nominated on the 46th ballot.

Bryan's platform formed much of what became known as Wilson's New Freedom. The platform called for tariff reform, antitrust legislation, constitutional amendments to allow the income tax and direct election of senators, independence for the Philippines, a ban on corporate political contributions, rural free delivery, conservation, a Department of Labor, vocational education and the exemption of unions from the antitrust laws.[131]

The Republicans were split with Taft being nominated by at the party convention and Theodore Roosevelt, the choice of most Republican voters, running as the Progressive Party nominee. Wilson won the election due to this Republican split, garnering 100,000 fewer votes that Bryan had won in 1908. After his election, Wilson began corresponding regularly with Bryan, noting, "I have thought of you very constantly through the campaign and have felt everyday strengthened and heartened by your active and generous support."[120]

Bryan accepted Wilson's offer to be Secretary of State. Bryan wrote to Wilson, "I would not accept a place in your official household if I did not feel as deeply interested in the success of your administration as you do yourself."[131] As secretary, Bryan pushed the idea of submitting international disputes to arbitration, negotiating arbitration treaties with thirty nations. Bryan argued that "The killing of human beings shall not be commenced by any nation until the world knows what crime has been committed that requires so high a penalty."[129] Bryan commented, "The proposed plan provided for the submission of all international disputes of every kind and character to a permanent tribunal for investigation, when not by other treaties submitted for arbitration."[120] The liberal journal *The Nation* commented that the treaties "constitute the great constructive achievement of Mr. Bryan's administration."[131]

Bryan proposed that there should be a mandatory cooling-off period when conflicts erupted between nations before they could resort to war. Wilson later commented that such a cooling-off period would have avoided World War I. British Ambassador Cecil Spring Rice agreed, telling Bryan,

"No one who has studied the diplomatic history of the events leading up to the present disastrous war can ever speak lightly of your idea again. For it is abundantly manifest that even one week's enforced delay would probably have saved the peace of the world."[131] Bryan's proposal for such a cooling-off period became a major part of the League of Nations following World War I. Historian Coletta commented, "As so often happened, Bryan's ideas were laughed at for the moment, then used at a later time."[131]

Former Filipino president Emilio Aguinaldo wrote to Secretary of State Bryan, saying, "May the right of the Filipinos to independence receive a friendly support in the Democratic Party."[131] Bryan replied, "It will take some time to pass the necessary measures and I trust you will use your great influence to encourage your people to be patient."[131] Bryan was able to persuade Wilson to grant immediate home rule to the Philippines with the plan for eventual independence. Bryan told Wilson, "It is a great joy to me…to have this country committed to independence—it has been on my heart for 15 years."[131]

Bryan spent a lot of time behind the scenes pushing the administration's reform agenda, including constitutional amendments that were successfully passed allowing for an income tax and popular election of senators. Bryan's support was also crucial in winning the support of liberals for the passage of the bill creating the Federal Reserve bank system.[129] Wilson admitted that he had "relied greatly upon Bryan for help in this Congressional crisis."[131] Coletta wrote, "[Bryan] paid little attention to personal criticisms, refused to dodge an issue and was perennially an optimist and generally a happy man…Bryan laughed heartily when the butt end of a joke was on him."[131]

When World War I broke out, Bryan urged strict neutrality, saying that the war is "so horrible that no man afford to take responsibility for continuing it for a single hour."[129] At Bryan's urging, in August 1914, Wilson asked Americans to be "impartial in thoughts as well as action."

Yet over time Wilson and Bryan's views drew farther apart. Bryan tried to block loans to the opposing sides, writing on August 10, 1914, "I know of nothing that would do more to prevent war than that neutral nations would not loan to the belligerents."[120] Wilson disagreed, being increasingly irritated by Bryan's opposition to American banks making large loans to Britain and France. While Bryan favored continued American neutrality,

Wilson increasingly came to favor Britain and its allies, viewing German submarine attacks on civilian ships as immoral.

On May 7, 1915, a German submarine sank the British passenger ship *Lusitania*, resulting in the deaths of 785 passengers, including 124 Americans. Wilson rejected Bryan's suggestion that Americans be asked not to travel on the ships of belligerents, instead issuing an ultimatum to Germany. Bryan unsuccessfully argued that the United States should rebuke both Germany for sinking the *Lusitania*, but also Britain for, "using our citizens to protect their ammunition," as the *Lusitania* had been carrying ammunition to Britain.[120]

Replying to the American diplomatic message, Germany refused to accept any responsibility for the sinking of the *Lusitania*. Wilson now prepared to send a second note to Germany. Bryan was convinced that a harsh letter from the United States to Germany over the *Lusitania* would lead to war. On June 5, Bryan told Wilson, "This may be our last chance to speak for peace."[131] Wilson refused Bryan's idea that a cooling-off period be implemented before war be declared if Germany refused to back down. Bryan decided to resign. Secretary of the Treasury William McAdoo, Wilson's son-in-law, tried to talk Bryan out of resigning, pointing out his resignation would destroy Bryan politically. Bryan replied, "I believe you are right. I think this will destroy me, but whether it does or not I must do my duty according to my conscience."[131] Bryan received very harsh criticism from the increasingly pro-war Republicans and Democrats and the press over his resignation. The *New York World* called him, "contemptible," while others accused him of treason.[131]

Out of office, Bryan continued to campaign to keep America out of the war. He supported Wilson's reelection in 1916 based on the slogan, "He kept us out of the war." In 1917, the United States severed diplomatic relations with Germany. Bryan wrote an open letter to Congress saying, "If we go to war, it should be for a cause which history will ratify."[129] Bryan joined a meeting of pacifists and socialists in New York that demanded a national referendum on the issue of going to war. Bryan again received severe criticism, with a Republican congressman suggesting that he be jailed.

When war was declared in April 1917, Bryan offered his services to Wilson. Wilson ignored Bryan and denied his request to be part of the American delegation to the peace conference. Bryan supported Wilson's proposed League of Nations. Wilson's refusal to accept Republican amendments to the peace treaty bringing the United States into the League of Nations led to its defeat.

Bryan campaigned for constitutional amendments for prohibition and women's suffrage, both of which passed in 1920. He also proposed that all forms of discrimination based on gender should be abolished.

Bryan continued to argue for government action to protect those at the bottom against the great corporations. He argued for nationalization of the railroads and a government-run telephone and telegraph. He urged Congress to subsidize farm prices, guarantee a living wage, and protect collective bargaining and the right to organize.

Bryan believed that humans and society were perfectible and that people were intrinsically good. He rejected Darwin's theory of evolution whose derivative, social Darwinism, argued that human affairs were governed by the law of the jungle where the strongest would dominate. Bryan felt that without God, there was no hope for reform of humanity and society.[128] Bryan opposed the eugenics movement, a component of social Darwinism that tried to prohibit the poor and "feebleminded" from having children.

While opposing evolution, Bryan also attacked religious prejudice, criticizing Henry Ford for reprinting a virulently anti-Semitic forgery. Bryan never worried much about the doctrinal issues dividing different faiths. Rather, as Michael Kazin wrote "Bryan cited Tolstoy's conviction that religion was a practical faith because it taught men how to love and live in harmony with those of different classes and beliefs."[129]

Bryan argued that the public schools should refrain from promoting a single faith or none, by which he meant Darwinism. In July 1925, Bryan agreed to serve as the prosecuting attorney in the trial of John Scopes, a teacher accused of violating a Tennessee state law against teaching evolution. Scopes, hired mainly to coach football, had unwittingly violated the law one day while substituting for the regular biology teacher. Bryan argued that the proper place to challenge laws against evolution was in legislature.

At the trial, opposing counsel Clarence Darrow humiliated Bryan by forcing him to try to defend the literal words of the Bible.[128] The *New York Times* called the confrontation "an absurdly pathetic performance with a famous American the chief actor and butt of the crowds' rude laughter."[129]

Bryan wrote, "Science is a magnificent material force, but it is not a teacher of morals…it adds no moral restraint to protect society from misuse of the machine."[129] Staying on in Tennessee after the trial ended on July 22, Bryan died in his sleep on July 26, 1925.

Bryan is too often remembered only for this last battle. The Bryan who was the passionate crusader for social justice and the greatest liberal of his day is too often forgotten. Many of the great reforms of Franklin Roosevelt's New Deal, such as insurance for bank deposits, protection for workers and crop subsidies for farmers, were derived from Bryan's proposals. It was Bryan who helped set the Democratic Party on its new path, evolving from the party of limited government to using government to protect the weaker members in society.

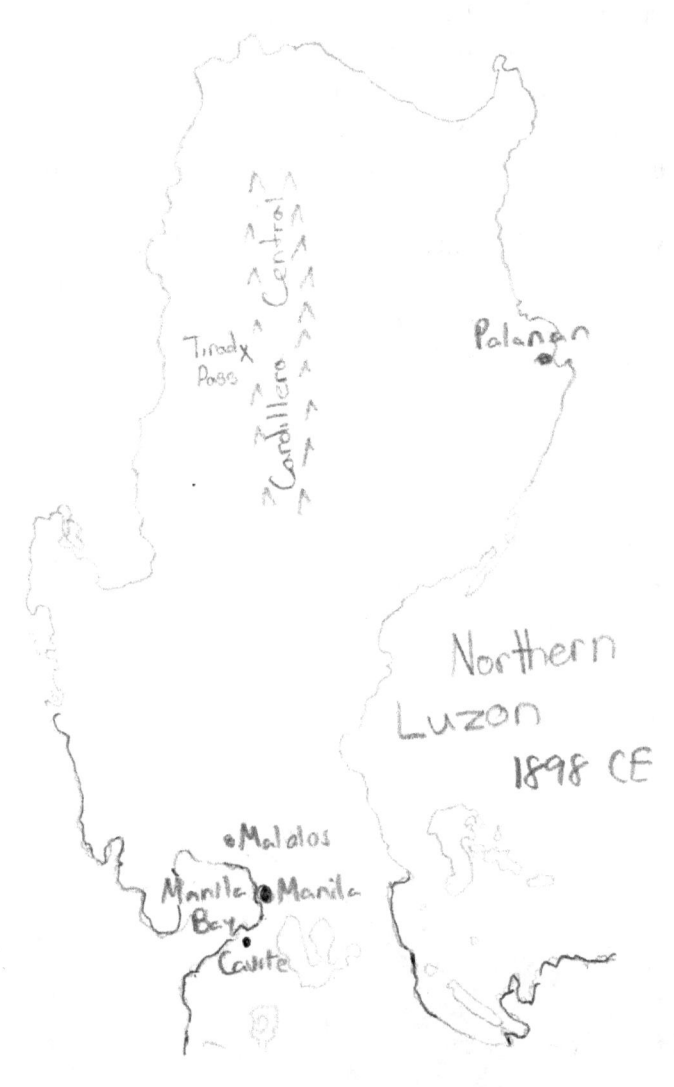

Chapter 19: Emilio Aguinaldo
The First Philippine Republic, 1898 CE, Philippines

EMILIO AGUINALDO is a name known to few Americans. Yet, America's longest war between Lees' surrender at Appomattox in 1865 and the Japanese attack at Pearl Harbor in 1941 was against this small, quiet man, whose face was scarred from smallpox. Aguinaldo fought first against the Spanish and then against the United States in a bid to bring freedom and independence to his nation of the Philippines.

The Philippines, an archipelago of some 7100 islands, about 1000 of which are inhabited, lies southeast of the continent of Asia. It stretches approximately 1150 miles from north to south. The Philippines were discovered by Ferdinand Magellan, a Portuguese explorer in the service of Spain, in 1521. The Spanish claimed the islands, founding their first colony in 1565 and then building the city of Manila on the large island of Luzon as their capital.

The Spanish rule was based on a feudal system, where vast estates were given to the Spanish. The native Filipinos were conscripted into forced labor and forced to pay taxes and tribute to their Spanish rulers. Many estates were ruled by Spanish clergy, or friars, who often were particularly hated. Historian David H. Bain wrote, "They instituted taxes, cheated peasants out of their land and imposed harsh penalties for the most minor offenses, all the while preaching Christian charity, meekness and forgiveness."[133] The Spanish government officials were also known for their corruption. The result was series of peasant revolts in multiple provinces, which were harshly suppressed. Peaceful attempts for reform did not fare better. In the late 1800s Dr. Jose Rizal formed the Liga Filipina, dedicated to bettering the Filipinos lives peacefully within the context of Spanish rule. The Spanish responded by banishing Rizal to an isolated southern island.[134]

Emilio Aguinaldo was born, the sixth of eight children, on March 22, 1859, in the town of Kawit in the province of Cavite on the eastern shore of Manila Bay. The brutal suppression of an earlier revolt in the province left few Filipinos there supportive of Spanish rule. Never the most attentive student, Emilio quit high school to assist his older brothers in the family businesses of transporting goods between the islands. Emilio's father had been mayor of Kawit. Through family connections, Emilio was appointed the local tax collector. After eight years in this post, Emilio Aguinaldo was elected mayor of Kawit.

Soon afterwards, Aguinaldo joined a secret society, the Katipunan, led by a man named Andres Bonifacio. The Katipunan advocated Filipino autonomy and, ideally, independence by any possible means, including violent revolt. After passing a series of secret tests, Aguinaldo was inducted on March 14, 1895. Aguinaldo began to recruit others for the Katipunan.

The Katipunan spread to many provinces as it gained adherents. In August 1896, the Spanish authorities learned about the society. The authorities responded by rounding up hundreds of suspects. Many were exiled or executed. The Katipunan responded by declaring rebellion on August 29, 1896. The Katipunan had few modern weapons. Bonifacio led several hundred rebels to attack a Spanish arms depot to secure more weapons, but was routed with major losses. Subsequent defeats followed.

The Katipunan rebellion in the province of Cavite started on August 31. As the mayor of Kawit, Aguinaldo went to the Spanish governor of Cavite to request troops to help fight any rebels should they appear. Aguinaldo was told that most of the troops had been sent to Manila.

Now that he knew of the Spanish weakness, Aguinaldo led the local Katipunan to take over control of Kawit and two other nearby towns from the few remaining Spaniards, almost without bloodshed. The rebels published a manifesto, urging all provincial towns in Cavite to "break the chains of slavery that have bound us…to rebel against this tyrannical race."[133]

In his first military campaign, Aguinaldo led a force of some 2000 poorly armed rebels to liberate the town of Imus. The Spanish retreated to a fortified hacienda, but Aguinaldo lit a next-door warehouse on fire. The smoke forced the Spanish to surrender.

Aguinaldo's next battle was less successful. Leading some five hundred rebels he encountered a well-armed Spanish column. The Spanish fired, causing the rebels to flee. Aguinaldo, who had not run, only escaped by pretending to be dead. The Spanish now marched on Imus. Aguinaldo, who had rejoined his men, broke the bridge that led into the town. When the Spanish unexpectedly had to stop because of the broken bridge, Aguinaldo led the rebels to wade across the river to attack the Spanish in the flank. The Spanish panicked and fled across the rice fields. Within a few weeks nearly all the towns in Cavite had been liberated. Aguinaldo was acclaimed for his generalship, which stood in contrast to Bonifacio's failures.[133]

With most of Cavite under his control, in October 1896 Aguinaldo announced his plan to create a government similar to "that of the United States."[135] The Spanish responded by wholesale slaughter of suspected rebels, convincing Aguinaldo that the Philippines must become independent. On October 31, 1896, Aguinaldo proclaimed, "People of the Philippines, open your eyes! The blood of your innocent brothers must leave an indelible mark upon your soul. From this day onwards the blood on our side and the tyranny on their side shall serve as an impossible barrier between the Philippines and Spain."[134]

The Spanish, led personally by the governor-general of the Philippines, landed a force of 2000 men along the coast of Cavite. Aguinaldo's forces drew them on, then suddenly attacked. Five hundred Spaniards were killed or wounded and the rest were forced to flee.[135] In retaliation for the revolt, the Spanish executed Jose Rizal on December 30, 1896.

Even as the rebellion continued, the Katipunan had broken into two factions, one favoring Aguinaldo and the other loyal to Bonifacio. A convention was held in March 1897 to consolidate the two factions into a united front and decide on further moves. Aguinaldo was absent, leading his troops against the Spanish in the north of the province. Bonifacio presided over the meeting. The delegates voted to declare the Republic of the Philippines. Aguinaldo was elected president, while a prime minister and cabinet were also selected. Bonifacio, furious at being passed over as leader, left and declared that the assembly was dissolved and its actions annulled. Aguinaldo tried to ignore Bonifacio's actions to maintain a united front against the Spanish, saying, "I patiently accepted this difficult situation so that petty jealousies and recriminations of brother against brother [could] be stopped."[133]

The Spanish had named a new governor, General Polavieja, who directed his troops "to wash all offenses in blood."[135] Polavieja had been heavily reinforced from Spain. He had over 17,000 well-armed troops against some 10,000–30,000 rebels, most with minimal weapons. Aguinaldo adopted tactics of trying to get close enough to the Spanish to be able to surprise them and allow the rebels, many of whom were armed only with the knife-like bolo, to engage in hand-to-hand combat. This tactic was successful at the battle at Zapote, where Aguinaldo killed three Spaniards with his Spanish-made sword.[134] At Imus, the Filipinos under Aguinaldo dug trenches, fending off repeated Spanish attacks on these trenches. The Spanish were finally forced to retreat.

Nevertheless, the better-armed Spanish began to make progress against the rebels. Aguinaldo had dispatched reinforcements to his brother Crispulo, whose forces had come under heavy Spanish attack. Bonifacio, however, intercepted these troops and instead ordered them to protect the town he was in. The Spanish defeated Crispulo, who was killed in the fighting. Aguinaldo went north in an unsuccessful attempt to recover his brother's body, but fell ill with malaria. While he lay ill, the Spanish advanced south, recapturing many towns and burning Aguinaldo's home town of Kawit to the ground.[134]

Aguinaldo heard that additional rebel troops had been detained by Bonifacio. Aguinaldo, accompanied by his troops, went to the hacienda where Bonifacio was staying. Here he found the missing troops sequestered and Bonifacio meeting privately with two of Aguinaldo's generals. Bonifacio and his supporters escaped through the cordon of troops surrounding the house. Bonifacio went to the neighboring province of Batangas, where it was rumored that he would declare himself the true president. Aguinaldo now sent troops to arrest Bonifacio and his brother, who were brought before a military tribunal. Bonifacio clearly had denounced the new republican government while recklessly interfering with military decisions. The chief witness was one of Bonifacio's own men, Lieutenant Colonel Pedro Giron. The military tribunal ordered the brothers executed. Aguinaldo commuted the sentence to banishment. However, he was persuaded to rescind this change after heavy lobbying, much from Bonifacio's former supporters as well as the two generals who had been found meeting with him. On May 10, 1897, Andres Bonifacio and his brother were executed.

Spanish pressure forced Aguinaldo to leave Cavite. He traveled to Biyak-na-Bato, a well-defended area in central Luzon that was controlled by Aguinaldo's supporter, General Mamerto Navidad. Advent of the rainy season caused a lull in hostilities. Aguinaldo offered to compromise, asking as condition for ending the rebellion the expulsion of the Spanish friars, the establishment of press and speech freedoms, restitution of land and parliamentary representation for the Filipinos. The Spanish rejected these terms. Aguinaldo tried to persuade the United States to intervene against Spain, but was unsuccessful.

When fighting resumed the tide turned against the rebels. General Navidad was killed in battle in November. Aguinaldo's forces desperately fought off repeated Spanish assaults. The rebels remained critically short of weapons. Increasing numbers of men began to desert from their ranks. Aguinaldo at last agreed to end the rebellion. Aguinaldo and nineteen other key leaders agreed to go into exile in Hong Kong in exchange for 800,000 pesos, proclamation of a general amnesty and distribution of an additional 900,000 pesos to be given to civilian victims of the war. Aguinaldo claimed that the Spanish promised further reforms, but reneged on these verbal promises. The rebels intended to use the money to purchase weapons to be able to renew the fight for independence later.[133] On December 27, 1897, Aguinaldo and his deputies boarded a British ship to travel to Hong Kong.

On the other side of the world, Cubans were also rebelling against Spanish colonial rule. When the US cruiser *Maine*, on a courtesy visit to Cuba, exploded, many in the United States blamed the Spanish. In March 1898 an American naval officer, Captain Edwin P. Wood, met with Aguinaldo. Wood suggested that Aguinaldo return to the Philippines to reassemble his army with arms supplied by the United States. When Aguinaldo asked about the Americans' intentions, Wood answered, "The United States, my general, is a great and rich nation, and neither needs nor desires colonies."

Shortly afterward, Aguinaldo traveled to Singapore, where he was found by the American Consul General, E. Spencer Pratt. Pratt informed him, "As of the other day, April 19th, Spain and America have been at war. Now is the time to strike. Ally yourselves with America and you will surely defeat the Spaniards."[133] Aguinaldo asked if the American commander in the region, Admiral Dewey, would issue an official invitation. Dewey telegrammed, "Send Aguinaldo at once."[133] Pratt told Aguinaldo that Dewey had said that the United States "would at least recognize the independence of the Philippines under the protection of the United States Navy."[133] Aguinaldo answered, "If I can secure arms, I promise that my people will rise as one man against the Spaniards."[133] On May 7, the US Navy ship *McCullouch* arrived in Hong Kong with news that Dewey had annihilated the Spanish fleet on May 1.

Aguinaldo and seventeen associates traveled on the *McCullouch* back to the Philippines, arriving in Manila Bay on May 19, 1898. Aguinaldo was invited onto Admiral Dewey's flagship. Dewey urged him to go fight the Spanish. While the American fleet controlled the waters around the islands, the Americans did not have any troops in the region to defeat the Spanish army. Aguinaldo noted that Dewey told him that "the United States had come to the Philippines to free the Filipinos from the yoke of Spain," and needed no colonies.[133] None of the American leaders—Wood, Pratt or Dewey—would make a written agreement with Aguinaldo. Dewey told Aguinaldo that "the word of honor of Americans was more positive, more irrevocable than a written agreement."[133]

Aguinaldo landed and immediately found fresh volunteers. On May 20, 1898, Aguinaldo issued a proclamation urging the Filipinos to ally themselves with America, declaring, "To the Revolutionary Leaders of the Philippines: Divine Providence is about to place independence within our reach. Alliance with the Americans has assured us of this. Therefore, do not align yourself with the Spanish, our oppressors for three hundred years, but rather look to the American flag."[134]

Aguinaldo's first attack resulted in the liberation of Kawit on May 28. Only some 2800 Spanish troops were scattered in small garrisons through the province of Cavite. Half of these troops were native Filipinos, many of whom deserted. Within a few days, Cavite had been liberated. By June 30, Aguinaldo's troops had liberated all of Luzon except the capital of Manila, into which the Spaniards had retreated. Nine thousand Spanish troops were prisoners of war. Aguinaldo ordered that property and prisoners should be protected. Thirty thousand Filipino troops under General Antonio Luna now surrounded Manila in fourteen miles of trenches and had cut off the city's water supply. Dewey praised the Filipinos encircling the city as, "our friends assisting us [and] doing our work."[135] Aguinaldo wrote to the Spanish in Manila asking them to consider, "an honorable capitulation," but the Spanish refused to answer.[134]

Now controlling most of Luzon, on June 6, 1898, Aguinaldo led the Filipinos in proclaiming their independence. The Filipino Declaration of Independence was based on the American document. Admiral Dewey said he was too busy to attend the ceremony. The new Filipino government printed postage stamps and restarted telegraph and ferry service. Expeditions were sent to the other islands to free them.

Worried about American intentions, Aguinaldo sent a letter to President McKinley thanking America for its help in ejecting the Spanish, but also saying that the Philippines "should not be sold as if it were a lamb to be sacrificed and exploited for the greed of another nation."[136] McKinley initially did not intend for the United States to retain the Philippines after the war, but pressure from his advisors and what he took as public opinion had changed his mind. Not advising Aguinaldo of his views, McKinley wrote his commanders that the United States must control Manila, noting, "The insurgents and all others must recognize the military occupation and authority of the United States."[135]

American troops now began to arrive in the Philippines. They ordered the Filipino troops to move aside to let the better-armed Americans launch the final assault on Manila. The initial American commander, General Anderson, wired the War Department on July 9, 1898, noting, "Aguinaldo, who was at first suspicious, is now friendly and willing to cooperate. He is making every effort, however, to take Manila without American help. The establishment of a provisional government on our part will probably bring us into conflict with the insurgents, now in active hostility to Spain."[134]

On August 13, the Spanish surrendered Manila to the Americans after a sham battle to preserve Spanish honor. The Filipinos were unaware of this arrangement. When they captured several Manila suburbs, they were pushed back by American troops. The Filipinos were upset that the Americans kept the Filipino forces out of Manila. Dewey and General Merritt, the new American army commander, barred Aguinaldo from the surrender ceremony. Aguinaldo's Prime Minister Apolinario Mabini told him, "The conflict is coming sooner or later, and we shall gain nothing by asking as favors of them what are really our rights."[135]

Aguinaldo meanwhile assembled a constitutional convention at Malolos on September 15, calling for "the Philippines for the Filipinos."[133] Aguinaldo, and especially Mabini, advocated a populist philosophy. However, the constitutional convention was dominated by the "illustrados," the wealthy Hispanicized Filipinos, many of whom had originally opposed the revolt against Spain. The constitution that was adopted limited Aguinaldo's power, while restricting suffrage to wealthy landowners.

More and more American troops landed. Successive American commanders assured Aguinaldo that they were not there to take over, even while further displacing the Filipino troops from their positions. In France,

Spain and the United States were negotiating a peace treaty. McKinley met with Aguinaldo's representative Felipe Agoncillo, but rejected Filipino representation at the talks or even letting the Filipinos talk to the American delegation.[135] On October 26, McKinley wrote to his negotiators in Paris about the Philippines, ordering "the cessation must be of the whole archipelago."[135]

The final peace treaty, signed December 10, 1898, provided for the cession of the Philippines to America in exchange for a token payment of twenty million dollars. President McKinley called for "benevolent assimilation" of the Philippines. The Filipinos were outraged. Aguinaldo responded that he had never agreed to or recognized the sovereignty of America over the islands, noting, "My government is disposed to open hostilities if the American troops attempt to take forcible possession…upon their heads be all the blood that may be shed."[133] Aguinaldo ordered his provincial commanders to stockpile supplies. Aguinaldo also tried to increase support from the Filipino peasantry by proclaiming the end of the forced labor that had been a hated feature of Spanish rule. On January 20, 1899, the Philippine Congress gave Aguinaldo authority to declare war if necessary. Aguinaldo said, "We are no longer insurgents, we are no longer revolutionaries…no longer is there anything lacking in order that we be recognized and admitted as a free and independent nation."[134]

Aguinaldo waited to see if the US Senate would ratify the treaty, which had generated vociferous opposition in the United States from those opposing the annexation of the Philippines. Labor leader Samuel Gompers said that retention of the Philippines would show that "our war was without just cause."[126] Industrialist Andrew Carnegie telegraphed his agreement, saying, "Let us stand together to save the Republic."[126] A petition signed by ex-President Cleveland and other national leaders noted, "In accordance with the principles upon which the Republic was founded we are duty bound to recognize the rights of the inhabitants…to independence and self-government."[126] Some Americans opposed the absorption of more non-whites, while others proclaimed the right and duty of white America to rule over a lesser people.

An uneasy standoff existed between the American and Filipino forces on Luzon. On the night of February 4, 1899, two American sentries opened fire on four men approaching in the darkness, killing several Filipino soldiers. Soon firing erupted all through the lines. Full-scale battles between the Americans and Filipinos on February 5 led to the deaths of over 3000 Filipinos compared to sixty American dead. General Otis, the American commander, refused Aguinaldo's proposal for a ceasefire. Otis replied that "the fighting having begun, must go to the grim end."[133] Aguinaldo wrote, "we had no honorable course, but to sell our lives dearly."[133]

On February 6, the peace treaty was very narrowly approved in the US Senate, with the tiebreaking vote being cast by the vice president. Republican House Speaker Thomas Reed, who privately opposed annexation, commented, "We have bought ten million Malays at $2 a head unpicked and nobody know what it will cost to pick them."[126] Reed soon retired from Congress rather than support the McKinley administration policy. Speaking on February 16, 1899, President McKinley said Filipinos "shall for ages hence bless the American Republic because it emancipated and redeemed their fatherland and set them in the pathway of the world's best civilization."[136]

The Americans blamed the Filipinos for starting the war. Secretary of War Elihu Root stated, "On the night of February 4, two days before the United States Senate approved the treaty, an army of Tagalogs, under the leadership of Aguinaldo, a Chinese half breed, attacked in vastly superior numbers our little army in the possession of Manila."[133] The *New York Times* described Aguinaldo as nothing but "a vain popinjay, a wicked liar and a perfectly incapable leader" whose men were "dupes, a foolish incredulous mob" and stated that the "mischievous influence of this tricky little man must be broken."[137] Admiral Dewey now said that Aguinaldo was interested only in, "revenge, plunder and pillage."[137]

In fact, the poorly armed Filipino army of some 80,000 men was scattered across Luzon. The Philippine population was divided into eleven major language groups as well as between Catholics and Muslims, who predominated on the most southern islands. The nationalist forces were dominated by Tagalog speakers, which aroused the resentment of other ethnic groups. The Americans secured the cooperation of the Muslims in the south by promising autonomy.[136]

The well-armed American forces pushed the Filipinos back. At the end of March, American forces under General Arthur MacArthur attacked and captured the Filipino capital of Malolos. The Filipino commander, General Luna, burned Malolos to the ground before retreating.[134] Aguinaldo had abandoned the capital the day before. The Americans captured the relocated

Philippine capital at San Isidro on May 17. On June 16, 1899, Aguinaldo personally led a force of seven thousand men attacking MacArthur's headquarters in San Fernando. After fierce fighting, the Filipinos were forced to retreat. The arrival of the summer monsoon created a lull in the fighting. Atrocities by the American forces were met by atrocities ordered by General Luna against American prisoners and Filipinos whom he suspected of cooperating with the Americans.[134]

An American peace commission arrived in Manila. After interviewing mainly Westerners and a few conservative illustrados, the commission proposed limited Filipino autonomy under American rule. Aguinaldo proposed a three-month truce to allow the Filipinos to decide whether to accept this proposal. The Americans refused to agree. However, a rump group of the Filipino legislature, comprised of illustrados, voted to accept the autonomy and end the war. Shortly afterward, the hot-tempered General Luna was murdered by his enemies among the army. Aguinaldo said, "The loss of Luna was, of course, a very heavy blow to our armed efforts."[133]

By the summer of 1899, 60,000 American troops were in the Philippines, a number that would grow to 75,000 in 1900, or about three-quarters of the whole American army.[135] In June 1899, John Bass, a correspondent for *Harpers* wrote that the United States controlled a region no farther than thirty miles from Manila, noting that the population supported Aguinaldo and that "only those natives whose immediate self-interest requires it are friendly to us."[135]

The addition of more troops allowed the Americans to resume their advance in October. Historian Stanley Karnow argued that Aguinaldo, by focusing only on independence and not on social, and particularly not on agrarian reforms, lost the active support of much of the peasantry.[135] Aguinaldo decided to break up his armies into small groups of guerrillas to harass the Americans, rather than lose more men in open battles. Aguinaldo, accompanied by his family and 1200 men, headed north for the mountains. He was pursued by American troops. During the retreat, Aguinaldo's infant daughter Flora died of fever. The rear guard, along with Aguinaldo's son and the national printing press, was overtaken and captured by the Americans. Aguinaldo, his wife and sister and 250 men under the command of the young and charismatic General Gregorio del Pilar entered the mountains. The American pursuit did not slacken. Aguinaldo's force blocked the high cliffs of Tirad Pass, but was driven back after General Pilar was killed by a sniper. Aguinaldo and his remaining men climbed higher into the mountains.

Aguinaldo and his men spent the next five months moving from village to village in the high mountains of the Central Cordillera. These mountains were inhabited by many distinct and more primitive tribes, ethnically distinct from the Tagalog majority. The tribes were hostile to outsiders, tolerating Aguinaldo's forces only due to their superior weaponry and numbers.

Aguinaldo's men existed in an uneasy truce with villagers with whom they stayed. Soldiers on patrol stood a chance of being ambushed by people from other villages. Just before Christmas, Aguinaldo sent his wife, sisters and the other women in the group to give themselves up to the Americans. Aguinaldo and his troops, having crossed the mountains, descended into the vast Cagayan Valley, where the Filipino inhabitants greeted them as heroes. It did not take long before the Americans learned of his presence and resumed the pursuit.

Aguinaldo's forces headed back into the mountains. The trip through the mountains was a nightmarish journey that involved crossing swollen rivers and climbing steep mountain trails, all while being closely pursued by American troops. Many of the men fell ill with malaria. Aguinaldo was forced to abandon fourteen soldiers too ill with malaria to be moved. They were killed by the pursuing troops. At last the Americans caught up with them. The Filipino soldiers scattered to avoid being captured.

Aguinaldo and sixty-one survivors escaped into a forest near the town of Naguilian, where they remained for almost three months. On August 26 Aguinaldo learned that the Americans had discovered his location. Aguinaldo left most of the men to operate as guerrillas. With only twenty men, Aguinaldo set out through the mountains, heading for a remote area near the eastern coast of Luzon. At last, on September 3, 1900, they reached the isolated settlement of Palanan. Here Aguinaldo set up his base.

Aguinaldo hoped that a protracted war with increasing American casualties would gradually erode support for the war in the United States. He was also hoping that William Jennings Bryan, who opposed annexation, would win the American presidential election in 1900. Aguinaldo proclaimed, "In America there is a great party that insists on the United States government recognizing Filipino independence. They will compel their country to fulfill the promises made to us in all solemnity and faith...[The] great Democratic party of the United States will win the next fall election...Imperialism will fail in its mad attempts to subjugate us by force of arms."[137] Filipino soldiers chanted, "Aguinaldo-Bryan."[126]

By now some 70,000 American troops were occupied trying to put down what they called the Philippine Insurrection.[125] Guerrilla attacks on American forces resulted in increased mistreatment by the Americans of civilians and captured soldiers. The American army rounded up populations in the most affected areas, such as Cavite, and moved them into towns under American control, aiming at severing the population's support of the resistance. Towns not under American control were burned down. The Filipinos intensified their guerrilla attacks on the American forces in September and October of 1900. Yet they were disappointed as William McKinley won reelection in November 1900.

The year 1900 had been marked by Filipino guerrilla attacks and an American counterinsurgency campaign. The whereabouts of Aguinaldo remained elusive. Although General Otis, on leaving the Philippines in the spring of 1900, commented that Aguinaldo was, "probably dead," the new American commanders viewed Aguinaldo as the key to ending the war.[137] General Frederick Funston wrote, "As [Aguinaldo] was insistent that the Filipinos should not accept American rule, and as he was still recognized as the head and front of the insurrection, many of us had long felt that the thing would not end until he was either out of the way or a prisoner in our hands."[133]

Early in 1901, Aguinaldo received a letter from one of his generals letting him know that a band of Filipino guerrillas had captured five Americans and was bringing them to him. On March 23, 1901, the guerrillas arrived in the village of Palanan, where they were warmly greeted by Aguinaldo's men. Aguinaldo himself received the leaders of the band. Suddenly these guerrillas started firing on Aguinaldo's men while their officers pulled guns on Aguinaldo. It had been a ruse. The Americans had captured one of Aguinaldo's couriers the month before. The courier had revealed Aguinaldo's location. The letter from Aguinaldo's general was an American forgery. The "captured" Americans, led by General Frederick Funston, had captured Aguinaldo.

Aguinaldo reportedly said, "the whole thing seems yet to be a nightmare. I can hardly believe myself to be a prisoner."[133] He later admitted that he had "a feeling of disgust and despair for I had failed my people and my motherland."[133] Funston noted of Aguinaldo, "His gameness and general bearing won our hearts."[133] Aguinaldo was taken to the coast, where an American naval ship was waiting to take him to Manila.

The news of Aguinaldo's capture was greeted with banner headlines in the United States. Those in the United States opposed to annexation did not abandon their stance. William Jennings Bryan said that while Aguinaldo's capture "may end the war for the present," he could derive no satisfaction, for "we cannot administer an empire in the Orient and maintain a republic in America."[133]

In Manila, Aguinaldo was kept in seclusion under heavy guard. The US Army commander, General Arthur MacArthur, visited Aguinaldo daily and explained "the US point of view, the glories and prosperity that would follow as soon as the fighting ended, and the hopelessness of allowing the struggle to continue."[137] The Americans argued about what to do with Aguinaldo. Admiral Dewey suggested that he be shot, while others suggested that he be exiled to Guam. Aguinaldo, after intense lobbying by his family, issued a proclamation on April 19, 1901, saying, "The country had declared unmistakably in favor of peace; so be it. Enough of blood: enough of tears and desolation…by acknowledging and accepting the sovereignty of the United States throughout the entire Archipelago, as I do now, without any reservation whatsoever, I believe I am serving thee, my beloved country. May happiness be thine."[133] Over 20,000 Filipinos now surrendered, but others continued resistance.

The center of the insurgency shifted to Batangas Province, where 5000 guerrillas under General Malvar regained control of most of the area south of Manila by the summer of 1901. The United States responded with a brutal counterinsurgency campaign that resulted in the deaths of 54,000 civilians in Batangas. Malvar and his forces surrendered on April 16, 1902. Continued fighting on a lesser scale would not end for another ten years.[137] The war would ultimately cost America some 4000 dead while Filipino deaths were estimated to include 20,000 soldiers and some 200,000 civilians.[135]

Whatever his private misgivings, Aguinaldo had made no further efforts to rouse Filipino resistance to American rule. American attitudes toward Aguinaldo improved. MacArthur acknowledged in August 1901 that "Aguinaldo is a better man than we gave him credit for."[137] The *New York Times* now described Aguinaldo as a "warm, friendly, intelligent, trustworthy and reasonable person—a man of honor with the best interests of his countrymen at heart."[137] Admiral Dewey testified before a Senate committee on January 28, 1902, stating, "I never dreamed that they wanted independence...He [Aguinaldo] whipped the Spaniards in battle after battle...He and I were always on the most friendly terms; we never had any differences."[134]

Aguinaldo was finally released from house arrest on July 4, 1902. He returned to Kawit, where he managed the family plantation. In 1907, he was visited by William Jennings Bryan, who commented on the injustice of American rule.[129] Aguinaldo lobbied to set up rural development banks and for Filipino veterans, becoming head of the Association of the Veterans of the Revolution in 1915. Aguinaldo always wore a black bow tie of mourning for the lost republic.

Aguinaldo attempted to return to politics in the 1930s. The Philippines had become a commonwealth with a plan for independence many years in the future. Aguinaldo ran for president of the commonwealth, advocating a shortened transition period before independence. He was decisively defeated by Manuel Quezon, who stood for the status quo.

In 1942 Japan captured the Philippines. Aguinaldo, now in his seventies, broadcast a plea for General Douglas MacArthur to stop his resistance, stating that Japan had promised independence. Many top commonwealth officials also worked for the Japanese. Numerous Americans denounced Aguinaldo and the others as traitors. However, after the war many of the collaborators with the Japanese were pardoned, some reentering the government. Aguinaldo was not prosecuted.

The Philippines received independence after the end of World War II. During the Independence Day parade of July 4, 1946, Aguinaldo carried the same revolutionary flag he had carried against the Spanish in 1898 and removed his black tie. Aguinaldo, who did not smoke or drink, remained in good health, exercising daily. Emilio Aguinaldo died on February 6, 1964, just short of his 95th birthday.

Aguinaldo and the First Philippine Republic had been defeated in 1901. However, Aguinaldo survived to see an independent Republic of the Philippines declared forty-five years later.

Europe
1914 CE

Chapter 20: Jean Jaurès
Justice, Not War, 1914 CE, France

THE END OF THE NINETEENTH CENTURY in Europe was marked by industrial revolution and social disruption. The general European peace, excluding wars between individual countries, had lasted since 1815. This was to end in 1914 in the cataclysm of World War I. No man fought harder against world war and came closer to preventing it than Jean Jaurès.[138–141]

Jean Jaurès was born on September 3, 1859, in the city of Castres in the primarily agricultural Department of Tarn in southern France. His middle-class family divided its time between Castres and the countryside. Jean was delighted by the outdoors and had spent enough time among country folk to be able to appreciate the struggles of the peasants. During his youth, Tarn was being altered by the development of mining and metallurgy, which was dominated by the very wealthy Solages clan.[138]

Jean Jaurès started at the College de Castres, a high school, in October 1869. Jaurès was the most outstanding student during his seven years there, achieving an unmatched record of scholastic achievement at the college.[138]

In 1876, Jaurès was recruited for the Ecole Normale Superieure, which trained the future professors of France. Jaurès entered the Ecole Normale in 1878, deciding eventually to specialize in philosophy. Historian Harold Weinstein described him, writing, "Jaurès passionately loved nature; and nature, art, music, literature and the company of his friends were his greatest pleasures. He was utterly indifferent to money, luxury and the haute monde."[142]

Jaurès also became a staunch supporter of the French Republic, which had only been established after the demise of the French Empire in the Franco-Prussian War of 1870. For most intellectuals, the republic was associated with a more just social order. Many conservative French preferred the empire or a monarchy.

After graduation in 1881, Jaurès became a professor of philosophy at the lycée of Albi, near his parents, where he was an outstanding and popular teacher.[139] In 1883, following the death of his father, Jaurès moved to join the teaching faculty at Toulouse. He became interested in politics, writing, "I cannot deny that from time to time I turn my ear to the noise of politics, and then I think I could move into that world; yet I'm not really sure."[138] In 1885 Jaurès met Louise Blois, the daughter of a wholesale cheese merchant, whom he was to marry the next year.

One day, after teaching his philosophy class, Jaurès heard the noise of a large crowd in a nearby amphitheater. Jaurès went to the meeting where the speaker was attacking the republic. Jaurès stood up in the audience and gave a vigorous defense of the French Republic. A witness recalled, "It was a spectacular success. Jaurès thawed his audience, so cold at first, and at the end of his wonderful improvisation, there was a tremendous ovation."[138]

Impressed by his speech, the local pro-republican party picked Jaurès to run as one of six representatives for the Department of Tarn in the Chamber of Deputies, the French legislature. Jaurès campaigned enthusiastically for the ticket, defending it from attacks from both the right and left. He proposed the enactment of reforms to benefit the poor, saying, "I will vote for all reforms that will improve the lot of the suffering."[138] Jaurès won the most votes of all the candidates in Tarn and became the youngest member of the legislature at age 26.

Jaurès' main goals were economic reforms to help the poor and effective ways to protect the republic against its monarchist opponents.[138] The French Republic at the time was dominated by moderate conservatives who backed secular education and universal suffrage, but did not push social or economic reforms. In 1887 Jaurès commented, "It is necessary that the Republic, by showing its affection for the workers of the cities and the workers of the fields and by giving benefits to both groups, attach them to itself."[142] Jaurès argued for a reduction of taxes on land to help the peasants, legalization of unions for agricultural workers, an eight-hour work day and a system of social insurance to counter "the consequences of illness, accident, old age, prolonged unemployment."[142] Foreshadowing his later socialism, Jaurès suggested that the government provide pensions to workers, which would allow them to purchase ownership of factories.[142] Jaurès was disenchanted by the failure of the dominant republicans to enact social reforms, but remained a staunch supporter of the republic.

Many on both left and right denounced the republic as corrupt, instead idealizing a French general, Boulanger, whom they imagined an incorruptible strongman who should take over rule. Jaurès took the lead in opposing General Boulanger, denouncing him as a potential despot, saying, "Despotism is the most monstrous of inequalities, since there are millions of men who can do nothing while one man can do anything."[138] The government finally moved to arrest Boulanger and the general, accompanied by his mistress, fled France on April 1, 1889.

Legislative elections were held in 1889. Jaurès was opposed by the Reille-Solages family, long the dominant political and economic force in the Tarn. Jaurès opened his campaign saying, "I carry with me a dream of fraternity and justice and toward these goals I want to work."[138] Jaurès argued for increased government supervision of large private businesses, for strong independent unions and extensive social security. The Reille-Solages family threatened the workers working in their factories and mines, saying their jobs depended on voting against Jaurès.[138] Jaurès was narrowly defeated in the election in September, 1889.

Jaurès resumed his position as professor of philosophy at Toulouse. In 1889, Jaurès became friends with the librarian of the École Normale Superiéure, Lucien Herr. Herr, a socialist, persuaded Jaurès to study Marx and other socialist thinkers. Jaurès became persuaded that socialism was the best hope of achieving improvements in the lives of ordinary people. On

February 25, 1890, Jaurès published a column in which he identified himself as a socialist.

Yet, Jaurès frequently disagreed with Marxist orthodoxy. Historian Barbara Tuchman wrote, "He believed that man was good, that society could be made good and the struggle to make it so was to be fought daily…Of all Socialists he was most pragmatic, never a doctrinaire, always a man of action…He was a working idealist."[132] Marxist dogma predicted the eventual emergence of a worker-ruled state. Jaurès disagreed, writing that the latter "would simply mean the replacement of one tyranny by another, one oppression by another."[138] Jaurès instead argued that socialists "must strive for the fusion of classes in the common defense of liberty, in the common quest for justice."[142]

Jaurès also saw practical issues as more important than theoretical positions. Hence, in November 1891 he opposed a proposal to rid relief houses of all religious personnel as the principle of secularization, which Jaurès supported, was less important to him than the immediate relief of the needy.

Orthodox Marxism argued that education under capitalism was of little value. Jaurès argued strongly for education, saying, "The intellectual equality of all will make social equality untenable."[138] Jaurès commented, "There are not some who are common and others who are intellectual. Within each man is both the commoner and the philosopher."[138] Against those who postulated the workers were inferior in intellect, Jaurès retorted, "How can you expect that after twelve, fourteen or fifteen hours of work in a factory…man's thoughts will rise, dreamlike, above all the raucous noise of the machines?"[138] Jaurès summed up his version of socialism, stating, "It seeks to develop the faculties of man, his power to think, to love and to will."[138]

Marxist orthodoxy held that the fall of capitalism and the triumph of socialism was an inevitable fact of history independent of any human intervention. Jaurès instead argued that people's efforts could bring about reform and the improvement in people's lives. Jaurès told his students, "Before evidence of evil, a man must neither fall silent nor compromise; he would be denying his reason and wasting his chance to act."[138]

The failure of the Paris Commune in 1870 affected socialists in different ways. While orthodox Marxists saw this as evidence of the permanent antagonism between the classes, reform-minded Socialists saw this as evidence that reform by means of the political system was more likely to be successful than a violent uprising.[142] Jaurès said that the socialism would result "not from the violent and exclusive agitation of a social fraction, but from a kind of national movement."[142] While the hard core Marxists repudiated the French Republic as a bourgeois creation, the more liberal Socialists, including Jaurès, saw in the republic the tradition of the French Revolution and the Declaration of the Rights of Man. Jaurès disagreed with the notion that all non-Socialist states were equally bad, stating that it was crucial for the workers whether they were "in a nation as free or slave, autonomous or conquered, rich or poor, enlightened or ignorant."[142]

Jaurès believed in the idea of the French nation, anthropomorphizing France into a living organism with a heart and conscience.[142] He argued that social justice would give "to our well-beloved France the most glorious position to which a glorious nation can aspire."[142] Where many socialists felt that nation states would disappear after the advent of socialism, Jaurès argued that independent nations would be beneficial in the future as the choice would be between "a crushing planetary bureaucracy and the federation of autonomous nations harmoniously associated in the common work of humanity."[142] Jaurès also argued for a uniquely French form of socialism, stating, "All socialism, all collectivism, is not in Marx. It comes in France from French conceptions and French traditions."[142]

Unions had been legalized in France in 1884. Employers resisted both workers' specific demands and their right to unionize. In the Tarn, the mines were largely owned by the Marquis de Solages and Baron Reille, who had almost feudal control over the workers. When the secretary-general of the miners' union, Jean Baptiste Calvignac, was elected mayor of Carmaux, Reille refused to give him time for his mayoral duties and fired him when he took time for these duties. On August 16, 1892, the miners started a strike in response. This Jaurès enthusiastically supported. After ten weeks of the strike, Reille was forced to agree to arbitration when the French government threatened to seize the mines. During the strike the Marquis de Solages had been widely criticized for the company's position. He resigned from the Chamber of Deputies in October, 1892, causing a special election to be called. Against the opposition of the more doctrinaire socialists, Jaurès was chosen as the candidate of the socialists. Jaurès then won the special election on January 8, 1893, and returned to the Chamber of Deputies.

Jaurès felt that the chamber had continued to follow a conservative course in the years since he had left, noting that the majority had "consistently capitulated before the power of money."[138] The general election held in the fall of 1893 left the moderate republicans dominant with 275 deputies, while the socialists, including Jaurès, increased from twelve to thirty-seven. French governments tended to be weak and short lived, as one faction fought others for power.

Thus, when a new prime minister, Charles Dupuy, opened the meeting of the chamber in November 1893 with a declaration of a conservative program, Jaurès effectively rebutted him, instead laying out the case for reform. After four days of attacks from Jaurès, Dupuy resigned. Jaurès gained immense prestige among the socialists.

This period was also the height of the anarchist movement, which favored abolition of all government. The anarchist movement was suffused with the idea of the propaganda of the deed, in which individual acts of violence would lead to a revolution. On December 9, 1893, an anarchist threw a bomb in the Chamber of Deputies, which fortunately only resulted in wounding one deputy. The government now enacted legislation allowing suppression of newspapers for "indirect provocation" and allowing the government to outlaw organizations and forbid meetings suspected of hatching criminal plots.

While the laws were overtly aimed at the anarchists, they also threatened the socialists who shared the anarchists' opposition to capitalism. Jaurès asked the government ministers, "Why, why in these past few months have you become so suspicious of the militant workers? Why have you multiplied searches and arrests among the poor on the basis of the vaguest standards, the silliest pretexts and completely anonymous charges?"[138] Jaurès also stressed the importance of academic freedom in response to the government surveillance of the political activities of teachers and professors.

On June 24, 1894, the French president, Sadi Carnot, was stabbed to death by an anarchist. The government, with the support of the public, now proposed to suppress any source of anarchist ideas, including the press, meetings, private gatherings and even letters. Jaurès offered an amendment that "All men in public life who have sold their votes—or have been involved in financial scandals—will be judged as the real cause of the anarchist propaganda."[138]

Jaurès's oratory had few rivals in the legislature. Historian Barbara Tuchman wrote, "In the Chamber when he climbed with heavy, purposeful steps to the tribune and tossed off a glass of red wine before speaking, auditors tensed with expectancy…He could speak at this pitch for an hour and a half to two hours at a time. Using no notes he could not be fazed by interruptions."[126] The socialist Leon Trotsky called Jaurès "the most powerful speaker of his time and perhaps of all times."[138] The government measure ended up being passed without Jaurès's amendment, but not before the government escaped censure by one vote. In September 1894, a socialist editor was arrested for criticizing the new president. Defending the editor, Jaurès argued that the president should not be immune from criticism.

Jaurès continued to attack the control of the wealthy over the government, stating, "In French society a group of men, privileged through education and wealth, wields the decisive political and economic power…the peasants and workers comprise two thirds of the nation, yet there is hardly a handful of workers in the parliament and not a single peasant."[138]

On January 1, 1895, a ministry of Radicals, who would be considered liberals in today's America, took over. This government proposed progressive taxation, pensions for workers and arbitration of strikes. Jaurès supported this government in the face of criticism by the orthodox socialists who refused to cooperate with a "bourgeois" government. The Chamber of Deputies passed the progressive income tax only to see it blocked in the more conservative upper chamber of the parliament, the Senate. By the next year, a more conservative government took over.

Another conflict for the socialists concerned their prescription of collectively owned farms as the solution for agriculture. Most peasants, however, wanted to own their own farms. Jaurès' country background gave him more understanding and sympathy toward the peasants than the more orthodox socialists from urban areas. Jaurès suggested that a socialist France could have room for both "what we call small family operations and then we can call collective farms."[138] Jaurès pointed out that the 28,000 richest owners in France, however, held as much property as the six million poorest farmers.[138] Jaurès proposed a minimum wage for farm workers, extension of cheap credit and community ownership of processing plants.

To his advocacy of improved social conditions, Jaurès added the importance of avoiding war. France wanted revenge on Germany for the

1870 Franco-Prussian conflict, during which Germany had seized the two French provinces of Alsace and Lorraine. To achieve this, France reached a military alliance with Russia. Jaurès was suspicious of this secret diplomacy as well as the alliance with the ultra-reactionary Tsarist regime in Russia. Then, in September 1898, France came to the brink of war with the British Empire over ownership of territory in the Sudan in Africa. France backed down, narrowly avoiding war. Jaurès commented that peace "has been left to the whim of chance. But if war breaks out, it will be vast and terrible. For the first time, it will be universal, sucking in all the continents…no more terrible accusation can be made against this social system."[138]

Anti-Semitism had been growing in France as the Jewish population grew near the end of the century. Jaurès first spoke out against it in 1892, responding to the anti-Semitic leader Édouard Drumont, "You only want to oust Jewish financiers from places of privilege. But once the Jews are eliminated, there will be Christians to take their place."[138] Jaurès continued, "I have no prejudice against Jews; in fact, I favor them, since they have long been among my best friends. I don't like racial arguments, and I adhere to the idea of the French Revolution, however outmoded it may seem today, that there is only one race and it is mankind."[138]

On October 15, 1894, Alfred Dreyfus, a Jewish army captain on the French general staff was arrested on charges of treason for spying for Germany. Jaurès initially viewed this as a conflict within the bourgeois. Dreyfus was convicted in a closed court martial and sentenced to a lifetime of solitary imprisonment on Devil's Island.

However, arguments to revisit the Dreyfus verdict began to be raised. In the autumn of 1897, Lucien Herr, the librarian of the École Normale, tried to persuade Jaurès of Dreyfus's innocence. Jaurès began to consider that the verdict may have been wrong. When his friend Peguy urged Jaurès to speak out, Jaurès replied, "You can hardly imagine how tormented I am…our enemies are nothing. But our friends! You can't know how battered I am. They devour me because they are all afraid of not being elected."[138] Public opinion was strongly anti-Dreyfus as the election approached in the spring of 1898.

On January 13, 1898, Émile Zola, France's most renowned novelist, wrote "J'Accuse," a letter attacking the government and army for persecuting Dreyfus and protecting the real traitor, Esterhazy. The government arrested and put Zola on trial for libel. A wave of anti-Semitism swept through France. On January 22, 1898, Jaurès spoke in the Chamber of Deputies, addressing the conservative premier Meline, "The cry of 'Death to the Jews' has howled through the streets and those responsible are your supporters. The charges against Zola are based on nothing but lies and cowardice."[138] The Chamber broke up in a near riot. The next day Jaurès asked Meline whether the defense had been denied access to evidence in the Dreyfus court martial, which indeed had been the case. Meline refused to answer.

Jaurès testified in Zola's trial in February 1898. He pointed out how the sham trial of Esterhazy "was conducted, not to reach the truth and justice, but exonerate the great military chiefs."[138] Of Zola, Jaurès said, "They can prosecute him, they can hunt him down, but I think I speak for all free citizens in saying that we bow before him in deference."[138] The court found Zola guilty. Zola answered, "France will one day thank me for having helped to save her honor."[126]

Jaurès' defense of the truth was to cost him. In the election of April 7, 1898, the business moguls of Carmaux spent thousands of francs to defeat Jaurès. He was called an enemy of religion and an agent of freemasons and Jews.[138] Jaurès was defeated by the Marquis of Solages, 6702 to 5515 votes. Jaurès found consolation after setbacks in work, writing, "Work...is an interior light, a defense against stupidity, vilification, cowardice and betrayal; it brings serenity and frees one of bitterness."[138]

Jaurès now began to write the daily editorial for the left wing paper *La Petite Republique*. A new government was formed after the election. The new minister of war, Cavaignac, appeared in the Chamber to show new evidence against Dreyfus. The Chamber endorsed his findings almost unanimously. That evening the pro-Dreyfus forces were distraught when Jaurès appeared at the home of Leon Blum, where Lucien Herr and Mathieu Dreyfus, Alfred's brother, were gathered. Jaurès, beaming, told his friends, "Meline was invulnerable because he kept quiet. Cavaignac is talking, debating and so he will be beaten. The documents which he has just adduced—well! I tell you they're forgeries...And I will prove it...Don't despair any more. Join me and rejoice."[138]

Other socialists told Jaurès that he shouldn't waste his time fighting for a bourgeois. Jaurès answered, "If Dreyfus has been illegally convicted and if, as I will prove, he is actually innocent, then he is no longer an officer or bourgeois; in his misery, he has been stripped of all class character; he is nothing less than mankind itself in its deepest pit of despair."[138] Over a three-week stretch from August 9 to 29, 1898, Jaurès wrote "*Les Preuves*" (The Proofs), an article each day demonstrating the weakness of the case against Dreyfus.

Initially, Cavaignac was enraged by the attacks on his position, yet Jaurès's article caused Cavaignac to order a reevaluation of the evidence. It became clear that the key evidence against Dreyfus had been fabricated. The army officer, Major Henry, who had forged the central evidence was arrested and admitted the forgery. Henry then committed suicide in jail. Esterhazy, the actual traitor, fled France.

However, the conservative premier Charles Dupuy still wouldn't act on the Dreyfus case. Jaurès addressed a meeting of 30,000 people in Marseille about the continuing denial of justice, describing this "ignominious drama which has been unfolding for two long years."[138] During the turmoil, French President Faure died in the arms of his mistress.

Then the new president, Loubet, a staunch republican, was assaulted at the steeplechase by a monarchist, the Baron de Christiani. The fall of the cane of the baron on the top hat of the president was considered an attack on the Republic itself. Dupuy received a vote of no confidence, and was succeeded by Rene Waldeck-Rousseau, a moderate. Jaurès felt that the Republic was threatened enough to demand a strong government. He supported Waldeck-Rousseau and his ministry. At last a new trial was ordered for Dreyfus.

The second court martial of Dreyfus began on August 7, 1899. Dreyfus had been brought back from Devil's Island for the trial. Jaurès wrote, "I cannot describe how deep my feeling of pity was when I first saw him a week ago. His whole presence reveals depths of unspeakable suffering."[138] Once again, to the surprise of the world, the army officers sitting in judgement convicted Dreyfus by a five-to-two vote. The court changed the terms of the sentence to ten years due to unspecified "extenuating circumstances."[138]

Jaurès called the decision "monstrous. To convict an innocent man a second time is a crime without precedent."[138] Seeing how much Dreyfus had suffered, his supporters asked for presidential pardon rather than continuing to fight the case. Dreyfus was pardoned on September 19.

In December 1899, the French socialists met. The seven hundred delegates represented 1452 different socialist groups. There was a sharp division on whether socialists should ally with liberal non-socialists. Jaurès stated, "if we can't predict exactly when and how capitalism will collapse, we must always be ready for it, but we must also work for those reforms which…will prepare the way."[138] Jaurès continued, "We must not fight from a futile distance, but from the heart of the citadel."[132] The division on this issue was temporarily papered over, but in 1900 the hardliners, led by Jules Guesde, left to form a new Socialist Party.

The elections of 1902 resulted in Jaurès beating the Marquis de Solages to recapture his seat in the Chamber of Deputies. The new premier, Émile Combes, of the Radical Party, was most impassioned about limiting the influence of the Church. Jaurès too saw the Church, which tended to favor monarchists and conservatives, as the, "core of counter-revolution."[142] Jaurès supported Combes's efforts to close religious schools, writing, "In a system of education where the minds of the young are formed, there must be state control; education must be free of dogma."[138] Jaurès was disappointed that the Radicals did not enact more economic reforms to help the poorer part of the population.

Jaurès tried to maintain unity within the Socialist Party between those who favored collaboration with non-socialist reformers and those arguing against it. Goldberg wrote, "The socialist house, he argued, was large enough for all its tenants. So he deplored the folly, indeed the sheer laziness of hewing to a single narrow line of socialist thought and dismissing all others."[138] The Russian socialist Leon Trotsky later wrote of Jaurès, "He had a physical repulsion for all sectarianism…He was an eclectic, but an eclectic of genius."[138]

Jaurès continued to warn against France allying with Russia, fearing that the alliance would increase the risk of war as France would be forced to support Russian objectives of little benefit to France. Jaurès detested the repressive Tsarist government of Russia, attributing the Kishinev pogroms of 1903 to "the systemic spirit of savage reaction that the Russian government has unchained in order to distract attention from its own despotism."[142]

In response, the conservative paper *Les Débats* stated, "Universal peace is a dream…even if socialism should one day triumph, we are not convinced that human nature would have changed so much as to eliminate war from society."[138] Jaurès replied, "If it is true that nations will forever be forced to kill in order to defend themselves; if it is true that the spirit of fraternity will never win over man's aggressive nature, then humanity has embarked on a futile journey...I reject such foregone conclusions."[138] Addressing his old lycée in Albi, Jaurès said, "Peace is difficult, but not impossible...humanity is doomed if, in order to prove its courage, it must eternally kill...Courage is not to let force resolve conflicts which reason can solve."[138] Jaurès argued that France should renounce the idea of military revenge against Germany, commenting, "No nation has now a vital interest in altering the map of Europe."[138] Jaurès was joined by Guesde and the more left-wing socialists in arguing the growth of socialism in Germany would eventually lead to Germany peacefully returning Alsace-Lorraine.

Jaurès spoke out for the textile workers when they went on a large-scale strike in northern France. In reply to management claims of poverty, Jaurès answered, "An industry which cannot survive without constantly lowering the wages of its workers is finished. There is a level below which human beings cannot sink."[138]

In 1903, Jaurès' friends Lucien Herr and Leon Blum proposed the creation of a new daily paper that Jaurès would edit. The first issue of *L'Humanité* appeared April 18, 1904. Jaurès attracted a talented group of political and intellectual contributors. He remained as editor over the next decade, using the paper to push his ideas for social reform and rejection of war.

Jaurès remained optimistic about the future. In 1904 he wrote, "If we thought that man was now permanently evil and the human conscience powerless, we would despair of love and we would abandon the great hope of socialism. On the contrary we note with joy countless examples of human nobility...in spite of the human capacity for good, Socialism will triumph only because all the victims of the social order are uniting to overthrow it."[138]

After repeated attacks, Premier Combes resigned on January 18, 1905, and a more conservative government took over. The various socialist parties of France could now agree to be in the opposition, formally uniting on April 25, 1905. French historian Daniele Halevy later wrote, "What, then, was this [socialist] party? I will define it in a word: it was Jaurès. it was his reflection. He created it. He kept it together."[138]

In the summer of 1905 a crisis over who would dominate Morocco brought France and Germany to the brink of war. Jaurès denounced the imperialists of each nation as being responsible for the quarrel, and was attacked as unpatriotic and pro-German. The 1906 elections resulted with Jaurès's reelection and an increase in the number of Socialist deputies to 84.

The dominant force in the government remained the Radicals, who now adopted a more conservative platform. When the miners struck, the government brought in troops. The new premier, Georges Clémenceau, once known as an impassioned supporter of the poor, broke several strikes in the name of order.[141]

Jaurès led the opposition in the legislature, advocating a five-and-a-half-day work week, a minimum wage, an income tax and pensions for old age. The author Marcel Proust described Jaurès as "wonderfully gifted for thought, action and oratory."[138] Trotsky commented, "one had only to listen to the ringing voice of Jaurès, to see his enlightened look, his imperious note, his thick and unyoked neck to say to himself: There is a Man."[138] Tuchman said of Jaurès, "Short, stocky, strong, red faced and jovial, he radiated the joy of battle. With his big head, rough beard and careless clothes finished off with drooping white socks, he looked like the accepted image of a labor leader."[126]

Jaurès worried about the increasing signs of war throughout Europe. The French Socialist congress of November 1906 was divided about how to respond to the threat of a war involving France. Some delegates thought a war inevitable and unpreventable under capitalism while others proposed a revolutionary strike in the event of any conflict. Jaurès persuaded the delegates to agree to affirm that the workers would defend France against unprovoked attacks, but would also take every action possible to prevent wars of aggression. Goldberg wrote, "It was Jaurès who came to symbolize the Socialist resolve for peace. From one end of France to another, he traveled, a propagandist for peace, a patriot, an internationalist, a voice of conscience. To some, whether sincere nationalists or untamed chauvinists, he seemed dangerous, even treasonable."[138] Clémenceau later said that it was Jaurès's fate "to preach the brotherhood of nations with unswerving faith…that he was not daunted by the brutal reality of facts."[126] Later in the decade, it was shown how close to war France had come. Jaurès wrote, "Clémenceau has thus revealed that if France had been stronger, she would have fought England at Fashoda and Germany at Tangier."[138]

Jaurès supported the idea of treaties requiring nations to take their disputes to arbitration. Jaurès argued that these treaties were "the rudiments of a first attempt at the organization of peace against violence and against the menace of unleashed war" and that they could lead to stronger measures later.[142]

Jaurès thought and read extensively about the military, searching for ways to lessen the chance of war. He proposed to replace standing regular armies that could be used in an attack with popular militias that could guarantee defense. He co-authored *The New Army*, a 700-page volume giving his rationale for such a change. Jaurès noted that German war plans postulated a rapid offensive, which France's smaller frontline army would be unable to stop. Instead, Jaurès suggested an army made up of the whole nation, of trained reserves, might eventually slow down and defeat the enemy. Jaurès introduced a detailed proposal along these lines in the Chamber on November 14, 1910. The proposal was met with ridicule by the more conservative deputies and press. Yet the events of 1914 saw the initial German thrust defeat the French regular forces only to be slowed down and reversed in large part to the use of trained reserve French troops.

The end of the first decade of the twentieth century saw a rebound of the right-wing nationalists. They postulated the creed called "vitalism," that war was needed to regenerate and reenergize France. Jaurès denounced this philosophy as senseless and likely to lead to catastrophe. Meanwhile Jaurès attacked the government for its neglect of the poor, stating, "The pleasures of life, which both dazzle and dull the rich, blind them to the untold miseries of daily existence [of the poor]."[138]

In the beginning of 1910 Jaurès helped enact a law providing compulsory pensions to workers at retirement. Jaurès wrote that the pension law "signals the increasing influence of the Socialist Party. It is our victory. Only our presence and our pressure forced republicans, who scorn our ideal of social justice, to take another step toward it."[138]

In 1912, war in the Balkans now threatened to drag in the larger powers. A generalized European war was only narrowly avoided when the other great powers arranged a conference to enforce a Balkan settlement.

Socialists from across Europe organized an emergency congress to try to oppose war. In late November 1912, 555 delegates from twenty-three countries met in Basel. Historian R. W. Brogan wrote that Jaurès "was more and more convinced that the immediate menace of the capitalist system was not the direct impoverishment of the worker, but his death and mutilation in a fratricidal war with his fellow workers [from other nations]."[143] Jaurès said, "I call upon the living that they may defend themselves from the monster who appears on the horizon. I weep for the countless dead now rotting in the east. I will break the thunderbolts of war which menace from the skies."[126] Jaurès concluded, "We will leave this hall committed to the salvation of peace and civilization."[138] Privately, Jaurès was pessimistic that war could be prevented. He told Camille Huysmans, the Belgian secretary of the International Socialist Bureau, "If war breaks out, we don't know what effect such an event may have on those who now seem to be the strongest internationalists."[138]

In the Chamber of Deputies, Jaurès argued against a proposal to lengthen army service from two to three years, thus increasing the size of the regular army. Jaurès noted that the extra expenditure would not add to the army's quality or strength, while encouraging French leaders to be more open to a military showdown with Germany. Jaurès's position enraged the French right. Wherever Jaurès spoke in public, hecklers attacked him as pro-German and a traitor to France. The conservative paper *L'Écho de Paris* editorialized, "France is speaking, so keep quiet, Mr. Jaurès!!"[138] Jaurès refused to be silent. Soon after, Jaurès spoke to a crowd of 150,000 supporters in Paris to emphasize the importance of peace and reform.

The right wing continued their harsh rhetoric against Jaurès and the Socialists. Speaking in the chamber on July 4, 1913, Jaurès said, "Day after day, you gentlemen of the right and your supporters agitate for our assassination."[138] Jaurès addressed the nationalist rhetoric in a speech to students on January 22, 1914, saying, "Today you are told: act, always act! But what is action without thought. It is the barbarism born of inertia. You are told: brush aside the party of peace: it saps your courage. But I tell you that to stand for peace today is to wage the most heroic of battles."[140]

The election of 1914 was a decisive victory for the left. While the Radicals remained dominant with 239 deputies, the Socialists saw a huge increase in support, winning 1.4 million votes and 103 deputies. The conservative paper *L'Écho de Paris* stated, "The progress of revolution and Socialism among the villagers is a significant and frightening development."[138] The victory was credited to Jaurès.

The Radical leader Joseph Caillaux now told Jaurès, "As soon as possible we form a strong leftist ministry which will press for a policy of European peace…But it is only possible if the Socialist party offers its unqualified support…I would never assume power as Premier, for example, unless you entered the Cabinet as Minister for Foreign Affairs."[138] Jaurès pledged to support Caillaux and his program for peace. However, President Poincaré refused to offer the premiership unto anyone but a more nationalistic moderate or conservative. Poincaré had three premier designates rejected. At last however, Vivani, a Socialist turned moderate, won the support of enough Radicals who were unwilling to prolong the political crisis to form a government on June 14, 1914.

On June 28, the Austrian heir to the throne, Archduke Francis Ferdinand, was assassinated by a Serbian nationalist. Austria agitated for war against Serbia and was told that Germany would back it in the face of Russian support for Serbia. On July 7, the French government asked for money to send President Poincaré and Premier Vivani to Russia for consultation. Jaurès unsuccessfully objected, stating, "We find it inadmissible that France should become involved in wild Balkan adventures because of treaties of which she knows neither the text, nor the sense, nor the limits, nor the consequences."[138] Writing in *L'Humanité* that summer, Jaurès proclaimed, "The true strength of states no longer resides in the pride of conquest and the brutality of oppression, but in the respect for liberties, in the concern for justice and peace."[140]

On July 14, the French Socialist Party held their annual meeting. Like the socialists in many countries, the delegates said they would consider a general strike, if necessary, to influence the French government against war. Jaurès stated, "We have often agreed that the general strike is one way of influencing and warning our rulers." The newspaper *Le Temps* denounced the Socialists' "treason against their homeland."[138] Jaurès replied on July 18, "The general strike will never be unilateral…No matter what our enemies say, there is no contradiction between the maximum effort for peace and, if we should be invaded, the maximum effort for national independence."[138]

Austria gave Serbia an ultimatum on July 24 and followed this with a declaration of war on July 28. In Russia, on July 29, Poincaré affirmed French support for Russia to act against Austria and, if necessary, Germany. While the nations were speeding toward war, the socialists in Europe tried to rouse the workers to oppose any war. Campaigning for a Socialist candidate, Jaurès talked to a crowd near Lyon about the horror of a general war, saying, "Think of what that disaster would mean for Europe…What a massacre, what destruction, what barbarism? That is why I still fervently hope, even as the black clouds threaten, that we can prevent the catastrophe."[138]

Once again, the socialists across Europe called an emergency meeting, this time in Brussels. Jaurès spoke to the delegates, "When typhus finishes the work begun by bullets, disillusioned men will turn on their rulers, whether German, French, Russian or Italian and demand their explanation for all these corpses. But if we avoid the storm, I hope the masses will not forget and will say: We must prevent this specter from rising out of its grave every six months to terrify the world."[138]

Jaurès returned home to Paris on July 30. He led a delegation of Socialists to meet with Premier Vivani, who did not reveal the pledge of alliance to Russia. After dinner, Jaurès returned to his office at *L'Humanité*, where he composed his lead article for the next day. Unknown to Jaurès, he was being stalked by a 29-year-old rightist named Raoul Villain who had decided to assassinate Jaurès. When Jaurès and friends had drinks at the Café du Croissant, Villain waited outside, but eventually gave up and left.

On July 31 Germany demanded that Russia suspend mobilization or face a declaration of war. Unable to see the premier, Jaurès spoke to Undersecretary of State Abel Ferry, who asked what the Socialists were going to do. Jaurès replied, "We will clear our party of any guilt; to the very end, we will continue to struggle against war."[138] Ferry answered, "No, you won't be able to continue. You will be assassinated on the nearest street corner."[138]

Jaurès returned to *L'Humanité* after 8 PM, where he told the staff, "Tonight I'm going to write a new 'J'Accuse.' I will expose everyone responsible for this crisis."[138] The Socialist journalists decided to have dinner before composing the issue of the paper. They returned to Café du Croissant. Jaurès had his back to the street, separated from the outside only by a screen. Suddenly the screen was pulled away by Villain, who then shot Jaurès twice from behind. Jaurès slumped down, dead.

Trotsky wrote, "Jaurès…fell on the fighting field while struggling against the worst scourge of mankind—war."[138] Premier Vivani commented, "M. Jaurès, the great orator…has been treacherously assassinated. He…struggled for noble causes."[138] Historian Goldberg wrote, "Yet peace, the greatest of those causes, died with him. Even as men eulogized Jaurès and praised his purposes, they rallied, almost without exception to the standards of war."[138] When Germany mobilized on August 1, France followed the same day. Jean Longuet, Karl Marx's grandson spoke for many on August 2, 1914, when he said, "If France is invaded, how could

Socialists not be the first to defend the France of the Revolution and of Democracy…of Jaurès."[140] France was to suffer 200,000–300,000 casualties in August 1914 alone.[141] Later the war would claim the life of Louis Jaurès, the only son of Jean Jaurès.

To the other "what ifs" that historians mention that might have prevented the First World War was Poincaré's decision to ignore the will of the Chamber of Deputies and not pick Caillaux as premier and hence Jaurès as foreign minister. If Jaurès had been in that post, he would never have pledged that France would follow Russia into war. Absent that pledge, Russia would never have challenged Germany alone. Instead the conflict would have been localized to Austria versus Serbia and millions of lives might not have been lost.

A decade after his assassination, Jaurès's remains were transferred to the Pantheon, the mausoleum that holds the nation's heroes. If Jaurès had prevented World War I, he might be considered one of France's greatest heroes of all.

Chapter 21: Epilogue

THE COST OF THE IDEALISM was high for these fighters for a better world. At best, like Clay, Stanton, Howard, Garibaldi, Debs and Bryan, they ended their lives with a degree of disillusionment and disappointment. Others ended their days in exile, such as Kossuth, or in prison like L'Ouverture. For the majority, including the Gracchi, Boudica, Akiba, Mazdak, Wat Tyler, Razin, Warren, Tone, Amaru, Tecumseh and Jaurès, the struggle was to cost them their lives. Aguinaldo was unique in living long enough to see his dream become a reality fifty years later.

If they would have known how it would all turn out, would they have done things differently? Being human, they might have hesitated. Yet, being who they were, many would have chosen to follow the same or a similar course. These were men and women who deeply believed in what they fought for. They believed that their ideal, of a better world, was worth fighting for. These are among the greatest of heroes, men and women who followed their course, no matter how perilous, knowing that success might elude them.

Our modern world puts a heavy emphasis on the ideal of satisfying oneself, of making oneself happy as among the highest goals. Many of us, especially as we get older, are cynical that the world can ever be changed, that wars can be stopped or justice achieved. It seemed fitting to stop this book at the onset of World War I, which perhaps more than any other event seemed to give the lie to idealism and prove the truth of cynicism.

From another perspective, these figures did not lose. Each contributed an idea whose day was to come. The Gracchi showed how an unequal society could consider the needs of its poorer members. The nations of Israel, Ireland, Hungary and the Philippines owe some part of their independence to the deeds of Akiba, Tone, Kossuth and Aguinaldo. Amaru, Tecumseh, L'Ouverture and Howard helped discredit the racist concept of white superiority. The rights of women, of labor and the dream of a more equal society were greatly advanced by Stanton, Debs and Jaurès. It is not that the twentieth century and beyond were not full of other magnificent losers. That, however, is a topic for another day. Now it is worth remembering these twenty-plus men and women whose efforts, even if partially or completely unsuccessful, helped make ours a better world. All of us are in their debt.

References

1. The Gracchi, Henry Boren, Twayne Publishers, Inc., New York, 1968
2. Makers of Rome: Nine Lives, Plutarch, Penguin Books, London, 1965 (translated by Ian Scott-Kilvert)
3. The Roman Republic, David M. Gwynn, Oxford University Press, London, 2012
4. SPQR: A History of Ancient Rome, Mary Beard, Liveright Publishing, New York, 2015
5. The Civil Wars, Appian, Penguin Classics, London, 1996 (translated by John Carter)
6. Rome: An Empire's Story, Greg Woolf, Oxford University Press, London, 2012
7. How to Run a Country, Marcus Tullius Cicero, Princeton University Press, 2013 (translated by Phillip Freeman)
8. The Jugurthine War, Sallust (Gaius Sallustius Crispus), Penguin Classics, London, 2007 (translated by A.J. Woodman)
9. Boudica: The Life of Britain's Legendary Warrior Queen, Vanessa Collingridge, The Overlook Press, 2005
10. The Gallic War, Julius Caesar, Harvard University Press, 1917, (translated by H.R. Edwards)
11. Julius Caesar in Gaul and Britain, Stephen Ridd, Raintree Steck-Vaughn Publishers, 1995
12. The Lives of the Twelve Caesars, Suetonius, Modern Library, New York, 1931
13. The Annals of Imperial Rome, Publius Cornelius Tacitus, Penguin Classics, London, 1956 (translated by Michael Grant)
14. Roman History, Cassius Dio, GP Putnam and Sons, 1925 (translated by Earnest Cary)
15. Roman Britain, Peter Salway, Clarendon Press, Oxford, 1981
16. The Isles: A History, Norman Davies, Oxford University Press, London, 1999
17. The Britons, Christopher A. Snyder, Blackwell Publishing, Oxford, 2003
18. The Indestructible Jews, Max Dimont, Signet/The New American Library, New York, 1971
19. The Story of the Jews, Simon Schama, Harper-Collins, Publishers, New York, 2013
20. A History of the Jews, Abram Sachar, Alfred A. Knopf, Publishers, New York, 1967
21. The Jewish Wars, Flavius Josephus, Penguin Classics, London, 1959 (translated by G.A. Williamson)
22. The Jews: Story of a People, Howard Fast, The Dial Press, New York, 1968
23. Jews, God and History, Max Dimont, Signet, New York, 1962
24. Jewish Heroes, Sadie Rose Weilerstein, The United Synagogues of America, New York, 1956
25. Akiva: Life, Legend, Legacy, Reubven Hammer, The Jewish Publishing Society, Philadelphia, 2015
26. Digging through the Bible, Richard A. Freund, Rowman and Littlefield, Publishers, Lanham, MD, 2009
27. The Secrets of the Cave of Letters: A Dead Sea Mystery Uncovered, Richard A. Freund, Humanity Books, New York, 2004
28. A History of the Jewish Experience, Leo Trepp, Behrman House, Inc., 1973
29. Rome and Jerusalem, The Clash of Ancient Civilizations, Martin Goodman, Alfred A. Knopf, New York, 2007

30. Religions of Iran, From Prehistory to the Present, Richard Foltz, Oneworld Publications, London, 2013
31. Shahnameh, The Persian Book of Kings, Abolqasem Ferdowsi, Penguin Classics, London, 1997 (translated by Dick Davis)
32. The Cambridge History of Iran: The Seleucid, Parthian and Sasanian periods, Ehsan Yarshater, editor, Cambridge University Press, Cambridge, 1983
33. A History of Iran, Michael Axworthy, Basic Books, New York, 2008
34. Kavad's Heresy and Mazdak's Revolt, Patricia Crone, Journal of Persian Studies 1991, (29) 21-40
35. In the Shadow of the Sword, Tom Holland, Little, Brown Book Group, London, 2012
36. The Last Plantagenets, Thomas Costain, Popular Library, New York,1962
37. The Story of England, Michael Wood, Penguin Books, London, 2010
38. The Royal Policy of Richard II: Absolutism in the Later Middle Ages, Richard H. Jones, Barnes and Noble, Inc., New York, 1968
39. The Hollow Crown, Harold F. Hutchinson, The John Day Company, New York, 1961
40. Foundation: The History of England from its Earliest Beginnings to the Tudors, Peter Ackroyd, St. Martin's Press, New York, 2011
41. England in the Age of Wycliffe, 1368-1520, G. M. Trevelyan, Harper Torchbooks, New York, 1963
42. The Three Richards, Nigel Saul, Hambledon and London, London, 2005
43. 1381: The Year of the Peasant's Revolt, Juliet Barker, Harvard University Press, Cambridge, 2014
44. A Distant Mirror, Barbara Tuchman, Alfred A. Knopf, New York, 1978
45. Russian Rebels 1600-1800, Paul Avrich, W.W. Norton and Company, New York, 1972
46. A History of Russia and its Empire, Kees Boterbloem, Rowman and Littlefield Publishers, Inc., Lanham, 2014
47. A History of Russia, Nicholas V. Riasanovsky, Oxford University Press, 3rd edition, New York, 1977
48. A History of Russia, Roger Bartlett, Palgrave MacMillan, New York, 2005
49. Horsemen of the Steppes; The Story of the Cossacks, Albert Seaton, Hippocreme Books, New York,1985
50. A History of Russia, George Vernadsky, Yale University Press, New Haven, 6th edition, 1969
51. Peter the Great and the Emergence of Russia, B.H. Sumner, Collier Books, New York, 1962
52. The Icon and the Axe, James Billington, Alfred A. Knopf, New York, 1966
53. With Fire and Sword, James L. Nelson, St. Martin's Press, New York, 2011
54. A History of the American Revolution, John R. Alden, Da Capo Press, New York, 1969
55. Whirlwind: The American Revolution and the War that Won it, John Ferling, Bloomsbury Press, New York, 2015
56. Bunker Hill: A City, A Siege, A Revolution, Nathaniel Philbrick, Viking, New York, 2013
57. The Oxford History of the American People, Samuel Eliot Morrison, The New American Library, New York, 1972
58. The Spirit of 'Seventy-Six, edited by Henry Steele Commager and Richard B. Morris, Harper and Row, New York, 1967

59. The Spirit of '74, Ray and Marie Raphael, The New Press, New York, 2015
60. Patriots: The Men Who Started the American Revolution, A.J. Langguth, Simon and Schuster, New York, 1988
61. The Life and Times of Joseph Warren, Richard Frothingham, Little, Brown and Company, Boston, 1865
62. The Last Inca Revolt, Lillian Estelle Fisher, University of Oklahoma Press, Norman, OK, 1966
63. The History of Peru, Daniel Masterson, Greenwood Press, Westport, CT, 2009
64. The Rebellion of Tupac Amaru II, 1780-1, Phillip Ainsworth Means, Hispanic American Historical review, vol. 2, #1, 1-25, February, 1919
65. Ireland: A History, Thomas Bartlett, Cambridge University Press, Cambridge, 2010
66. History of Ireland, Malachy McCovert, Running Press, Philadelphia, 2004
67. The Course of Irish History, 4th edition, T.W. Moody and F.X. Martin, Robert Rinehart Publishers, Lanham, MD, 2001
68. Wolfe Tone: Prophet of Irish Independence, Marianne Elliot, Yale University Press, New Haven, 1989
69. A History of Ireland, Mike Cronin, Palgrave, New York, 2001
70. Invisible Armies, Max Boot, Liveright Publishing, New York, 2013
71. This Gilded African, Toussaint L'Ouverture, Wenda Parkinson, Quartet Books, London, 1978
72. Haiti, Phillipe Girard, Palgrave MacMillan, New York, 2005
73. Haiti: The Aftershocks of History, Laurent Dubois, Metropolitan Books, New York, 2012
74. Avengers of the New World, Laurent Dubois, Harvard University Press, Cambridge, 2004
75. The Black Jacobins, C.L. R. James, Vintage Books, 2nd edition, 1989
76. Open the Door to Liberty, Anne Rockwell, Houghton Mifflin, Boston, 2009
77. Great Chiefs, Tony Hollihan, Folklore Publishing, Edmonton, 2002
78. Tecumseh, Chief of the Shawnee, C. Ann Fitterer, The Child's World, Chanhassan, 2003
79. Tecumseh, Shooting Star of the Shawnee, Dwight Jon Zimmerman, Sterling Publishing, New York, 2010
80. Tecumseh and the Dream of an American Indian Nation, Russell Shorto, Silver Burdett Press, Engelwood Cliffs, NJ, 1989
81. Tecumseh: A Life, John Sugden, Henry Holt and Company, New York, 1997
82. The Shawnees and War for America, Colin G. Calloway, Penguin Library of American Indian History, New York, 2007
83. The Shawnee Prophet, R. David Edmunds, University of Nebraska Press, 1983
84. The Gods of Prophetstown, Adam Jortner, Oxford University Press, 2012
85. Henry Clay: The Essential American, David S. and Jeanne T. Heidler, Random House, New York, 2010
86. Henry Clay, America's Greatest Statesman, Harlow Giles Unger, Da Capo Press, Philadelphia, 2015
87. The Great Triumvirate: Webster, Clay and Calhoun, Merrill D. Peterson, Oxford University Press, Oxford, 1987
88. Henry Clay and the War of 1812, Quentin Scott King, MacFarland and Company, Jefferson, North Carolina, 2014
89. The Edge of the Precipice, Robert V. Remini, Basic Books, New York, 2010

90. The Age of Jackson, Arthur M. Schlesinger, Jr., Mentor Books, New York, 1945
91. America's Great Debate: Henry Clay, Stephen Douglas and Compromise that Preserved the Union, Fergus M. Bordewich, Simon and Schuster, New York, 2012
92. The Lawful Revolution, István Deák, Columbia University Press, New York, 1979
93. The Age of Revolutions, Eric Hobsbawn, Vintage Books, 1962, New York
94. Revolutions of 1848: A Social History, Priscilla Robertson, Princeton University Press, Princeton, New Jersey, 1952
95. 1848 Year of Revolution, Mike Rapport, Basic Books, Philadelphia, 2008
96. Austria in 1848-9, William H. Stiles, Sampson Low, London, 1852
97. Elizabeth Cady Stanton: An American Life, Lori D. Ginzberg, Hill and Wang, New York, 2009
98. Elizabeth Cady Stanton and Susan B. Anthony: A Friendship that Changed the World, Penny Colman, Henry Holt and Company, New York, 2011
99. The Political Thought of Elizabeth Cady Stanton, Sue Davis, New York University Press, New York, 2008
100. Mrs. Stanton's Bible, Kathi Kern, Cornell University Press, 2001
101. Yankee Stepfather: General O.O. Howard and the Freedmen, Willian S. McFeely, Yale University Press, New Haven, 1968
102. Sword and Olive Branch: Oliver Otis Howard, Fordham University Press, New York, 1999
103. This Hallowed Ground, Bruce Catton, Vintage Books, New York, 1955
104. Hearts Touched by Fire, edited by Harold Holzer, the Modern Library, New York, 2011
105. Bury Me Not in a Land of Slaves, Joyce Hansen, Franklin Watts, New York, 2000
106. A History of the Freedmen's Bureau, George R. Bentley, The American Historical Association, Philadelphia, 1955
107. The Wars of Reconstruction, Douglas R. Egerton, Bloomsbury Press, New York, 2014
108. Reconstruction: America's Unfinished Revolution, Eric Foner, Perennial Classics, New York, 1988
109. American Voices from Reconstruction, Adriane Ruggiero, Marshall Cavendish, New York, 2007
110. General Howard's Own Story, Oliver Otis Howard, Bear Creek Press, Wallowa, Oregon, 2001
111. Garibaldi: Citizen of the World, Alfonso Scirocco, Princeton University Press, Princeton, NJ, 2007
112. Garibaldi's Defense of the Roman Republic, George MaCauley Trevelyan, Phoenix Press, London, 1907
113. Garibaldi's Memoirs, Elpis Melena, International Institute of Garibaldian Studies, Sarasota, Florida, 1981
114. Garibaldi and the Making of Italy, G.M. Trevelyan, Longmans, Green and Company, London, 1911
115. Garibaldi, Jasper Ridley, The Viking Press, New York, 1974
116. The Bending Cross, Ray Ginger, Haymarket Books, Chicago, 1947
117. The Land of Orange Groves and Jails: Upton Sinclair's California, edited by Lauren Coodley, Heyday Books, Berkley, California, 2004
118. 1912: Wilson, Roosevelt, Taft and Debs: The Election that Changed the Country, James Chace, Simon and Shuster, 2004

119. Democracy's Prisoner: Eugene Debs, The Great War and the Right to Dissent, Ernest Freeberg, Harvard University Press, Cambridge, Massachusetts, 2008
120. Wilson, A. Scott Berg, G.P. Putnam' Sons, New York, 2013
121. Eugene V. Debs, Citizen and Socialist, 2nd edition, Nick Salvatore, University of Illinois Press, Chicago, 2007
122. Debs: His Life, Writings and Speeches, Eugene V. Debs and Others, University Press of the Pacific, Honolulu, 2002
123. The Pullman Case, David Ray Papke, University Press of Kansas, Lawrence, Kansas, 1999
124. Eugene V. Debs: Spokesman for Labor and Socialism, Bernard Brommel, Charles H. Kerr Publishing Company, Chicago, 1978
125. The Golden Door, Isaac Asimov, Houghton Mifflin Company, Boston, 1977
126. The Proud Tower, Barbara W. Tuchman, Bantam Books, New York, 1966
127. Autobiography of Upton Sinclair, Upton Sinclair, Harcourt, Brace and World, New York, 1962
128. American Portraits, Volume 1, edited by Donald W. Whisenhunt, Kendall/Hunt Publishing Company, Dubuque, Iowa, 1993
129. A Godly Hero: The Life of William Jennings Bryan, Michael Kazin, Alfred A. Knopf, New York, 2006
130. William Jennings Bryan, volume 1, Paolo E. Coletta, University of Nebraska Press, Lincoln, Nebraska, 1964
131. William Jennings Bryan, volume 2, Paolo E. Coletta, University of Nebraska Press, Lincoln, Nebraska, 1969
132. Age of Betrayal: The Triumph of Money in America, Jack Beatty, Alfred A. Knopf, New York, 2007
133. Sitting in Darkness: Americans in the Philippines, David Howard Bain, Houghton Mifflin Company, Boston, 1984
134. Magdalo: The story of Emilio Aguinaldo, Don Skillin, PublishAmerica, Baltimore, 2006
135. In Our Image: America's Empire in the Philippines, Stanley Karnow, Ballantine Books, New York, 1989
136. Arc of Empire: America's Wars in Asia from the Philippines to Vietnam, Michael H. Hunt and Steven I. Levine, The University of North Carolina Press, Chapel Hill, 2012
137. Wanted Dead or Alive, Benjamin Runkle, Palgrave McMillan, New York, 2011
138. The Life of Jean Jaurès, Harvey Goldberg, University of Wisconsin Press, Madison, Wisconsin, 1968
139. A Concise History of France, Roger Price, Cambridge University Press, Cambridge, UK, 2005
140. The Embrace of Unreason: France 1914-1940, Frederick Brown, Alfred A. Knopf, New York, 2014
141. Twilight of the Belle Epoque, Mary McAuliffe, Rowman and Littlefield, Lanham, MD, 2014
142. Jean Jaurès: A Study of Patriotism in the French Socialist Movement, Harold R. Weinstein, Octagon Books, New York, 1973
143. France Under the Republic, D.W. Brogan, Harper and Brothers, New York, 1940

INDEX

A
Adams, Abigail, 85
Adams, John, 67, 72, 74, 75, 78, 117
Adams, John Quincy, 144–145
Adams, Sam, 68, 70, 71, 72, 74, 75, 76
Address to the Throne (Hungary), 159
Adet, Pierre, 102
Aelia Captolina (Jerusalem), 32
AERA (American Equal Rights Association), 176, 177
AFL (American Federation of Labor), 221, 224, 227, 231, 232, 235, 254
after-life, 36
Agoncillo, Felipe, 268
Aguinaldo, Crispulo, 264
Aguinaldo, Emilio
    background of, 261–262
    Bryan and, 256, 271, 273, 274
    death of, 274
    efforts of and opposition to, 262–273
    vindication of, 273–274
Ahura Mazda, 35, 36
Akiba, Rabbi
    arrest, imprisonment and death of, 33–34
    background, 29, 30–31
    efforts of and opposition to, 29–33
    vindication of, 34
Alabama, 195
Alden, John, 71, 85
Alexis, Tsar (Russia), 57, 64–65
Alien and Sedition laws (US), 140
Altgeld, John, 227, 229
American Colonization Society, 143
American Equal Rights Association (AERA), 176, 177
American Federation of Labor (AFL), 221, 224, 227, 231, 232, 235, 254
American Legion, 238
American Railroad Union (ARU), 223–224, 224–225, 226, 229, 234
American Revolution, 110, 125. *see also* Warren, Joseph *and other revolutionaries*
Amnesty Proclamation (US 1865), 188
anarchist movement, 280
Anderson, Thomas, 267
Anglesey (island), 20
Anra Mainyu, 35, 36
Anthony, Susan B., 174, 175, 176, 177, 178–179, 181, 231
Antyllius, Quintus, 15
Apache, 198

Appian, 7
Appian (Roman historian), 8
Apponyi, Chancellor, 159
Arad, fortress of, 168–169
arbitration, 224, 225, 251, 252, 255, 279, 281
Areche, Jose Antonio de, 88, 92, 93, 95
Argentina , 93, 204, 205–206
"An Argument on Behalf of the Catholics in Ireland" (Tone), 99
Aristobulus, 29
Armedaris, Jose de, 87
armies, soldiers, and war. *see also* protests, revolts, revolutions and riots (civil strife); World War I *and other wars*
    American colonies and, 67–68, 78, 81
    Bar Kochba and, 32
    Britain and, 42, 43, 46, 47, 67–68, 99, 101
    Bryan and, 255–256, 256–257, 256–258
    Clay and, 141–142, 143, 144
    Debs on, 230, 234–235, 236
    France, 42, 43, 47, 101
    Freedman's Bureau and, 197–198
    Gaius and, 5, 15, 16
    Garibaldi on, 216
    Howard on, 185
    Hungary and, 157
    Jaurès on, 281–282, 285–286, 287, 288–289
    Kossuth and, 165, 167
    Philippines and, 251
    Rome and, 6–7, 16, 19–20, 21–22, 29–30, 33
    Russia and, 57–58, 290, 292
    Social Democrats and, 230
    strikes and, 226–227, 249
    Tiberius and, 5, 6, 7
    Union soldiers (US), 191, 197, 214
    US in Philippines and, 230
    Warren and, 81–82, 84
Arnold, Benedict, 80, 84
Arriaga, Antonio de, 89–90
Arsen'ev, A.V., 65
Arthur, P.M., 221
ARU (American Railroad Union), 223–224, 224–225, 226, 229, 234
Association of the Beterans of the Revolution (Philippines), 274
Astrakhan, 60, 61–62
Austria, 165, 203, 207–211, 214–215, 290, 292. *see also* Habsburg Empire
authoritarianism, 65
autocracies, 65
Aux Canard River, 133

the Avesta, 36
Avrich, Paul, 60, 61, 64

B
Baird, Absalom, 191
Baird, Mary, 244, 250, 253
Balkans, 288
Ball, John
    background, 44
    death of, 55
    efforts of and opposition to, 44–49, 55
    vindication of, 2, 55
Bancroft, George, 71, 141
Bank of the United States, 145, 147–148
banks, 254, 259, 274
banks , 256
Bariatinsky, Yuri, 63
Barker, Juliet, 54
Bar Kochba, Simeon, 29, 32–33, 34
Bass, John, 270
Bastidas, Micaela, 89, 90, 93
Batthyány, Count, 160, 161, 163–164, 167, 169
Battle of Fallen Timbers, 126
Battle of New Orleans, 142
Battle of San Antonio, 206
Battle of the Wabash River, 126
Battle of Volturno, 213
Bentley, George, 189, 198
Benton, Thomas Hart, 144
Betar, fortress of, 33
Billings, J.B., 195
Billington, James, 65
bimetallism (gold and silver), 250
Birth of a Nation (movie), 232
Bismarck, 170
Bizefrance, Etienne, 112
Black Codes (US), 190
Blackheath, 48
Black Plague, 41, 42, 43
blacks (US), 187–188, 197. *see also* Freedman's Bureau
    American Railroad Union and, 223
    Bryan and, 253
    Debs and, 231, 232
    Freedman's Bureau and, 193, 195
    Howard on, 199
    racial violence against, 197
    railroad brotherhoods and, 229

voting rights and, 176–177, 187, 197
Blatch, Harriet Stanton, 179, 181, 238
BLF (Brotherhood of Locomotive Firemen), 220, 221, 222–223
Blois, Louise, 276
Blue Jacket, 126
Blum, Leon, 283, 286
B'nai Brak, 30
Bohemia, 160
Bois, Louise, 275
Bolingbroke, Henry, 52
Bolivia, 87
Bolsheviks, 236
Bonifacio, Andres, 262, 263, 264
Book of Mazdak, 36
boons, 42
Boot, Max, 205, 217
Boston, 66m, 67
Boston Committee of Correspondence, 70
Boston Massacre, 69, 75, 76
Boston Port Bill SAME AS? Port Act, 75
Boston Tea Party, 69, 71
Boudica
    death of, 25
    described, 19, 23–24
    efforts of and opposition to, 20–25
    vindication of, 25–26
"Boudica" (Tennyson), 25
Boudica and Her Daughters (sculpture), 25
Boukman, 111
Boulanger, Georges Ernest, 277
Brampton, John, 45
Brant, Joseph, 128
Brazil, 204–205
Britain (British Empire, England, Great Britain, United Kingdom). *see also* Boudica; Ireland; London; Peasants' Revolt (England, 1381); Sudan; Warren, Joseph; World War I
    61 CE, 18m
    Clay and, 139, 141–142, 144, 145
    France and, 287
    Hungary and, 168, 169
    Indian allies and, 125
    Ireland and, 97, 98, 103–104, 105
    Kossuth and, 169–170
    national identity and, 25
    Oregon and, 148
    Roman invasion of, 19
    Saint Domingue and, 114–115, 116

Tecumseh and, 129, 130, 133–136
Tupac Amaru's revolt and, 91
Brock, Isaac, 133, 134
Brogan, R.W., 288
Brooks, Robert, 139
Brotherhood (magazine), 220
Brotherhood of Locomotive Firemen (BLF), 220, 221, 222–223
Bryan, Charles, 250
Bryan, William Jennings
    Aguinaldo and, 256, 271, 273, 274
    background of, 243–244
    character of, 255, 256
    death of, 259
    Debs and, 229–230, 232
    efforts of and opposition to, 244–259
    vindication of, 256, 259
Buda-Pest Committee of Public Safety, 161
Buffalo strike, 223
Bunker Hill (Massachusetts), 82–85
Bureau of Refugees, Freedmen and Abandoned Lands. *see* Freedman's Bureau
Burgoyne, John, 81, 83
Burley, Simon, 46
Burnett, David, 188
Butler, Andrew Pickens, 151

C
Caesar, Gaius Julius, 19
Caillaux, Joseph, 289–290, 292
caiques, 88
Calhoun, John, 144, 145, 146, 150, 151
California, 149, 150
Caligula, 16
Calvignac, Jean Baptiste, 279
Cambridge, 47
Cambridge History of Iran (Yarshater), 39
Camulodunum, 19–20, 21–22
Canterbury, 47
capitalism, 229, 230, 234, 278, 280, 285, 287. *see also* corporations; imperialism;
        monopolies
Caribbean, 108m
Carnegie, Andrew, 254, 268
Carnegie Steel Homestead plant, 222
Carnot, Sadi, 280
Carpenter, John, 185–186, 190, 198
Carthage, 5, 14
Castle Hill (Budapest), 167
Catholic Convention, 101, 102

Catholicism, 42, 97, 99–100, 105, 157, 158, 216. *see also* papal rule
Catholic-Presbyterian alliance, 100
Catuvellauni tribe, 22
Cavaignac, Godefroy, 283
Cavite (Philippines), 261, 262, 263, 264, 266, 272
Cavour, Camillio di, 210–211, 213
Celts, 19
Cerealis, Petrilus, 22
Charles Albert of Piedmont, 207
Charles II (England), 65
Charles III (Spain), 88, 93
Chatham, 136
Cheeseekau, 125, 126
Chief Joseph, 199
Christiani, Baron de, 284
Christophe, Henri, 117, 119, 120
Cicero, 15
CIO (Congress of Industrial Organizations), 240
Circular 13 (Howard), 188–189
circumcision, 32
Civil Rights Bil of 1866 (US), 193, 196
Civil War (US), 150–152, 175, 185–186
Claudians, 8
Claudius, 20
Clay, Henry
    background of, 139–140
    death of, 153
    efforts of and opposition to, 140–152
    on Mexican War, 236
    vindication of, 151, 152–153
Clay, Junior, Henry, 149
Clémenceau, Georges, 287
Cleveland, Grover, 226, 228, 229, 245–246, 247, 250, 268
Cochise, 198
Cockayne, John, 101, 102
Coletta, Raymond, 243, 249, 253, 256
colonialism, 253
Colorado, 227
Combes, Émile, 285, 286
Committee of Security (Austria), 163
The Commoner (newspaper), 251–252
common people. *see* poor (common) people
communism, 35–41, 239, 251. *see also* land and property ownership
compromise, 140, 146, 150–152. *see also* Missouri Compromise *and others*
Compromise of 1833 (US), 146
Compromise of 1850 (US), 152
Concord (Massachusetts), 76, 77, 81

Congress of Industrial Organizations (CIO), 240
Conservative Party (Hungary), 157, 158, 163
Conway, Thomas, 190
Cooke, Henry, 198
Cooke, Jay, 198
Cornelia, 16
Cornwallis, General, 105
corporations, 246, 249, 250, 252, 253, 254, 258. *see also* capitalism; monopolies
corregidores, 88, 95
corvee, 42, 51
Cossacks, 58–60, 63, 64, 65
Crawford, William, 144
Creeks, 132
Creoles, 90, 91, 95
Croats, 162, 163, 164
Croix, Teodoro de, 95
Cuba, 250, 265
Cuneo, Giovan, 203–204
Cuzco, 91–92
Czechs, 159, 160

D
daevas, 35
Daily Tribune (newspaper), 210, 212
Darrow, Clarence, 226, 232, 238, 239, 258
Dartmouth, Lord, 74, 76
Darwinism, 258
Daugherty, Harry, 238
Dawes, William, 76
Dayton Republican (Ohio newspaper), 137
Deák, István, 156–157, 160, 164, 167
death, 36
Debs, Eugene
    arrest, trial, and imprisonment of, 236–239
    background of, 219–220
    Bryan and, 249
    character of, 224, 233–234, 237, 238, 239
    death of, 239
    efforts of and opposition to, 220–239
    vindication of, 239–240
Debs and the Poets (Sinclair), 238
Decianus, Caius, 21
Declaration of Sentiments (US), 173–174
Declaration of the Rights of Man (France), 110
Declaratory Act (Britain), 69
Degow, James, 192
Democratic Party (US)

    Aguinaldo and, 271–272
    Bryan and, 229, 244, 246, 247–248, 249–250, 251, 252, 253, 254, 256, 257, 259
    Debs and, 220, 235, 243
Democratic-Republican Party (US), 102, 140, 145, 148, 151
Department of Labor (US), 255
depressions, 247, 250
Dessalines, 117, 120, 122
Dewey, George, 265–266, 269, 273, 274
Dio, Cassius, 22, 25, 33
Diophanes, 11
District of Columbia, 150, 198
divorce, 174, 175, 178
Douglas, Frederick, 151, 176, 177, 193
Douglas, Stephen, 152
The Dream of John Ball (Morris), 44
Dreyfus, Alfred, 282–284
Dreyfus, Mathieu, 283
Druids, 20
Drumont, Édouard, 282
Drusus, M. Livius, 14
Dubois, Laurent, 116
DuBois, W.E.B., 199–200, 253
Dudley, William, 135
dues and services, 157, 158, 160
Dupuy, Charles, 280, 284

E
Earl of Salisbury, 50, 51
Easton, Amos, 194
L' Echo de Paris (newspaper), 289
education, 179, 194–195, 207, 278, 281, 285. *see also* public schools
Eighty Years and More (Stanton), 181
Elizabeth I (England), 25
Elliot, Mariane, 99, 104
Emancipation Proclamation (US), 175
encomienda system, 87
Engels, Friedrich, 212
England. *see* Britain
Enlightenment, 89
Epictetus, 110–111
Espionage Act (US, 1917), 236
Essex (England), 45, 48, 50, 54
Esterhazy, Ferdinand, 282–283, 284
ethnicity, 269, 271
eugenics, 258
Europe, 275m. *see also* France *and other countries;* World War I

F
Fabritius, Ludwig, 61–62
farmers. *see also* land and property ownership
    Akiba and, 32, 33
    Boudica and, 23, 24
    Bryan and, 243, 244, 245, 247, 252, 258, 259
    Cossacks and, 58–59
    Debs and, 229
    Gracchus reforms and, 6–9, 13, 16–17
    Hispaniola and, 109
    Howard and, 188, 189, 191, 194, 198
    Jaurès and, 277, 281
    Peasants' Revolt (Britain) and, 42, 43, 44
    Toussaint and, 118
    Tupac and, 91
Faure, Félix, 284
Federalist Party (US), 102, 140, 142, 172
Federal Reserve bank system (US), 256
Federated Trades and Labor Council (US), 221
Ferdowski, Abolqasem, 36–39
Ferry, Abel, 291
Fillmore, Millard, 152
Finney, Charles G., 243
The First Battle (Bryan and Bryan), 250
First Congregational Church (D.C.), 198
First Continental Congress (US), 71
Fischer, Adolf, 162
Fisher, Lillian, 90, 92–93, 94–95
FitzGerald, Edward, 104
Fitzgibbon, John, 101
Fitzwilliam, Earl, 102
Flaccus, Fulvius, 10, 14, 15
Florida, 143
Florus, Gesius, 29
Foner, Eric, 195
food and hunger. *see also* farmers; land and property ownership; poor people
    Boudica's army and, 23
    Bryan and, 252, 253
    Debs on, 219
    Freedman's Bureau and, 187, 194
    Gracchus reforms and, 12, 17
    Judean Revolts and, 33
    Kossuth and, 158
    Mazdak and, 36–37, 38
    Peasants' Revolt and, 43, 47, 50
    revolts of 1848 and, 158

Rome and, 7, 8, 14
Tecumseh and, 127, 129
food stamps, 2
Foote, Henry, 151
Ford, Henry, 258
Fort Dearborn, 134
Fort Detroit, 133, 134
Fortescue, John W., 115
Fort Malden, 133, 135
Fort Meigs, 134–135
Fort Miami, 126, 135
Fort Michilimackinac, 134
Fort Stephenson, 135
Fort Wayne Treaty (1809), 129, 130
Forward (newspaper), 234
Founding Fathers (US), 67–85
Fox, Ebenezer, 67
France. *see also* Jaurès, Jean; World War I
    Austria and, 211
    Catholicism and, 99
    Clay on, 141, 145
    England and, 287
    Garibaldi and, 210–211, 215–216
    Germany and, 281–282, 286–287
    Hispaniola and, 114
    Hungary and, 158
    invasion of Ireland and, 101–104, 105
    Kossuth and, 169–170
    L'Ouverture and, 115
    map, 275m
    1914 CE, 275–292
    Roman Republic and, 208–209
    Saint Domingue and, 110, 113, 118–120, 119, 122
    1381 CE, 42, 46
    Tone and, 102–103
    unions and, 279
    wars and, 42, 43, 47, 101
Francis Ferdinand (Austria), 290
Francis II (Bourbon king), 212
Francois, Jean, 111
Franco-Prussian War (1870), 275, 282
Franz Joseph (Austria), 167, 168
Freeberg, Ernest, 232–233
Freedman's Bureau (US), 185, 186–198, 199–200
Freedmen's Saving Bank (US), 197, 198
freedom of speech/press, 158, 159, 160, 236, 237, 264, 280
Freemen's Inquiry Commission (US), 186

French Empire, 275
French Republic, 275, 276, 277, 279
French Revolution, 101, 110
Frick, Henry, 222
Froissart, Jean, 48–49
Frugi, Lucius Calpurnius Piso, 12–13
fugitive slave laws (US), 150–151
Fullerton, James, 189, 190, 192–193
Funston, Frederick, 272, 273
Fyodor, Tsar (Russia), 57

G
Gage, Thomas, 72, 74–75, 76, 79, 80, 81, 85
Galloway, Joseph, 74
Garibaldi, Giuseppe
    background of, 203–204
    character of, 205–206, 208, 209, 212, 213, 214, 217
    death of, 217
    efforts of and opposition to, 203, 204–217
    vindication of, 217
Garibaldi, Minotti, 205, 211
Gaul, 19
General Managers Association, 229
General Managers Association (US), 225
Geoffrey the Litster (England), 47
George III, 81
Georgia (US), 196
Germany, 163, 235, 281–282, 286, 288. *see also* World War I
Gerry, Elbridge, 84
Ghent, treaty at, 136
Ginger, Ray, 222, 229, 230, 232, 237
Ginzberg, Lori, 173, 174, 182
Girard, Phillipe, 122
Giron, Pedro, 264
Goethe, 219
gold, 245
gold and silver (bimetallism), 250
Goldberg, Harvey, 285, 287, 291
gold rush, 150
golytha, 59
Gompers, Samuel, 221, 227, 268
Gore, Francis, 129
Gorgey, Arthur, 165, 167–168, 168–169
Gower, John, 43, 55
Gracchus, Gaius
    background of, 6, 11–12
    death of, 15–16

efforts of and opposition to, 11–16
vindication of, 1–2, 6, 16–17
Gracchus, Tiberius
background of, 5, 6
death of, 11
efforts of and opposition to, 5–11
vindication of, 1–2, 6, 16–17
Great Britain. *see* Britain
Great Northern Railroad, 223–224
Greeley, Horace, 176–177
Greenwich, 49–50
Gregory, Edward, 188
Grindecobbe, William, 54
guerrilla warfare, 111–112, 120, 204, 209, 211, 215–216, 270, 271, 272, 273
Guesde, Jules, 285, 286

H
Habsburg Empire, 154m, 158, 159–160, 162–170, 163. *see also* Austria
Hadrian, 32, 34
Haiti, 122. *see also* L'Ouverture, Toussaint
Hales, Robert, 50, 52
Halevy, Daniele, 286
Hancock, John, 71, 72, 75, 76, 78
Hanna, Mark, 249
Harding, Warren, 237, 238
Hardy, General, 105
Harpers Weekly (periodical), 249, 270
Harrison, William Henry, 127, 128, 129–130, 130–132, 133, 134–135, 136, 147
Hart, Lucretia, 140
Haynu, General, 167, 168, 169
Haywood, Bill, 231–232
health care, 194–195
Heath, William, 77, 83
Hedoubille, Comte, 116
Heidler, Daniel and Jeannette, 140
Henry, Hubert-Joseph, 284
Henry IV, 52, 55
Herr, Lucien, 277, 282, 283, 286
Herzen, Alexander, 210
Hill, George, 105
Hill, James J., 223–224
Hispaniola, 109–110, 117
History of Women's Suffrage (Stanton and Anthony), 178–179
Hoche (ship), 105
Hoche, Louis, 103, 104
Hog and Noddles islands, 81
Homestead Steel strike, 245

Hooton, Elizabeth, 67, 70
Horne, John, 49
Howard, Oliver Otis
    background, 185–186
    efforts of and opposition to, 186–199
    vindication of, 199–200
Howard University, 195
Howden, Lord, 206
Howe, General, 85
Hugo, Victor, 212, 216, 217, 219
Hull, William, 133, 134
L' Humanité (journal), 290, 291
Hundred Years War, 41
Hungarian Declaration of Independence, 167
Hungarian Diet, 156, 157, 158–160, 160–161, 164
Hungarian House of Representatives, 163, 164
Hungarian National Assembly, 164–165, 167, 168, 169
Hungary (1848 CE), 154m, 165, 167, 171. *see also* Kossuth, Louis
hunger. *see* food and hunger
Hutchinson, Thomas, 67, 70
Hyrcanus II (Judea), 29

I
Iceni, 19, 20–21
Idaho, 231
Idahos strike, 222
Illinois, 227
immigrants, 179, 199. *see also* golytha
imperialism, 122, 251, 272, 286. *see also* capitalism
Imus, battle of, 263–264
Imworth, Richard, 52
Incas, 87
India, 253
Indiana, 127, 149, 221
Industrial Workers of the World (IWW), 219, 231, 232, 236
injunctions, 227
Insurrection Act (Britain), 104
International Congress for Peace and Freedom (1967), 216
Interstate Commerce Commission (US), 246
Intolerable Acts (Britain), 71–72
Ireland, 95m, 97, 98–99. *see also* Tone, Wolfe
Israel, 34
Italian Emancipation Association, 214
Italian Legion, 205, 206
Italian revolution, 158, 160, 163, 164
Italy, 202m, 203, 206–208, 212, 214–215, 217. *see also* Garibaldi, Giuseppe
Ivan the Terrible (Russia), 57

IWW (Industrial Workers of the World), 219, 231, 232, 236

J
Jackson, Andrew, 139–140, 142, 143, 144–146, 247
Jackson, William, 101, 102
James, C.L.R., 120
James Redpath Lyceum Bureau, 178
Japan, 274
Jaurès, Jean
    background of, 275–276
    death of, 291
    efforts of and opposition to, 277–291
    vindication of, 291–292
Jaurès, Louis, 292
Jefferson, Thomas, 245, 247
Jeffries, John, 82
Jelačić, Josip, 164
Jerusalem, 29–30
Jewish populations. *see also* Torah
    Austrians and, 166
    Bryan and, 248, 258
    Debs and, 234
    Dreyfus case and, 282–283
    Hungarian, 155, 161, 162, 168
    Jaurès and, 282
    Papal rule and, 210
    Rome and, 29–30, 31, 32–34
    Russia and, 65
    Stanton and, 178, 181
John of Gaunt, 47, 50
Johnson, Andrew, 187, 188–190, 191, 192–193, 196
Johnson, Edward, 185
Judean Revolts (131 CE), 28m, 29–34

K
Kansas, 177, 227
Karnow, Stanley, 270
Karsner, David, 239
Katipunan, 262, 263
Kawit (Philippines), 261–262, 264, 266, 274
Kazan Stepana Razina (Shostakovich), 65
Kazin, Michael, 243, 244, 248, 249, 253, 258
Kent, 45–46, 47
Kentucky, 125, 139, 141, 149, 153, 192
Kentucky Gazette (Clay), 140
Kerverseau, General, 116
Kesra, Prince, 38–39, 40

Kingdom of Italy, 213, 214
Kirker, Thomas, 128–129
Kishinev pogroms, 285
Knighton, Henry, 42
Knowles, Robert, 54
Knowlton, Thomas, 83
Kossuth, Louis
    arrest and imprisonment, 156–157
    background of, 155, 156
    death of, 170
    efforts of and opposition to, 155–170
    Garibaldi and, 213–214
    vindication of, 170–171
Krug (Cossack general assembly), 58, 59, 60, 61, 62

L

labor. *see also* Debs, Eugene; farmers; poor people; serfdom; slavery; strikes;
    unions
    Bryan on, 252
    child, 252
    Debs on, 219
    in England (1381 CE), 42–43
    freed slaves and, 188
    Garibaldi and, 214
    Hispaniola and, 109
    Howard and, 195–196
    Jaurès and, 277, 278, 281, 286, 287, 288
    non-socialist states and, 279
    Philippines and, 261, 268
    Spanish rule and, 87–88
Lacroix, Pamphile, 112
Laenas, P. Popillus, 11
Lake, Gerard (General), 104
Lake Erie, 135
Lake Titicaca, 91
Lalawe'thika (The Prophet), 127–128, 128–129, 130, 131–132, 136
land and property ownership. *see also* farmers; food and hunger; serfdom; taxes
    Aguinaldo and, 264–265, 266
    Bryan and, 252, 253
    Clay on, 140
    English (1381 CE), 42, 49
    Freedman's Bureau and, 186–189, 188, 191, 194, 195, 199
    Garibaldi and, 205–206
    goods held in common, 2, 48
    Irish religions and, 97
    Jaurès and, 277, 281
    Kentucky lawyers and, 139

Kossuth and, 157, 161
  Mazdak and, 2, 35, 36, 38, 39, 40
  Peasants' Revolt and, 50–51, 53
  Philippines and, 261
  Roman Republic (1848) and, 207, 208
  Rome and, 6
  slavery and, 7, 118
  Spanish churches in Peru and, 88
  strikes and, 226, 227, 234
  suffrage and (US), 173, 174
  Tecumseh and, 127, 128–129, 130
  Tupac and, 92
  Tyler and, 53
  US, 173, 174, 175
Langland, William, 43
Langston, John, 193
La Petite Republique, 283
Latifundia, 7
Latin America, 153
Laveaux, Compte of, 112, 113, 114, 115
laws. *see also* Civil Rights Bill of 1866 *and other laws;* taxes
  anarchism and, 280–281
  Bryan on, 252
  divorce and, 178
  English (circa 1381 CE), 42–44
  Freedman's Bureau and, 196
  Garibaldi and, 214
  Hispaniola and, 110, 114
  Hungary and, 160–161, 164
  Irish and, 102, 104
  Jaurès and, 288
  Jewish (*see* Torah)
  labor and, 221
  Peasants' Revolt and, 45, 52, 53, 54, 55
  Rome and, 8–9
  Russia (circa 1670) and, 57
  South Carolina, 146
  Tupac Amaru on, 90
  US, 140, 150–151
  women and, 175
Leach, Joshua, 220
League of Democracy (Italy), 216
League of Nations, 256, 258
Le Cap, 111–112, 119
Leclerc, Charles, 119, 120, 121, 122
Legge, John, 46, 52
Lenin, Vladimir, 56

Les Débats (newspaper), 285
Le Temps (newspaper), 290
Lexington, 77–80
Lex Kossuth, 170
L'Humanité (newspaper), 286
Liberal Nationalism (Hungary), 155–172
Libertas, Bayon de, 111
Licinia, 15
Liga Filipina, 261
Lincoln, Abraham, 150, 153, 175, 200, 236
Lincoln Memorial University, 195, 199
Londinium, 22, 25
London, 41m, 47, 48, 49, 50–51, 54
Longuet, Jean, 291–292
Loubet, Émile, 284
Louisiana, 190, 197
Louis Napoleon, 215
L'Ouverture, Toussaint
    arrest, imprisonment and death of, 121
    background of, 110–111
    character of, 110–111, 112, 113, 114, 115, 116, 120
    efforts of and opposition to, 109–120
    vindication of, 2, 122–123
Luna, Antonio, 266, 269, 270
Lusitania, 235, 257
Luzon, Northern, 260m, 266, 268–269

M
Mabini, Apolinario, 267
MacArthur, Arthur, 269, 273
MacArthur, Douglas, 274
Maccabee brothers, 29
Mackenzie, Frederick, 76
Madison, James, 129, 141, 142
Maine (cruiser), 265
Malolos (Philippines), 269
Malvar, Miguel, 273
Manila (Philippines), 266, 267, 269
marriage, 39, 42, 174. *see also* divorce
Married Women's Property Act (1860), 175
martyrs, 34, 204
Marxism, 277–279
Massachusetts (1775 CE), 67–85
Massachusetts Provincial Congress, 72, 73, 74, 75, 76, 79, 80, 81, 82, 84
Mazdak
    background, 35–37
    death of, 39

efforts of and opposition to, 37–39
vindication of, 2, 40
Mazzini, Giuseppe, 204, 207, 208, 209, 213, 214, 216
McAdoo, William, 257
McDonald, John, 128
McKinley, William, 249–250, 251, 267, 268, 272
McParlan, James, 232
Meline, Jules, 283
Memphis (TN), 197
Memphis Avalanche (newspaper), 197
Mencken, H.L., 252
Merritt, Wesley, 267
Meszlenyi, Terez, 157
Metternich, Prince, 157, 159, 204
Metzel, Kate, 221
Mexican War (US), 236
Mexico, 148–149, 234
middle class, 158, 159
Milan, 160, 206, 207
Milchrist, Thomas, 225–226
Mile End meeting (London), 51
Military Reconstruction Act (US) (1867), 197
Miller, Elizabeth Smith, 180
Miloslavsky, Ivan, 63
Milton, John, 25
Mine Owners Association (US), 232
miners, 222, 230, 279
mines in Peru, 87, 91
minorities, Hungarian, 155, 162–163, 168, 178
Mirebelais Valley, 114
Les Miserables (Hugo), 219
Mississippi, 188, 195
Missouri Compromise, 143–144
mita system (Peru), 87, 88, 89, 90, 95
Moise, 116, 118, 119
money supply, 245, 246, 251. *see also* bimetallism (gold and silver)
monopolies, 47, 52, 70, 161, 251. *see also* corporations
Monroe, James, 103, 142, 143
Montevideo, siege of, 206
Moraviantown, 136, 160
Morocco, 286–287
Morris, William, 44
Moscono, Bishop of Cuzco, 89–90, 91, 95
Mott, Lucretia, 173
Moundsville state prison (West Virginia), 237
Moyer, Charles, 231–232
mulattoes, 110, 111, 112, 115, 116, 117, 119

Municipal Reports (Kossuth), 156
mutinies, 204–205

N
Naples, 208, 211–213
Napoleon Bonaparte, 118, 119, 123, 142
Napoleonic wars, 141
Napoleon III, 170
Nasica, Cipio, 10–11
The Nation (journal), 255
National American Women's Suffrage Association (NAWSA), 178–179, 181
National Association of Manufacturers (US), 254
National Defense Committee (Hungary), 164, 167
National Democratic Party (US), 248
nationalism, 171, 289
National Silver Party (US), 248, 250
National Woman Suffrage Association (NWSA), 178
Native Americans, 95, 125–138, 198–199. *see also* Tecumseh *and others*
Navidad, Mamerto, 264, 265
Nebraska, 244, 246
Nelson, James L., 73, 77, 83, 84, 85
Nero, 16, 21
The New Army (Jaurès), 288
New Deal (US), 259
New Freedom platform (US), 255
New Mexico, 149, 150
Newton, John, 49–50
New York Times (newspaper), 226, 227, 248, 269, 273
New York World (newspaper), 247, 248, 257
Nez Perce, 199
Nicholas I, 168
Noe, Comte de, 110
Norfolk, 47
North Carolina, 191, 194
Northern Star (Irish newspaper), 100
Nullification Crisis (US), 146

O
Octabius, Marcus, 8–9
Oliver, Peter, 85
Olney, Richard, 226
Omaha World-Herald (newspaper), 246
Optimus, Lucius, 14, 15, 16
Orchard, Harry, 231, 232
Oregon, 148, 227
Otis, Elwell, 269, 272
Otis, John, 185

Ottomans, 169
Owsley, Alan, 238

P
Pacific Northwest (US), 148, 199
Paine, Thomas, 55
Palermo, 211–212
Palmer, Attorney General, 238
Panic of 1837 (US), 146
Panic of 1907 (US), 254
pan-Indian confederacy, 128, 129, 136
papal rule, 206, 207–208, 210, 213, 214, 215, 216
Papke, David, 225–226
Paris Commune (1870), 278–279
Parker, Alton B., 252
Parkinson, Wenda, 118, 120
Parmelee, T.N., 147
Party of United Opposition (Hungary), 157–158
Paukeesa, 136
Paulinus, Suetonius, 20, 21, 22, 23, 25
Peace Party (Hungary), 167
peasants. *see also* land and property ownership; poor people; serfdom
    Hungarian, 155, 162
    Jaurès and, 275, 281
    Kossuth and, 164
Peasants' Revolt (England, 1381), 41–55
Peasants' Revolt (England, 1381 CE), 41–55
Peguy, Charles, 282
Penal Laws, anti-Catholic, 102
Pennsylvania Railroad, 220
pensions, 252
People's Party (Populists) (US), 229
Percy, Lord, 77
Pergamum, 9
Perry, Oliver, 135
Persia, 36, 65. *see also* Mazdak
Persian Empire, 35
Peru (1781 CE), 86m, 87–96. *see also* Tupac Amaru, Jose Gabriel
Pest City Hall, march on, 159, 161
Pest Hilo (Pest News) (Kossuth), 157
Peter III (Russia), 62
Peterson, Merrill, 139
Peton, Sándor, 159, 161, 168
Pettibone, George, 231–232
Philbrick, Nathaniel, 69, 79, 80, 81
Philippines, 16–17, 230, 251, 252, 255, 256, 260m, 261. *see also* Aguinaldo, Emilio
Piedmont, 213

Piedmont-Sardinia, 160, 170, 203, 207, 210–211
Pierre Baptiste, 110
Piers Plowman (Langland), 43
Pilar, Gregorio del, 270–271
Pinkertons, 222
Pitt, William, 74
Pius, Pope, 208
Pizarro, Francisco, 87
Plautius, Aulus, 19–20
Plutarch, 6, 11, 12, 14
Poincaré, Raymond, 290, 292
Polevieja, Camilo, 263
Polk, James, 148–149
Pompey, 29
poor (common) people. *see also* food and hunger; labor; land and property ownership; peasants; serfdom; urban poor
    Bryan and, 243, 246–247, 248–249
    Debs and, 219, 220, 227, 230, 239
    G. Gracchus and, 7–8, 12–13, 16
    T. Gracchus and, 5–6, 7–8, 9
    Howard and, 187, 189, 194, 199
    Jaurès and, 276, 277, 278, 280, 285, 288
    Kossuth and, 157, 158, 161
    Mazdak and, 35, 36, 39
    Razin and, 60
    Roman land reform and, 16
    Russia and, 57–58, 58–59
    slavery and, 7
    war and, 230
    Warren and, 67
    wars and, 6–7
    wealthy people and, 9
    whites (US) as, 187, 194
Populists Party (People's Party) (US), 229, 248, 249, 250
Port Act (Britain), 71, 72
Potawatomis, 133–134
Prastagus, 20
Pratt, E. Spencer, 265, 266
Prescott, Samuel, 76, 84
Presidential Reconstruction, 190

"Les Preuves" (Jaurès), 284

Prior John, 46
Proctor, Henry, 134–136
prohibition (US), 254
property rights. *see* land and property ownership
The Prophet (Lalawe'thika), 127–128, 128–129, 130, 131–132, 136

Prophetstown, 132
prostitutes, 234
protests, revolts, revolutions and riots (civil strife). *see also* Garibaldi, Giuseppe;
        Judean Revolts; mutinies; Peasants' Revolt; Razin, Stenka; strikes;
        Warren, Joseph
    Austria and, 159, 165
    Ball and, 41
    Gracchus brothers and, 11, 15
    in Hungary, 159
    Hungary and, 161, 170
    Irish, 104–105
    Judea and, 29
    L'Ouverture and, 111
    Philippines and, 261, 262–263, 263–264
    Russia and, 58
    Sicily and, 211
Proust, Marcel, 287
Prussians, 170, 214–215
public schools, 258
public works projects, 246
Pugachev, 62
Pukeshinwau, 125
Pullman, George, 224–225, 226
Pullman strike, 219, 224–228, 231, 246, 254
Pushkin, Alexander, 56
Putnam, Israel, 81, 82, 84

Q
Qobad, King, 36–37, 37–38, 40
Quezon, Manuel, 274
Quiquijana, 90

R
rabbis, 30–31
race, 221, 268, 282
Rachel, 30, 31
racial violence, 197
Radical Party (France), 285, 287, 289
railroad brotherhoods, 221, 222, 223, 224, 225, 229, 235, 253. *see also* Brotherhood
        of Locomotive Firemen *and other unions*
railroads (US), 243, 248, 250, 251, 253, 258. *see also* Union Pacific *and other*
        railroad companies
railroad workers (US), 219–221. *see also* Debs, Eugene
Railway Times (newspaper), 230
Randolph, John, 141, 146
Raphael, Ray and Marie, 67
Rawdon, Lord, 85

Raynal, Abbot, 111
Razin, Frolka, 64–65
Razin, Stenka
    Alexis' "son" and, 62–63
    background, 58
    described, 59, 60, 61
    efforts of and opposition to, 59–64
    imprisonment and death of, 64–65
    vindication of, 65
Redshirts, 211–212
Reed, Thomas, 269
Regio (Italy), 212
Reille-Solages family, 277, 279
religion and churches. *see also* Catholicism; Jewish populations; Zoroastrianism
    Arriaga and, 89–90
    Ball and, 44
    Bryan and, 243, 248, 249, 254, 258–259
    Ireland and, 98
    Jaurès and, 278, 285
    Kesra on, 38–39
    Kossuth and, 160, 163
    Mazdak on, 36
    Peasants' Revolt and, 47, 53, 55
    Philippines and, 261, 264, 269
    Razin and, 62
    South America and, 88
    Stanton and, 172, 180–181
    Tone and, 99–100, 106
    Tupac Amaru and, 91
    Tyler and, 52
repartimiento (1781), 88
Republican Army (Ireland), 97
republicanism
    Garibaldi's, 204, 207, 210–211, 216
    Jaurès and, 276, 277, 280, 284, 288
    Philippines and, 264, 269
    Tone and, 99, 100
Republican Party (US). *see also* Democratic-Republican Party
    Bryan and, 230, 232, 235, 237, 244–245, 246, 248, 249, 257–258
    Freedmen's Bureau and, 191, 192
    voting rights and, 176–177, 197
    Wilson's election and, 255
Revere, Paul, 67, 73–74, 76
The Revolution (newspaper), 178
revolutions. *see* protests, revolts, revolutions and riots (civil strife)
Revolutions of 1848, 158, 163, 206, 219
Riasanovsky, Nicholas, 57

Rice, Cecil Spring, 255
Richard II, 47, 49, 50, 51–55
Richardson, Priscilla, 161, 165, 167, 169–170
Ridley, Jasper, 212, 214
Rigaud, André, 116–117, 119
Riley, James, 223
riots. *see* protests, revolts, revolutions and riots (civil strife)
Rizal, Jose, 261, 263
Rochester castle, 47
Rockefellers, 234, 235, 254
Roman Empire, 34. *see also* Akiba, Rabbi; Boudica; Judean Revolts
Romanians, 162
Romanov dynasty, 57
Roman Republic(s), 4m, 11, 16, 208. *see also* Gracchus, Gaius; Gracchus, Tiberius
Rome, city of, 7, 215
Roosevelt, Franklin, 259
Roosevelt, Theodore, 2, 233, 251, 252, 253, 254, 255
Roosevelt-Bryan Merger, 253
Root, Elihu, 269
Rossi, Pellegrino, 208
Rowan, Hamilton, 101, 102
Ruddell, Stephen, 126
Rufus, Tineius, 33–34
Rum Raisin, battle of, 134
Russia. *see also* Razin, Stenka
    1533-1669, 56m, 57–60
    Hungary and, 168–169
    Jaurès on, 282, 285
    19th century pogroms of, 65
    socialists and (US), 236
    Tiberius' land reforms and, 17
    World War I and, 290, 292

S
Saint Domingue, 108m. *see also* L'Ouverture, Toussaint
Saint Simonians, 203
salvation, 36
Salvatore, Nick, 223, 239
Sandburg, Carl, 232
Sangarara battle, 91
Santo Domingo, 117
Sasanian Dynasty, 35, 36, 40
Sassoon, Siegfried, 238
Savawaseeku, 126
Saxton, Rufus, 187, 189, 190
Scaevola, 10–11, 140
Schlesinger, Junior, Arthur, 233

Schoefield, John, 196
Scirocco, Alfonso, 203, 205, 210, 211, 213, 216
Scopes, John, 258, 259–260
Sea Islands (S.C.), 187, 189
Senate (bill) 60 (US) (1866), 191–192
Senate (bill) 61 (US) (1866), 193
senators, direct election of (US), 255, 256
senatus consultum ultimum, 15
Seneca Falls meeting (US), 173
Septimuleius, 16
Serbs, 162–163, 290, 292
serfdom, 48, 54, 57, 58, 156, 162, 170–171. *see also* peasants; poor people
services and dues, 157, 158, 160
Severus, Julius, 33
Shahnameh (Ferdowski), 36–39
Shane, Anthony, 126
Shawnees, 125–126, 136
Sheridan, Phillip, 197
Sherman, William Tecumseh, 186, 187
Shostakovich, Dmitri, 65
Sibley, Walter, 50
Sicily, 211–212, 213, 214
Silva, Anita Maria Riberio da (Anna), 205–206, 209, 210
silver, 249, 251
Silver Purchase Act, 245–246
Simbirsk battle, 63
Simeon, 32–33
Sinclair, Upton, 238, 239
Sinnamatha, 126
slavery. *see also* Civil War (US); World Anti-Slavery Convention (1840)
    Akiba and, 31
    Civil War and, 185, 186
    Clay and, 139, 140, 143–144, 146–147, 148, 149–150
    ended in Saint Domingue, 112–113, 115, 118
    ended in Santo Domingo, 117
    Freedman's Bureau and, 195
    freed slaves, 187–188
    Garibaldi on, 214
    Haiti and, 122
    Hispaniola and, 109–110, 114
    Kesra on, 38
    L'Ouverture and, 111
    Pullman workers compared, 225
    by Romans, 7, 21
    Stanton on, 175–176
Smith, Francis, 76, 77
Smithfield conference, 52–53

social Darwinism, 258
Social Democratic Party (US), 230
socialism
    Bryan and, 246, 248, 249, 251, 257
    Debs and, 228, 230, 231
    Jaurès and, 277–280, 283–287, 283–292, 290
    Roman Republic and, 208
    World War I and, 290–291
Socialist Party (France), 284–285, 287, 288–292
Socialist Party (US), 230, 231, 232–233, 235–236, 237, 238, 239. *see also* Debs, Eugene
Society of United Irishmen, 100, 101, 102, 103, 104
Solages clan, 275, 277, 283, 285. *see also* Reille-Solages family
soldiers. *see* armies, soldiers, and war
Sonthonax, Commissioner, 112–113
South America, 86m, 143
South Carolina, 146, 151, 187, 189, 194
Southern Homestead Act (US) (1866), 194
Southwark, 49
Spain
    Clay on, 143
    Cuba and, 265
    Hispaniola and, 109
    L'Ouverture and, 113
    papal rule and, 208
    Philippines and, 261, 261–263, 262, 264–265, 265–266
    Saint Domingue and, 114
    South America and, 87–88
    US war with, 230, 250–251
Spanish-American War, 230, 250–251, 265, 268
Spenser, Edmund, 25
St. Albans, 47, 54
Stamp Act, 68, 69
Standard Oil Company, 234, 254
Stanton, Edwin, 186–187, 190, 191
Stanton, Elizabeth Cady
    background of, 172–173, 174–175
    death of, 181
    efforts of and opposition to, 173–181
    vindication of, 2, 181, 182
Stanton, Henry Brewster, 172, 173, 175, 178
Stanton, Neil, 176
Stark, John, 83, 84
states' rights (US), 145, 146, 148, 190, 192, 244
Statute of Labourers (Britain), 42, 43
Steedman, General, 192–193
Stephen, Archduke (Habsburg Empire), 160

Steunenberg, Frank, 231
Stiles, William, 164, 165, 166, 167
St. Paul Chamber of Commerce, 224
strikebreakers, 225–226, 249
strikes
    Aguinaldo and, 265
    Bryan on, 245, 246, 249
    Clémenceau and, 287
    Debs and, 219, 220–228, 230, 231, 235
    French Socialist Party and, 290
    Hungary and, 162
    Jaurès and, 279, 281, 286, 287
    Taft on, 254
    Vienna and, 163
Strong, William, 187–188
Struys, Jan, 59, 62
Sudan, 282
Sudbury, Simon, 44, 52
Suffolk (England), 46, 47
Suffolk Resolves (US), 73–74
suffrage. *see* voting rights
sugar cane, 109
Sugden, John, 136–137
Sumner, Charles, 236
Suzanne, 111
Syria, 29
Syria Palestina, 34
Széchenyi, István, 155, 156, 160

T
Tacitus, 20, 25
Taft, William Howard, 232, 254, 255
Talbot, Adolphus, 244
Tallmadge, James, 143
Talmud, 34
tariffs, 143, 144, 145, 146, 244–245, 255
taxes. *see also* dues and services; tithes
    American colonies and, 68, 69–70
    Bryan on, 246, 247, 249, 250, 251, 252, 253, 255, 256
    Hispaniola and, 114
    Hungary and, 155
    Jaurès and, 281
    Kossuth and, 157, 158, 161, 163
    Peasants' Revolt and, 43–44, 45–46, 52
    Philippines and, 261
    Radicals and (France), 281
    Roman, 31

Russia and, 57, 58
Spanish in South America and, 88
Warren and, 68
women and, 174
Taylor, A.J.P., 217
Taylor, Zachary, 149, 152
Tea Act (US), 70
Tecumseh
    background and character of, 125–126, 128–129, 131, 135
    death of, 136
    efforts of and opposition to, 126–136
    vindication of, 136–137
temperance, 174, 175
Temple in Jerusalem, 29, 30, 31, 34
Temple of Jupiter, 32
Tennyson, Alfred, 25
term limits, 252
Texas, 148, 150, 187–188, 227
Thomas, Samuel, 188
the Thousand, 211
Thurston, John, 246
Ticonderoga, 80
Tillson, David, 196
tithes, 160
Tolstoy, Leo, 253, 258
Tone, Wolfe
    background, 97–99
    efforts of and opposition to, 100–106
    exile in America, 102–103
    on religion, 99–100, 106
    trial and death of, 105–106
    vindication of, 97, 106
Tonge, William, 50
Torah, 30, 31, 32, 33
Torta, Yohanan Ben, 32
Tower of London, 51, 52
Townsend, Charles and Townsend duties, 69–70
Train, George, 177, 178
Trajan, 32
treaties, 287–288
treaty at Ghent (1814), 136
Treaty of Greenville, 126–127
Treaty of Paris (1783), 125
Tresilian, Robert, 54, 55
Trevelyan, G.M., 206, 207, 208, 209, 212
Tribal Assembly (Roman), 8–9
Tribune (Chicago), 226

Tribune (New Orleans black newspaper), 190
Trinovantes, 21, 22
Trotsky, Leon, 281, 285, 287, 291
Trumbull, Lyman, 191–192, 243
trusts (US), 228, 250, 251, 254, 255
Tsaritsyn, 61
Tuchman, Barbara, 55, 278, 281, 287
Tupac Amaru, Diego, 92, 94–95
Tupac Amaru, Glas, 89
Tupac Amaru, Jose Gabriel
    background, 89
    death of, 93
    efforts of and opposition to, 89–95
    vindication of, 2, 94, 95
Turpilianus, Petronius, 25
Twelve Demands (Hungary), 159
Tyler, John, 147–148
Tyler, Wat
    death of, 54
    efforts of and opposition to, 46–53, 55
    vindication of, 55

U

Union Pacific Railroad, 246
unions, 220, 240, 246, 255, 258, 279. *see also* American Federation of Labor *and other unions;* strikes
Union soldiers (US), 191, 197, 214
United Kingdom. *see* Britain
United Orders of Railway Employees, 222
United States. *see also* American Revolution *and other wars;* Founding Fathers (US); Native Americans; Warren, Joseph *and other Americans*
    Aguinaldo and, 256, 263, 265–274
    Cuba and, 265
    eastern, 184m
    1824, 138m
    1896, 242m
    Garibaldi and, 210
    Kossuth and, 169–170
    Midwest, 218m
    The Northwest, 124m, 148
    Tone and, 102
United States Congress, 141
universities (US), 195
urban poor, 7, 12. *see also* poor people
Uruguay, 205–206, 207
US Congress, 176, 191, 244–245, 268, 269
US Constitution and amendments
    black rights and, 192, 197

Bryan and, 252, 255, 256, 258
   Clay and, 141–142, 142–143, 144, 146, 147, 148, 150, 151
   Debs and, 236
   slavery and, 143, 150, 176, 228
   state's rights and, 146
   strikes and, 227, 228
   women's suffrage and, 176, 177, 178, 179, 181
US Declaration of Independence, 173
US district attorney (Chicago), 225–226
US senators, election of, 252
US Steel, 254
utilities, ownership of (US), 252, 253

V
Valle, General del, 92, 93
Van Buren, Martin, 146
Van Cleve, James, 254
vegetarianism, 36
Velletri, 208
Venice, 215
Verulamium, 22
Victor Emanuel II, 211, 213, 214, 216
Vienna, 159–160
Villain, Raoul, 291
villeins, 42–43, 51, 55
Vincent, General, 119
vindication of ideas, 1–2
violence, 227, 236–237, 280. *see also* armies, soldiers, and war
Virginia, 191
vitalism, 288
Vivani, René, 290, 291
Volga River expedition, 59–60
voting rights (suffrage)
   blacks and, 176, 177, 187, 197
   Bryan and, 254, 258
   Debs on, 231
   Declaration of Sentiments and, 173
   Garibaldi on, 216
   Howard on, 199
   Hungary and, 160, 161
   Ireland and, 101
   Philippines and, 267
   Stanton and, 175, 176–177
   women's, 221

W
Waibel, Paul, 247

Waldeck-Rousseau, Rene, 284
Walsingham, Thomas, 46, 52, 54, 55
Walworth, William, 49, 51, 53
Ward, Artemus, 82, 83
War of 1812, 133, 142
Warren, Joseph
    background, 67, 68–69
    death of, 84
    described, 69
    efforts of and opposition to, 68–85
    soldiers and, 81–82, 84
    vindication of, 85
wars. *see* armies, soldiers, and war; protests, revolts, revolutions and riots (civil strife)
Washington, George, 80, 85, 102
Waterloo Quaker Meeting House speech (US), 174
Watson, James, 196
Wayne, Anthony, 126
Webster, Daniel, 148, 150, 151, 236
Weinstein, Harold, 275
welfare state, 17
Western Federation of Miners, 231, 232
West Virginia strikes, 230, 234
Whig Party (US), 146, 147–148, 149, 151
White, William Allen, 248–249
Wilmot Proviso (US), 149
Wilson, Henry, 191
Wilson, Woodrow, 219, 233, 234, 235, 237–238, 251, 254–258
Windisch-Graetz, Alfred 1, 165, 167
Witherington, Matilda, 98, 102, 106
women, 31, 38, 39, 62, 230. *see also* Stanton, Elizabeth Cady *and other women*
Women's Bible (Stanton), 180–181
Women's Loyal National League, 175–176
Women's New York State Temperance Society, 174
women's rights, 172–183, 199, 221
Wood, Edwin P., 265, 266
Wood, Fernando, 198
World Anti-Slavery Convention (1840), 173
World War I, 234–236, 255–258, 275, 288–290
Wrawe, John, 46
Wythe, George, 139

Y
Yaitsk, 60
Yakolev, Kronilo, 64, 65
Yarshater, Ehsan, 39
Yavneh (school), 30

yazotas, 35
Young Hungary, 159
Young Italy, 203–204

Z
Zapote, battle of, 263–264
Zola, Émile, 282–283
Zoroastrianism, 35–36, 39

www.ingramcontent.com/pod-product-compliance
Lightning Source LLC
Chambersburg PA
CBHW050527300426
44113CB00012B/1989